Nigeria's Policy Response to COVID-19 Pandemic

Adonis & Abbey Publishers Ltd
24 Old Queen Street, London SW1H 9HP United Kingdom
Website: http://www.adonis-abbey.com
E-mail Address: editor@adonis-abbey.com

Nigeria:
Plot 2560, Hassan Musa Katsina Street, Asokoro, Abuja, Nigeria
Tel: +234 (0) 7058078841/08052035034

British Library Cataloguing-in-Publication Data
A catalogue record for this book is available from the British Library

ISBN: 9781913976217

Nigeria's Policy Response to COVID-19 Pandemic

Isaac N. Obasi

Table of Contents

Part Four: COVID-19 Policy Response at the Sub-National Level

Part Five: Private Sector Policy Response (CACOVID), and Citizens' uncooperative Behaviour to COVID-19 Policy Interventions

Dedication

❖ To the Glory of Almighty God for His Mercy, Faithfulness and Love,

❖ Beloved members of my Family:

 ✓ My wife Prof. (Mrs.) Susan Nwakego Obasi
 ✓ Francis Chidiebere Obasi
 ✓ Pamela Chinenye Obasi
 ✓ Eric Chiemeka Nwokoma Obasi &
 ✓ Susan (Jr.) Chioma Nwanyioma Obasi

❖ All health workers in Nigeria who risked their lives during the lockdown period, and all those who lost their precious lives to COVID-19 pandemic (2020-2022).

Acknowledgements

All who survived the most dreaded period of COVID-19 pandemic in Nigeria particularly during the lockdown, would remember very well that it was a period characterized by uncertainty of life, occasioned by the heightened fear of whether one would be the next victim of the virus or not. It was also a period that a good number of people experienced depression for lack of adjustment to a life of confinement (like in a prison) that the lockdown policy imposed. It was again a period that some hitherto peaceful couples were reported to be having disagreements in the absence of serious engagements in their careers. The lockdown period was indeed a challenging one for many who could not quickly adjust to the changing circumstances. However, for some intellectually-minded people, it was a period to engage their minds productively. This was the path that this author chose during that most difficult period.

The writing of this book therefore started when this author took a column in the *Sundiata Post Online newspaper* in 2020 to focus on the evolving and then highly dreaded coronavirus (COVID-19) pandemic. The main focus of the column was on Nigeria's policy response to the pandemic and other related issues. Be that as it may, my profound gratitude goes to Mr. Max Amuchie Founder/CEO of Sundiata Post Media Ltd (Abuja & London) who graciously provided the opportunity to publish the articles that appeared during the lockdown period. As the Editor-in-Chief of the newspaper, he was overstretched going through each submitted article on every other days. It was his habit not to go to bed until he read the NCDC COVID-19 Update which appeared every night of the week.

My beloved family was very supportive during this period of serious intellectual engagement. First, the spiritual support of almost every one of them in their participation in the Mid-Day Mass by the Holy Cross Cathedral (Catholic) Church, Lagos, and aired on the Lumen Christi Television, DSTV Channel 350 every day, was spiritually regenerative and awakening in a period of uncertainty of life. Like in many other families, God demonstrated His sustaining power in the life of our family during the lockdown. Secondly, the excellent role of my wife Prof. Susan N. Obasi in making sure that the body was also well nourished with the right food to keep me strong in the writing exercise is very noteworthy and well appreciated. Special thanks go to Pamela Chinenye and her younger sister Susan (Jr.) Chioma, who steadily ensured that my meals were ready at the right time to sustain the tempo and flow of the writings. Along with Eric Chiemeka the three of them (though not working and earning income then) voluntarily ensured that my wife and I did not go out either to the bank physically or to the ATM in search of money during that risky period. They generously provided the money the family needed from the various savings they prudently kept while studying in the universities. This very thoughtful gesture has remained evergreen in my mind for which I am very grateful. I am equally indebted to Eric Chiemeka who downloaded all the published versions of the articles for a period of two years, and then arranged them orderly to enable me to do the re-writing required for this book.

I shared a good number of the published articles with selected scholars who provided feedback and for which I am immensely grateful. My profound gratitude therefore goes to Prof. Ladipo Adamolekun (former World Bank public sector management specialist and a distinguished Public Administration scholar) for his encouragement in the writing of this book.

I am most grateful to Dr. Joseph Ene, MD/CEO of Well-Point Hospital, Gwarimpa, Abuja who enthusiastically engaged me in robust and sometimes critical discussions that sharpened some of my thoughts during the earlier writing period. My special thanks go to Prof. Nze Cletus Aguwa, former Dean, Faculty of Pharmaceutical Sciences, University of Nigeria, Nsukka (UNN) with whom I bounced off ideas every Sunday of the week. My immense thanks also go to Prof. Zeph Njoku (Professor of Science Education at the University of Nigeria Nsukka) who was very active in giving me helpful feedback. His reactions served as a tonic to my writing spirit then.

Furthermore, I remain profoundly grateful, Dr. Joe Abah - *the Country Director of Development Alternatives Incorporated (DAI)* – who sometimes provided feedback each time I sent to him few of the articles. I am equally very grateful to Prof. Eric C. Eboh who was very engaging and constructive in his reactions to the articles which he found time to read out of his crowded engagement as the Chief Job and Wealth Creation Officer of Delta State. I sincerely appreciate the encouragement I received from the following: Prof. G. A. Chukwu (formerly of the African University of Science and Technology, Abuja); Chief C. C. Iwuaru, (retired Director, Central Bank of Nigeria and President, Ugwu Mbaise Abuja), and Mr. Charles Nwachukwu, (retired senior federal civil servant, Abuja) all of whom gave me encouragement during the writing of the newspaper articles.

My utmost gratitude goes to the entire print and broadcast media for the excellent reporting of the COVID-19 pandemic even at the grave risk to the lives of their courageous staff. My profound thanks go to all the editors and their reporters.

Lastly but by no means the least, my utmost gratitude goes to Roseline Yacim Ph.D (Head of Department of Theatre Arts, University of Abuja) for painstakingly carrying out the professional proofreading of the manuscript. Her ability to go through all the 65 chapters of the book within a short period of time was highly commendable. Other authors and publishers will find in her a capable professional partner.

Isaac Nnamdi Obasi
University of Abuja,
August, 2022

Preface

This book dwells on how the Nigerian federal and state governments as well as the citizens fought the battle against the coronavirus (COVID-19) pandemic within the framework of public policy. The book provides a historical analysis of Nigeria's policy response to the COVID-19 pandemic and other related issues from 2020 to 2022. It covers critical problems that confronted the Nigerian government and her people in their responses to the challenges posed by the pandemic. Specifically, the problems encountered in the implementation of the polices such as the lockdown policy and its associated issues of re-opening of offices, schools, markets, churches and mosques, entertainment and event centres; observance of the Non-Pharmaceutical Interventions (NPIs); enforcement of the wearing of face mask; vaccination mandate; welfare of health workers; the existing weak health system, etc., were critically discussed. The book also discussed the management of COVID-19 in few other countries (the US, Brazil, etc) that in one way or the other had impact on how people behaved in Nigeria when the battle against the virus was raging. In all of the issues covered, the underlying focus was on the big policy lessons that Nigeria could learn from the COVID-19 pandemic experience.

The book contains 65 chapters within the structural framework of ten major parts which are: (1) introductory and background issues, (2) COVID-19 and Nigeria's atypical governance challenge; (3) Nigeria's COVID-19 policy management; (4) COVID-19 policy response at the sub-national level; (5) Private sector response (CACOVID), and citizens' uncooperative behaviour to Nigeria's COVID-19 policy interventions; (6) Transformation of PTF to PSC on COVID-19, and the verdict by the Global Normalcy Index on Nigeria's policy response; (7) COVID-19 vaccine and its controversies; (8) Cross-cutting and general issues; (9) COVID-19 policy response in some countries; and lastly (10) Managing the return to normalcy to a receding COVID-19 pandemic.

Although, many more issues could have been covered, but as we know, COVID-19 pandemic itself is a multi-disciplinary issue which also involves multi-disciplinary interventions. This is because the impact of the virus is all encompassing in such areas as health, economic, political, educational, social, and religious spheres of life. COVID-19 policy response therefore cannot be comprehensively analysed from one disciplinary perspective or lens. A single book can hardly do justice to all the issues involved in the wider subject matter of COVID-19 pandemic.

This book therefore adopts a social science-wide policy perspective in its analysis. Be that as it may, other writers (particularly those from the wider medical and allied sciences) can examine the same issue from their own disciplinary perspectives which would no doubt enrich our understanding of the subject matter.

Nigeria's coordinating institutional response to COVID-19 emergency was called the Presidential Task Force on COVID-19 (PTF on COVID-19). This was later changed cosmetically to the Presidential Steering Committee on COVID-19 (PSC on COVID-19). Most of Nigeria's policy interventions to COVID-19, were initiated by this body with the approval of the president. And as a result of this, an important section of this book called Appendices contain some of the policy interventions released by the Presidential Task Force/Steering Committee during its National Briefings. The president's addresses to the nation on the pandemic are also included for the benefit of readers who may be interested in the original versions of such addresses.

How did COVID-19 pandemic affect the world and especially Nigeria in terms of number of cases of infection confirmed as well as fatalities? As of the time this author ended commentaries on COVID-19 in his column in March 2022 – the end-period covered by this book - the world had a little over 468 million confirmed cases of the virus, and a little over 6 million deaths according to the statistics of the World Health Organization (WHO). The same period, Nigeria recorded 255,415 confirmed cases with 3,142 deaths according to the statistics of the Nigeria Centre for Disease Control (NCDC). As of 20 August 2022 when the author concluded the manuscript of this book, Nigeria had 262,748 confirmed cases and 3,147 deaths. Generally speaking, in relations to other countries particularly outside of Africa, Nigeria was not so badly affected by the pandemic. But this conclusion raises the issue of the accuracy of Nigeria's data. This controversial issue was the subject of discussion in one of the chapters.

The subject matter covered by this book is a public health issue which concerns everyone. Consequently, no one can afford not to be interested in such a matter. Be that as it may, the book took the reading interest of the general public into account as well as policy makers and students of public policy in both public and private sectors of the economy. And since the major policy lessons contained in the book are intended to promote public health, the book is highly recommended for every family for the benefit of posterity. Furthermore, all students in the Social Science discipline will find the book very useful in carrying out research on many issues of interest to them. Finally, the book is valuable to students in the wider medical sciences and allied disciplines.

Part One
Introductory and Background Issues

CHAPTER ONE

Introduction

The Outbreak of COVID-19 and World Health Organization's (WHO) Response

The outbreak of Coronavirus (COVID-19) pandemic in Wuhan, China in December 2019 shook China to its foundations. The entire world watched China vigorously battling with the virus not knowing that it would soon reach everywhere in the world. Truly and shortly, it spread to every nooks and crannies of the world in 2020. Consequently, the World Health Organization (WHO) declared the novel coronavirus (COVID-19) as a "Public Health Emergency of International Concern" (PHEIC) on January 30, 2020, and shortly later as a *pandemic* on March 11, 2020.

The two declarations by WHO on January 30, and March 11, 2020, were accompanied by certain measures which all countries of the world were expected to adopt as immediate policy responses to help control the spread of the coronavirus (COVID-19).

First, when WHO declared COVID-19 a PHEIC in January 30, after the meeting of the International Health Regulations (IHR) (2005) Emergency Committee on the outbreak of the virus, it called all countries of the world (through a Statement issued by its Director-General Dr. Tedros Adhanom Ghebreyesus) to among others:

- ✓ implement decisions that are evidence-based and consistent,
- ✓ support countries with weaker health systems,
- ✓ accelerate the development of vaccines, therapeutics and diagnostics,
- ✓ combat the spread of rumours and misinformation,
- ✓ review preparedness plans, identify gaps and evaluate the resources needed to identify, isolate and care for cases, and prevent transmission,
- ✓ share data, knowledge and experience with WHO and the world,

✓ work together in a spirit of solidarity and cooperation.[1]

Consequently, the WHO concluded by saying that:

> we are all in this together, and
> we can only stop it together.
> This is the time for facts, not fear.
> This is the time for science, not rumours.
> This is the time for solidarity, not stigma.[2]

Secondly, when WHO declared COVID-19, a pandemic on March 11, 2020, it said in its very powerful confidence-building statement that:

> In the past two weeks, the number of cases of COVID-19 outside China has increased 13-fold, and the number of affected countries has tripled. There are now more than 118,000 cases in 114 countries, and 4,291 people have lost their lives. Thousands more are fighting for their lives in hospitals. In the days and weeks ahead, we expect to see the number of cases, the number of deaths, and the number of affected countries climb even higher. WHO has been assessing this outbreak around the clock and we are deeply concerned both by the alarming levels of spread and severity, and by the alarming levels of inaction. We have therefore made the assessment that COVID-19 can be characterized as a pandemic... We have never before seen a pandemic sparked by a coronavirus. This is the first pandemic caused by a coronavirus. And we have never before seen a pandemic that can be controlled, at the same time. WHO has been in full response mode since we were notified of the first cases. And we have called every day for countries to take urgent and aggressive action. We have rung the alarm bell loud and clear.[3] (Emphasis added).

---

[1] WHO (2020): WHO Director-General's statement on IHR Emergency Committee on Novel Coronavirus (2019-nCoV). Available at: https://www.who.int/director- general/speeches/detail/who-director-general-s-statement-on-ihr-emergency-committee-on-novel-coronavirus-(2019-ncov).

[2] Ibid.

[3] WHO (2020): WHO Director-General's opening remarks at the media briefing on COVID-19 - 11 March 2020. Available at: https://www.who.int/director-general/speeches/detail/who-director-general-s-opening-remarks-at-the-media-briefing-on-covid-19---11-march-2020.

Furthermore, WHO persuasively remarked:

> …we cannot say this loudly enough, or clearly enough, or often enough: all countries can still change the course of this pandemic. If countries detect, test, treat, isolate, trace, and mobilize their people in the response, those with a handful of cases can prevent those cases becoming clusters, and those clusters becoming community transmission. Even those countries with community transmission or large clusters can turn the tide on this virus. Several countries have demonstrated that this virus can be suppressed and controlled. The challenge for many countries who are now dealing with large clusters or community transmission is not whether they can do the same – it's whether they will.
> Some countries are struggling with a lack of capacity.
> Some countries are struggling with a lack of resources.
> Some countries are struggling with a lack of resolve.[4]

Commending the measures taken in some countries at this initial stage of the pandemic, the Director-General said:

> We are grateful for the measures being taken in Iran, Italy and the Republic of Korea to slow the virus and control their epidemics. We know that these measures are taking a heavy toll on societies and economies, just as they did in China. All countries must strike a fine balance between protecting health, minimizing economic and social disruption, and respecting human rights. WHO's mandate is public health. But we're working with many partners across all sectors to mitigate the social and economic consequences of this pandemic. This is not just a public health crisis, it is a crisis that will touch every sector – so every sector and every individual must be involved in the fight. I have said from the beginning that countries must take a whole-of-government, whole-of-society approach, built around a comprehensive strategy to prevent infections, save lives and minimize impact.[5]

Finally, the Director-General persuasively summarized his ideas in four key areas. First, all countries should prepare and be ready. Second, they

---

[4] Ibid.
[5] Ibid

should detect, protect and treat. Third, they should reduce transmission, and fourth, they should innovate and learn. He then reminded all countries to activate and scale up their emergency response mechanisms which would involve communicating with their people about the risks and how they can protect themselves. Again, they should find, isolate, test and treat every case and trace every contact. They should also get their hospitals ready, protect and train their health workers. Other important and actionable measures he listed are: prevention, preparedness, public health, and political leadership.[6]

With these very powerful confidence-building statements, WHO energized and mobilized the world to confront a novel pandemic that had never been seen before. As a follow-up, WHO swiftly announced some non-pharmaceutical safety measures to reduce the rapid spread of the virus across the world. Consequently, many countries announced their national policy responses in line with WHO's advice contained in its very powerful statements above.

Nigeria's National Policy Response

Nigeria quick response was the setting up of the Presidential Task Force on COVID-19 (PTF on COVID-19) by President Muhammadu Buhari on March 9, 2020, to serve as Nigeria's coordinating institutional response to COVID-19 emergency. This Task Force was established also "to coordinate and oversee Nigeria's multi-sectoral inter-governmental efforts to contain the spread and mitigate the impact of the Covid-19 pandemic." The Nigeria Centre for Disease Control (NCDC) – a parastatal under the Federal Ministry of Health – remained the 'foot soldier' of this very important Task Force.

For two years, Nigeria fought the battle against the devastating effects of COVID-19 with vigour. This is a pandemic which according to the WHO claimed over 6 million deaths and over 468 million confirmed cases across the globe as of 20 March 2022[7]. Nigeria like many other

---

[6] Ibid.

[7] WHO (2022): *COVID-19 Weekly Epidemiological Update*, Edition 84, published 22 March 2022. See https://www.who.int/publications/m/item/weekly-epidemiological-update-on-covid-19---22-march-2022

countries, passed through difficult period in the implementation of its policy response particularly in the areas of the economically devastating and socially dislocating lockdown policy, wearing of face masks, obeying the social distancing protocol, and vaccination policy among many others.

What was Nigeria's experience in the implementation of its policy response? Put differently, how effective was the implementation of Nigeria's policy response at the national and sub-national levels of governance? How did for instance, Nigeria's atypical governance mentality and challenge affect the implementation of the COVID-19 policy response? Again, to what extent did the Nigerian citizens cooperate with the government in the implementation of Nigeria's policy response? These and many other issues with their policy lessons were the subject of discussions in this book.

Scope of the Book

Although, many more issues could have been covered on the subject matter of this book, but as we know, COVID-19 pandemic itself is a multi-disciplinary issue which also involves multi-disciplinary policy interventions. This is because the impact of the virus is all encompassing in such areas as health, economic, political, educational, social, and religious spheres of life. COVID-19 policy response therefore cannot be comprehensively analysed from one disciplinary perspective or lens. A single book can hardly achieve such an ambitious goal. This book therefore adopts a social science-wide policy perspective in its analysis. Be that as it may, other writers (particularly those from the wider medical and allied sciences) can examine the same issue from their own disciplinary lens and perspectives which will no doubt enrich our understanding of the subject matter.

This book is made up of ten parts comprising of 65 chapters inclusive of introductory chapter. The length of all the other relatively shorter chapters reflected largely the original newspaper articles the author published in his column on COVID-19 pandemic in the *Sundiata Post* online newspaper from 2020 to 2022. During that period, the column steadily and consistently followed the emergence of COVID-19 pandemic, its spread and devastating impact, policy response, citizens' reactions, discovery of COVID-19 vaccine, implementation of vaccination policy and its resistance, and the eventual relaxation of restrictive policy measures following the receding of COVID-19 pandemic.

Part 1 of the book, deals with *Introductory and Background Issues* which elucidate the main themes and components of the book, as well as the origin of COVID-19. It also covers the emergence of a new culture of social interaction called social distancing introduced by the World Health Organization (WHO). From the book's insight, many Nigerians found it very difficult to comply with the social distancing policy in their daily activities because they preferred to carry on with their *business-as-usual-mentality* thereby validating the phrase that *old habits die hard*. It was difficult getting many Nigerians to comply even among those in government.

Thereafter, Part 2 focuses on *Covid-19 and Nigeria's Atypical Governance Challenge*. This part demonstrates the fact that governance in Nigeria runs in cycles with simple problems allowed to fester and become complex and seemingly unresolvable. Such phenomenon has become atypical over the years because many countries experiencing similar problems do find easy solutions while Nigeria's problems are allowed to fester. The first case (outside the scope of this book) is the non-functioning of Nigeria's refineries over the years amidst huge sums of money budgeted for their maintenance without results, and its concomitant costly and corruption-ridden importation of fuel, subsidy and fuel scarcity saga. The second is the perennial strikes by the Academic Staff Union of Universities (ASUU) which successive governments have over the years allowed to persist and run in cycles. Both problems and many others have persisted for a long period of time regardless of the regime or political party in power. This is atypical of Nigerian governance system.

Within the period of COVID-19 lockdown, some issues exposed the atypical nature of Nigeria's governance system on the side of the government and that of the governed also. Specifically, the COVID-19 lockdown in 2020 exposed some aspects of the governance weaknesses in Nigeria at both the national and sub-national levels. At the national level for example, issues such as trust-deficit, impunity and abuse of power, widespread tendency of citizens to disobey lockdown rules and safety protocols, became very glaring. And at the sub-national level, there was evidence of lack of cooperation and collaboration with the federal government's efforts to contain the spread of the virus. The Federal and state governments were at times not on the same speed level in implementing the appropriate policy response against COVID-19. Some chapters in this part of the book support the hypothesis of an atypical nature of Nigeria's governance system where over-temporizing attitude to decision making, disobedience to laws and flouting of presidential directives, poor enforcement of laws and public policies, citizens' distrust of government, and impunity on both part of public officials and the citizens, held sway.

Part 3 which is titled *Nigeria's COVID-19 Policy Management* discusses a wide range of issues on policy coordination in the management of COVID-19 pandemic from a national perspective. It starts by examining the *Presidential Task Force (PTF) on COVID-19* established to serve as Nigeria's coordinating institutional response to COVID-19 emergency. As a federation, Nigeria needed such a body to coordinate and oversee multi-sectoral inter-governmental efforts to contain the spread and mitigate the impact of the COVID-19 pandemic.[8] On the one hand, there was a lot of policy measures adopted and implemented by the *PTF on COVID-19* to accomplish its very important mandate, and on the other hand, there was a good number of attendant issues, challenges and even reactions by the citizens (particularly workers) towards the implemented policy measures by the PTF as well as the federal and state governments. One issue of particular concern which was addressed in this section was the question of implementing COVID-19 policies in Nigeria's weak health system. Another issue was how to manage COVID-19 induced austerity budget in a widely perceived over-bloated federal bureaucracy over which the *Report of the Presidential Committee on the Restructuring and Rationalization of Federal Government Parastatals, Commissions and Agencies* (Stephen Oronsaye Report, 2012) had addressed but not yet implemented. Nigeria is still living with the costly effects of an over-bloated federal bureaucracy with its concomitant corruption and high cost of governance.

---

[8] Presidential Task Force on COVID-19 (2020): 'About the PTF'. Available at: http://www.statehouse.gov.ng.

Chapter One | Isaac Nnamdi Obasi

Other attendant issues examined in Part 3 include (a) the controversial lockdown exit policy for educational institutions; (b) the problem of resolving the initial dilemma of lifting the lockdown policy; (c) the issue of violation of presidential ban on inter-state movement, which some have argued was the time Boko Haran insurgents, bandits and other criminally-minded people moved illegally from the far Northern part to the Central/Middle-Belt and Southern parts of the country (e.g. the menace of many criminally-minded motorcyclists in Lagos - who appear not to be Nigerians – is one case of such illegally transported people during the lockdown); (d) the question of poor compliance with COVID-19 safety protocols and guidelines in spite of the plethora of risk communication messages put out by relevant authorities; (e) the troubling issue of low COVID-19 testing exercises on the one hand, and the unethical practice of adopted but later abandoned policy of charging students for testing services on the other hand; (f) the very controversial issue (dilemma and politics) of school reopening under COVID-19 lockdown – an issue that would have prevented Nigeria's SS3 students from taking the West African Senior School Certificate Examinations (WASSCE) conducted by West African Examination Council (WAEC); and (g) the important issue of safety and welfare of health workers, as well as the welfare of Nigerian workers generally under a pandemic. All these identified and well-discussed issues constitute important factors in assessing Nigeria's response to COVID-19 pandemic.

Part 4 focuses on *COVID-19 Policy Response at the Sub-national Level.* It starts with a discussion on what this author calls 'COVID-19 pandemic and the Kano State Debacle' referring to a situation that was reported in the media as 'mysterious deaths' in Kano which nevertheless were majorly related to COVID-19. This COVID-19 sub-national level experience reflected a clear case of poor response to the pandemic. For example, the lockdown order by the Kano State Government came so late that it made no significant impact in minimizing the spread of COVID-19. Like many other states in Nigeria, Kano State government was unprepared when the incidence of COVID-19 were recorded in its domain. Again, its people ignored all social and physical distancing protocols and moved with a business-as-usual mentality.

Other issues examined in this Part 4 include (a) Rivers State

Governor Nyesom Wike's overzealous style of punishing COVID-19 lockdown violators; as compared with (b) the gentle fighting style of Governor Babajide Sanwo-Olu of Lagos, which led admirers of Governor Sanwo-Olu to call him a democrat, and Wike a despot. This specific reaction followed the flouting of the restriction order in Lagos State by two hotels which the governor reacted by closing them down, as against a similar case in Rivers State which attracted instant demolition by governor Wike. In other words, faced with the same situations where two hotels flouted the lockdown restrictions in their different domains, Governor Sanwo-Olu shut them down, while Governor Wike demolished them; (c) the issue of what this author calls bad politics which has been one of the atypical features of Nigeria's governance system and which also was at play in the lopsided distribution of COVID-19 palliatives, illegal movement of criminally-minded people during the lockdown against presidential directive, the alleged lopsided distribution of conditional cash transfer across the country during the lockdown, among other things. In fact, it was as result of bad politics that some people spread COVID-19 during lockdown in the name of transporting cows, agricultural products and cement. The effects of such spread were highly palpable especially in River State where the number rose sharply thereafter in spite of the spirited efforts of Governor Wike to stop the spread of the virus through his draconian style. Bad politics contributed to the spread of the COVID-19 pandemic in Nigeria, but it also did across the world, as the example of the United States under Donald Trump demonstrated; (d) the issue of the low verve of inter-governmental cooperation that affected federal government's efforts to contain the spread of the virus; (e) the assessment of COVID-19 fight at the sub-national levels; (f) a specific focus on Kogi State and its weird style of fighting the COVID-19 pandemic; and (g) the analysis of ten leading states in terms of COVID-19 number of infections and deaths in the first year (Feb. 2020 – Feb. 2021) which was the most dreaded period in the fight against the virus. The ten leading states were Lagos, FCT, Plateau, Kaduna, Oyo, Rivers, Edo, Ogun, Kano and Ondo. All the chapters in this part 4 underscore the need for effective inter-governmental cooperation and collaboration in a federation when faced with a national emergency like the outbreak of a pandemic.

Part 5 deals with the contributions of organized private sector to Nigeria's policy response against the pandemic, and how the citizens reacted to Nigeria's policy response. It is titled *Private Sector Response (CACOVID), and Citizens' uncooperative Behaviour, to Nigeria's COVID-19 Policy Interventions.* The private sector's contributions were made through its newly created body called the Coalition Against COVID-19 (CACOVID). With respect to CACOVID, the private sector mobilized tremendous support in both the fight against COVID-19 itself (coronavirus) and against hunger (hunger-virus). Its fight against hunger-virus was through the massive distribution of palliatives to indigent Nigerians during the lockdown. In 2020 alone, CACOVID mobilized nearly N39 million to execute its seven identified projects namely welfare, case management, IPC, laboratory, logistics, branding and communication, and surveillance. It spent over N22 billion (approximately 58%) on welfare of Nigerians, and close to N9 billion (N22%) on case management. It also spent close to N3 billion (approximately 7%) on Laboratory support, among the other seven items of expenditure.

The second segment of Part 5 which discusses citizens' uncooperative behaviour towards Nigeria's COVID-19 policy response, identified how such lack of cooperation by the citizens hindered a concerted fight against the pandemic. The first challenge it discussed was the holding of mega political rallies in September and October 2020 in Edo and Ondo states respectively for the governorship election campaigns. The huge crowds that attended the rallies made the gathering super-spreader events and compounded further efforts to stop the spread of the virus. The second challenge was the *#EndSARS* massive peaceful protests against police brutality across many parts of the country. Altogether, these events led to the emergence of the second wave of the pandemic in Nigeria. In actual fact, the mammoth crowds of people at the Edo and Ondo governorship campaign rallies as well as at the #EndSARS protests, were in complete violation of COVID-19 safety guidelines and non-pharmaceutical protocols. The hijack of the #EndSARS peaceful protests subsequently by hoodlums (hooligans) led to massive destruction of properties, looting of government and CACOVID stored - yet to be distributed - palliatives across the country. There was also the looting of medical stores which adversely impacted on public health management, and ultimately constituted major setbacks in the management of COVID-19 in Nigeria.

In addition to all these, the sudden emergence of a culture of vanishing fear of COVID-19 by the people at a time when the virus was still devastating nations across the world including Nigeria, became a big problem in the efforts to stop the spread of the virus. Towards the last quarter of 2020, Nigerians started behaving as if the pandemic was over. This was reflected in their low level of compliance to the risk communication messages by the Presidential Task Force on COVID-19 and the Nigeria Centre for Disease Control (NCDC). The premature vanishing of fear was perhaps simply because the lockdown was gradually being eased out, and as this was happening, some people started talking about Coronavirus in past tense as if it had gone finally.

Another area of uncooperative behaviour, was the case of a widespread disobedience (non-compliant behaviour) by international air passengers to the requirement for a mandatory COVID-19 PCR test. This prompted the *PTF on COVID19* to raise an alarm that the level of non-compliance was very high. Lastly, there was the bigger challenge of many people not being able to adjust their social behaviour to the demands of the new normal, such as wearing of face masks, maintaining social distancing, and observance of other non-pharmaceutical protocols. All these were signs of non-cooperative behaviour by the people to Nigeria's policy response to COVID-19 pandemic.

Part 6, is titled *Transformation of PTF to PSC on COVID-19, and the Verdict by the Global Normalcy Index on Nigeria's Policy Response*. In detail, this section deals with why the Presidential Task Force (PTF) on COVID-19 was changed to Presidential Steering Committee (PSC) on COVID-19. It is argued that the change of name which occurred after about a year (April 1, 2021) of the existence of PTF, was a smart move to retain the tenure of the PTF which was adjudged to be doing relatively well by those who were keenly following its activities. It is important to state that there was no substantial difference in the functions performed by the two bodies, but the nomenclatural change was to offer the new body the flexibility to stay longer than an *ad hoc* body like PTF would have enjoyed. By its very nature, a task force is an *ad hoc* body which should not be allowed to exist for a long time if it is to perform effectively.

The second major issue examined in this section was a verdict on Nigeria's policy response to COVID-19 pandemic by the Global

Normalcy Index which ranked Nigeria's response to COVID-19 as the fourth most successful in the world. This was a very encouraging pronouncement that warranted a scrutiny in this book. An assessment of this positive rating by this author in this section lends credence to the verdict. The third and last issue discussed in this section was the appointment of the former Director General of the Nigeria Centre for Disease Control (NCDC) Dr. Chikwe Ihekweazu by WHO as its Assistant Director-General for Health Emergency Intelligence with effect from November 1, 2021. This appointment given to *Nigeria's dogged fighter against COVID-19* did not come to many discerning minds as a surprise. Dr. Ihekweazu according to WHO "will lead the work on strengthening pandemic and epidemic intelligence globally, including heading the WHO Hub for Pandemic and Epidemic Intelligence in Berlin." Again, this appointment lends credence to our thesis in this book that Nigeria's policy response to the pandemic was on balance, commendable. The additional responsibilities given to Dr. Ihekweazu by the WHO, was a clear evidence of his courageous and excellent performance at home.

Part 7 titled *COVID-19 Vaccine and its Controversies* discusses emerging issues around the discovery of COVID-19 vaccine. Ordinarily, the scientific world expected everyone to be excited with the discovery of a COVID-19 vaccine as the entire humanity was badly in need of a vaccine to win the war against the ravaging effects of the pandemic. When one was eventually found, many people expressed overwhelming relief and outright joy. However and surprisingly, some others did not welcome the arrival of a vaccine. They even went ahead to stage protests against the vaccine and its use in midst of a ravaging pandemic. This author considers such behaviour as weird, retrogressive and counter-productive to public health. Specifically, this section examines the controversies surrounding the discovery and use of COVID-19 vaccine nationally and internationally, as well as other related issues such as (a) vaccine euphoria in Nigeria amidst scepticisms of some others; (b) vexed question of local production of COVID-19 vaccine in Nigeria; (c) vaccine nationalism vs equity; (d) resistance to government's enforcement of compulsory vaccination policy by some Nigerians; and lastly (e) the important question of averting the 'pandemic of the unvaccinated' if resistance against the use of COVID-19 vaccine is not defeated.

Part 8 focuses on a wide range of themes the author calls *Cross-cutting and General Issues*. The first issue examined is the *spiritual dimension of COVID-19 pandemic* where we argued that across the world, the policy response to COVID-19 pandemic was not strictly limited to pharmaceutical and non-pharmaceutical interventions, as some countries adopted a spiritual approach to the problem. Nigeria was one of the countries that did so, as the Federal Government at a point in 2020 resorted to a spiritual intervention calling on God to stem the tide of the then rising cases of infection and death. Seen against the fact that there is an omniscient and omnipotent God, this spiritual approach was not bad in itself when done with a sincere heart and also following science. However, in two African countries (Tanzania and Burundi) for example, this approach was taken too far thereby leading to the avoidable death of their presidents. In Nigeria, where the approach was combined with science, the action still generated controversies among critics who accused the government of running out of ideas of how to handle the COVID-19 crisis. The chapter on this, underscores the importance of the spiritual dimension of COVID-19 when the approach is combined with science.

The second issue examined is the celebration of *World Mask Week* amidst reluctance or outright resistance to wear face mask across the world. The third issue discussed is the adoption of Nigeria Economic Sustainability Plan to cope with the harsh realities of the pandemic. The fourth is the adoption of the Safe School Declaration by Nigeria to minimize the further disruption of school calendar under a pandemic. This was against the widespread insecurity that disrupted schooling since the Boko Haram abducted the Chibok schoolgirls in Borno State in 2014. The fifth issue is an interrogation of COVID-19 data on infections and deaths in Nigeria, where we argued that Nigeria's reported low cases of infection and death in comparison to other countries appeared not to have reflected fully the reality on the ground. The numbers were more likely to be much higher than reported for reasons that had to do with low testing nationwide, reporting of certain deaths as mysterious rather than attributing them to COVID-19, among many other factors. Lastly, the section discussed what the author calls *A Week-Like-no-Other in Nigeria*, which tried to show that the month of December 2020, was the most devastating in terms of high profile deaths, high profile infections, and general high rates of infections as at that time, among other reasons. Specifically, the week of 7-13 December, 2020 with very high rising cases of infection is described in the book as 'a week like no other.'

Part 9 which is titled *COVID-19 Policy Response in some Countries* presents an analysis of how selected countries responded to the pandemic. The countries and their presidents were selected because of policy lessons that Nigeria and other countries could learn from their experience. However, New York State in the United States (which is not a country) was selected for its experience as an epicentre of the virus in the US and whose, then Governor Andrew Cuomo fought doggedly to win the battle of reducing the devastating effects of the virus. Cuomo's exemplary leadership during the pandemic deserves to be highlighted in any serious book on policy response to the COVID-19 pandemic. It is not by sheer coincidence therefore that Part 9 started its discussion with a chapter titled *COVID-19 'War': New York State as Most Dreaded Battleground*.

The second issue examined in this section was on former president Donald Trump's misplaced anger against China over the origin of the pandemic as a cover up of his abysmal failure at home to control the spread of the virus. Since Trump's words and actions then attracted global attention with China responding and taking strategic steps to outshine the US on matters related to COVID-19 pandemic, this chapter was appropriately titled *COVID-19 Global Politics*. In addition to Trump, whose critical views against China had self-serving motive, there were however genuine criticisms against China from some other people. One notable person was Dr. Oby Ezekwezili, Nigeria's former Minister of Education who asked China to "demonstrate world leadership by acknowledging its failures to be transparent on covid-19." She specifically asked China to pay reparation to Africa for the incalculable damages the Wuhan-originated virus had done to African economies.

China's undiplomatic reaction to Dr. Oby Ezekwesili's criticisms formed the basis of a discussion of another chapter titled *COVID-19 Pandemic and China's New Conciliatory Tone on Africa*. Given the quick reactions that trailed China's unfriendly statement (including the one by this author in an opinion article), China promptly changed its rhetoric. During the Virtual Event of the 73rd World Health Assembly on Monday, 18 May 2020, Chinese President Xi Jinping struck the right chord by promising that China would provide greater support to Africa.

The fourth issue examined under this section was on New York State again but this time on how its then governor was able to tame the beast of coronavirus that hitherto constituted a nightmare to the State.

The effectiveness of Governor Andrew Cuomo's policy response needed to be highlighted in details for the benefit of posterity. Quite unlike former president Trump who jettisoned science, Governor Cuomo adopted a science-based and knowledge-driven policy response to COVID-19 pandemic. He was extra-ordinarily exemplary in providing leadership in the war against COVID-19. History would be kind to him in the way and manner he fought COVID-19 pandemic, regardless of the circumstances that forced him to leave Office later.

The fifth issue examined is titled *COVID-19 Policy Response in Brazil: Irrational Scepticism and its Repercussions.* The discussion here underscores the fact that President Bolsonaro (like Donald Trump of the United States) lived in denial of the existence of COVID-19 pandemic and downplayed its ravaging impact since its outbreak in China. He was widely reported for calling the coronavirus 'a little flu' also just like Trump. Afterwards, he began to have problems with his health professionals over the management of COVID-19 pandemic. He sacked his health minister following disagreement over social isolation measures which he dismissed as unnecessary. In less than a month (May, 2020), a second minister (the successor of the sacked minister) voluntarily resigned following also a disagreement with the president over the management of COVID-19 issues. This was at a time when Brazil recorded 844 new deaths in 24 hours (recording a total death toll then at 13,993), and a total number of infections at 202,918 then. At this time too, Brazil was the sixth most infected country in the world. With the exit of two health ministers (who were health professionals) driving the fight against the virus, and the appointment of non-health professional (with a military background), Brazil began to witness the worst in total number of infections and fatalities. With President Bolsonaro's defiant attitude and not-well-thought out statements about the coronavirus, it was not surprising that Brazil began to face calamitous repercussions. It was just a matter of time that he himself got the infection and not even once. He was lucky to have escaped death.

The sixth issue in this section (Part 9) is *The US Policy Response to COVID-19 Pandemic under the Trump Administration.* The discussion here made the point that except for the diehard supporters of former President Trump, there is consensus that Trump failed in his fight against the COVID-19 pandemic in the US. His former security adviser,

John Bolton, said as much when he appeared on CNN's *The Situation Room* anchored by Wolf Blitzer on 24 June 2020. Bolton accused Trump of showing no strong leadership in fighting the virus. Secondly, Trump turned a blind eye to COVID-19 pandemic at the initial period. Thirdly, he politicised every move he made on the fight against the COVID-19, as political calculations went into every decision and policy made on the virus. Lastly, he was erratic in the way he was reacting to the pandemic, as he had no comprehensive strategy to fight it.

The seventh issue focused again on Trump's total disregard for science as he consistently mocked science. More importantly, his ill-advised actions put many to great risk. For example, a hospital worker died after getting infected by a patient who refused to put face mask simply because according to him, Trump was not wearing a face mask. Trump's bad example therefore was certainly sending many people to avoidable early graves. Yet when he eventually got the virus, he received preferential treatment at the Walter Reed National Medical Centre in Maryland. Trump unilaterally left the hospital (while still on admission and treatment) to go on a show in a motorcade and waving to his supporters. By this action, Trump simply mocked science.

Subsequently, the eight issue examined under this section was on how the US tried to restore its battered image under the Trump administration. A golden opportunity came with the election of Joe Biden on November 7, 2020. By his various policy actions taken so far on mask mandate, vaccination and others, Biden was effective in fighting the virus thereby bringing the numbers down in the areas of infections, deaths and hospitalizations. By his policy response, Biden was able to demonstrate that America could do better than many other countries in fighting the pandemic, given her past spectacular achievements in the field of medicine, science and technology.

The ninth issue was a focus on *COVID-19 and Fate of Sceptical Political Leaders*. This discussion was prompted following the death of COVID-19 sceptical political leaders in Africa. The untimely and shocking death of two East African controversial political leaders one at 61 and the other at 55, is an unforgettable lesson in the misuse of Godly faith as well as a total disdain for science which itself is a gift and a power given to man by God himself at creation. The death of COVID-19 sceptic President John Magufuli of Tanzania on 17 March 2021 at the age of 61 years, and the earlier death of another COVID-19 sceptic President Pierre Nkurunziza of Burundi on 8 June 2020 at the age of 55 years (both of which shrouded in controversial circumstances) demonstrated a clear case of pushing scepticism beyond limit.

The last two chapters in Part 9 focused on the Delta and Omicron variants of COVID-19. Among others issues, it discussed the principle behind the naming of variants in a COVID-19 pandemic, as well as the controversies surrounding the emergence of Omicron variant in South Africa. Some developed countries wasted no time in imposing travel restrictions against selected Southern African countries of which South Africa was the main target and big economic loser. The pattern of travel restrictions and the hasty manner of their imposition re-enkindled the ever present and hidden racial divisions among developed and developed countries.

Part 10 is the last section of the book and it is titled *Managing the Return to Normalcy*. First, this section examines some appropriate policy response to a receding COVID-19 pandemic. It observes that many countries across the world were lifting the restrictions previously imposed to reduce the spread of the virus. This policy reversal meant that going forward the major concern should be on how to manage a gradual return to normalcy. Nigeria was not an exception to this policy reversal. It is important to note particularly that Nigeria had gone through a full circle in its policy response namely (a) lockdown stage (most dangerous period) when restrictions were fully imposed, (b) lifting of lockdown and relaxation of restriction stage (imposition of mask mandate and other Non-pharmaceutical interventions), (c) vaccination stage (combined with the observance of Non-pharmaceutical interventions), (d) stage of near full lifting of many of the hitherto imposed restrictions, and lastly (e) the cautious return to normalcy stage.

The gradual return to normalcy implies that all Nigerians have the personal responsibility to manage their adaptation to a gradual return to normalcy. The PSC and NCDC should not be left alone with this responsibility. People should therefore allow part of the new normal behaviour (wearing of mask in crowded places, and observance of other non-pharmaceutical interventions which displaced the old way of life) to still be part of their behaviour in public places as they gradually move into the old way of life. But more importantly, increased efforts at massive vaccination of people is key in the management of the gradual return to normalcy. The book concludes with a chapter on *Major Policy Lessons.*

Notes on Methodological Approach

This book is mainly a product of a documentary research which obtained, selected, compiled, organised, interpreted and analysed[9] needed data and information on Nigeria's policy response to COVID-19 pandemic and other related issues within and outside Nigeria. This documentary methodology was supported by a triangulation method that comprised of direct scientific observations of what actually happened as COVID-19 was unfolding across Nigeria in such places as organizational environment (public and private), churches and mosques, markets, conferences, workshops, event and other entertainment centres, major streets, buses and other means of public transportation.

The print and electronic media (television and newspapers mainly) were veritable sources of some of the observations and collection of relevant information. The daily tracking of the NCDC COVID-19 Case Update whose sample is shown below was one of the major sources of reported data in this book. Furthermore, the tracking and use of the global data provided by the Johns Hopkins University Coronavirus Resources Centre, made comparative analysis not only possible but very easy.

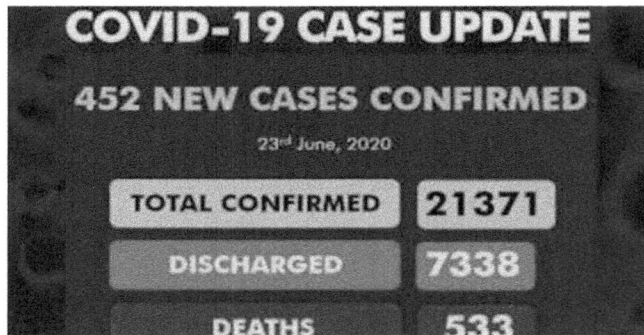

Sample of the Nigeria Centre for Disease Control (NCDC) COVID-19 Case Update that everyone anxiously waited for each passing day during the lockdown period and thereafter. Source: NCDC

---

[9] Adapted from Isabella Network (2020): 'Documentary research: what it is, characteristics and types', See http://www.takecareofmoney.com.

What constituted the first draft of this book were opinion articles that appeared in the author's column in *Sundiata Post* (Online Newspaper: www.sundiadatpost.com). Furthermore, the articles were meticulously edited from March to August, 2022.

Although the book is a product of a painstaking research and may appear a little technical in some areas, it is nevertheless meant to be of interest to the general public because of its public health focus and orientation. As a result of this, some strict bibliographical citation canons were not observed as obtainable in strict academic research and books. For example, the use of titles and full names of public officials or some other private sector actors, were retained as against the canons of strict academic writings. Again, internet sources which formed a larger part of the sources of cited materials (for example) were simply reproduced and prefixed with Via, or See or Available at, rather than the practice of saying when retrieved since the sources reflected happenings at the time of the research or writing (i.e. between 2020 and 2022). It is hoped that readers will enjoy reading through the book without obfuscations.

CHAPTER TWO

The Origin of Coronavirus (COVID-19) Pandemic

Though it is common knowledge that the novel coronavirus (COVID-19) emanated from Wuhan, China, its real origin or source within China has remained controversial even among distinguished members of the scientific communities across the world. For instance, within the World Health Organization (WHO) itself, all possible explanations made so far, still remain hypotheses in its informed opinion. This was why the WHO called for further studies and data on origin of COVID-19 (scientifically called SARS-CoV-2 virus).

Why Knowledge of the Origin of COVID-19 Is Important

Peter B. Embarek of the WHO advances three key reasons why it is important to know the origin of COVID-19. The first is if we find the source and if it's still out there, we can prevent future reintroduction of the same virus into the human population. The second reason is that if we understand how this one jumped from bats origin into humans, we can perhaps prevent similar events in the future. And the third reason is that if we can find the virus, what it looked like before it jumped to the human population, we could potentially be in a better position to develop more efficient treatments and vaccines for this disease.[10] It is clear that those who are of the view that it is sheer waste of precious time and resources to continue seeking an understanding of the origin of this novel virus, are completely missing the point. It is in the interest of public health and indeed humanity to continue the inquiry into the origins of the virus in China. More importantly, in the interest of posterity, it is necessary to ensure that there is transparency in laboratory experiments and the interactions between scientists and the animal world.

---

[10] Embarek, P. B. (2021): *Science in 5* (Episode #21 - COVID-19) - Origins of the SARS-CoV-2 virus. Available at: https://www.who.int/emergencies/diseases/novel-coronavirus-2019/media-resources/science-in-5/episode-21---covid-19---origins-of-the-sars-cov-2-virus

The Controversy itself

With respect to the controversial origin of the virus, two distinguished members of the American National Academy of Sciences, Harrison & Sachs have called for "an independent inquiry into the origin of the SARS-CoV-2 virus."[11] According to them, the origin of the virus has been a topic of intense scientific debate and public speculation. The two main hypotheses they said, are that "the virus emerged from human exposure to an infected animal" or "that it emerged in a research-related incident"[12] (ie the laboratory).

Perhaps against the background of conspiracy theorists who offer divergent views of these origins, a WHO expert Peter B. Embarek persuasively argued that:

> …we have now the tools that allow us to look at the genetic makeup of these viruses.
> And when we look at our virus, the COVID-19 virus, there is nothing in its makeup that would indicate that it has been manufactured. It's clearly a natural virus and there are many of these around, we have seen several of them in the past…laboratory accidents happen unfortunately once in a while. It has happened many times in the past... We have to look at this as a possibility. So, we will of course also look at that hypothesis among many others, even if it's an unlikely one. There is no evidence so far indicating that anybody was working with this virus in the past. There is no evidence to indicate that it would have escaped a laboratory in any way, but of course we will have that in mind when we look at the origin of this virus.[13]

World Health Assembly Resolution WHA73.1

In actual fact, the pathway to unraveling of the origin of the COVID-19 started with the World Health Assembly's request that the Director-

---

[11] Harrison, N. L. & Sachs, J. D. (2022): "A call for an independent inquiry into the origin of the SARS-CoV-2 virus." Available at: https://www.pnas.org/doi/10.1073/pnas.2202769119
[12] Ibid
[13] Embarek, P. B. (2021), *op cit.*

General of WHO should identify the zoonotic source of the virus as follows:

> In May 2020, the World Health Assembly in resolution WHA73.1 requested the Director-General of the World Health Organization (WHO) to continue to work closely with the World Organization for Animal Health (OIE), the Food and Agriculture Organization of the United Nations (FAO) and countries, as part of the One Health approach, to identify the zoonotic source of the virus and the route of introduction to the human population, including the possible role of intermediate hosts. The aim is to prevent both reinfection with the virus in animals and humans and the establishment of new zoonotic reservoirs, thereby reducing further risks of the emergence and transmission of zoonotic diseases.[14]

Key Findings of the WHO Report of the Global Study of the Origins of COVID-19

The report of the *WHO-conveyed global study of the origins of SARS-CoV-2* was published on March 30, 2021 with no conclusive evidence as the source of its origin. It was on the basis of this that the WHO called for further studies and data on origin of SARS-CoV-2 virus, and reiterating that all hypotheses remain open.[15] With respect to the substantive findings, the report first of all observed that:

> The epidemiology working group closely examined the possibilities of identifying earlier cases of COVID-19 through studies from surveillance of morbidity due to respiratory diseases in and around Wuhan in late 2019. It also drew on national sentinel surveillance data; laboratory confirmations of disease; reports of retail pharmacy purchases for antipyretics, cold and cough medications; a convenience

---

[14] WHO (2021): *WHO-conveyed global study of the origins of SARS-CoV-2: China Part. Joint WHO-China Study*, 14 January – 10 February, 2021. Joint Report. Available at: https://www.who.int /emergencies/diseases/novel-coronavirus-2019/origins-of-the-virus

[15] WHO (2021): "WHO calls for further studies, data on origin of SARS-CoV-2 virus, reiterates that all hypotheses remain open." Available at: https://www.who.int/news/item/30-03-2021-who-calls-for-further-studies-data-on-origin-of-sars-cov-2-virus-reiterates-that-all-hypotheses-remain-open

subset of stored samples of more than 4500 research project samples from the second halfof 2019 stored at various hospitals in Wuhan, the rest of Hubei Province and other provinces. In none of these studies was there evidence of an impact of the causative agent of COVID-19 on morbidity in the months before the outbreak of COVID-19.[16]

Secondly, under the review of surveillance data on all-cause Mortality and Pneumonia-specific Mortality, the report concluded that "the steep increase in mortality that occurred one to two weeks later among the population in the Hubei Province outside Wuhan suggested that the epidemic in Wuhan preceded the spread in the rest of Hubei Province."[17]

Thirdly, with respect to the clinical review of surveillance data and cases, the report affirmed that:

> Although 92 cases were considered to be compatible with SARS-CoV-2 infection after review, subsequent testing and further external multidisciplinary clinical review determined that none was in fact due to SARS-CoV-2 infection. Based on the analysis of this and other surveillance data, it is considered unlikely that any substantial transmission of SARS-CoV-2 infection was occurring in Wuhan during those two months.[18]

Fourthly, in the examination of the genomic data of viruses collected from animals, the report declared that "neither of the identified so far from these mammalian species is sufficiently similar to SARS-CoV-2 to serve as its direct progenitor." Fifthly, with respect to the review of data from published studies from different countries, the report concluded that "so far, however the quality of studies is limited. Nonetheless, it is important to investigate these potential early events." Lastly, the report suggested the need for a next-phase studies to help trace the origin of

---

[16] Ibid.
[17] Ibid.
[18] Ibid.

SARS-CoV-2 and the closest common ancestor to the virus, including analysis of trade and history of trade in animals and production in other markets, among others.[19]

[19] Ibid.

CHAPTER THREE

Nigerians and WHO'S COVID-19 Social Distancing Safety Protocol

Following the discovery of the index case of COVID-19 in Nigeria on 27 February 2020, the month of March 2020 marked the beginning of the palpable anxieties associated with the outbreak of the pandemic in Nigeria. One immediate global response that affected Nigerians was what the WHO called social distancing - a new way of life of keeping a distance from people in public. The implementation of this social distancing protocol announced by WHO became a big challenge to many Nigerians. This chapter reflects on how Nigerians initially observed this social distancing etiquette outside their homes against the rising cases of COVID-19.

Immediate Policy Response to the Early Rise of COVID-19 in Nigeria

The week of Monday March 16, to Sunday March 22, 2020, marked a turning point in both the rising cases of coronavirus (COVID-19) in Nigeria, and the concomitant swift public policy response both at the federal and state government levels to the pandemic. As of Saturday March 21, 10 new cases were added to the existing number (12 then) thereby bringing the total number of those who tested positive for the coronavirus to 22. Before 12 noon on Sunday, March 22, the total confirmed and reported cases jumped to 25, and by evening period it went to 27. The numbers were uncontrollably and dreadfully rising by the day.

This dreadful situation indeed, constituted a serious matter of public policy concerns that warranted the adoption of bold public policy response at both the national and sub-national levels of government. One of the first COVID-19 coordinated policy responses (interventions) was President Muhammad Buhari's address to the nation on Sunday 29th March, 2020[20]. In that address, the President announced *inter*

---

[20] See full address in Appendix 1.

alia the following policy measures: (a) the banning of travellers entering into Nigeria from 13 countries (originally announced) and later to 15 countries all of which as at that time recorded over 1,000 cases at their domestic levels, (b) the closure of educational institutions (at all levels and across both public and private sectors in Nigeria), (c) the banning of large crowds in churches and mosques, as well as places of entertainment, and (d) the closure of international flights at three airports (in Kano, Enugu and Port Harcourt, (originally announced) and later Lagos and Abuja airports.

At the African level, the World Health Organization (WHO) reported on Friday, March 20, 2020 that 12 African countries were already experiencing local transmission of COVID-19. The report further said that as at March 19, 2020, more than 600 cases were already confirmed in 34 African countries.[21] This report underscored the frightening number at which the virus was increasing as well as the fastness of the spread within African countries. However, the number appeared apparently low because the Nigerian situation had not yet escalated in proportion to her population. Surprisingly, it turned out in the end that the African situation was not as terribly bad as it was widely believed during the early period of the pandemic. For example, Melinda Gates had said that we should expect dead bodies in the streets of African countries during the pandemic[22], as a result of their weak health systems.

The Introduction of WHO's Social Distancing Advisory

Seen against this background, the release by the WHO of the social distancing etiquette as an effective measure to check the spread of the coronavirus was quite in order. However, a close observation of what was happening among individuals and groups in Nigeria during that early stage of WHO's announcement, revealed that the *business-as-usual* (BAU) mentality still dominated the social interaction space. In particular, WHO

[21] *Saturday Sun*, March 21, 2020.
[22] Channels Television (2020): 'COVID-19: Expect Dead Bodies in the Streets of African Countries, Melinda Gate Warms'. www.channelstv.com, 2020/04/13. As the Channels' Television said, this was a snapshot of Melinda Gates in an interview with CNN.

had advised that social distancing of at least 1 metre (i.e. 3 feet) should be observed when coming in contact with people whether in a queue or in midst of large number of people. Although modified a little much later, the social distancing protocol remained one of the most effective non-pharmaceutical interventions throughout the most risky period of the pandemic. It was a good precautionary measure against contacting the virus from infected people coughing or sneezing.

The Persistence of Business-As-Usual Mentality

There was no doubt that the *business-as-usual-mentality* amply validates the phrase *old habits die hard*. Many Nigerians observed this safety rule in the breach in such places as in Churches and Mosques, offices, public transportation (buses, taxis, crowding at bus stops, etc). Yet, the frightening COVID-19 pandemic situation, called for (and still calls for) a radical and far-reaching change of attitude and habits regardless of how deeply ingrained such habits are in our social life. It was even not cheering at all watching government officials who were giving update on COVID-19 on a number of times, disregarding (perhaps unknowingly) the social distancing etiquette.

The pandemic which was fast changing the normal way of social interaction therefore required corresponding adjustments in culturally-ingrained behaviours. However, many Nigerians were still sticking to their old ways of relating with one another. Shaking of hands and hugging were still prevalent (done unconsciously by some). Buses in Lagos were for instance carrying what is commonly called overload with commuters crammed in the bus as usual.

All hope was not lost then as one particular good example was noticed. It was gladdening that the practice of exchanging the *Sign of Peace* during the celebration of the Holy Mass in the Catholic Church, was temporarily suspended in some parishes. This practice involved the shaking of hands with some hugging themselves. It was noteworthy for instance that the Catholic Archdioceses of Lagos was excellently complying with the social distancing etiquette at this early period of the pandemic when others were paying lip-service. Its response was very innovative, comprehensive and brilliantly rationalized theologically. This was what was expected from other dioceses that only paid lip service to the social distancing etiquette then.

Chapter Three | Isaac Nnamdi Obasi

Looking at the social character of the transmission of coronavirus in Nigeria at its early stage, the virus could be classified as a 'big man and woman' disease. For example, the cases in Nigeria were mostly brought in by those who had returned from other parts of the world, and these were mostly people in the middle and higher income groups. While these people remained the primary purveyors of the virus, its further spread largely depended on those who came in contact with them. This happened in their homes, places of work, churches, mosques, schools, markets, places of entertainment, venues of conferences/seminars/works hops, and even on the roads, among others.

Given the fact that this category of people (higher social economic status) is to a large extent enlightened and therefore understood the public health implications of the outbreak of this virus vis-à-vis Nigeria's weak health system, it was shocking that many of them were not complying. Yet it was in their enlightened self-interest (for the common good) that they should strictly comply with the COVID-19 social distancing advice of self-isolation and voluntary cooperation with health authorities while in such self-isolation. Unfortunately, quite a good number failed to meet this expectation. This was one major disappointment that emerged from the observation of the observance of the WHO's social distancing safety measure among Nigerians.

Conclusion

The experience of various nations during the early stage of the pandemic revealed that proactive and preventive measures were very central to reducing the spread of the virus. Following the social distancing safety protocol of the WHO was one of the initial non-pharmaceutical interventions that nations followed in checking the spread of the virus at that early stage. As the former Governor of New York, Andrew M. Cuomo rightly said during his COVID-19 update,[23] time matters, minutes count, and the time for action was now. Unfortunately many failed to observe the protocol including those in Nigeria.

---

[23] Andrew Cuomo (Governor of New York State) COVID-19 Update, Sunday, March 22, 2020 via CNN.

Part Two
COVID-19 and Nigeria's Atypical Governance Challenges

CHAPTER FOUR

COVID-19 and Temporizing Style of President Muhammadu Buhari

It was Benjamin Franklin (one of the most influential founding fathers of the United States) who said that "you may delay, but time will not, and lost time is never found again."[24] For Napoleon Bonaparte (a French Military General and a very notable Emperor) "take time to deliberate, but when the time for action arrives, stop thinking and go in."[25] Furthermore, Theodore Roosevelt (the 26th president of the United States), summed it up when he advised that "in any moment of decision, the best thing you can do is the right thing to do, the next best thing is the wrong thing, and the worst thing you can do is nothing."[26] These wise sayings speak directly to leaders who delay in taking decisions when confronted with hard choices in governance circle.

Temporizing is the name for such behaviour in governance. In actual fact, temporizing can be said to be a trademark of some politicians in governance. Many countries would always have in abundance such politicians who like to buy time over a pressing knotty public policy problem hoping it will disappear from public space. In Nigeria and in our time, President Muhammadu Buhari's style of governance typifies such. Former President Trump of the United States adopted this style at the early stage of the pandemic in February, 2020 when he kept wishing away the imminent COVID-19 with such statement as "America is fine" thereby denying reality. Unfortunately following this denial of reality, COVID-19 hit the United States disastrously.

---

[24] See Brainy Quote via https://www.brainyquote.com/quotes/benjamin_franklin_101831
[25] See Goodreads via https://www.goodreads.com/quotes/17300-take-time-to-deliberate-but-when-the-time-for-action#...
[26] Theodore Roosevelt Center via https://www.theodorerooseveltcenter.org/Learn-About-TR/TR-Quotes/..

President Buhari's Temporizing Attitude

In the case of President Buhari, his temporizing style manifested more openly after his inauguration in 2015. Everyone then expected him to hit the ground running with the appointment of ministers but unfortunately, it took him several months to do so. As if to corroborate Roosevelt's saying, his 'best decision' (appointment of ministers) taken at a 'wrong time' (after much procrastination) ended up not satisfying the expectations of a wide spectrum of Nigerians. During that period of procrastination, he rationalized his temporizing style with the statement that permanent secretaries are the ones who do the enormous work, while ministers do the talking. He created the wrong impression that having ministers was a burden to his administration.

Yet across much of the world, whether in republics, constitutional monarchies or even in what Niccolo Machiavelli (in his famous book *The Prince)* called principalities (which are hereditary), heads of government need to appoint a Cabinet (made up of able assistants called also Council of Ministers). The roots of President Buhari's temporizing style with respect to the outbreak of COVID-19 could be traced to the early part of his administration in 2015. Ironically, this temporizing manner of his, remained his idiosyncratic style in the early management of COVID-19. The temporizing style was at the root of the inability of the president to address Nigerians on COVID-19 pandemic much earlier as widely demanded by many Nigerians.

COVID-19 more than anything else in Nigeria's governance history exposed President Buhari's administration as the most temporizing of our time. This is in spite of the quality and commendable nature of his eventual address on COVID-19 on Sunday March 29, 2020. For all intents and purposes, his COVID-19 nation-wide address put a lie to the view that he was a 'working and not a talking president'. In actual fact, an effectively working president is also a sensibly and shrewdly talking president. This is a good governance principle which all heads of government consciously or unconsciously obey. Again, this is the *raison d'etre* for appointment of chief press secretaries, media advisers or spokespersons.

This was why it was wrong for the Special Adviser to President Buhari, Femi Adesina to tell Nigerians during the ensuing cut-and-thrust debate (prior to the address) that the president's style of not addressing

Nigerians was simply idiosyncratic. Although, President Buhari is a reticent politician, this should in no way make him the most temporizing politician of our time. Any president who loves delaying taking decisions when needed most, or who ignores public opinion when a matter needs his urgent attention, could be said to be miles away from delivering good governance in a timely manner. Unfortunately, when the same president turned around to belatedly take decisions on such matter, he ended up being more reactive than proactive. This invariably reduced the quality of his governance regardless of his good intensions, because time is of essence in governance and more so in times of COVID-19 emergency.

Impact of President Buhari's Temporizing Style on the early rise of COVID-19

The price that Nigeria paid for the President's temporizing style on responding to crucial issues that required his stamp of authority at the outset of COVID-19 pandemic could be gleaned from the following: As at 11:15am Tuesday, March 31, 2020,[27] there was a total number of 135 cases across 11 states and the FCT. Ironically, the resultant policy response in the President's address (namely the targeted lockdown of three states, banning of domestic air travels among others as shown in Chapter Three) would have proactively reduced (by hindsight now) this rising curve of COVID-19 infection.

If these policy interventions were taken a week earlier for example, we would not have perhaps recorded as high as these 135 cases. Again, if these well targeted policy measures were taken two weeks back, those who returned with the last flights following the banning of international flights into Nigeria, would not have been among the purveyors of this spread as at March. In fact, if the policy measures were taken three weeks earlier, Nigeria by the month of March would have recorded far less number. The high number of cases was the price Nigeria paid as a result of the temporizing style of the president.

Although the policy measures contained in the President Buhari's address (as listed in Chapter Three) were commendable, however, they were majorly *reactive*. This is because, the COVID-19 rising infections

---

[27] *Punch* newspaper, Tuesday, March 31, 2020.

Chapter Four | Isaac Nnamdi Obasi

then were by far ahead of those commendable policy responses due to the temporizing style of President Buhari. Once again, we recall former Governor of New York, Andrew M. Cuomo's statement that "time matters, minutes count...[28]"as well as Benjamin Franklin who also said that "you may delay, but time will not, and lost time is never found again."

---

[28] Andrew Cuomo, *op cit.*

Chapter Four | Isaac Nnamdi Obasi

CHAPTER FIVE

COVID-19 Health Emergency and Nigeria's Social Investment Programme

The declaration of COVID-19 as a *pandemic* by the World Health Organization (WHO) on March 11, 2020, meant that various nations were going to experience differential impact of its devastation based on the strength of their health systems, resource endowment, health human resource capability and political will. As WHO rightly stated then, COVID-19 is not just a public health crisis, but it is also a crisis that will touch every sector. It is important to note from the onset that COVID-19 pandemic by its very nature was a health emergency where normal conditions were no longer normal.

President Buhari's First Address to the Nation on COVID-19

Consequently, in his first address[29] to the nation on the COVID-19 pandemic on Sunday 29th March, 2020, President Muhammadu Buhari rightly described Coronavirus (COVID-19) as both a *health emergency* and an *economic crisis* in line with WHO's earlier declaration. As expected, the president rolled out policy measures to mitigate different areas of COVID-19 negative impact. First, the federal government ordered a lockdown on Lagos and Ogun States as well as the Federal Capital Territory (FCT). Secondly, the federal government ordered the closure of all educational institutions at all levels. Thirdly, public worships in Churches and Mosques were suspended. Fourthly, non-essential businesses were put on lockdown. Lastly, in line with WHO's advisory, people's cultural ways of live were ordered to be modified to conform to social distancing etiquette.

More importantly, as economic livelihood was hugely affected, the need for appropriate policy response to alleviate widespread poverty among the most vulnerable members of the society became imperative. In response to this, the federal government announced a special focus on

---

[29] See full address in Appendix 1.

the Social Investment Programme (SIP) of the Buhari administration. It was deemed very relevant and exigent to focus on the badly affected economic livelihood of the people particularly the poor and marginalized. It was on the strength of this that the president "instructed the Ministry of Humanitarian Affairs, Disaster Management and Social Development to work with State Governments in developing a strategy on how to sustain the school feeding programme …without compromising our social distancing policies."

Furthermore, the president directed that a three month repayment moratorium for all *TraderMoni*, *MarketMoni* and *Farmermoni* loans (all under the Social Investment Programme) be implemented with immediate effect. Lastly, the president "directed that a similar moratorium be given to all Federal Government funded loans issued by the Bank of Industry, Bank of Agriculture and the Nigerian Export Import Bank."

Using Social Investment Programme (SIP) to fight 'Hunger-Virus'

It is important to recall that the Social Investment Programme (SIP) was adopted as an omnibus initiative of the Buhari administration comprising such components as (a) *N-Power*: a fixed employment and skills acquisition initiative targeted at Nigerian youths, (b) *National Home Grown School Feeding Programme* (NHGSFP): targeted at pupils at the universal basic education level, (c) *Conditional Cash Transfer* (CCT): targeted at the poor and most vulnerable Nigerians, and (d) *Government Enterprise and Empowerment Programme* (GEEP): business empowerment initiative with various components as *TraderMoni*, *MarketMoni* and *Farmermoni*, which are targeted at the micro and small enterprises.

The president's directives then raised some implementation issues. Critics wondered how some of these directives would be carried out under the COVID-19 public health emergency without violating the lockdown order and the social distancing etiquette. Truly, critics were right. First, in carrying out the president's directives, the officials of the Ministry of Humanitarian Affairs, Disaster Management and Social Development were seen in a national television network news disbursing money to beneficiaries of the CCT initiative (on Wednesday, April 1, 2020) in a manner that flagrantly violated the social distancing etiquette and its concomitant government order against large gathering of people.

During this activity in FCT, 100 beneficiaries as reported (in addition to government officials) were gathered for the disbursement. This was a violation of the social distancing etiquette, as it was akin to complying with one presidential directive and at the same time disobeying another one that prohibits gathering of a large number of people. This flagrant violation of presidential order was not only unnecessary but was also completely avoidable, because before this particular time, the disbursement of money to CCT beneficiaries was done electronically. The question that arose then was: why was there a direct and physical disbursement of cash to beneficiaries during the exercise? What happened to the electronic register of CCT beneficiaries? Why was there no social distancing-compliant alternative method explored?

Flagrant Violation of Presidential Directive

This flagrant violation of presidential directive was not an isolated occurrence, as some ministers and couple of Ministries, Department and Agencies (MDAs) obeyed such directives in the breach. Since public officials discovered that violators of such directives were not sanctioned, some others joined in disobeying directives even with impunity. The implementation COVID-19 programmes and policies helped to expose some of these misdeeds of top government officials.

With respect to the Homegrown School Feeding Initiative, the implementation of presidential directive was a bit challenging given the fact that schools had already been shut down. The federal government was encouraged to go ahead with the implementation of this initiative since it was an important poverty alleviation intervention. This was exigent also because there were many low income earners employed in the food supply chain of the Initiative. But the major implementation question then was, how would the funds be disbursed when the schools were closed because of the COVID-19 pandemic?

It was our thinking then that the presidential directive could still be carried out if corruption was removed out of the implementation process. For instance, the school records of the pupils were available and so were the records of school food vendors. The federal government had the option of collaborating with the participating states and the school authorities to remit the equivalent of feeding money to the pupils through their parents who should be known in the school communities.

In getting access to the parents, the school authorities had the option of inviting the parents without compromising the social distancing safety protocol.

It is important to point out that it is wrong to question or doubt that the presidential directive on school feeding was implementable in a period of lockdown when schools were closed. As a poverty alleviation measure, the implementation of school feeding could take place with or without schools being in session. The feeding money rather than the food itself could be sent to the pupils while at home since some States ran their school through different electronic platforms during the lockdown period. Unfortunately on the implementation of the school feeding exercise itself, news report alleged that there were large scale frauds in funds disbursement. However, we are not in a position here to confirm whether this allegation was true or not.

Conclusion

Finally, the twin-pronged government approach of attacking COVID-19 disease and at the same time improving economic livelihood of the people was good and deep thinking, as a neglect of either of them could lead to death whether through disease or through hunger. Since none of these is desirable and acceptable, the government was on good and solid ground to continue to give priority to its social investment programme during the period of COVID-19 pandemic.

CHAPTER SIX

COVID-19 Health Emergency and Relative Importance of Occupational Groups

Following the outbreak of COVID-19, in Wuhan, China, and the declaration of a global health emergency by WHO many nations including Nigeria declared a total lockdown in their countries. The COVID-19 lockdown brought to the limelight how relatively important or less important different occupational groups that were hitherto involved in supremacy battles in the nation's industrial relations system, actually were, not only in the fight against the ravaging virus, but also in the economy generally. It is noteworthy that before the outbreak of COVID-19, many occupational groups through their labour unions were often involved in one form of inter-union (or sometimes intra-organizational) conflicts over their relative importance in the Nigerian governance system. Their fight for superiority over the others especially in the fight for higher remuneration and welfare for their members has for long created an unstable industrial relations system in Nigeria. The governance system has been worse for it particularly in the social sector namely education and health.

This chapter reflects on a moral lesson from the lockdown experience in 2020. More importantly and specifically, it stresses the need for civility of conduct in the way some occupational groups fight for their rights against some other occupational groups in the industrial relations system. The fight for such rights has always been characterized by the wrong feeling of aura of indispensability of their role in national development.

A Helpful Background

We are all aware of the incessant inter-union squabbles in the health sector between the medical doctors and other health sector unions. Health professionals such as pharmacists, physiotherapists, nurses and midwives, radiographers, laboratory scientists and some others had at one time or the other been at loggerheads with the government over how they felt treated in relation to medical doctors. Some of their unions include Nigeria Union of Allied Health Professionals (NUAHP), Medical and Health Workers Union of Nigeria (MHWUN), National Association of Nigerian Nurses and Midwives (NANNM), Association of Medical Laboratory Scientists of Nigeria (AMLSN), and Senior Staff Association of University Teaching Hospitals, Research and Associated institutions. Some of these unions usually confronted the government through the Joint Health Sector Unions (JOHESU) of which some of them are members. Some strikes by doctors themselves in furtherance of their interests or by other unions had led to avoidable deaths of patients. This therefore shows how serious this matter is in our country.

Furthermore, we are also very familiar with the incessant inter-union conflict between the Academic Staff Union of Universities (ASUU) on one side, and Senior Staff Association of Nigerian universities, (SSANU) and the Non-Academic Staff Union of Educational and Associated Institutions (NASU) on the other side. This is to mention just a few. In some instances, these inter-union and intra-organizational disputes (or squabbles) had often led to a long period of closure (or sometimes inactivity when not closed) in the public university system with students experiencing untold hardship. In all of these cited examples (in either educational or health institutions), the government had often acted in ways that did not help matters thereby leaving the elephants to fight intermittently while the grass suffered.

Dynamics of Unhealthy and Unnecessary Occupational Rivalries

The dynamics of the unhealthy and unnecessary occupational rivalries have greatly affected the quality of professional services by various occupational groups. Based on the experience of COVID-19, this chapter reflects on the need to appreciate *the dignity of labour* generally whether one is talking about truck pushers, cleaners, subsistence farmers, petty traders, drivers, carpenters, plumbers as well as professional groups. The chapter supports the view that "a man's dignity depends not upon his wealth or rank but upon his character." [30] More importantly, the chapter further makes the point that well-organized societies give some modicum of respect to workers in every

---

[30] See Oxford Advanced Learner's Dictionary of Current English, Revised Third Edition, p 241.

Chapter Six | Isaac Nnamdi Obasi

occupation that serves the society. Every occupation is therefore considered relatively important given their complementary contributions in keeping the society going. However, the ravaging COVID-19 pandemic shockingly exposed how some occupational groups which hitherto over- exaggerated their importance suddenly became non-essential in the fight to arrest the menace of the virus that was perceived then to be the catalyst of extinction of humanity.

The reality during the COVID-19 lockdown was that social life was no longer the same. Virtually all aspects of social life were negatively affected. People were asked to re-adjust their cultural ways of life, their daily work activities and means of livelihood, their other social events such as wedding, burial, naming, and birthday ceremonies. Except for workers who were performing essential duties, others were asked to stay at home or work from home if extremely necessary. Suddenly, workers in many occupational groups found themselves idle at home doing nothing and contributing nothing. It was obvious that some workers including lecturers and legislators (in national and state assemblies) were nowhere close to providing *'real essential services'* to the society. COVID-19 health emergency suddenly made them less important in keeping the society going.

However, workers who were in the officially-designated Essential Services were in demand for societal survival. For example, some groups in the health sector were in high demand to save lives. Those in the power sector were needed to support the maintenance of power, while those in the water and other infrastructural facilities were also in need. Furthermore, workers in the financial, telecommunication and mass communication industries, as well as agricultural products supply chain services, were all essentially needed for survival of society. All the workers in educational institutions including universities, polytechnics, colleges of education, and secondary, primary and nursery schools became 'less important' in the fight against COVID-19 pandemic and survival of society. COVID-19 made all these occupational groups less important in the scheme of things as against workers in the health sector or those providing essential services that kept the society going.

Aside from the occupational groups already mentioned because of their recurring inter-union conflict, there are other groups that palled into insignificance during the lockdown period. Yet some of these occupational cum professional groups are about the most prestigious, respected and well-remunerated in relation to others. Take the case of the legal profession for instance, it was not in the forefront of the fight against COVID-19 during the lockdown. Does this mean that the legal profession is not important? It is not a matter of yes or no but the fact is that it palled into insignificance in that fight to save Nigerians from the ravaging scourge of COVID-19. Members of the legal profession rather looked unto other occupational groups in the health sector to save Nigerians.

Take again the case of international professional footballers who are fabulously paid to entertain their fans (or 'worshipers') at football matches. During normal times, the matches played by these footballers sometimes could 'disorganize' some families every weekend especially young couples that needed to be together but could not. The matches are not even played in Nigeria and yet people idolize the players. However, during the COVID-19 lookdown period,[31] no one cared about these footballers. Their occupation palled into insignificance even though some of them were donating money to help save lives. This was a period when the United States of America for example shockingly and embarrassingly recorded over 1,000 deaths in ONE DAY (i.e. Friday, April 3, 2020) under the watch of former President Trump.

Take another case and this time Nigerian politicians who are fabulously paid in the various legislative arms of federal and state governments. Our distinguished senators and honourable members literally disappeared from the scene during the lockdown. None of them could go to the 'war front' of fighting COVID-19 to demonstrate how extremely important they claim to be in normal times. All of them during the lockdown period were at mercy of our neglected first responders (namely our heroic health workers) not minding the consistently abysmally low budgetary allocation to the health sector over the years. The lockdown period made medical tourism impossible for distinguished personalities as they had little or no choice but to remain in Nigeria for any medical treatment. We can only remember one high profile exception during that period in what remains a wasteful medical treatment abroad.

For the members of the Academic Staff Union of Universities (ASUU)[32] whose members regularly embark on strikes, as they were

---

[31] This was a period Fola Ojo called 'Pandemic Pandemonium', Punch newspaper, April 3, 2020.
[32] This is my own union as an academic.

always found restating how important the academic profession is to the progress of the society. Their profession palled into insignificance during the lockdown. In actual fact, ASUU chose this lockdown period to embark on one of longest strikes in its history. Aside from their members in the medical profession, the COVID-19 war went virtually successfully without ASUU members. Like the members of the legal profession, the politicians, admired footballers among others, ASUU members (non-medical experts) depended on the medical profession to save everyone from the COVID-19 scourge. This statement does not mean that our eggheads are not important any longer. Far from this, the same message remains and that is everyone has their own role to play and some play more important role than others at a particular point in time.

Secondly, there is complementarity of role in keeping the society going and no labour union (not even those in the health sector) should hold society to ransom through prolonged strikes. More importantly, the government officials on their part should do the needful in resolving industrial crisis, as they are not more important than any of these occupational groups mentioned here. Government officials should know that they were all helpless during the period of the lockdown and looked for help from health professionals.

A Word of Advice for Workers in the Health Sector

Finally, there is a word of advice for all the workers in the health sector who became heroes during the lockdown. If these workers have a sense of occupational importance, they would not be mistaken. However, they should not carry their feeling of importance too far. First, the food they were eating (to remain alive) to offer their essential services, were produced by the poor farmers who are also important in their own right but yet remain uncelebrated. Secondly, they were taught by teachers from nursery to the university levels before they became very important. So the poor farmer and the poorly paid and less-respected teacher (which spinsters run away from marrying by the way) helped to feed and produce them. One may ask if they are more important than their teachers, which in any case is the irony of life.

CHAPTER SEVEN

COVID-19 Pandemic and Social Class

In the preceding chapter, the relative importance of different occupations in the fight against COVID-19, particularly during the period of the lockdown, was examined. The chapter singled out occupational groups in the health sector as the most important groups, while some other occupational groups that provided other essential services that kept the society going, occupied the next important position in the fight against COVID-19 pandemic. The present chapter re-enforces the fact that one of the numerous lessons from COVID-19 pandemic is that human relations (both in organizations and the wider society) should be guided by the principle of respect for human dignity which should depend on character of the person and not upon possession of wealth or the social class or position of a person in society.

Social Class in Nigeria

In Nigeria for example, one's social class in society is everything. It defines the person. It is either one occupies a position of note or one is treated as 'Mr. or Mrs. nobody'. This has made some people to use the symbols of influence or higher positions like big cars (even when they can ill-afford to maintain such), flamboyant dressings, or other forms of regalia, to announce their presence and attract commensurate respect in society whether legitimately earned or not. There is yet a bigger problem associated with this mind-set of being an important person or the mentality of seeking to be recognized as one.

Quite a good number of Nigerians misuse their positions to commit all types of impunity that are hurtful to others thereby obstructing the common good. For example, some use security men to harass others, or use Siren to break traffic rules (e.g. traffic lights). Many use their privileged positions to grab everything, or influence many other things in their favour thereby blocking others from getting their legitimate fair share. People's position in the society has been a major driver of their uncivilized and barbaric behaviours (such as cheating others, maltreating them like taking over their properties and land). Although no society is perfect or completely free from these, but civilized societies have maintained some level of sanity through effective enforcement of laws and rules. This strict enforcement considerably reduces the damaging influence of impunity in their public space.

COVID-19 pandemic demonstrated beyond doubt that the virus does not respect anyone's position in the same way that death does not. Unlike death, COVID-19 does its own in a more dramatic and embarrassing manner at a time for example one may be feeling and showing a sense of good health. Think of the gregarious and ebullient British Prime Minister Mr. Boris Johnson and how COVID-19 sent him to the Intensive Care Unit (ICU) and one gets a sense of what is being said here. Again, think of our own very politically powerful Chief of Staff to President Muhammadu Buhari (late Abba Kyari), and one would also get the right sense that COVID-19 is no respecter of positions. Some Governors including those of Bauchi, Kaduna, Edo, and Oyo States, tested positive for COVID-19 regardless of their privileged positions. Although the virus respected and still respects no one,[33] some people regrettably felt that the positions they occupy could exempt them from obeying the lockdown order of the government. Few examples will illustrate this point clearer.

The Case of Violation of COVID-19 Rules by a Nigerian Celebrity and a Scottish Chief Medical Officer

During the weekend of April 4 & 5, 2020, two 'role models' in the fight against COVID-19 pandemic (one in Nigeria and the other in Scotland, United Kingdom) disappointed the public because they did not live by example. One of the incidences in Nigeria, concerns a Nollywood actress, Mrs Funke Akindele-Bollo who organized a birthday party in honour of her husband on Saturday (April 4th) with sizeable number of people that violated *The Lagos State Infectious Diseases Regulations 2020*. The video of the party that was circulated in the social media showed that the lockdown as well as the social distancing rule were violated. The party was considered more embarrassing or even scandalous because Mrs.

---

[33] The Queen of England (Queen Elizabeth) tested positive for COVID-19 with mild symptoms in February, 2022. And in March, 2022 also Barack Obama, former president of the United States of America tested positive. Furthermore, months later in 2022, President Joe Biden and his amiable wife tested positive.

Chapter Seven ｜ Isaac Nnamdi Obasi

Akindele-Bello was at that material time serving as the Face of Dettol Nigeria campaign in a television public enlightenment programme. The Campaign was advising people on how to stay safe and stop the spread of COVID-19 pandemic through improved hygiene. Yet the face of this campaign probably felt she was above the law.

The incident attracted public condemnation with Mrs. Akindele-Bello apologizing profusely soon after. The police swiftly arrested her and her husband for breaking the law. They were subsequently prosecuted in the Court and found guilty. However, it was reported much later that the government granted her and the husband pardon. It was commendable that the police and the Court of law worked effectively to convict them to serve as a lesson to those who think that their *position in society* is a license to act with impunity in violating the law of the land.

In somewhat similar incidence in Scotland, United Kingdom, the then Chief Medical Officer of Scotland Dr. Catherine Calderwood who had been the official face of the government issuing guidelines against the spread of the dreaded virus, violated the same rules she helped to make by travelling to her second home reportedly "a drive of more than an hour from her Edinburgh" residence. The rules prohibited people from traveling out to such a distance during the period in question. Although, she apologized profusely and admitted that she was very wrong, but as a rule-based society, certain actions followed immediately. First, the police visited her and issued her a warning about her conduct. Secondly, a decision was taken to remove her as the government 'face of the coronavirus public information campaign' to regain and retain public confidence.

Subsequently, Dr. Calderwood was advised by the Scottish First Minister Nicola Sturgeon to resign on the ground that her mistake would undermine public confidence in the government's effort to fight COVID-19 pandemic. Dr. Calderwood herself did realize that it would be "impossible for the public to have confidence in her official advice… if she remained in post"[34] Although, the Scottish First Minister wanted to retain Dr. Calderwood because of what she called her invaluable expertise and advice in fighting the coronavirus scourge, but the issue of betraying public trust could not be sacrificed on the altar of invaluable

---

[34] The Guardian (London) via https://www.theguardian.com/uk-news/2020/apr/05/…

expertise and advice. This singular reason more than demonstrated the importance attached to the maintenance of public confidence by government officials in the implementation of policies not minding anyone's expertise or assumed air of indispensability

Although, the First Minister was sympathetic and tried to save her[35] but ultimately the right thing was done by her resigning from office[36]. This is a case of burden of public morality on her conscience. It is important to note that in this case, hypocrisy and impunity in high position appear to be a natural tendency in man and woman,[37] which only effective enforcement of the law in civilized societies amply checkmates and minimizes.

This is the way for Nigeria to follow in post-COVID-19 pandemic period. Presently in Nigeria, no one resigns on grounds of burden of conscience. This is because impunity has been a way of life for many top officials of the government. This has made impunity of actions a major driver of governance deficit, which itself is a product of huge deficit of public morality in the Nigerian governance system. The wider society has been the worse for it over the years. It has now come to the point that the impunity disease afflicts both officials in high position and ordinary citizens. We see this for example, in the way many tricycle drivers in Abuja totally disregard traffic light in broad day light. Many other motorists do this also across Nigeria. In fact, everyone behaves as if rules are meant only for others to obey.

Conclusion

The impunity disease in Nigeria is as bad as the COVID-19 disease itself. There is a need for total transformation of this attitude and mentality of always *I* or *self-first, and others to hell*. It is this mentality and the absence of empathetic concern for the public interest (which also manifests in both petty and grand corruption), that has crippled the 'Giant of Africa' to its

---

[35] Our own interpretation of a news source namely https://www.aol.co.uk

[36] This is again our own interpretation from a news source namely *BBC World News*: https://www.bbc.com/news/uk-scotland-52177171.

[37] Again, the case can be cited of British Prime Minister Boris Johnson who also was accused of attending a party during the lockdown period, a scandal that led to resignation of couple of his aides and later affected him.

dwarfed status in all ramifications of its national life. One major lesson from COVID-19 is that everyone should work for the common good because one might be the victim of a poor public health system (for instance) that one helped to create or sustain through corruption or through other acts of negligence.

CHAPTER EIGHT

Public Trust and Implementation of COVID-19 Policy Response

In the preceding chapter which examined COVID-19 pandemic and social class, a very important point was made that a swift and impartial enforcement of laws by government effectively checkmates and minimizes the reckless display of impunity by both top public officials and the ordinary citizens. The example of the swift response by the police in Lagos in arresting and eventual prosecution of a popular Nollywood actress Mrs. Funke Akindele-Bello and her husband for violating the COVID-19 safety protocols was commended as a good deterrent measure against impunity. Also the case of the resignation of the Chief Medical Officer of Scotland Dr. Catherine Calderwood, who violated the social distancing guidelines she played key role in preparing and publicizing, was equally mentioned as a good deterrence to acts of hypocrisy by those in higher position. Her resignation was to retain public confidence in the implementation of COVID-19 safety guidelines in Scotland. The way her case in Scotland and that of Mrs. Funke Akindel-Bello in Nigeria, were handled is a good example of how the Nigerian governance system should strive to operate in order to retain public trust.

Importance of Public Trust in Government

Public trust or confidence in government is therefore very essential for effective implementation of public policies. This is why the Organisation for Economic Co-operation and Development (OECD) in its document titled: *Trust in Government,* says that: (a) trust is important for the success of a wide range of public policies that depend on behavioural responses from the public, (b) trust is necessary to increase the confidence of investors and consumers, (c) trust is essential for key economic activities, most notably finance, and (d) trust in institutions is important for the success of many government policies, programmes and regulations that depend on cooperation and compliance of citizens.[38]

---

[38] OECD via https://www.oecd.org/gov/trust-in-government.htm

To underscore the importance of trust in government, the Commonwealth Association for Public Administration and Management (CAPAM) held one of its regional conferences in 2010 in Abuja Nigeria, on the theme: *Good Governance, Accountability and Trust*. It was as if the organizers knew that trust-deficit has been a major hindrance to the effective implementation of government policies in Nigeria. The problem however is a world-wide phenomenon, for as an OECD study revealed "Only 43% of citizens trust their government." It observed further that "trust in government is deteriorating in many OECD countries," not minding that "lack of trust compromises the willingness of citizens and business to respond to public policies and contribute to a sustainable economic recovery."[39]

Nigeria's High Level of Trust Deficit

Nigeria is one of the countries where trust deficit has been high over many decades. It has even grown to an all-time high under COVID-19 policy implementation. For example, the Federal Minister of Information and Culture, Alhaji. Lai Mohammed in 2020 debunked the news making the rounds in the social media that members of the Presidential Taskforce on COVID-19,[40] were paid N500,000 each, per day. This wide allegation amply demonstrates the lack of public trust on government officials and pathetically in this case on these officials who were even risking their lives in the fight against COVID-19 pandemic.

Another example of the high level of distrust even among public officials and among different arms of government is the case of the leadership of the National Assembly dismissing the implementation of the National Social Investment Programme (NSIP) which it alleged was a failure after gulping about N2trillion. The important issue for us here is on the embarrassment of a high level of distrust among such top officials of government. It might well be that this was simply a case of a distrust which arose probably because they were 'not involved' (i.e. taken along in the implementation of the programme). The issue of 'not being involved'

---

[39] Ibid
[40] The Presidential Taskforce on COVID-19 (PTF on COVID-19) will be a subject of assessment and discussion later.

might simply mean that their oversight functions (and possibly interests) were not accommodated in the implementation of the NSIP.

These two cited examples of lack of trust raise the bigger question as to why there is lack of trust by the people on their government in Nigeria? The Organisation for Economic Co-operation and Development (OECD) once again provides a general answer to the crucial question which is very much applicable to Nigeria. According to it, public trust is a function of reliability, responsiveness, openness, better regulation, integrity and fairness, and lastly inclusive policy making. Put differently, public trust is low in the absence of reliability, poor responsiveness by the government to the needs of the people, lack of openness, poor regulation, lack of integrity and fairness, and lastly lack of inclusive policy making.[41]

Why would for instance, a people trust their government when they know from experience that its officials are not reliable, responsive, and open, or where they regulate discriminatorily, lack integrity and fairness, and are not inclusive in policy making? When the people know or simply perceive that their government is not always telling them the truth but only gives them assurances (which experience makes them not to believe), then trust-deficit would continue to grow and widen. For example, how many people listen and trust government's mass media outfits apart from its party supporters? These are the basis of trust deficit in Nigeria. Why would one government institution trust another, when that government institution knows that it lacks itself these indicators of good governance? Trust is essential for government policies to succeed. This is why another OECD (2017) report[42] said that 'trust plays a very tangible role in the effectiveness of government. Few perceptions are more palpable than that of trust or its absence. Governments ignore this at their peril'.

In Nigeria, the management of COVID-19 pandemic affected public trust in government in two understandably opposite directions. Management of COVID-19 is both increasing and eroding public trust in government. In Lagos State for instance, while many are praising the efforts of the government in managing the ravaging virus, some others

---

[41] OECD via https://www.oecd.org/gov/trust-in-government.htm.
[42] OECD (2017): *Trust and Public Policy. How Better Governance Can Help Rebuild Public Trust*, See https://www.oecd.org/gov/trust-and-public-policy-9789264268920-en.htm.

Chapter Eight | Isaac Nnamdi Obasi

are expressing loss of confidence over the distribution of the COVID-19 emergency palliatives. At the federal level, a mixed bag of reactions is also following its handling of the pandemic so far. Initially, there was displeasure over the temporizing style of the Buhari administration in announcing appropriate measures to control the spread of the virus. However, public trust started increasing following the President's address on the pandemic. For instance, the government received kudos for its serious concern for the poor and the most vulnerable in the society who were the targets of its national social investment programme, among other targeted interventions.

The Bigger lesson

However, much later when the disbursement of the conditional cash transfers started (following the president's directive), public confidence waned as people began to raise questions over the physical cash disbursement method that violated the social distancing order of the same government. More serious issues of transparency and fairness were raised and the case of distrust among two arms of government began to manifest as we observed earlier in this chapter. All these leave us with one lesson and that is – drawing from the OECD's admonition – all levels of government in Nigeria should use the instrumentality of good governance as an effective tool for rebuilding public trust.

CHAPTER NINE

COVID-19 Safety Rules and Psychology of Public Officials

Public officials in most developing countries feel and behave as if they are above the law. Put differently, the psychology of public office holders is that it is their duty to make laws, policies, regulations, guidelines, rules and procedures, while it is the duty of the citizens to obey. This simply translates to a mentality of master-servant relationship which is antithetical to the governing psychology in democratic and republican nations, where everybody (rulers and the ruled) are governed by the universally accepted principle of equality under the law. Although critics are quick to add that this *equality before the law thesis* holds more in theory than in practice, but it is gratifying that its ideals and aspirational value give a good measure of hope to the ordinary citizens.

Feeling of 'Bigmanism': A major Driver of Impunity in Nigeria

In Nigeria, people who see themselves as 'big-men' and 'big-women' (i.e. wealthy, powerful and influential) many a times exhibit a feeling of what Nigerians call 'bigmanism'. This sense confers on them the mentality of feeling and behaving above the law and this phenomenon is rife. Regrettably, this is one of the major drivers of impunity and all other attributes of bad governance at both the federal and state government levels. COVID-19 containment efforts by public officials in Nigeria had glaringly exposed the widespread nature of this psychology of acting above the law. For instance, a good number of officials who were discharging their duties of appealing to citizens to obey COVID-19 safety rules (such as social/physical distancing) were seen sitting or standing (on national television) in a manner that violated the same safety rules they were promoting. Perhaps we might excuse them to say that the act was unconscious (a kind of reflex action), but when it repeated itself, the justification became untenable.

In April 2020, there was a case of one state governor for instance who while issuing out COVID-19 safety rules (he was asking people in his state to obey), was at the same time seen violating one of the rules. He was seen right there touching his nose freely in a manner that suggested that he was not among those required to obey the safety rules that advised people not to touch their mouth, eyes and nose. Perhaps this business-as-usual mentality was again a *reflex action* or perhaps still, the case of the saying *old habits die hard*. Yet as leaders, the principle of leadership-by-example demands greater responsibility which again requires being conscious of one's position and role at all times.

It was Ittai Bar-Siman-Tov (2010) who in an article titled 'Lawmakers as Lawbreakers' argued that lawmakers are themselves (leading) lawbreakers.[43] The point resonates well with the behaviour of public officials in Nigeria which was exposed more during the period of the COVID-19 lockdown. This was the case of public officials who disobeyed the law, regulations and guidelines they themselves made and were propagating in the fight against COVID-19. The case of some of the members of the Presidential Task Force on COVID-19, who violated part of the COVID-19 safety guidelines while attending the burial of Mallam Abba Kyari (the late Chief of Staff to President Muhammadu Buhari), is a good example. Although these officials apologized to the nation for such violation, they still failed to quarantine themselves as required of them. This is a clear manifestation of a psychology of impunity which generally characterizes the behaviour of public officials in Nigeria.

What may worry some law abiding Nigerians is the ease with which some very senior appointees of the President disobeyed his directives without any sanctions. A former Inspector-General of Police who was directed by President Buhari to relocate to Benue State in the wake of the gruesome killings of many Benue indigenes by herdsmen few years ago, failed to obey the directive and nothing happened after that. This recalcitrant behaviour raised the question as to whether there was something some top public officials know about the running of the government generally that ordinary Nigerians outside the corridors of power do not know. This is because the culture of impunity was rampantly displayed for a quite a while without any punishment.

As we noted in an earlier Chapter, although COVID-19 respects no one, some people regrettably felt that their position could exempt them from complying with the lockdown order of the government. Some

---

[43] Ittai, Bar-Siman-Tov (2010): 'Lawmakers as Lawbreakers', *William and Mary Law Review*, Vol. 52,(Availableat: https://www.researchgate.net/publication/43292179_Lawmakers_as_Lawbrea kers).

public officials think their position can immune them from being infected with the coronavirus because they are above the law. But regrettably, many examples of high profile cases of infection abound across the world. COVID-19 pandemic should make everyone to fall under the law, and those who decide to act as if they are above the law would have themselves to blame because many have paid dearly for it both in Nigeria and across the world.

Fighting Impunity

Dealing with impunity, the case of the Chief Medical Officer of Scotland in the UK who lost her job after flouting the same COVID-19 safety guidelines she played key role in developing and propagating, is a good example of how civilised nations confront acts of impunity. Over here in Nigeria, public officials get away with impunity thereby emboldening many more people to continue committing acts of impunity. Generally, such widespread acts of impunity destroy public trust (as we argued earlier in Chapter 8) thereby jeopardising citizens' support towards effective public policy implementation.

The disobedience by many people to the lockdown order in Abuja for example was a painful illustration of the widespread acts of impunity among Nigerians. During the lockdown, only those on Essential Services were lawfully allowed to be on the road, however, many people suddenly became employees on Essential Services in Abuja. In all the major expressways into the City-centre of Abuja (Zuba-Kubwa-Gwarinpa axis, Airport road axis, and the Nyanya-Karu-AYA axis), heavy traffic was consistently observed in spite of the lockdown restrictions. This reflects again, the widespread acts of impunity.

Although the agitation for the lifting of the lockdown restrictions did not only happen in Nigeria, but the impunity-dimension of the agitation, was observed to be exceptional among many Nigerians. For example, men in uniform (Army, police etc, for example) were seen driving against the traffic (on one-way) with an air of impunity. Their behaviour created more traffic chaos for the real workers on Essential Services going to work. Although, some of these violators were arrested, but the damage they has already caused was incalculable. For example, one staff of the National Hospital in Abuja was seen and heard complaining on national television over how she spent three hours on the road to work because of both the traffic congestion and the attendant road blocks mounted by security personnel checking violators.

Conclusion

Impunity among public officials as well as among the ordinary people, is one of the major governance challenges in Nigeria. The number of people arrested and subsequently prosecuted by the Mobile Courts for violating the lockdown order in the FCT, Abuja, was a clear evidence of widespread disobedience to the law. This typical Nigerian way of behaving with impunity needs to be curbed seriously. Chapter 10 below provides additional evidence of the high level of impunity committed by some public officials who go by the appellation Very Important Persons (VIPs).

CHAPTER TEN

COVID-19 Safety Protocols and the Disdain by very Important Persons (VIPS)

A further demonstration of the public officials' mentality of exempting themselves from obeying the law was the growing disdain through flagrant disregard of the safety protocol by the privileged class especially the Very Important Persons (VIPs), in spite of the high volume of risk communication messages directed at all Nigerians on a daily basis through a multiplicity of media channels. Unfortunately, this flagrant disregard of the safety protocols was happening when new cases of COVID-19 infections were steadily on the rise. It was as if the VIPs wanted to return to their normal lives by force without following the existing safety guidelines that would make such desired normal lives safer and more meaningful. A few examples would suffice to illustrate this point in this chapter.

Flagrant Violation of Safety Rules by VIPs

In the month of July 2020, two governors (a former governor and a serving governor) flagrantly violated the COVID-19 safety protocols at two different airports. As *Nairametrics*[44] reported (in one of the cases on July 15):

> …the management of the Federal Airports Authority of Nigeria (FAAN)…strongly condemned the conduct of the former Governor of Zamfara State, Alh. Abdulaziz Yari, for blatantly violating the Public Health procedures (COVID-19) on travels at the Malam Aminu Kano International Airport.

The report also said that the former governor "reportedly refused to adhere to the protocols by forcefully pushing away an officer of the

---

[44] See Nairametrics, (2020) via https://nairametrics.com/2020/07/15/faan-condemns-fmr-gov-yari-misconduct-at-kano-international-airport/.

Environment Department when he (the officer) insisted that his (former governor's) luggage must be disinfected". Then in the atypical (acting with impunity) for which many Nigerian public officers are well known for, FAAN reported that "the former governor said the officer should have known he is a VIP. *This irresponsible act"*, FAAN rightly concluded, "endangers all other airport users, it is unacceptable."[45]

In the second case, *Premium Times*[46] (16 July 2020) reported the case vividly as follows:

> The Federal Airports Authority of Nigeria, FAAN, has again condemned the conduct of a governor, this time, the Governor of Adamawa State, Ahmadu Fintiri. He was alleged to have violated public health protocols on COVID-19 at the Port Harcourt Airport on Tuesday by refusing to have his temperature checked or be sanitised by health officials. FAAN noted that the governor's entourage did exactly as the governor did as the team that came to receive them drove through the barricades up to the terminal building, ignoring traffic and aviation security instructions. The agency said such acts of irresponsibili ty displayed by the governor and his entourage endangers the lives of other airport users, adding that it is unacceptable. FAAN called on airport users, especially VIPs, to adhere to the protocols and procedures on COVID-19 prevention.

In the third case for our illustration, *The Cable*[47] (2 July 2020) reported that:

> on June 16, 2020 Governor Akeredolu of Ondo State, who was seeking another term, submitted his expression of interest and nomination forms at the APC national secretariat in Abuja. Before heading to the headquarters of the ruling party, the governor was seen in the midst of the lawmakers who sang his praise. Neither the governor nor the lawmakers observed the safety protocols listed by the Nigeria Centre

---

[45] Ibid

[46] Premium Times (2020): 'COVID-19: FAAN berates another Nigerian governor for violating airport protocols' Via https://www.premiumtimesng.com/news/more-news/403250-covid-19-faan-berates-another-nigerian-governor-for-violating-airport-protocols.html.

[47] The Cable (2020) via https://www.thecable.ng/sources-four-lawmakers-in-video-where-akeredolu-sneezed-refuse-covid-19-test-despite-falling-ill.

for Disease Control (NCDC). They did not wear face masks or maintain social distance and shortly after, governor Akeredolu sneezed on his palm. Then one of the lawmakers reached for his hand which he raised high as others acknowledged the governor who beamed with smiles. Two weeks after the incident, the governor announced that he had tested positive for COVID-19 and directed members of his cabinet to self-isolate and also go for test.

In chapter 9, we decried the psychology of top government officials whose behaviour gave the false impression that they have immunity against the virus. We also observed that there are no significant changes in the attitude and behaviour of the people towards complying with the guidelines for containing the spread of COVID-19. One major reason why many Nigerians were not complying with the COVID-19 safety guidelines was the low level of public trust in the governance system. A key factor accounting for the low level of people's trust in the government is lack of leadership-by-example, as exemplified by the wide abuse of powers by public officers.

Lack of Leadership-by-Example

Put differently, those in power do not practise what they preach hence many people take a cue from that. For example, laws which are meant to be obeyed by everyone are not obeyed by many of those in power, as they see themselves being above the law. Another major reason for low level of compliance is weak enforcement of laws and the safety guidelines particularly as it applied to top public officials. Ample evidence during the lockdown period suggest that both of these causal factors became very pronounced. Both impunity of actions by those in power and their families, and weak enforcement of safety protocols in public places, all combined to lower the compliance level more, as more people became emboldened to show flagrant disdain for the safety rules without qualms. There are two areas of societal lives where these flagrant disdain become more pronounced.

The first is in the organisation of, and attendance to, wedding ceremonies. There was the case of the son of the Attorney-General of the Federation and Minister of Justice, Abubakar Malami, SAN, whose wedding activities violated the social gathering requirement of the guidelines which allowed only 20 people to be in attendance.[48] As the video of the ceremony circulated in the social media showed, this rule was very flagrantly violated, and unfortunately the large gathering remained a purveyor of the spread of COVID-19. Again, the physical distancing requirement of the guidelines, was also flagrantly violated, as the large crowd in attendance made such impossible to observe.[49] This singular act emanating from the home of such a highly placed public officer was capable of creating ripple effects thereby multiplying the virus more.

The second area of societal life where there was increasing disdain for the safety protocols was with respect to burial ceremonies. Across the country, people found it difficult to comply with the NCDC guidelines of allowing 20 people also in attendance during burial ceremonies. Starting with the burial of Malam Abba Kyari (late Chief of Staff to President Muhammadu Buhari), the flagrant disdain and blatant violation of NCDC safety protocols continued with burials of many other VIPS across the country. Who were these safety protocols meant for if those who were expected to lead-by-example flagrantly violated them? Does anyone still wonder why laws, rules and policies are not effectively implemented in Nigeria?

In conclusion, the flagrant display of impunity and that of a feeling of being above the law, is not how to build a society of law and order, a failure of which is one of the atypical features of the Nigeria's governance system. President Muhammadu Buhari himself rightly pointed out that "the irresponsibility of few can lead to the death of many."[50] This proved to be so even in other countries such as the United States of America under former president Donald Trump.

---

[48] For details of this report, see Daily Post (2020): 'How Malami, son flouted COVID-19 rules at wedding ceremony'. July 11.

[49] Ibid.

[50] See his address on the extension of the COVID-19 pandemic lockdown on Monday, 13 April 2020. Appendix 2.

CHAPTER ELEVEN

Naira Marley, Marlians and COVID-19 War
in Nigeria

This chapter presents one of the consequences of the failure of public officials to provide leadership-by-example, as demonstrated in chapter 10. This is a case of a particular citizen called Naira Marley and his supporters who followed the footsteps of some of the VIPs to flagrantly disobey COVID-19 safety protocols and possibly assured themselves that nothing would happen. While the VIPs were reprimanded or not charged to court beyond mere public condemnation, Naira Marley was charged to a Mobil Court and convicted with a fine of N200,000 and a public apology to the federal government. This was a typical case of the atypical nature of Nigeria's bad governance system, where different laws apply to the rich and the poor.

No One should pose a threat to Public Health

'Black Lives Matter' and 'Áll Lives Matter', are popular slogans used by protesters to signal the importance of respecting and preserving all human lives regardless of whether the person in question is black, white or coloured. And if we apply these catchphrases to public health during the period of COVID-19 pandemic, it implies that all people have their rights, but nobody should under any circumstance jeopardise the lives of others by failing to take personal responsibility. It is unacceptable for anyone to pose a threat to public health in the pursuit of economic and social fame, revelry or merriment in a crowd-pulling environment, in total disregard to social and physical distancing protocols and other PTF, NCDC, Federal Capital Territory (FCT) guidelines. The pursuit of pleasure (by some) that poses potential risk to the health of many, cannot be tolerated or defended in an organised or rule-based society not to talk of, in a COVID-19 pandemic.

During the lockdown and presidential ban on inter-state travels, Naira Marley and his musical crew came into Abuja in a chartered aircraft from Lagos to hold a drive-in concert at the Jabi Lake Mall. The holding of the event attracted public opprobrium which the VIPs' (equally irresponsible acts) though attracted but failed below what was expected. Naira Marley was subsequently charged to FCT Mobile Court and convicted for violating[51] (a) presidential ban on inter-state travelling, (b) not wearing a face mask contrary to the Presidential Order enforcing compulsory wearing of face mask on all persons within Abuja the Federal Capital Territory, (c) violating social distance order, and (d) violating the dusk to dawn curfew in the Territory. In each of these four count charges, he was to pay N50,000, and to tender a public apology to the Federal Government of Nigeria in a national daily.[52]

The hosting of a concert (a crowd-pulling event) was not only illegal and repugnant, but it was also morally, socially and spiritually reprehensible, as it violated public health protocols and denigrated all the efforts that were made to contain the dreaded and deadly COVID-19 pandemic. This particular case was considered important to be discussed in this book because Naira Marley and his followers (a growing large fan base called Marlians) posed enormous risk to public health during the COVID-19 lockdown. The health risk posed by Marlians in Lagos then made people in the state to be greatly worried given the rising cases of COVID-19 infections there, and the fact that Lagos was the epicentre of the virus in Nigeria.

About Naira Marley and Marlians

Naira Marley is a Lagos-based musician whose peculiar form of musical performance exhibited in an antisocial behavioural pattern, attracts a good number of fans among the youths. These followers of his are called Marlians. According to Olugbile,[53] the Marlians "are a rambunctious presence anywhere" Naira Marley performs. "They revel in being 'outsiders', and as a trademark, they are disrespectful of rules and agents of law enforcement," he added.

---

[51] See Vanguard newspaper (2020): 'Lockdown violation: FCT Court convicts Naira Marley, to pay N200,000 fine'. August 7.
[52] Ibid.
[53] Femi Olugbile (2020): *'Naira Marley and the 'Marlian' counter-culture', Business Day*, January 17.

Furthermore, a greater concern is that "the craze of proudly pronouncing themselves Marlians and damning the consequence is spreading through schools and neighbourhoods among teenagers and young adults, and it has left many parents scratching their heads", Olugbile again added. As he finally pointed out,

> ...the defining attributes of Marlians are roughly said to include the following: 'NO MANAZ' – any effort to behave like 'decent' youth is frowned up; No Belt: Marlians would not be caught dead wearing a belt on their trousers; Smoke Weed, and perhaps use other drugs of abuse, such as 'Coke' and Tramadol; Respect nobody; Eager to go clubbing every weekend; Crazy hairstyle – dreadlocks or scruffy; Don't fear anything, even death (MA FO); Must love Naira Marley's music and be ready to stand up for him; Not to pay excessive attention to studies (most 'Marlians' are students); Strong focus on sex, including masturbation...[54]

In an earlier chapter on *COVID-19 pandemic and social class,* we condemned the attitude of those who consider themselves above the law by flouting the PTF and NCDC guidelines. The chapter specifically mentioned among others the birthday party organised by a Nollywood actress Mrs. Funke Akindele-Bello where many people gathered against the presidential lockdown order on Lagos, as well as against the social and physical distancing protocols. It is on record that Naira Marley was among those who attended that party. It is obvious that he and his group are keeping to their peculiar characteristics of disrespecting the laws of the land. Although, they were mildly sanctioned, there appears to be no lessons learned from that experience that was nationally condemned. In the case of the Jabi Lake Mall event, in Abuja, Naira Marley wrongly thought he would circumvent the law. Perhaps, this was why his lawyer in reacting to the judgment claimed that 'we were given the assurance that all the approvals from the government had been procured to him to be in Abuja and at the concert.'[55] His lawyer might not be wrong since some corrupt public officials might have assured them that its business-as-usual circumvention of the law would hold sway. The Chairman of

---

[54] Ibid
[55] Vanguard newspaper (2020), *op cit,*' Lockdown violation: FCT Court...'

Chapter Eleven | Isaac Nnamdi Obasi

FCT Ministerial Enforcement Task Team on COVID-19 Mr. Ikharo Attah and his hardworking team as well as the security agencies, did a highly commendable job.

Nigeria needs to be 'sanitised' from the impunity in the land with appropriate legal sanctions. Enforcement of the laws is therefore key to achieving this. Another form of 'sanitisation' is through all manner of deterrent measures. The protection of our public health is a key and primary function of the government. Protection covers all manner of preventive measures for keeping the citizens healthy and alive in such a mixture of areas as protection against hunger, physical attacks by bandits, herdsmen, members of Boko Haran, armed robbers, kidnappers, social miscreants of whatever types, outlaws, among host of others.

In conclusion, if Naira Marley and his Marlians are careless about dying, many other citizens care much about their own lives. Consequently, the Marlians should not jeopardise the lives of others in the name of entertainment, and pursuit of wealth and fame in a period of the deadly COVID-19 pandemic. The Federal Government and its sub-national counterparts should demonstrate the expected strong leadership in this situation by putting a stop to the display of impunity by any group that takes to anti-social behaviour inimical to efforts to contain the spread of COVID-19. This would however be effective if it is carried out through leadership-by-example.

Part Three
Nigeria's COVID-19 Policy Management

CHAPTER TWELVE

Task Force Model For COVID-19 Policy Emergency Management

COVID-19 pandemic as a war against humanity created an emergency situation by its dynamics. This emergency situation in turn required an emergency approach to manage and contain the virus. An emergency in common dictionary parlance is a serious situation that requires prompt or immediate action. According to the World Health Organisation (WHO) however, an emergency is a term describing a state, and as a managerial term, it demands decision and follow-up actions of extra-ordinary measures. Emergency, the WHO added, requires 'a threshold values to be recognised, and it implies rules of engagement and an exit strategy'. Put differently, 'an emergency is a situation that poses immediate risk to health, life, property or environment', and would therefore require 'urgent intervention to prevent the worsening of the situation.'[56]

Under emergencies, times are not normal and this suggests that in governance terms, extra-bureaucratic measures may be put in place to respond quickly to situations and prevent escalation of the problems so created. In normal times, a bureaucracy (i.e. civil or public service) commonly referred to as Ministries, Departments and Agencies (MDAs) in Nigeria, is the subsisting conventional machinery for implementing government policies. However, in 'abnormal' times as in COVID-19 pandemic era, this long-established and traditional structure is usually found to be inhibitory for timely and effective policy implementation, because of its rigidity, lethargy, conservativeness, and sometimes unnecessarily very legalistic. Consequently, in times of emergencies, extra-bureaucratic bodies such as *ad hoc* commissions and task forces may be established as a result of these dysfunctional elements of a traditional bureaucratic institution.[57] This was the major justification for the

---

[56] *Wikipedia, the Free Encyclopaedia.*
[57] See Obasi, I. N. & N. O. Yaqub, (eds.) (1998): *Local Government Policy Making and Execution in Nigeria.* Ibadan:
Sam Bookman Publishers, Bookman Social Science Series.

establishment of the Presidential Task Force on COVID-19 (PTF on COVID-19).

Origin, Overarching Objectives and Mandates of PTF on COVID-19

The Presidential Task Force on COVID-19 (PTF on COVID-19) was established to serve as Nigeria's coordinating institutional response to COVID-19 emergency. This Task Force was set up by President Muhammadu Buhari on March 9, 2020, "to coordinate and oversee Nigeria's multi-sectoral inter-governmental efforts to contain the spread and mitigate the impact of the Covid-19 pandemic."[58] The Secretary to the Government of the Federation (SGF), Mr. Boss Mustapha, was appointed as the Chairman of the PTF made up of 12 members drawn from various ministerial and disciplinary backgrounds as well as from a development partner[59]. The PTF was created to be a scalable structure with various Working Groups assisting it at the operational level.

The three-fold overarching objectives of PTF are[60]: (a) Advising the President on the National Response to the pandemic; (b) Assessing the needs of State and Federal Governments, and liaising with the private sector and multilateral partners to mobilise needed resources; and (c) Accreditation of Isolation and Treatment Centres nationwide. At inception and during the lockdown, the PTF was holding daily briefings to update the nation on the national response to the COVID-19 pandemic.

The full mandates of the PTF on COVID-19 and its functional areas are as follows[61]:

---

[58] Presidential Task Force on COVID-19 (2020): 'About the PTF'. Available at: http://www.statehouse.gov.ng.

[59] The other members of the PTF on COVID-19 were: Dr. Sani Aliyu (National Coordinator); Dr. Osagie Ehanire (Hon. Minister of Health); Ogbeni Rauf Aregbesola (Hon. Minister of Interior); Sen. Sirika Hadi (Hon. Minister of Aviation); Hajia Sadiya Umar Farouq (Hon. Minister of Humanitarian Affairs, Disaster Management and Social Services); Malam Adamu Adamu (Hon. Minister of Education); Alh. Lai Mohammed (Hon. Minister of Information and Culture); Dr. Mohammad M. Abubakar (Hon. Minister of Environment); Alhaji Yusuf Magaji Bichi (Director-General, State Services); Dr. Chikwe Ihekweazu (Director-General, Nigeria Centre for Disease Control); and Dr. Fiona Braka (WHO Acting Country Representative).

[60] Ibid

[61] Ibid

The first of the seven broad list of mandates of the Task Force is to:

> ...provide overall policy direction, guidance, and continuous support to the National Emergency Operations Center (EOC) at the NCDC, and other Ministries and Government Agencies involved in response activities, and ensure their coordination towards a single set of national strategic objectives.

The second is to "enable the delivery of national and state-level outbreak control priorities which include": (a) "Effective and safe treatment centres to ensure capacity to manage outbreaks"; (b) 'Coordination of National and State Emergency Operation Centres"; (c) "Response commodities for case management, infection prevention and control, diagnostics, etc"; (d) "Sensitisation and awareness campaigns for the general public on prevention measures and response activities'; and (e) 'Diagnostic laboratories and deployment strategies."

The third is to: "review and make approval recommendations for implementing country-wide or regional non-pharmaceutical interventions if and when needed; such as school closures, suspension of large gatherings, implementation of social distancing, flight limitations etc."

The fourth is to:

> ...provide recommendations for the provision of direct funding and technical support to states and local governments to strengthen their preparedness capacity and mobilise human, material and financial resources from within and outside the country for effective national and state-level preparedness.

The fifth is to "define targets and monitor the progress in the delivery of these targets to meet the minimum requirements for a satisfactory performance and use this to advise the Presidency on the overall national response to COVID-19." The sixth is to "coordinate Nigeria's engagement with other countries' bilateral and multilateral bodies, international organisations to share lessons, best practices, and technical assistance;" and the last, is to "keep the public abreast of strategic progress with Nigeria's response, and emerging developments regarding preparedness and response."

Both the three over-arching objectives and the seven mandates of the PTF are implemented through the following eleven functional areas:[62]

- ✓ PTF National Pandemic Response Center (NPRC) Coordination;
- ✓ Epidemiology & Surveillance;
- ✓ Risk Communication & Community Engagement;
- ✓ Laboratory;
- ✓ Security, Logistics & Mass Care;
- ✓ Points of Entry;
- ✓ Resource Mobilization;
- ✓ Infection, Prevention & Control;
- ✓ Research;
- ✓ Case Management; and lastly
- ✓ Finance Monitoring & Compliance.

Appropriateness and Advantages of a Task force

A task force is a special purpose *ad hoc* body of people with diverse disciplinary background for accomplishing a matter of urgent concern whether in public or private sphere of human endeavour. Rightly seen, a task force has certain advantages in emergency situations.[63] First, it is composed of expert and competent hands from relevant disciplinary backgrounds to accomplish an urgent task.

Secondly, such an expert group enjoys greater degree of autonomy than the traditional bureaucracy. Thirdly, the group performs assigned functions with greater degree of speed, precision, flexibility and adaptability. Fourthly, the task group is usually well resourced (financially, materially and humanly speaking) to enable it execute the desired assignment. And lastly, the group has greater capacity to be more perceptive and innovative than the traditional bureaucracy.

Governments across the world have created one form of mechanism or the other to fight this ravaging COVID-19 pandemic emergency. Some use what is called Emergency Management Team, others Emergency Operations Task Force, while some others just call theirs

---

[62] Ibid
[63] Ibid

Task Force or Presidential Task Force as in the case of Nigeria. Whatever name this emergency team is called, it is basically meant to quickly respond and mitigate a crisis situation as COVID-19 Emergency.

The institutional structure of a task Force offers a flexible, innovative and effective model for public policy implementation during an emergency situation. A task force, therefore, is suitable for a project-like emergency situation such as COVID-19 pandemic. A project-like emergency situation means that there is an end-date of the operation of any task force. A task force unlike a normal bureaucratic organisation is therefore time-bound. At the time of creation, the 'expected' end-date of the Presidential Task Force on COVID-19 was when Nigeria's policy response has effectively and satisfactorily contained the ravaging virus to a level where the relevant bureaucratic machinery (namely the Federal Ministry of Health and its agencies) can routinely handle.

Consequently, a longer-term end-date for the life of the PTF on COVID-19 would put a lot of stress on its members, as no task force is established to last for a long and unspecified period of time.[64] As the time went on, the PTF was faced with a dilemma. On the one hand, it would be premature and unwise to disband the task force when the virus was still ravaging the population, and on the other hand, the task force would become over-stressed if left to work for a longer time. If it exists for a longer period of time, its members would suffer fatigue, and gradually end up becoming lethargic like the bureaucracy it supplanted.

Assessment of PTF Membership and Expertise

The membership of the PTF met to a reasonable degree the criterion of inter-disciplinary and inter-ministerial composition with the needed relevant and varying expertise and experience. Although there is a good mix of technical (professionals, specialists or technocrats) versus strong political membership necessary to drive the activities, one could only have wished for a stronger representation from the technocratic/specialist side as against the over-representation of the political/administrative

---

[64] This point will be taken up for discussion in a subsequent chapter as the name *PTF on COVID-19* was actually changed to *Presidential Steering Committee on COVID-19* later to accommodate this fear raised here.

side. Having only one member from the donor community (development partners namely WHO for example) was not enough. More representation should have come from some other members of the donor community. In the alternative, representation from the pool of epidemiologists, virologists, immunologists, laboratory scientists or even from the Nigerian Medical Association (NMA) etc, would have given more balance and vigour, which would be inevitably needed to fight fatigue and lethargy that would surely set in.

With regards to the deployment of expertise to fight COVID-19, PTF confronted the fight against the virus with extra-ordinary and commendable sense of commitment expected of task force members anywhere.[65] During the entire period of the lockdown, members of the PTF were visible in carrying out their duties (such as attendance to daily national briefings) even to a point of exhaustion and putting their lives at great risk. For those who had a good sense of understanding of PTF's work, there was enormous intellectual and physical energy involved. It should be acknowledged that every member of the body demonstrated the possession of both of these qualities to execute the equally enormous tasks involved. These members discharged their functions in a sustained manner as at the time of this assessment.

Concluding observations

Members of the PTF worked like the Faculty and Departmental Examination Officers in the Universities who administer or oversee the conduct of examinations (conducted three times a day, morning, afternoon and evening), and sometimes for one good month without rest. We know what happened to some of them at times when adequate support and incentives were grossly lacking. For members of the PTF, watching some of the faces of the twelve members during the daily national briefings, one could see exhaustion all over, for no fault of theirs as they had been over-worked and over-stressed. We should bear in mind also that these members were at the same time still discharging their role

---

[65] The assessment of PTF was carried out in stages as would be clearer later. This particular assessment was based on approximately two months of its existence during the lockdown period.

in various Ministries, Departments and Agencies (MDAs). It is also important to take note of the active participation of the members of the mass media at the daily briefings, and their subsequent coverage of the dynamics of the pandemic. Their role was equally heroic like that of the members of the PTF itself.

CHAPTER THIRTEEN

COVID-19 FG-Induced 2020 Austerity Budget and Presidential Directive on Oronsaye Report

During the first week of June 2020, the Minister of Information and Culture, Alhaji Lai Mohammed, revealed that the COVID-19 pandemic had attacked all revenue sources of the Federal Government. The 2020 budget of the Federal Government he said had become an austerity one, as the original budget of N10.59 trillion presented to the National Assembly with fanfare in October 2019 and passed by it in December 2019, had been revised in May 2020 in line with the COVID-19-induced economic reality.

According to Lai Mohammed, the budget was earlier based on a crude oil benchmark of $57 per barrel but now:

> …we are praying that the crude oil will go to $30 per barrel. All sources of revenue has been attacked by COVID-19"…"this is why the minister of finance at the last council meeting, informed all of us that they will slash every ministry's budget by 20 percent capital and 16 percent overhead.[66]

The Minister's observations form the background of our discussion in this chapter that exposes the fact that the social sector (education and health) ended up as usual bearing the brunt of the imposed austerity budget.

Effects of Austerity Budget on Education and Health

The palpable negative effects of this revision on the original allocations to various competing sectors of the government were very incontrovertible. Unfortunately, education and health sectors appear to be bearing the brunt. For example, the allocations to education (UBE)

---

[66] See Daily Sun (2020): '…COVID-19 has attacked all revenue sources'. June 4.

and health (Basic health care) were considerably reduced to as much as 54.25% and 42.5% respectively. Consequently, the government was frantically exploring ways of increasing its revenue and reducing wastage in its expenditure. One of the options that the government adopted was to revisit the Report of the Presidential Committee on the Restructuring and Rationalisation of Federal Government Parastatals, Commissions and Agencies (The Stephen Oronsaye Report) of 2012. It was not surprising therefore that President Muhammadu Buhari directed that the Oronsaye Report should be implemented but it ended up not implemented then, due to lack of political will.

The implementation of the Oronsaye Report: A classic case of lack Political Will

It would be recalled that the Oronsaye Report had been reviewed under both the Jonathan and Buhari administrations. The Jonathan administration that established the Committee released a White Paper on it, and also established four sub-committees to oversee its implementation before leaving office. This was the stage of the Report when President Buhari came into power in 2015. The Report had been reviewed twice under the Buhari administration but unfortunately without releasing a White Paper to guide its implementation. Although, it was reported that the president directed that it should be implemented, the policy statements that followed this directive suggested that another review was going on. It was announced couple of times that the government planned to complete the process of implementation by October, 2020.[67]

This is where one gets worried as to why another long review would be needed for a report that has benefited from an independent review of experts (third in the line of reviews) in 2017. That independent review was supported by one of Nigeria's development partners, which insulated the process from the controversial territorial protection of institutional interests by politicians and bureaucrats always in competition among themselves. By the way, what would have been an implementation of

---

[67] However, implementation was yet to commence as at June 2022.

win-win recommendations (i.e. national interests and that of labour) contained in the independent review suffered serious set-backs due to political interference. Indeed, the protection of the personal interests of politicians and bureaucrats against national interests had always been the cause of lack of political will which is one of the typical features of Nigeria's atypical governance system.

This chapter is an advocacy intervention against the waste of public funds through a politically-led and interest-driven circuitous review of the Report without any tangible results. Over the years, the review of Oronsaye Report was an endless wasteful exercise that kept recurring because of lack of political will to implement what already exists. Such wasteful circuitous reviews actually defeat the main purpose of the Oronsaye Report which set out primarily to curtail waste of public resources.[68] It was therefore painful watching a government that said it had no money to be wasting additional resources to embark on a long process of reviewing a Report that had been previously reviewed twice under the same government. It was even unacceptable that this was happening under a COVID-19-induced austerity budget.

Duplication of Agencies and Overlapping Functions Vs Other Drivers of High Cost of Governance

If there is political will, what are the very clear (though controversial) issues for implementation without wasting much time and resources? The first is that the structure of governance is wasteful. People wrongly assume that the main issues centre more on duplications of agencies and their overlapping functions. Yes, they exist but they are not the main conduit pipes that drain the resources per se. One of the main problems is the existence of top-heavy manning levels with humongous expenses made on the allowances of top public officials (the elected, appointed and career officials) in the executive and legislative arms of government.

---

[68] As of August 2022, the Buhari administration was still considering implementing the latest White Paper on the Report before leaving office in 2023. We see this as simply an attempt to shift the actual political burden of such implementation to the in-coming administration in 2023 because there is hardly much the government could achieve on it before leaving office.

With respect to these officials, the Adamu Fika Committee Report of 2011 for example in its review of expenditures for the Federal Government held that a total of N1.13Trillion was expended on 18,000 top public servants including politicians. This represented over 25% of the National Budget during that period under review. The committee also found out that out of that sum, only N95billion was expended on salaries for these 18,000 top officials. This means that 91% of that huge sum was wasted on perquisites (allowances) of these officials.[69] The clear message is that it is not the sheer numbers of poor public servants that matter, but the inequities in expenses of those at the top. The government should do the needful in cost reduction.

Think of the number of SUVs being used by these top officers across the entire public service, and you will get a sense of the enormous waste of resources. There is a growing culture of entitlement mentality which needs to be checked as a cost saving measure. So a low hanging fruit begging for immediate implementation is the abolition of the use of SUV cars in the public sector. This means that any proposed and indiscriminate sacking of poor public servants is out of the question in the implementation of the Oronsaye Report. There are also areas of rationalisation and/or merging of institutional duplications with clear options of how the affected staff should be moved to other needed areas, as many areas are grossly under-staffed in the entire public service (e.g. in education and health, the security services generally).

There is no reason for a country that cannot fund education and health adequately, to be having large, unwieldy and expensive governing boards and councils. Some Federal Commissions have 36 members with one member from each state. This is completely unnecessary and wasteful. If we are serious in cutting cost drastically, all such boards, councils and commissions should be limited to seven members including the chairman. This will take care of the six geo-political zones in the

---

[69] Federal Republic of Nigeria (2012): Presidential Committee on the Review of the Reform Processes in the Nigerian Public Service. Abuja: OSGF Final Report.

country. If anyone doubts what these large boards cost Nigeria, the person can carry out an independent research on the expenses to maintain them. This recommendation can only be done anyway, if there is political will. However if the politicians hijack the implementation of the presidential directive, we will end up the same way like in the past.

One important area of cutting cost which was not in the Terms of Reference (TOR) of Oronsaye Report, but which is relevant for our purpose here, is the structure and composition of the National Assembly. As presently constituted, it is a big conduit pipe for draining resources. It should be restructured and reconstituted. The Senate should have only one member from a state, why the House of Representatives should be reduced to 30-50% of its membership now. So a state with 15 members in the House of Representatives for example should have a maximum of five members. Additional thinking needs to go on here if we are serious at reducing cost of governance at the federal level.

In conclusion, all that Nigeria needs to implement the Oronsaye Report is just political will. So far, such political will has been lacking. In the absence of such political will, it was unwise for the Buhari administration to be wasting additional scarce resources carrying out further circuitous review of the report.

CHAPTER FOURTEEN

The COVID-19 Management Challenge in Nigeria's Weak Health System

During the COVID-19 lockdown, health workers in Nigeria revealed the dilemma in which they found themselves namely having to watch out for their safety while treating patients – a situation they found strenuous. This reported reality brought to the fore, the poor state of Nigeria's health infrastructure and weak health system generally, which incidentally shocked Boss Mustapha, the Secretary to the Government of the Federation (SGF) and Chairman of the Presidential Task Force on COVID-19. Health professionals across the country had bemoaned their plight over shortages of personal protective equipment (PPE) and supplies in hospitals. Specifically, staff of one of the Federal Medical Centres in the country had complained that 'gloves, sanitizers, are luxuries here' while reporting their challenges in treating patients.[70]

The WHO's Single Framework for understanding a Health System

In one of its remarkable publications[71] in 2007, the World Health Organisation (WHO) aptly said that 'a health system consists of all organisations, people and actions whose primary intent is to promote, restore or maintain health'. According to it, a health system goes beyond 'the pyramid of publicly owned health facilities that deliver personal health services' to include a wide range of other complementary things as "private providers, behaviour change programmes, vector-control campaigns, health insurance organisations, occupational health and safety regulation", among others. Going further to operationalise this

---

[70] See Vanguard newspaper of Friday, April 10, 2020 in a news report titled: 'COVID-19: Our challenges treating patients'.
[71] WHO, (2007): Everybody's Business: Strengthening Health Systems to Improve Health Outcomes (WHO's Framework for Action). See https://www.who.int/alliance-hpsr/resources/Strengthening_complet.pdf).

definition, WHO in this publication, presented what it calls "a single framework with six building blocks" comprising (a) service delivery, (b) health workforce, (c) information, (d) medical products, vaccines and technologies, (e) financing and (f) leadership/governance.

In this context, this single framework is key to rebuilding or strengthening Nigeria's weak health system. One can only talk of rebuilding or strengthening of a weak health system of a country when there is a clear understanding among all stakeholders of the various components of the health system that require remedial attention. These stakeholders that need common understanding are policy makers, practitioners and health system policy researchers.

The reality of Nigeria's weak Health System

It was actually shocking to hear Mr. Boss Mustapha (The SGF) on national television (April 9, 2020) make an open confession that he never knew our healthcare infrastructure was in such bad condition until he was appointed Chairman PTF on COVID-19. According to him, 'I can tell you for sure, I never knew that our entire healthcare infrastructure was in the state in which it is.' [72] Although the SGF reacted later on April 10 that he was quoted out of context, many Nigerians would not believe this revision of his earlier honest admission of inadequate knowledge of Nigeria's poor health infrastructure. This is not surprising because it reflects the typical nature of those occupying political offices.

This is again because by wearing their political garbs, politicians (even the most sincere ones) hardly see issues beyond their narrow and partisan lens. Their overriding political interest hardly allows them to see and comprehend issues and occurrences objectively. For example, the manner in which the leadership crisis in the National Health Insurance Scheme (NIHS) (which lingered on in 2018 and 2019), was eventually 'resolved', was a demonstrative evidence of how top political office holders mostly see things from their narrow and partisan lens. How else can one explain a situation where an executive secretary of the agency

---

[72] See https://www.premiumtimesng.com/health/health-news/387036-i-never-knew-nigerias-healthcare-infrastructure-was-in-such-bad-state-sgf.html

Chapter Fourteen | Isaac Nnamdi Obasi

had (a) running battle with his minister (who suspended him), (b) had fierce and long running battles with labour union under his agency, (c) had problems with the Health Maintenance Organizations (HMOs), and above all (d) had serious problem with his Governing Council, when he was sacked, he had to go along with others (members of Governing Council and some others). Then who was wrong in the whole saga? This is indeed not how to enthrone a good governance culture in a public health agency thereby negating one of WHO's six building blocks identified above.

Another example demonstrates how parochialism sometimes hold sway in governance. In March 2020, 25 elders drawn from various tribes in Taraba State (a highly multi-ethnic state with about 50 tribes) sent a petition to President Muhammadu Buhari over what they observed to be a "consistent lop-sidedness in federal appointments in the state". This followed the appointment of a Chief Medical Director of the Federal Medical Centre, Jalingo. They complained that the leadership of that Medical Centre had come from a senatorial zone and from one particular ethnic group for a long time now.[73] The point here again is about the issue of leadership, which when poorly handled impacts negatively on the other five building blocks (WHO's concept of a health system) with the health system generally weaker for it. The lesson here is that for the government to achieve its strategic goal of strengthening our weak health system, it has to be holistic by adopting WHO's single framework of six building blocks that complementarily strengthens the system.

With respect to the state of Nigeria's health infrastructure, many Nigerians already knew long ago that their leaders are far removed from those they govern. Many Nigerians also knew long ago that a good number of their leaders do not go to hospitals in Nigeria when they are sick, and that many of them do not have their children in secondary and tertiary institutions in Nigeria. This is probably one of the reasons why annual budgetary allocations to the social sector have remained abysmally low ranging between 5-10% thereby leaving the country with poor human capital development. This is in spite of the fact that health professionals and professors have been at the head of the ministries of

---

[73] See http://www.news-af.feednews.com.

health and education. They, as individuals, could not influence in any significant manner budgetary allocations to either health or education despite their knowledge of the poor state of the sectors. This was because of the reactionary character of the ruling class that has long dominated the Nigerian public governance system.

The Imperative Need for Rebuilding Nigeria's Weak Health System

The importance of rebuilding Nigeria's weak health system cannot be over-emphasized if one recalls what happened during the lockdown. During that particular period when the epicenter of COVID-19 was in China, later in Europe and much later in the United States of America, it sounded strange that some foreign embassies of countries such as France, USA, UK, Israel, and even South Africa took permission (after Nigeria's airspace had been closed) to airlift their nationals back home. Actually some Nigerians were wondering why. These were countries where citizens were dying in several hundreds, within 24 hours. Take the case of the United States for example, which recorded 2,492 deaths within 24 hours as of Saturday, April 25, 2020. The reason for their leaving Nigeria was simply the fear that Nigeria's weak health system would not be able to cope if it became overwhelmed by COVID-19 patients. They feared perhaps that what Mrs. Melinda Gates said about dead bodies littering the streets of Africa under COVID-19, would come to pass. Nobody should blame them for after all, our own leaders do not trust our health system by going for their medical treatment abroad.

This shows that there is no alternative to fixing and strengthening Nigeria's weak health system. Nigeria's COVID-19 experience revealed that research has not been feeding very well into policy and practice in Nigeria. 'Getting research into policy and practice' (GRIPP) was a point well made in a publication titled: *Strengthening Health Systems: The Role and Promise of Policy and Systems Research* under the auspices of the Alliance for Health Policy and Systems Research in collaboration with WHO in 2004. Indeed, the importance of getting the findings of health systems research into policy and practice in Nigeria is urgent now than ever before. Rebuilding Nigeria's weak health system requires that the earlier identified tripod (policy makers, practitioners and health system policy researchers) need to work more collaboratively in the task of rebuilding the weak health system.

It was heart-warming that the PTF on COVID–19 adopted a strategic approach in utilizing available funds towards strengthening the health infrastructure across the country. There is need for example for massive expansion of our health infrastructure at the tertiary level for specialist training. Presently many new medical graduates find it extremely difficult to secure places to do their compulsory house-manship. This is should not be so, as it is a national embarrassment to say the least.

Regardless of achievements recorded so far, there is still room to establish more Federal Medical Centres across the country. There might also be need to explore partnering with tested private sector health institutions towards achieving the goal of having more tertiary level health institutions for specialist training.

Conclusion

The WHO's 'Single Framework' comprising six building blocks should serve as strategic reference point for rebuilding Nigeria's weak health system, as it is not only about buildings and facilities. Issues of leadership and management are also key in creating the required organizational climate capable of motivating health professionals to put in their best in service delivery. More importantly, capacity building of the entire health workforce (in all occupational groups) should be aggressively pursued, as they perform complementary functions in strengthening the weak health system.

CHAPTER FIFTEEN

COVID-19 Lockdown Exit Policy For Nigerian Educational Institutions

Less than a month after the implementation of Nigeria's lockdown policy in Lagos and Ogun States as well as in FCT, Abuja, there were agitations across sections of the society against the lockdown. It is noteworthy that agitations and protests against the lockdown policy, was not entirely a Nigerian problem. There were also agitations and even protests by some citizens in other countries. The major problem faced by various governments across the world then, was how to rationally review the subsisting lockdown policy that was impacting negatively on economic prosperity and lives of their citizens. Surely no government would want her citizens to die so easily either through coronavirus itself or 'hunger-virus' due to prolonged lockdown of the economy.

It was therefore understandable that across the world, the subsisting lockdown policies generated palpable restiveness, some mildly expressed (through non-violent protests) while some others manifested through violent demonstrations. In some countries (like Nigeria for instance), youth restiveness gave rise to daring street-level armed robbery attacks on many homes, breaking of shops and looting of goods, and other acts of hooliganism such as attacking of lorries carrying food items designated as palliatives for the people. As a result of these backlashes, governments started reconsidering the lockdown policy towards opening the economy.

Lockdown Exit Plan in international Perspective

In Germany, the then Chancellor Angela Merkel announced a lockdown exit plan to reopen schools, shops among others. In the United States, President Donald Trump equally announced a phased lockdown exit plan for opening up of the economy. The various states in the US were given the responsibility to decide when and how to implement the policy based on unique circumstances. The European Union also prepared a lockdown exit strategy for its member states to follow in a more coordinated approach.

It was against the background of all these, that the World Health Organization (WHO) announced six conditions for ending the COVID-19 lockdown. The conditions were meant to prevent a resurgence of COVID-19 and stop its dangerous spread that would reverse some of the hard won gains the world had recorded so far. Nations were expected to meet the conditions before announcing the lifting of the lockdown order in their different jurisdictions. The six conditions issued by WHO for relaxing the lockdown restrictions were as follows:

> ➤ Disease transmission is under control;
> ➤ Health systems are able to "detect, test, isolate and treat every case and trace every contact;"
> ➤ Hot spot risks are minimised in vulnerable places, such as nursing homes;
> ➤ Schools, workplaces and other essential places have established preventive measures;
> ➤ The risk of importing new cases "can be managed;"
> ➤ Communities are fully educated, engaged and empowered to live under a new normal.[74]

The Nigerian situation as at this period (April 2020) was far from meeting the six conditions of WHO. For examples, new cases of infections were still on the rise with community infections emerging as a worrying threat. At this time too, the Buhari administration was still strategizing on its exit plan at the end of the two weeks' lockdown extension which the President announced on Monday April 13, 2020, for Lagos and Ogun states, as well as the FCT, Abuja. One of the most challenging problems involved in this strategizing efforts, was how to re-open educational institutions.

---

[74] See: https://www.who.int/dg/speeches/detail… (version of this summary here was made by National Public Radio (NPR) Washington, Available at: https://www.npr.org/sections/g oatsandsoda/2020/04/15/834021103/who-sets-6-conditions-for-ending-a-coronavirus-lockdown.

Like the markets, churches, mosques, entertainment houses, and other crowd-pulling events, educational institutions constituted potential high risk areas for spread of COVID-19. It was on account of this fear (in the first place) that the federal government wisely ordered the closure all tertiary institutions for a period of one month with effect from Monday, March 23, 2020. The government also ordered the closure of all Unity Schools latest by Friday, March 26, 2020. The various state governments also closed educational institutions in their domain. These institutions were to remain closed until the governments review their lockdown order, probably when the spread of the virus had been reasonably contained.

Crucial Questions that faced Lockdown Exit Policy for Educational Institutions

Whatever was the case, the decision to review the lockdown policy or announce the reopening of educational institutions would surely be made some day. This decision required a customized well-thought out lockdown exit policy for these institutions. Some important questions that were raised then include first, how would the exit policy address the modus operandi of lecturers-students interactions in educational institutions? For example, how would interaction patterns in the crowded lecture rooms and halls in tertiary institutions be made, to conform to the social/physical distancing etiquette? Secondly, with respect to secondary schools, how would existing crowded dormitories (without additional ones) cope with social/physical distancing requirements? Thirdly, how would pupils in primary schools be controlled by adults who might be carrying the virus?

Fourthly, how would the school buses protect pupils from one another to avoid easy spreading of the virus that might have been contacted from their parents? Would the children for instance, be made to carry and use sanitizers while using the school buses? Fifthly, would our poorly-funded educational institutions be in the position to make sanitizers available to hundreds of their students and pupils bearing in mind the standard hygiene protocols that were required? Sixth question, would enough water and soaps be provided for regular washing of hands in line with the hygiene protocol?

The seventh question, how would examinations be conducted in crowded lecture halls with question papers and answer scripts distributed by lecturers who might unknowingly spread the virus to their students and vice-versa? Would enough sanitizers be made available for the invigilators to use before the distribution of examination scripts? Would the sanitizers be enough for use at the end of the examinations shortly before collecting back the answer scripts?

Lastly and more importantly, how would students conduct and protect themselves from one another in the lecture and examination halls, hostels/halls of residence, libraries, cafeterias/canteens, worship places, that are proliferated on campuses, business centres that also exist everywhere on campuses, etc? These crucial public health-related questions needed to be seriously considered and factored into the lockdown exit or reopening policy by the federal government and sent to all public and private educational institutions across the country. The various state governments should do the same for the educational institutions they regulate.

Conclusion

The various questions in the preceding paragraphs brought to mind the issue of inadequate infrastructure, facilities and working materials in both public and private educational institutions across the country. The federal government was challenged to use this period to do the needful in improving both infrastructure and other facilities in tertiary institutions. Some of the questions also raise the issue of how education regulatory authorities would ensure that private schools comply with the policy in the post-lockdown period? The federal and state governments were challenged to think very deeply in rolling out guidelines to stop the rapid spread of COVID-19 in educational institutions during the post-lockdown era.

CHAPTER SIXTEEN

The Challenge of Resolving Initial Dilemma
of Lifting the Lockdown Policy

One of earliest measures to check the spread of COVID-19 across the world was the adoption of the lockdown policy. Owing to its very controversial nature, this policy could rightly be described as a necessary evil that governments had to face during the early stage of the outbreak of COVID-19. The initial dilemma that confronted governments over its continued implementation amidst the controversy was analogous to a choice between the devil and the deep (blue) sea. It was what the then Australian Prime Minister Scott Morrison described as "weighing lives against livelihood."[75]

The challenge of controlling Corona-virus amidst Hunger-virus

In Nigeria (as in elsewhere), it was a big challenge struggling to save lives simultaneously from both corona-virus and hunger-virus. These two separate eleven letter words gave governments across the world serious challenge, simply because the strategies for attacking the two-pronged problems became mutually-contradictory. For example, on the one hand, a prolonged lockdown period (to stop the spread of the virus), prevented informal sector workers from engaging in their livelihood activities, and on the other hand, a premature easing of the lockdown restrictions by governments exposed more people to the infections leading to more deaths. What a dilemma?

Specifically in Nigeria, President Muhammadu Buhari faced this big challenge when he was contemplating what next to do as the country was anxiously waiting the expiration of the lockdown extension order on Lagos and Ogun states, as well as FCT, Abuja. At that material time, the dire situation in Kano State in what was described as mysterious deaths,

---

[75] See https://www.theguardian.com/world/2020/apr/19/...

and the rapid community spreading of the virus across the country, added to the challenge facing the president then in developing a lockdown exit strategy. Yet as a novel coronavirus, there were no ready-made text book solutions on any lockdown exit strategy. Scott Morrison rightly described the solution trajectory as completely 'an uncharted territory,'[76] which Ben Doherty equally called a 'long and winding' road.[77]

As noted earlier, one factor that complicated the decision dilemma of easing the lockdown restrictions, was the widespread discontent and agitations across sections of the people including the old and the young, men and women, people of different political and religious persuasions, labour unions etc. For example, Chief Executive Officers (CEOs) of private organisations in Nigeria pushed for an early restart of the economy,[78] in the same way as the Nigeria Labour Congress (NLC) warmed that the extension of lockdown would fuel unrest.[79]

Again, Governor Ben Ayade of Cross River State also warmed, that any further extension of the lockdown would spell doom for the nation, as it would give rise to uncontrollable youth restiveness.[80] In actual fact, some agitations that later happened were violent leading to many deaths that prompted the National Human Rights Commission (NHRC) to complain then that security personnel had killed more people than the COVID-19 itself during the period of the lockdown.[81]

A related and disturbing dimension to the challenge of developing a rational exit strategy was the flagrant disobedience to the lockdown order by many people who moved around in a business-as-usual mentality. This and other restive behaviour made decisions about how to ease the restrictions a bit more difficult. If there was premature easing of restrictions the gains achieved during the lockdown could be lost, and yet if the government extended the lockdown without accommodating the

---

[76] Ibid
[77] See *The Guardian* newspaper, UK, April 18, 2020.
[78] See *Daily Trust* newspaper, Thursday, April 23, 2020.
[79] See *THISDAY* newspaper, Thursday, April 23, 2020.
[80] See Daily Post via https://dailypost.ng/2020/04/22/…).
[81] See *Vanguard* newspaper: 'Security agents killed more Nigerians within 14 days than Coronavirus', April, 16, 2020. The *Punch* newspaper put in another way: 'Security agents, deadlier than COVID-19', April 21, 2020.

feelings of the agitated people, more social crisis (unrests) could result. Yet, the number of new cases kept rising for as at 11.30pm on Thursday, April 23, 2020, the total number of reported new cases had risen to 981.

Nigeria at this period in time had entered the dangerous stage of community infections. This prompted the Nigeria Governors' Forum (NGF) to adopt a decision to implement a two-week lockdown on inter-state movements. This was in essence to form part of President's nation-wide lockdown policy accommodating people on essential services such as those involved in the movement of agricultural goods, pharmaceuticals, security personnel etc. Although, many agitated citizens were further disappointed, the fact was that nations do not lift lockdown restrictions when the infections were spreading and the number rising dangerously as it was the case with Nigeria then. The NGF's decision appeared to have taken into cognizance of WHO's six conditions for relaxing the lockdown restrictions as noted earlier. As at that period, Nigeria was very far from fulfilling these conditions, as detecting and testing capacity was still very low, new hot spots were still emerging (e.g. Kano State), and schools were still closed because effective preventive measures were not yet in place, etc. Nigeria's lockdown policy response was quite in order then.

Global Examples of Middle-Ground Solutions to Resolving the Dilemma

Across much of the world, one could identify then some middle-point solutions to resolving the decision dilemma. Put differently, an overview of how some countries were reacting to the initial lockdown review showed that many were adopting a step-by-step precautionary approach with some doses of trial and error to see what the outcome would be before proceeding. For example, Australia was among the leading nations in this cautious approach. Germany also cautiously lifted restrictions on businesses dealing on cars, bike shops and bookshops, while restaurants, bars, gyms, large stores were to remain closed. In the same manner, the United States of America announced a phased exit strategy that allowed states to reopen the economy based on local conditions regarding the containment of the virus.

Norway allowed partial reopening of high schools, universities, hair, massage and beauty salons. In Denmark, Day care centres and primary schools were already reopened at this particular period, while restaurants, and other related businesses remain closed.[82] Spain following a different approach allowed some construction and factory workers to open, while keeping schools, restaurants and other related businesses closed. On its part, Italy kept factories closed while some other businesses such as bookshops, laundries, stores dealing on children's clothes were to open.[83]

In conclusion, these country-specific examples revealed a mixed-bag of approaches and solutions based on how each country weighed its strategic economic interests, vis-à-vis the efficacy of containment measures. The common-denominator, is that many of the countries demonstrated courageous leadership in confronting a very serious problem in a period of uncertainty or emergency.

---

[82] See for example: https://www.theguardian.com/world/2020/apr/19) for more detailed report.
[83] See also for example: https://inews.co.uk/news/world/how-spain-italy-easing-lockdown-restrictions-2537041.

CHAPTER SEVENTEEN

COVID-19 and the Violation of Presidential Ban on Inter-State Movement

In his third address to the nation on COVID-19 pandemic on 27 April 2020, President Muhammadu Buhari announced some key measures to contain the rapidly spreading cases of coronavirus (COVID-19) infection across the country. Among other things, the president announced the: (a) imposition of overnight curfew from 8pm to 6am. All movements were prohibited except for essential services; (b) ban on non-essential inter-state passenger travel until further notice; and (c) partial and controlled inter-state movement of goods and services from producers to consumers. Prior to the imposition of these measures, the president in his situation analysis (part of the address), revealed that exactly two weeks ago, there were 323 confirmed cases in 20 States and the Federal Capital Territory. At the morning of the address, the president regrettably reported that Nigeria had recorded 1,273 cases across 32 States and the FCT, and unfortunately with 40 deaths.

Boldness of President Buhari's Measures and their Flagrant Violations

Based on these dreadful statistics, the measures announced were well received across the country. Rightly too, inter-state movement particularly was seen to be among the key drivers of the rising number of cases of infection across the country. With the high number of deaths recorded in Kano State then, the ban on inter-state travels was also rightly seen as a major containment measure against the rapid spread of the virus. Barely two weeks after the presidential ban on inter-state travels, the total number of infections across the states increased from 1,273 to 4,339 as at Sunday 10 May 2020 with the number of deaths at 143. The virus had now spread to 34 states and the FCT. These statistics made people to wonder if the ban on inter-state movements had significant effect on reducing the rising cases of infection.

Regrettably, it was found out that this major containment measure was not effective as a result of the flagrant violation of the presidential ban. A close monitoring of the situation revealed that some categories of Nigerians were culprits across the country. The first identifiable group were businessmen whose vehicles were used to transport essential goods and services along with persons not authorised to travel under the inter-state lockdown order. Such unauthorised persons were unfortunately coming from states already highly infected with the virus. A lot of vehicles were actually intercepted conveying such people across the states. Quite a number of such vehicles made their way through from the far northern states (in spite of security check points or road blocks) into such southern states as Lagos and Port Harcourt.

The second category was commercial transporters who flouted the presidential ban by regularly embarking on their trips and setting money aside to bribe security personnel on their way. In a very insightful opinion piece by Nwamu,[84] the modus operandi of these commercial drivers came to light. They paid their way through at every checkpoint. Mr. Nwamu who was in one of the commercial vehicles counted 44 such checkpoints from Abuja to Obollo Afor (in Enugu State), where their driver settled all security agents. This point was collaborated by Governor Nyesom Wike of Rivers State who revealed that offering bribe to police authorities was a method by which the big lorries and commercial vehicles made their way through. He said a deputy commissioner of police in his state was collecting bribe and issuing permit for those illegal travels in disregard of the travel ban.[85]

The third group were few security personnel who mounted road blocks while pretending to be enforcing the presidential ban were busy collecting bribes from motorists namely big lorries, and commercial buses and cars. However, there were security operatives who actually did a good job by intercepting defaulters on the road. For example, the News Agency of Nigeria (NAN) on May 9, 2020 reported that the Federal

---

[84] Aniebo Nwamu, (2020): *44 Checkpoints* (See *Sundiata Post* via https://sundiatapost.com/44-checkpoints-by-aniebo-nwamu/)

[85] COVID-19: Police collecting bribe, sabotaging lockdown in Rivers Wike alleges, (See https://dailypost.ng/2020/05/08/covid-19-police-collecting-bribe-sabotaging-lockdown-in-rivers-wike-alleges/).

Road Safety Corps (FRSC) intercepted and turned back as many as 791 vehicles from Ogun and Lagos States' boundaries within five days, while enforcing the Federal Government's restrictions on inter-state movements.

The fourth group that disturbed people most then were those conveying large number of Almajiri children (street beggars) across the states mainly from the northern part of the country to the southern part. For example, the Police in Kwara State intercepted 200 such children, while a truck load of Almajiris concealed in cattle truck were intercepted also in Abia State. In Cross River and Enugu States, the stories were the same with many buses making such illegal travels. Incidentally, some of these Almajiris on transit originated from Kano where there were massive deaths taking place then.

The violators of lockdown restrictions were not only along the inter-state highways. In the cities, the authorities of the FCT for example, arrested 900 offenders in six weeks of the lockdown. The story of conviction of many offenders was the same in many other states. The high number of violators of inter-state travels and offenders of lockdown restrictions suggest clearly that ours is a lawless society. Nigerians have learnt (regrettably from long historical experience) that law breakers both in high and low places in our society get away with their acts. Many believed perhaps that the lockdown order would also be observed in the breach with their engrained business-as-usual-mentality. Unfortunately for some defaulters, this time around mobile courts were established to give them prompt trial. This is one of the gains of the lockdown experience in the enforcement of laws in Nigeria.

Some Useful Lessons

There are some other lessons we can learn from the flagrant violations of presidential ban on inter-state movements and lockdown restrictions within the areas affected (FCT, Lagos and Ogun States). One lesson is that if the government at every level enforces the laws without compromise, many Nigerians will also learn to obey. Secondly, prompt dispensation of justice (like the hot-stove theory of discipline) will send the message loud and clear. The example of Governor Nyesom Wike of Rivers State is very instructive. Offenders should be given instant justice and not the usual refrain that they will be brought to justice, a promise or assurance people have come to know hardly gets implemented.

The third lesson is that Nigerians will take obedience to the law seriously when they see leadership-by-example in action. This point resonates very well with Professor Chinua Achebe's book *The Trouble with Nigeria*. Prof. Achebe pungently observed that the bane of leadership in Nigeria is the inability to live up to the challenge of personal example that is the hallmark of true leadership. When we overcome this problem, many Nigerians will willingly obey the law without much coercion, and many more will obey by coercion knowing well that they will be brought to justice unfailingly.

CHAPTER EIGHTEEN

COVID-19 Risk Communication and Nigerians' Poor Compliance

A s the management of COVID-19 policies progressed, millions of Nigerians appeared to be hard of hearing over the deadly nature of the disease. Many Nigerians in our big cities could be observed (through national television stations) moving about as if they were completely in denial of the virus. Yet, there were aggressive risk communication programmes in various mass media channels to make the people fully aware of the risk. Risk communication was one of the core capacities to be developed by countries as required by the International Health Regulations (2005) that came into force on 15 June 2007. The International Health Regulations were developed to protect the global community from public health risks and emergencies that cross international borders.[86]

Risk Communication as a Two-Way Exchange of Information

Risk communication is defined as a two-way exchange of information between interested parties about the nature, significance and/or control of a risk.[87] As Lowbridge and Leask, further elaborated 'risk communication is fundamental to public health practice and critical to the success of any public health response'. This is because "effective risk communication is essential for improving public understanding of potential or actual health threats and helps the public to make informed decisions about risk mitigation measures."[88]

With the outbreak of the COVID-19 pandemic, the Nigeria Centre for Disease Control (NCDC) took the issue of risk communication as an important aspect of its response strategy. It has for example, a Risk

---

[86] See national Risk Communication Plan, India via https://ncdc.gov.in/WriteReadData/l892s/File593.pdf).

[87] Covello, V. T. (1993): 'Risk communication and occupational medicine', *Journal of Occupational Medicine*, Vol. 33, No. 1, pp.18-19. See also Lowbridge, C. & Leask, J. (2011): 'Risk communication in public health', *NSW Public Health Bulletin*. Vol. 22, Nos. 1-2.

[88] Lowbridge, C. & Leask, J. (2011): Ibid.

Communication Pillar in its National Emergency Operations Centre. The Presidential Task Force on COVID-19 established a Risk Communication Unit. Both the PTF and NCDC were involved in aggressive public enlightenment campaign on the serious threat to life posed by the COVID-19 disease.

The Central Message of Key Communication Campaign by Different Stakeholders

The central message of the campaign has been that all Nigerians should "adhere to the use of face masks when in public; wash hands frequently; and always observe physical distancing of at least 2 metres from others." They have also been communicating to the public on the need to take personal responsibility in fighting the spread of this deadly virus. Furthermore, they have been addressing the critical issue of public misconceptions, superstition and ignorance among some people. Above all, they have been strengthening response efforts and ensuring that members of the public have the confidence to take responsibility in the fight against COVID-19. Given these risk communication efforts of the government, one might be wondering and asking also why many Nigerians appeared to be deaf by not complying with the messages targeted at them.

CACOVID's Efforts

Going beyond the government, the private sector-driven Coalition Against COVID-19 (CA-COVID)[89] was also implementing an aggressive risk communication strategy in all the 774 Local Government Areas of Nigeria, using all known means of reaching the people and even in their local languages. For CA-COVID "the end of COVID-19 in Nigeria can only become visible when Nigerians, get more enlightened and fully adhere to the provided guidelines". Consequently, CA-COVID tried to quicken this process through its advocacy and enlightenment efforts across several media. To demonstrate further its seriousness, it has

---

[89] The discussion on CA-COVID would come later under private sector policy response against COVID-19.

"enlisted the help of CEOs, billionaires, and even celebrities to speak to Nigerians in the language they understand and get them to accept that this pandemic is not a joke."[90]

UNICEF's Efforts

Apart from government and private sector efforts, international development partners were not left out in the implementation of various risk and communication strategies against the spread of COVID-19. The United Nations Children's Fund (UNICEF) was doing spectacular work at the national level in the "risk communication and community engagement functional area in developing and disseminating COVID-19 messaging and infographics across the country."[91] According to it[92], over three million U-Reporters have been engaged on the U-Report platform to support information dissemination. At the state level, it is using unique and most relevant communicating channels to reach out to the people in states such as Kaduna, Bauchi, Gombe, Kano, Ekiti, Osun, Oyo, Enugu, Zamfara, Kebbi, Rivers, Sokoto, Borno and Yobe. How well did the people respond to the various risk communication messages?

In spite of all these risk communication efforts by the government, private sector and international development partners, there were no significant changes in the attitude and behaviour among Nigerians towards complying with the guidelines for containing the spread of COVID-19. For example, the business-as-usual mentality remained a standard practice for many Nigerians. One is at a great loss why this was so. Even in the churches and mosques during the brief period of the easing of the lockdown, people were not obeying the required NCDC protocols. There were instances when some church ministers appealed repeatedly to members to put on their masks but the appeal fell on deaf ears on some. So what were the responsible reasons for the poor compliance level among Nigerians?

---

[90] As report by Nairametrics (2020) via https://nairametrics.com/2020/05/12/.
[91] UNICEF Nigeria COVID-19 Situation Report, (2020) via:
   https://www.unicef.org/appeals/files/UNICEF_Nigeria_COVID19_Situation_Report_10_April_2020.pdf.

Reasons for Poor Compliance Level among Nigerians

First, the level of public trust of those in government is very low. This factor has already been analysed in earlier chapters. The main cause of the low level of people's trust in their government is lack of leadership-by-example, and wide abuse of powers. Those in power do not practise what they preach and the people take a cue from that. For example, laws which are meant to be obeyed by everyone are not obeyed by many of those in power.

The second reason for poor compliance is related to low enforcement capacity of laws. The enforcement of laws is very weak and the law enforcement agents are easily compromised by those who violate the laws. This exists in every aspect of life. The third reason is the high level on impunity among Nigerians. This factor has also been discussed extensively earlier. For example, when some people freely move about with AK-47 (which is unlawful) and then go further to harass innocent citizens boldly in their farms, then the victims can easily conclude that different laws exist for different people in the land.

Generally, Nigerians exhibit very high level of impunity because there is no leadership-by-example, and lastly there is the existence of wide spread corruption which is related to the other factors. With low level of enforcement and impunity, violators of laws know that with a little bribery, they could easily get away with their acts of lawlessness.

In conclusion, governments at all levels have a lot of job to do in getting Nigerians to comply with not just the risk communication messages but other laws of the land. They should start first by improving the level of public trust through good governance and through leadership-by-example. The poor level of enforcement of laws of the land should be significantly improved. All of these will significantly reduce the high level of impunity among Nigerians which will in turn possibly make them to begin to drop the idea that with bribery and corruption, one can easily get away with acts of impunity.

Chapter Eighteen | Isaac Nnamdi Obasi

CHAPTER NINETEEN

COVID-19 Testing Issues in Nigeria

The *National Strategy to Scale up Access to Coronavirus Disease Testing in Nigeria,* prioritized testing as one of the key interventions to the COVID-19 policy response in Nigeria.[93] It recognised that "diagnostic testing is essential response strategy to interrupt the transmission of the COVID-19 pandemic". Consequently, in order to rapidly contain the outbreak, the Federal Government planned to rapidly scale up diagnostic testing to cover all 36 States and the Federal Capital Territory FCT). Following this directive, the NCDC in line with best practice recommended and implemented COVID-19 diagnosis by molecular RT-PCR testing.[94] The main thrust of this policy document resonates well with the key message of the World Health Organisation (WHO) on testing which is: test, test, test, as a way of stopping the spread of the deadly coronavirus.

Testing as a big Challenge

In Nigeria, like in many other countries especially the developing ones, testing for the coronavirus was a big challenge under a weak public health system since the outbreak of the pandemic. Many factors conspired to complicate the problems aside from the well-known paucity of huge financial resources required. For example, the competition for the testing materials between the well-endowed nations and the poor ones, posed a bigger challenge. The fact that the manufacturers of such urgently needed materials were themselves impacted negatively in their operations by the virus also made matters worse. The inadequacy of specialised skills required to conduct the test itself in a pandemic

---

[93] Nigeria Centre for Disease Control (NCDC) (2020): 'National Strategy to Scale Up Access to Coronavirus Disease Testing in Nigeria', Abuja: Federal Ministry of Health.

[94] For this document, see https://covid19.ncdc.gov.ng/media/files/COVID19TestingStrategy_L z3ZVsT.pdf.

emergency was equally a critical factor. The poor health facilities and infrastructure constituted yet another. In all, Nigeria's public health system like in many other developing countries was not fully in a state of preparedness when the index case was recorded in February, 2020 in Nigeria.

As at the time the index case was recorded, there were only two laboratories where COVID-19 could be tested in Nigeria. However, according to NCDC website, as of July 2, 2020, there were forty (40) laboratories in Nigeria that could test for COVID-19 and they were all in the NCDC molecular laboratory network. These laboratories were then located in the following states of the federation namely Lagos and Kano with 5 laboratories each; FCT 4 laboratories; Kaduna 3 laboratories; Rivers, Edo, Oyo, & Ogun with 2 laboratories each; and one (1) laboratory each for Ebonyi, Osun, Plateau, Borno, Sokoto, Delta, Imo, Adamawa, Anambra, Katsina, Bauchi, Ekiti, Akwa Ibom, Jigawa and Ondo states.

Given the high number of COVID-19 testing laboratories established between February and early July 2020, the NCDC and their supporting partners deserve a big pat on the back for working very hard to achieve this within a very short period of time. Their tireless efforts did not therefore go unnoticed and history would be kind to them. Looking back now, some issues that happened need to be discussed for future lessons.

Some Major Concerns Regarding Location of Laboratories and Testing

First, the criteria for the location of the laboratories across the nation was not clear to the public. At that particular period in the fight against the virus, 14 states still did not have laboratories, while couple of others had more than one. For example, two states had up to 5 each, with others having between 4 and 1. A state like Taraba very far away from Abuja, and with large international borders with the Republic of Cameroun did not have one laboratory. This prompted the State Governor, Darius Ishaku to lament the absence of COVID-19 laboratory in his state. Another state (Kogi state) was not disposed to the establishment of NCDC laboratory with hoodlums attacking health workers. For example, according to the Chairman of the Presidential

Task Force on COVID-19 and Secretary to the Government of the Federation, Mr. Boss Mustapha, the PTF had received with great concern, reports about the attack on the Federal Medical Centre, Lokoja, Kogi State by some hoodlums. He said that the PTF was "distressed and regrets the trauma to which medical workers, patients and others who went on their legitimate businesses were subjected. He then assured that security agencies were looking at the matter very seriously…"[95]

Secondly, the slow pace of testing across the country was a major concern which did not in any reflect the worthy aspirations of the *National Strategy to Scale Up Access to Coronavirus Disease Testing in Nigeria*. As of July 1, 2020, the number tested (138,462) was incredibly too low. Again, the response time for a desperate person to establish meaningful contact with the testing officials via a phone call was to say the least very frustrating. At times there was absolutely no follow-up feedback from the officials even when such an official had promised to do so. This further frustrated the would-be COVID-19 patient. It was gratifying to note however that during the briefing of July 2, 2020, the Honourable Minister of Health, Dr. Osagie Ehanire assured that many hospitals in Abuja were going to serve as test collection centres. The National Coordinator, Dr. Sani Aliyu specifically mentioned that 7 new collection centres had been added then.

Conclusion

After two years of COVID-19 in Nigeria, the total number of people who have been tested stood at 4,589,726 as at Saturday, March 19, 2022 (12:30 am).[96] We can however conclude that this number was abysmally low as it is still far from what was envisaged in the Strategy policy document, but when seen against the difficulties encountered along the way, one could still commend the authorities for the efforts so far made.

---

[95] Sundiata Post, July 2, 2020. Report by Joyce Remi-Babayeju.
[96] NCDC, (2022): 'Samples Tested'. http://www.covid-19.ncdc.gov.ng.

CHAPTER TWENTY

COVID-19 Testing and the Unethical Practice
of Charging Students

Although the issues raised here - a reaction to the Ogun state government policy that made COVID-19 and malaria tests mandatory – were overtaken by events through the magnanimous reversal of the policy by Governor Dapo Abiodun, the lessons therein make the discussion in this chapter still relevant.

Governor Dapo Abiodun of Ogun state remained one of the governors known for their pro-activeness in the fight against the COVID-19. His government had consistently maintained its verve in fighting COVID-19 pandemic. Ordinarily, the news that his government adopted a policy which made COVID-19 and malaria tests mandatory as a condition for reopening of schools during the lockdown period in 2020, to enable SS3 boarding students to return, should have been a welcome one. The intent of the policy was also an indication that the government was consistently pro-active in stopping the spread of the virus thereby keeping the students healthy as they returned and prepared for their terminal examinations. However, the policy was ill-timed, and secondly, the charging of money for COVID-19 test, which also surprisingly applied discriminatorily between students in public and private schools, raised serious ethical questions.

Details of the Policy

According to news report [97] students were expected to resume on August 4, 2020, and according to the government the Ministry of Health had made provision for a COVID-19 and MALARIA TEST for all SS3 BOARDING students in Ogun State as part of the conditions for the

---

[97] *Premium Times* August 1, 2020 (report by Alfred Olufemi
via https://www.premiumtimesng.com/regional/south-west/406352-school-reopening-ogun-begins-mandatory-covid-19-malaria-tests-for-ss3-students.html.

reopening of schools in listed Public Health Care facilities between Friday 31st July & Monday 3rd August, 2020.[98] The three facilities listed were Ogun State General Hospital, Ota; the 250 MTR Okemosan, Abeokuta; and Olabisi Onabanjo University Teaching Hospital, Sagamu.

The policy specified that part of the strong condition of admittance to school for boarding students was the COVID-19 certificate showing 'Negative'. Consequently, all Principals were therefore directed to immediately disseminate the above important information to all SS3 learners in the State and to ensure that the above instructions were strictly adhered to as sanctions would be meted out to any defaulting school.[99] Furthermore, in its follow-up report (2 August 2020 by the same reporter) it was revealed that the COVID-19 test would cost twenty-five thousand naira (N25, 000) per student. More details revealed also that *only students in private secondary schools in the state would be charged for the test.*

Public Reactions and Government Explanations

The discriminatory policy of charging only a section of the students immediately attracted protects from parents of these students in private schools. Some of the parents who spoke to *Premium Times* "described the fee as insensitive on the part of the state government." However, government responded[100] to the criticisms saying that "private school students were meant to pay N25,000 because the government had subsidized the cost by 50 per cent."

Continuing, the government explained that:

> ...the COVID-19 test costs about N50,000. For the students in public schools, it was free but because the private schools could not provide

---

[98] Statement released by Ronke Soyombo, the Special Assistant to the Governor on Primary and Secondary Education, on Saturday, August 1, 2020. Based on premium Times report.

[99] Ibid.

[100] This response came through Remmy Hassan, the Special Assistant to the Governor on public communication, See https://www.premiumtimesng.com/news/headlines/406422-schools-reopening-parents-kick-as-schools-levy-n25000-for-covid-19-test-in-ogun.html

us with the total number of their students, we could only subsidize the cost by 50 per cent. The reagents for the test had to be made available by NCDC because the students needed to resume in the next 48 hours. All these were very important and it would cost money. That was why we decided that private schools should pay half of the cost since they were profit makers.

Critical Discussion

The Ogun State Government's intention to pro-actively stop the spread of the virus through making such a COVID-19 test mandatory was quite in order and reasonably justifiable. Such a massive test programme remained the wish and aspiration of many responsible governments all over the world given the devastating effects of the virus. At the time the Ogun State Government rolled out this policy, many governments did not have adequate testing materials to achieve this goal. The goal therefore was more aspirational than practically achievable. This was one serious shortcoming at that time, as it would lead to sharp practices that would eventually defeat the noble goal.

On a very serious note, the adoption of a commercialization policy on COVID-19 test (a public health disease) which was then being treated free of charge, raised serious ethical questions. First, it was not ethically advisable and defensible to adopt a commercialization policy on COVID-19 testing on students whose state of mind, could be disoriented by the hassles generated by the suddenness of the policy. We recall that the policy was announced on Saturday evening (1 August 2020), with parents given up to Monday, August 3, 2020, to complete the test so as to make it possible for the same students to resume on Tuesday, August 4. This raised the second moral question. Given the long waiting period for results of tests conducted by the Nigeria Centre for Disease Control (NCDC) then to come out, how realistic was this very tight deadline?

Thirdly, and deriving from the unrealistic deadline, was the policy meant to be implemented properly according to the standard procedures? In other words, was the policy designed to succeed or to achieve less than optimum result? For example, was the N25,000 meant to be paid across the counter in designated health facilities, and in return immediately issued a 'Negative test result' certificate without undergoing an actual test, as is the practice in most government hospitals that issue medical reports without actual test? Such reports end up being only a revenue generating activity for the government rather than a good public health maintenance policy.

Fourthly, were the tests designed to be carried out with COVID-19 Rapid Test Kits? The NCDC had been very conservative in this regard, as it had always insisted that COVID-19 tests should be conducted in its molecular laboratories which were highly reliable. For the NCDC, reliability of results could not be compromised if our understanding of the agency's position was correct. In any case, the NCDC in reaction to the Ogun State policy of charging fees for the test issued a statement immediately that COVID-19 tests conducted in any of its 61 molecular laboratories were free. This confirmed that there was an ethical problem with the commercialization of the test for students in either public or private schools.

Lastly, why was the policy discriminatory regardless of the explanation given by the government? The reason offered by the government was not too satisfactory. If the government was offering a public good, there should be no discrimination. Students in private schools in Ogun State are citizens of the state whose parents or guardians pay taxes. By the way, proprietors of private schools pay registration or licensing fee and perhaps other taxes annually to the government. So the charging of money for a public good which some citizens of the state were enjoying free already was ethically indefensible.

Conclusion: Governor Abiodun's Magnanimous Reversal of the Policy

Governor Abiodun's magnanimous stepping down of the mandatory COVID-19 test as a requirement for returning students in the exit classes,[101] demonstrated the power of citizen engagement in policy making. More importantly, it also showed that the governor was humane and had a listening ear. This quality is a major characteristic of

---

[101] Punch, August 3, 2020 via https://punchng.com/breaking-school-reopening-ogun-cancels-covid-19-test-requirement/.

participatory democracy. The policy reversal statement issued by the governor is as follows:

> After reviewing these developments, I have today immediately directed that the Government Laboratories carry out tests for all returning SS3 boarding students at no cost. I have also directed that all those who have paid for tests be refunded. The health of our children remains our utmost priority. However, in view of the total number of boarding students to be tested (5,340 private and 500 public), and bearing in mind the limitation of our installed testing capacity of 500 tests per day, it may not be feasible for all boarding students to get tested and get their results prior to resumption or even exams which commence on 17th August 2020.[102]

The discussions in this chapter are still relevant for other state governments that may contemplate similar policy on a public good in the future.

---

[102] Ibid.

CHAPTER TWENTY ONE

The Dilemma and Politics of School Reopening
Under COVID-19 Lockdown

Following the prolonged closure of schools as a result of the lockdown in Nigeria, there came palpable agitation for schools to reopen. This became intense as a result of the release by the West African Examinations Council (WAEC) of its time table for the 2020 West African Senior School Certificate Examinations (WASSCE). The Federal Government of Nigeria which was at the receiving end of the agitation could not pick up the gauntlet, but rather started temporizing over the reopening of schools. After such temporizing, it eventually announced conditions to be met before reopening schools on a particular date to be announced. Consequently, all owners of schools (federal, states and private proprietors) were expected to make preparations towards that date. And suddenly without any convincing reason, the federal government (through the Honourable Minister of Education Adamu Adamu) announced a reversal of school reopening date. The reactions to this volt face by some states that were making serious preparations towards the reopening of schools, were one of complete disappointment.

One state that felt highly disappointed was Oyo state which had announced its readiness to resume classes and had in fact started experimenting such resumption with examination classes. Unlike in some other states, education policy makers, executors and managers in Oyo State worked very hard to be in a state of preparedness for the anticipated reopening of schools closed in March 2020 across the nation. It was, therefore, understandable that Oyo State felt highly disappointed when the hope of reopening schools for examination classes was dashed by the Federal Government on Wednesday, July 8, 2020. The state of being in shock was the right phrase to describe how some other Nigerians.

The Dilemma of School Reopening or not Reopening

Prior to the reversal of reopening of schools, the recurring policy issue of whether to reopen schools (or not) for those in final examination classes, had remained a big public policy dilemma since April of that year. The issue had dominated discussions in the media. The sudden reversal by the Federal Government of its earlier announced decision to reopen schools for pupils and students to take their final examinations (in Primary 6, JS 3, and SS 3), was sudden and quite unexpected. As a result, the announcement sent shock waves to some state governments, parents and students anxiously waiting for the anticipated reopening particularly after the West African Examinations Council (WAEC) released its time table for the 2020 WASSCE.

The sudden policy reversal by the Federal Government came after it had already announced (over three weeks earlier ie middle of June, 2020) through the Minister of State for Education, Hon. Chukwuemeka Nwajiuba), six conditions that must be met before the reopening of schools. These conditions were that all educational institutions must have (a) Hand-washing facilities, (b) Body temperature checks, (c) Body disinfectants at all entering points to their major facilities including the gates, hostels, classes, offices, etc., (d) The whole premises of each institution must be decontaminated, (e) All efforts must be geared toward maintenance of the highest level of hygiene, and (f) Ensure Social and Physical Distancing in class sizes and meeting spaces.[103] These conditions gave hope that schools would soon reopen but it did not come to be by the sudden reversal.

The House of Representatives Committee on Basic Education and Services disagreed vehemently with the government's decision not to reopen schools for the examination classes. According to the chairman of the Committee, Prof. Julius Ihonvbere:

> ...this sudden policy reversal is not good for the country. It is bound to create further confusion in the education sector, create disappointment and suspicion among parents, frustrate the students, and show to our development partners and Nigerians that the distortions and disarticulations in the sector are only getting worse. The reversal also shows that our policy makers may just be adopting a laid-back

---

[103] Oyeleke Sodiq (2020): 'FG lists conditions for reopening schools, varsities', Punch, See: https://punchng.com/breaking-fg-lists-conditions-for-reopening-schools-varsities/

approach to the need to confront the novel coronavirus rather than taking proactive and creative steps to manage and contain it.[104]

The seemingly popular sentiment then was that schools should reopen particularly for the examination classes. However, there were equally other vocal voices that welcomed the reversal of school reopening with great joy and relief, arguing (like the Federal Government) that the time was not yet safe for the schools to reopen due to the continuous spread of coronavirus. Apparently speaking, in a situation of decision making under uncertainty, each side of the argument had some merits. However, the side that called for the reopening of schools specifically to enable students to revise and take their examinations, appeared to have more justifiable and progressive reasons than the other conservative side which appeared to be operating a policy of do-little or nothing until the virus goes away. This wait and see policy approach or at best a back-and-forth shaky attitude of preparedness, was criticized by many on the other side, because it would have more harmful effects on the SS 3 students, since WAEC was not going to wait for Nigeria or its students indefinitely.

Although the conservative side argued forcefully that the time was not ripe or safe to reopen schools, the progressive side argued persuasively also that given the uncertain and unpredictable way the coronavirus was still spreading in Nigeria, it was very likely (repeat very likely) that the first half of 2021 would still not be safe for the schools to reopen. This means that the phrase by the conservative side that 'the time was not yet ripe' to reopen schools in 2020 might still remain the same in 2021 if nothing significantly changed. Yet as we pointed out in earlier chapters, many Nigerians including those in authority have been very poor at obeying the COVID-19 safety guidelines. And so if they continued to disobey the safety guidelines (and they were more likely to do so), the virus would continue to spread, and the future of the SS 3 students would then hang in the air. In that case, such a potential

---

[104] Baiyewu Leke (2020): 'COVID-19: Reps fault FG's decision on school reopening', *Punch* See:https://punchng.com/covid-19-reps-fault-fgs-decision-on-school-reopening/

Chapter Twenty one | Isaac Nnamdi Obasi

situation would generate a bigger policy dilemma in 2021 than what existed in 2020.

What this meant also was that, two sets of Nigerian students for WASSCE (i.e. 2020 and 2021 sets) would be at a greater risk of not completing their secondary school education as social and physical distancing protocol would be more difficult to manage or maintain in such combined sets. The progressive side's argument that schools should reopen for the 2020 WASSCE (SS 3 set) within the strict compliance of the safety, was more justifiable.

There was no doubt that the issue of reopening schools then involved a policy dilemma namely a choice *between the devil and the deep (blue) sea*, but the idea of following science in controlling the spread of COVID-19, provides a safe window out of the dilemma. The reversal of announced reopening date, was simply not following science in the management of COVID-19. In actual fact, the reversal was like taking the nation three months back where it was in April 2020, when the government was talking about plans, policies and strategies of how to reopen the schools after the lockdown. By July, the various governments (federal and states) were expected to begin getting the schools ready for the new normal that required upgrading of infrastructure and provision of facilities to meet up the social and physical distancing and hygiene protocols. In fact, by July, the Federal Government should have been showing the lead by announcing the additional infrastructure and facilities it had put in place in its 104 Unity Schools to set the standard for the state and private schools to follow. This appeared not to be the case. By telling Nigerians that students would miss their WASSCE for safety reasons was like telling them that it had failed to provide the safety measures in the first place or that it had done nothing to get the schools ready in a safe manner.

The federal government failed to recognize that the idea of postponing WASSCE until 2021 might aggravate mental health problems for some of the students. More seriously, it would lead to serious and more dangerous congestion (i.e. combing of 2020 set with the 2021 set) which would breach social distancing protocol. Moreover, it would create more health hazards that the government was trying to run away from in 2020. The same logic applies to the other examination classes except that the difference was that they were all within the total control of Nigerian government while WASSCE is not strictly under Nigeria's total control, as it involves five West African governments/nations. The National Examinations Council (NECO) was not a major issue in the argument, because it is within Nigeria's exclusive control and the Federal Government could organise NECO examination at any time it chooses.

Given the facts raised in the preceding paragraphs so far, one was tempted to wonder why the Federal Government found it difficult to develop a progressive outlook towards reopening schools for final examinations classes then. This brought the issue of politics to the fore and how it kept the dilemma lingering for so long. One fact that emerged from the back and forth movement, was that the sudden volte-face by the Federal Government, exposed it's lack of preparedness in providing the required safety measures for schools reopening.

The Politics of School Reopening or not Reopening

The back and forth approach of the Federal Government attracted followers when Commissioners of Education in the 19 Northern States issued a statement[105] supporting the federal government's position of not reopening schools. The commissioners went further to request the Federal Government to grant financial support to them so that they would be in a position to provide the safety measures in their schools. The Commissioners' support and request generated more controversies as it raised more questions than answers.

First, if they were asking for financial support at a time when WASSCE was around the corner, then what preparations were they making since April? By this request (for funding support), they exposed their very high level of unpreparedness to reopen schools. Secondly, to make matters worse, the Federal Government itself was releasing the Guidelines for the safe reopening of schools about this period, and with the document containing phrases like the government will, which inadvertently revealed apparent lack of preparedness at that material time. The 52-page document (though comprehensive) was late in coming, as one expected such document to be out late April or sometimes in May, 2020.

---

[105]Report by *Sundiata Post*, See https://sundiatapost.com/wassce-19-states-back-fgs-suspension-of-school-resumption/.

Chapter Twenty one | Isaac Nnamdi Obasi

Expectedly, the position of Commissioners of Education in the 19 Northern States triggered off a political controversy between the Northern and Southern parts of Nigeria. Yet the public health issue involved was not such that should be viewed with sectional and geo-political lens. In reaction to the Commissioners' position for example, the six South-west states thereafter met and expressed their willingness to reopen schools to enable students in their geo-political zone to participate in the 2020 WASSCE.[106] Some state governments in other geo-political zones (for example Ebonyi State in the South-east) also announced their decision to reopen schools.

The Federal Government did not help matters in this regard through its back and forth approach. For example, much earlier, it was after the announcement of the six conditions that the Minister of State for Education Hon. Chukwuemeka Nwajiuba also further announced that the government had approved the resumption of schools for examination classes namely primary 6, JS 3 and SS 3. He equally announced the dates for the 2020 WASSCE following the release of the time table by the West African Examinations Council (WAEC). Furthermore, he provided details that the 2020 WASSCE would hold between August 4 and September 5. It would be recalled also that the government in its confidence and hope-building measures considered the idea of adopting the shift system (involving holding of morning and afternoon classes) when schools eventually resume. The Minister of State under the platform of the Presidential Task Force on COVID-19 was constantly updating the public every week on the plans being taken to reopen schools, and he pleaded for patience from all stakeholders. In deed the federal government left no one in doubt that it was on the trajectory of reopening schools.

Recall again that the same Minister of State for Education had much earlier briefed the Committee on Basic Education and Services of the House of Representatives on the Ministry's plans towards the reopening of schools. That meeting went well and members were satisfied. All these gave the hope that the government was indeed making serious preparations to put safety measures in place to contain the spread of the

---

[106] Report by *Punch*, See https://punchng.com/wassce-south-west-states-ready-to-reopen-schools/.

virus when schools resume. In actual fact, in some countries in Europe and Asia, where schools opened for graduation classes, it was the adoption of innovative measures that kept the spread of the virus low.

The coming of the Minister of Education, Adamu Adamu into the matter later, introduced another dimension that tried to scuttle efforts towards reopening. For example, while announcing the reversal of its earlier decision on reopening of schools, the minister created the impression that the government had issues with WAEC. According to him, WAEC would not dictate to Nigeria when schools should resume. He then accused WAEC of announcing the Examination Time-Time while the Nigerian government was still busy consulting its stakeholders. It was a known fact that WAEC gave over three months for such consultations before eventually releasing the time table. The fact was that these new dates came after three months of postponement.[107] This means that WAEC should not be blamed for government's own back and forth approach in handling the issue.

In spite the seeming reluctance of the federal government as discussed above, great relief came at last when the government finally capitulated to the wishes of the progressive side of the argument that Nigerian students should participate in the 2020 WAEC conducted examination for our SS 3 students.

From Dashed Hope, to Renewed Hope of School Reopening

As the dust raised by the news of the Federal Government reversal of its earlier decision to reopen schools for examination classes, was yet to settle down, the Minister of State for Education Hon. Chukwuemeka Nwajiuba issued a statement on July 17, 2020 that offered a ray of hope for school reopening. According to the statement, the government gave "school owners in the country up to July 29, 2020, to meet specific guidelines towards the reopening of schools at a date to be announced in due course."[108] The announcement of this deadline (to meet the necessary safety guidelines for reopening of schools) was a major policy shift from the government's earlier position that the condition was not

---

[107] See for instance Blueprint newspaper, July 6, 2020.
[108] See Vanguard, July 17, 2020.

Chapter   Twenty one ┃ Isaac Nnamdi Obasi

yet safe to reopen schools. The deadline also, was a positive signal or renewed hope towards the resumption of pupils and students in examination classes in 2020 rather than in 2021.

It was heartening to note that the details of the statement showed that the Federal Government had at that period adopted a proactive approach of doing-something and putting safety measures in place before reopening of schools. It is necessary to provide more details of the statement[109] by the Honourable Minister of State before making further analysis on the subject. According to him, the government had developed and circulated guidelines for the reopening of schools after consulting widely in collaboration with Federal Ministry of Health, Nigerian Centre for Disease Control (NCDC), and the Education in Emergencies Working Group. He therefore urged schools to undertake self-assessment and send feedback to state ministries of education, not later than 29 July 2020. Thereafter he said consultations with relevant stakeholders would be held to review the situation and decide on a specific date for reopening or otherwise.

Continuing the minister said, since July 14, 2020, the ministry had consulted widely with stakeholders in the sector, including commissioners of education in all the states of the federation, the Association of Private School Owners of Nigeria, (APSON), National Association of Proprietors of Private Schools, (NAPPS), provosts of colleges of education, rectors of polytechnics, Vice Chancellors of Universities, some State Governors, and development partners. With respect to WAEC, the minister said, that the government met with WAEC on July 13, 2020 and had agreed to further consult with four other countries on a new examination date. While appealing to parents, the minister conclusively said, parents should be rest assured that the safety of our students and teachers was paramount as we work assiduously towards speedy reopening of our schools for the exit classes to take external examinations.

Like we already said above, the government's new approach, was reassuring that all authorities (both public and private school owners) were working towards taking practical safety measures before reopening

---

[109] Leadership newspaper, July 18, 2020, via https://leadership.ng/2020/07/18/fg-gives-school-owners-july-29-to-meet-guidelines/.

schools. Nonetheless, one very important issue needs to be examined. Going by the statement in which the minister "urged schools to undertake self-assessment and send feedback to state ministries of education", it appeared that nothing was said about the Federal Government-owned 104 Unity Schools. A content analysis of the reports in many of the newspapers then showed that there was no mention of the Federal Government as a school owner. The news reports implied that the Federal Government was speaking as a regulator and not as an owner of schools itself. If the minister's statement deliberately talked about the Federal Government only as a regulator and not as well as a school owner, we considered this a big mistake. The Federal Government is both a regulator (through policies and laws) as well as an owner of schools. It should also be regulated by the policies it makes.

Some crucial questions that arose then were as follows: First, why did the Federal Government not mention that it was also undertaking a self-assessment of all its own Unity Schools to assure everyone that it was doing something meaningful as well, to put all the necessary safety measures in place? Second, was it that the federal government had already undertaken the self-assessment? If it had already done so, it should have been transparent enough to showcase what it had done for purpose of confidence-building among stakeholders particularly the parents. If it was just putting the measures in place at that time, it could still have shown a good example by showcasing such accomplishments for confidence-building sake. Whatever was the case, these questions were necessary because federal government leadership-by-example was necessary to motivate state governments and private school proprietors to work very hard to put their own safety measures in place. In the absence of such, many state government would just go on with the business-as-usual mentality, in view of the fact that many of them had already asked the federal government to give them funds to provide the needed infrastructure, facilities and safety measures.

One important point to make is that in this type of situation in future, parents should be given the freedom of choice to decide for their children to participate or not, in the various examinations (i.e. primary 6, JSS3, and SS3) to be taken under a pandemic emergency. This choice should not be made on behalf of the parents by the government because such would be an infringement on their democratic rights to take such important decision. It is better for the parents to take responsibility for such a highly risky decision to avoid blaming anybody. However, the various governments and private school proprietors have the very important responsibility to provide all the necessary safety measures in every school before reopening.

Eventual announcement of Resumption date

Eventually, the period of renewed hope led to the actual realization of the hope of school resumption. The news of the approval by the Federal Government of Nigeria that SS3 classes should reopen on August 4, 2020, to enable the students prepare for their final examinations was a huge relief and a welcome development. This development we must acknowledge exemplified government's responsiveness to public opinion that a progressive attitude should prevail.

In a statement released by the Federal Ministry of Education and titled "Exit Classes To Reopen August 4th"[110] reads:

> Secondary schools in the country are to reopen from the 4th of August 2020 for exit classes only. Students will have two weeks with which to prepare for the West African Examinations due to start on the 17th of August 2020. These were the unanimous decisions reached today at a virtual consultative meeting between the Federal Ministry of Education, Honourable Commissioners of Education of the 36 states, the Nigerian Union of Teachers, the proprietors of private schools and the Chief Executives of examination bodies. It was agreed that the exit classes should resume immediately after the Sallah break, from the 4th of August 2020, to enable them to prepare for the WAEC examinations scheduled to commence from the 17th of August 2020. The meeting also resolved that a passionate appeal be made to the Federal Government through the Presidential Task Force on Covid-19 and public-spirited Nigerians for assistance to schools across the country to enable them fast-track the preparation for safe reopening, as agreed. Another meeting is to be convened tomorrow between the Federal Ministry of Education and the Chief Executives of examination bodies namely, NECO, NABTEB and NBAIS to harmonise their examination

---

[110] For more details, see *Punch*, July 17, 2020, via: https://punchng.com/breaking-2020-wassce-to-begin-aug-17-fg/.

dates, which will be conveyed to stakeholders expeditiously by the Federal Ministry of Education.

With this announcement, the anxiety over the long awaited decision to reopen schools was then over. It was a long and tortuous journey by anxious parents and their children whose hope of school resumption had hitherto been hanging on the balance. We just hope that history would remember the progressive side of the argument which boldly and vigorously fought for the reopening of schools amidst uncertainty.

Conclusion

With hindsight now (in 2022) one recognizes that the reopening of schools for exit classes in 2020, was a bold and strategic decision. If that decision had not been taken, the future of about 3 million (two sets 2020 & 2021) Nigerian students would have been jeopardized. As we predicted in 2020, the COVID-19 was not in hurry to go, hence that bold and commendable decision saved Nigeria from the embarrassment that it would have experienced in 2021 when the Delta and Omicrom variants of the coronavirus were still ravaging the entire world (Nigeria inclusive) in even more ferocious way than in 2020. Looking back now, we can say here that the dilemma and politics of school reopening under the lockdown policy in 2020, was one of the most difficult policy responses by the Nigerian government to the COVID-19 pandemic.

CHAPTER TWENTY TWO

COVID-19 Pandemic and Safety and Welfare
of Nigerian Health Workers

The background

During part of the long period of implementation of the lockdown policy (from May to July, 2020 precisely), Nigeria witnessed a harvest of warning strikes, threat to embark on strikes, and actual strikes, by different health workers' unions in the health sector at both the federal and state levels of governance. Regrettably, part of the reasons for the strikes or threat of it had to do with the safety and welfare of health workers under the COVID-19 pandemic. One of the earliest threats of strike during this period, (which happened in May) came from the Joint Health Sector Unions (JOHESU) in the Federal Capital Territory (FCT), Abuja. The unions under JOHESU that issued the threat to go on strike then were the Medical and Health Workers Union of Nigeria, National Union of Allied Health Professionals (a combination of pharmacists, Medical Laboratory Scientists, Physiotherapists etc), and the National Association of Nigerian Nurses and Midwives.

In as much as Nigerians were shocked that a strike could be contemplated by JOHESU in a COVID-19 pandemic, the reality of the enormous risk to their safety and welfare at work, made their threat to embark on a strike understandable to discerning minds. Seem in this perspective therefore, these workers (who were among those rightly called heroes of our time by President Buhari during the early stage of the pandemic) are human beings with families (like any of us) to cater for during the trying times of the pandemic.

Widespread agitations

There were widespread agitations by health workers over the non-prioritization of their safety and welfare issues by both the federal and state governments. In actual fact, the threat by JOHESU in the FCT to go on strike opened up a floodgate of many threats to strike, warning strikes, and actual strikes that occurred in the months of June through September, 2020 at a time when the COVID-19 was still ravaging in the country. During this period, the Association of Resident Doctors Federal Capital Territory Administration (ARD-FCTA) actually embarked on a strike (on September 7 and called it off on September 9 2020), over the non-payment of their COVID-19 allowance, among other demands. The parent body - National Association of Resident Doctors (NARD) - had earlier in the year embarked on a couple of strikes in spite of their long drawn one in 2021.

At the state level, medical doctors in Delta State announced their intention to go on a three-day warning strike during the third week of July.[111] Earlier before that (13 July 2020), medical doctors in Lagos State under the umbrella of the Medical Guild also announced their intention to embark on a three-week warning strike. The Nigerian Medical Association (NMA), Ekiti State chapter, which had already been on strike vowed within the same period that its members would not call off their indefinite strike until its demands were met by the government. The Association complained of the poor welfare conditions of their members in the midst of COVID-9 challenges. And similarly JOHESU, Akwa Ibom State chapter which had also been on a two-week strike, suspended it on Wednesday, 29 July 2020. The list continued in many states on the same issue of neglect of safety and welfare of health workers under the COVID-19 dangerous working condition. The widespread agitations of health workers raises the important issue of whether federal and state governments really understand the concept of the health worker and the enormous health hazards they face in the workplace.

The Broad Concept of Health Worker

The concept of health worker is a complex one. People often think of medical doctors and nurses most of the time when safety and welfare issues are raised in the health sector. There are however, many other categories of health workers. According to the World Health Organization (WHO),[112] health workers are classified into five categories namely health professionals, health associate professionals, personal care workers in health services, health management and support personnel,

---

[111] TVC News of July 25, 2020.
[112] See https://www.who.int/hrh/statistics/Health_workers_classification.pdf?ua=1.

and lastly other health service providers. Many of those we know are in the category of health professionals comprising medical doctors (specialist and generalist practitioners, nursing and midwifery professionals, dentists, pharmacists, physiotherapists, dieticians and nutritionists, optometrists and ophthalmic opticians, etc.

In the category of health associate professionals are such important professionals that "perform technical and practical tasks to support diagnosis of illness, disease, injuries and impairments etc."[113] The list is endless and these ones mentioned suffice for our purpose. What is the common denominator of risks or hazards faced by most health workers (if not all) in their daily provision of services? The WHO in another document provides us with the needed guidance.

Health and safety hazards faced by Health workers

According to the WHO,[114] health workers across the world face a "complex variety of health and safety hazards everyday including":

- ✓ biological hazards, such as TB, Hepatitis, HIV/AIDS, SARS;
- ✓ chemical hazards, such as, glutaraldehyde, ethylene oxide;
- ✓ physical hazards, such as noise, radiation, slips trips and falls;
- ✓ ergonomic hazards, such as heavy lifting;
- ✓ psychosocial hazards, such as shift work, violence and stress;
- ✓ fire and explosion hazards, such as using oxygen, alcohol sanitizing gels; and electrical hazards, such as frayed electrical cords.

Then continuing, the WHO in its advocacy aptly said:

Health-care workers (HCWs) need protection from these workplace hazards just as much as do mining or construction workers. Yet, because their job is to care for the sick and injured, HCWs are often viewed as "immune" to injury or illness. Their patients come first. They are often expected to sacrifice their own well-being for the sake of their patients. Indeed health protecting health-care workers have the added benefit to contributing to quality patient care and health system

---

113 Ibid.

114 *See* https://www.who.int/occupational_health/topics/hcworkers/en/

strengthening. Some of the same measures to protect patients from infections, such as adequate staffing, protect health-care workers from injury…Unsafe working conditions contribute to health worker attrition in many countries due to work-related illness and injury and the resulting fear of health workers of occupational infection, including from HIV and Tuberculosis. The 2006 World Health Report Working Together for Health reported on a severe health workforce crisis in fifty-seven countries, most of them in Africa and Asia. Protecting the occupational health of health workers is critical to having an adequate workforce of trained and healthy health personnel.[115]

The Need to Prioritize Safety and Welfare of Health Workers

Given all the enumerated 'complex variety of health and safety hazards' faced everyday by health workers in Nigeria, we cannot in all honesty say that the different levels of government have been treating them well and fairly. These hazards pose existential threats to their lives and by extension to their families while rendering services to the public. Some of the health workers possess scarce skills which implies that issues concerning their safety and welfare need to be prioritised by the government, otherwise, there would be high level of brain drain or attrition within their group.

In one of our earlier chapters, we argued that under the COVID-19 pandemic, no occupational category should be given high priority more than the ones in the health sector. We argued further that our usual politically Very Important Persons (VIPs) in our society had suddenly under COVId-19, become Very Unimportant Persons (VUPs). This was because none of them could be in the front line in the war against the ravaging COVID-19 pandemic. If we may all recall, the fear of COVID-19 in the months of March and April (when health workers were called heroes), provided enough lessons on how to treat our health workers, but it appears that no serious lessons have been learnt.

For example, the provision and payment of special hazard allowances to those of them in the front line were still not well prioritized otherwise there would not have been harvests of strikes among the health workers

---

[115] Ibid.

across the nation. One of the issues complained about was the arrears of unpaid allowances to them. The non-provision, or delay in the provision of all safety materials such as Personal Protective Equipment (PPE) was a common occurrence in many states and also one of the major complaints and reasons responsible for the strikes across the states.

In conclusion, the need to prioritize the safety and welfare of health workers cannot be over-emphasized, as Nigeria cannot be talking of rebuilding the health system without prioritising the safety and welfare of all health workers. There is enough evidence under the COVID-19 pandemic that government across levels failed to prioritize the safety and welfare of health workers in Nigeria.

CHAPTER TWENTY THREE

COVID-19 Pandemic and Welfare of Nigerian Workers

Policy response to the COVID-19 pandemic across nations of the world, among other things separated governments that formulate and implement good welfare policies for workers, from those that formulate and implement anti-workers' welfare policies. In spite of this distinction, many governments across the world were compelled during the months of March, April and May, 2020 to adopt variety of policy responses such as stimulus package, cash transfers, public work programmes and other kinds of welfare palliatives, to reduce the harsh impact of COVID-19 pandemic on both the economy and workers. Be that as it may, this chapter focuses on how the federal and state governments in Nigeria handled the issue of the welfare of workers (including the pensioners) during the period of the pandemic.

Variety of Policy responses by Federal and State Governments

During the period of the lockdown, both the federal and state governments adopted a variety of policy measures to reduce the debilitating effects of the COVID-19 pandemic. The far-reaching impact of such policy responses varied vertically across levels of government (namely federal, state and local governments), and horizontally among the states, as well as among the local governments. For some obvious reasons (e.g more revenue available to the federal government than the states), the federal government adopted far-reaching measures than the state governments in protecting and promoting the welfare of workers particularly on the issue of payment of salaries.

There was little doubt that the economic fortunes of the various governments in Nigeria dwindled as a result of the COVID-19 pandemic. It all started with the dwindling price of oil in the international market. As the entire world entered into a total lockdown in the months of March and April (with only essential movements allowed across the world), the demand for crude oil as well as its prices, were drastically reduced. This immediately impacted negatively on Nigeria as crude oil remains its major source of revenue. Consequently, the federal and other levels of government had to revise their 2020 approved budget downward. The total amount of money shared during the monthly Federation Accounts Allocation Committee (FAAC) meetings also fell drastically. In spite of this obvious fiscal crisis, the federal government maintained the payment of salaries to its workers. Unfortunately, state governments started contemplating with the idea of salary cut for their workers, and this marked the beginning of the idea of anti-welfare policy under the COVID-19 period.

The Idea of cutting Salaries of Public Servants

Although a couple of state governments announced their intention to cut salaries of their workers in April 2020, states such as Kaduna, Nasarawa and Bauchi were ahead of many others in this regard. As Dataphyte[116] put it, 'the salary crisis began in April when some states hinted at a cut in pay. For example, Kaduna and Nasarawa in April announced a 25 percent cut. Both states claimed this was due to dwindling revenue because of the Coronavirus crisis'. But after its initial decision, the Bauchi state government reversed the decision to cut salary of its workers. Unfortunately, the Kaduna State Governor Nasir El-Rufai - a pace setter in public service reforms - surprised everyone when he announced that all state public servants earning, at least, N67, 000 per month will 'donate' 25 per cent of their salaries to the state government to help it fight the COVID-19 war. The Government actually went ahead to make this deduction with effect from April.

Across the nation, many state governments announced as much as a 50% pay cut, but only applicable to the politically appointed officials and this was considered as a worthy sacrifice by such officials. For example, Governor Seyi Makinde of Oyo state who also announced a 50 per cent pay slash for all senior political appointees in his administration, assured that the salary reduction will not affect civil servants in the state. According to him, "nothing will affect the welfare and payment of the workers' salary despite the dwindling economy."[117] The governor's

---

[116] Dataphyte, May 7, 2020.
[117] See Businessday, May 1, 2020 via https://businessday.ng/news/article/coronavirus-gov-makinde-slashes-salaries-of-senior-political-appointees-by-50/.

decision was a smart one primarily because civil and some other public servants in Nigeria are poorly paid.

The Akwa Ibom state government initially announced a pay cut policy to cover everyone (namely public and civil servants, as well as political appointees), however it reversed itself much later and limited the salary reduction to political appointees. This was also a smart decision. However, this was not the case with some other states. For example, the Delta state government – a late entrant into the pay cut controversy – went ahead to include workers on salary grade level 7 and above for a period of six months with effect from July 2020. It appeared that the government did not benefit from the lessons learnt with respect to the controversy characterizing the policy in states that adopted it much earlier. Some of such states became politically wise by limiting the cut to political appointees.

Aside from the fact that the pay cut policy was objectionable because public servants in Nigeria generally are poorly paid, the unilateral method of arriving at the policy in many states without broad-based consultations, was also objectionable. This is why the Bauchi government's consultative and consensus-building approach was commendable and worthy of note for the future. The initially agreed policy (though later reversed) was signed by the State Head of Civil Service, the State Chairman of the Nigeria Labour Congress, State Chairman of Trade Union Congress, and State Chairman, Joint Service Negotiation Council. This inclusive approach impacted positively on the quality and equitable nature of the policy. For example, according to The Eagle Online[118] Permanent Secretaries and their equivalents were meant to contribute 10 per cent of their salaries, while Directors on Grade Levels 16 to 17 at both the state and local governments were to contribute 5 per cent. Furthermore, Workers on Grade Levels 1 to 15 in the state and local governments were to contribute one per cent from their salaries for the same months of April, May and June.

---

[118] The Eagle Online, April 9, 2020.

Objectionable methods used to Subvert Workers' Welfare

Close observations of practices of some state governments during the COVID-19 lockdown period revealed that there were many objectionable methods that were used to subvert the welfare of workers who were already suffering so much under the pandemic. For example, some state governments were pretending to be paying salaries of their workers, when indeed what they were actually doing was to pay workers in a selective, staggered and phased manner or what can be described as payment in batches. This meant that some workers could be owed up to three months or even more in this manner of selective or staggered payment system and yet the government would be claiming to be paying salaries. This objectionable practice extended to pensioners in their states.

A noticeable carrot that some governments used, was to buy over union leaders who would then be reluctant to mobilize their members to agitate and protest against their inhuman treatment. As if this bribery and co-optation method was not enough, there was a more objectionable practice of hiring thugs to intimidate and even maltreat workers and pensioners protesting against their inhuman treatment. A report by Punch newspaper[119] revealed that hoodlums assaulted pensioners who were at the Imo State Government House, Owerri, (the state capital) to protest their five months unpaid pension and gratuities. The protest was the fifth time in less than a month that the senior citizens were protesting their non-payment of pensions and gratuities by the Hope Uzodinma administration. Trouble started when thugs clutching canes formed a barricade, stopping the pensioners from approaching the Government House's main gate. The senior citizens who were resolute in their demands defied the situation which led to their being flogged by the thugs.[120] The inexcusable excuse given by the government was that most of the protesters were 'ghost pensioners' who were being used by the opposition politicians to discredit the performances of the government.

---

[119] Punch newspaper, Tuesday, August 4, 2020.
[120] Ibid

The more substantive question of whether the pensioners were actually owed five months of their entitlements, became a secondary issue.

The NLC's position and reaction

The position and reaction of Organized Labour on the issue of reduction of workers' salary under COVID-19, was predictable. The Nigeria Labour Congress (NLC) warned employers against stoppage and reduction of workers salary in the country due to COVID-19 pandemic. The president of the NLC Ayuba Wabba, said workers' salaries are core elements of employment contracts and collective bargaining agreements, hence stopping it was illegal and would be resisted by workers whom he said had been directed to do so.[121] In conclusion, it cannot be over-emphasized that the prioritization of the welfare of workers is paramount in a good governance system. The swelling of the cost of governance in Nigeria for instance, has to be checked not through cut in workers' poor salaries but rather through drastically reducing the humongous waste and leakages in other areas particularly institutionalized grand corruption. The living conditions of pensioners who have been owed many months of arrears of their entitlements need to be addressed without delay by defaulting states even in the post-pandemic period.

---

[121] See Premium Times, April 29, 2020.

Part Four
COVID-19 Policy Response at the Sub-national Level

CHAPTER TWENTY FOUR

COVID-19 Pandemic and the 'Kano State Debacle'

Globalisation through the instrumentality of Information and Communications Technology (ICT) is widely said to have reduced the entire world to a global village, where the interconnectedness of people and nations has become a virtual reality. The wonders of ICT have really reduced physical distance and human separation to nothing. The term 'global village' (first used in the 1960s by Marshall McLuhan, a Canadian mass media theorist), acquired its current prevalent usage with the advent of globalisation through the instrumentality of the ICT. The 'globalisation' of disease as witnessed in coronavirus (COVID-19) that originated in faraway Wuhan, China, has further demonstrated the interconnectedness of peoples and nations in this new global village.

Popular Solidarity-Building Slogans for Organizing and Mobilizing of Workers

In labour relations' parlance, one very popular organising, mobilising and solidarity-building slogan is the saying that an injury to one is an injury to all, a quote originally credited to David Courtney Coates. Coates was an outstanding labour union leader who served as the president of the American Labour Union. As a socialist politician, he was the 11th Lieutenant Governor of the State of Colorado, USA from 1901 to 1903. However, this quote was popularised by the Industrial Workers of the World (IWW) which used it as its motto. Coates was said to have suggested the quote to IWW, a very powerful international labour union founded in Chicago, Illinois, USA in 1905. This quote is used nowadays by every labour union across the world.

A second related slogan by the International Labour Organisation (ILO) is that poverty anywhere is a threat to prosperity everywhere. This quote which came out of the ILO declaration of Philadelphia of 1944 has profoundly influenced social welfare thinking across the world. Thinking of humanity in the sense of a community is a way to promote peace across the world. It is perhaps in this sense that Kofi Annan (former UN

Secretary General) said in another catchphrase that extreme poverty anywhere is a threat to human security everywhere.

The idea of 'globalisation' of disease and these three slogans are very relevant to the topic of this chapter. The reported massive deaths that happened in Kano State in April and May 2020 concerned everyone in Nigeria whether residing in the far cities of Calabar, Uyo, Port Harcourt, Yenagoa, Lagos, Sokoto, Yola, or Maiduguri. Kano is no doubt far (distance-wise) just as Wuhan, China, appeared far away from the rest of the world. However, in a COVID-19 pandemic era, Kano is not far away from anybody anywhere in Nigeria. It would only take a bus or lorry load of Kano residents to travel out of the state and then the deadly virus would infect anyone in contact with them.

Dynamics of Kano State debacle

What we call here 'Kano State debacle' refers to what was then reported in the media as 'mysterious deaths'. Unfortunately, the lockdown order by the Kano State Government came so late that it made no significant impact in minimizing the spread of COVID-19. To make matters worse, like many other states in Nigeria, Kano State government was unprepared when COVID-19 arrived in its domain. Its people ignored all social and physical distancing protocols and moved with a business-as-usual mentality.

Matters degenerated when members of the State Task Force on COVID-19 contracted the virus thereby halting the coordinated fight against the disease. The disaster then came with the shutting down of the COVID-19 testing laboratory. As conflicting news of the state of the testing centre lingered (oscillating between functioning and not working), the next alarming news was the mystery death of 150 people within three days. This was again followed by news of the death of 12 prominent Kano indigenes within two days. As the dust raised by this startling news was just dying down amid conflicting official reactions, Nigerians woke up on Sunday April 26, 2020 to hear the news that a total of over 600 mysterious deaths had occurred in Kano.

These deaths were called mysterious because the causes were not ascertained then. It sounded unscientific for the State government to rule out COVID-19 as a possible cause of the deaths without investigation.

The mention of meningitis as one of the possible causes lacked deep thinking as these deaths involved high profile individuals such as the regional manager of a big bank, professors (one in medically-related discipline and the other in mass communication), former editor of a newspaper, top government officials, who presumably worked in air-conditioned offices and less exposed to heat (I stand to be corrected here). My doubt arose from the fact that after living in Sokoto, a place known extreme heat, for 14 years while lecturing at the Usmanu Danfodiyo University, Sokoto (UDUS), this story of meningitis appeared less convincing.

On the contrary, the views of two notable and knowledgeable people in Kano State appeared more plausible. Prof. Usman Yusuf (former Executive Secretary, National Health Insurance Scheme) who was one of the first to raise alarm argued earlier enough that the cause of the mysterious deaths was COVID-19. First, he alerted the nation in a headline tilted: "Kano city is now the killing fields of COVID-19 pandemic in Africa."[122] About a week later, he re-emphasized his point about the reality of COVID-19 in Kano State (which was in denial at that time in official quarters) in another alarming headline titled "Covid-19: Kano may set Nigeria on fire."[123]

The second notable voice was the former Governor of Kano State, Senator Rabiu Kwankwaso, who also contended that COVID-19 was the possible cause of death of many prominent citizens of the state. In a letter to President Muhammadu Buhari, he argued that since the announcement of the positive results of the members of the COVID-19 committee, no test was ever conducted in the entire state. This he said was very frightening as neither asymptomatic nor active cases of infected patients were being identified and isolated, and as such carriers of this dreaded virus were spreading it and causing the untimely death of people.

---

[122] Business Day, April 26, 2020. (See https://businessday.ng/opinion/article/kano-city-is-now-the-killing-fields-of-covid-19-pandemic-in-africa/).

[123] The Sun, May 2, 2020. (See https://www.sunnewsonline.com/covid-19-kano-may-set-nigeria-on-fire-prof-usman-yusuf-ex-nhis-boss/).

Federal Government commendable rescue efforts

Regardless of the controversy, the federal government took a decisive step to arrest the situation. First, it declared that it would focus attention on Kano State as the second epicentre of the COVID-19 pandemic in Nigeria. This declaration meant that the State would be given additional support and resources like Lagos State to fight this ravaging virus as an emergency. President Buhari (in his address to the nation on April 27, 2020) promised to "deploy all the necessary human, material and technical resources to support the state government in controlling and containing the pandemic and preventing the risk of further spread to neighbouring states." Secondly, the Federal Government dispatched high level group of experts to confront the situation in collaboration with the Kano State government. The group was made up of experts from the Federal Ministry of Health, PTF, NCDC, WHO among others. Thirdly, Mr. President directed that there should be a total lockdown in Kano for two weeks. These measures helped tremendously to contain the situation.

In conclusion, those in authority need to be transparent in governance matters. It is even unpardonable when it has to do with public health issues. COVID-19 pandemic exposed the fact that many of those in authority were not transparent thereby toying with the lives of the people with respect to public health issues. This is completely reprehensible and should be stopped going forward.

CHAPTER TWENTY FIVE

COVID-19 Lockdown and Governor Wike's Overzealous Style of Punishing Violators

From an unbiased analytical lens, Governor Nyesom Wike of Rivers State could be described as a very controversial and temperamental person who at the same time exhibited an uncommon sense of excellence in hard work driven by focused and purposeful leadership. Prior to the recording of an index case of coronavirus (COVID-19) in Rivers State, critics of Governor Wike described his style of governance in many uncomplimentary terms. Some critics saw him as being draconian in his style, citing couple of measures he adopted to solve pressing public policy problems, as good examples. In the same manner, some other critics described his approach as simply despotic for lacking essential democratic credentials. Some people (who may not even be his critics) just saw him as very temperamental, confrontational or provocative in his style of governance. These appellations gained greater visibility because of his dogged style and the unrepentant manner with which he fought against the spread of the coronavirus in his state.

Dynamics of Governor Wike's dogged efforts to control COVID-19

It is on record that the governor was the first (in Nigeria) to announce the closure of his state's land, sea and air borders in order to protect Rivers State people from getting infected with the ravaging virus. After doing that, he worked tirelessly and relentlessly against the spread of the virus, and also remained unapologetic when critics complained about the way he was going about it. He rather got emboldened and knowingly or unknowingly became overzealous in waging his very serious 'war' against violators of border closures and lockdown restrictions.

A good number of cases exposed his overzealous style of dealing with perceived offenders of the law in his state. Three of such cases are very noteworthy. The first was when he ordered the arrest of two pilots of Caverton Helicopters (with 10 other people on board) who flew into the state without the Rivers State government's knowledge and permission. As an active governor, (Barrister) Wike promptly ordered the arrest of the pilots and the 10 other people on board, they were subsequently charged to court. Then his altercation with the federal government started with accusations and counter-accusations. But at the end, the pilots were released, but not without getting an apology from the company.

A little background explanation is necessary. The Rivers State Commissioner for Information and Communications, Pastor Paulinus Nsirim offering a detailed explanation said:

> Contrary to the view being peddled by the Minister of Aviation, Alhaji Hadi Sirika, the two pilots of Caverton Helicopters and their 10 passengers were not arrested because they operated a permit granted them by the Ministry of Aviation. They were arrested because they constantly contravened the Executive Order issued by the Governor of Rivers State, His Excellency, Nyesom Ezenwo Wike, which requires that everyone coming into the state for essential duties subject themselves to mandatory health checks to ascertain their coronavirus status…Before their arrests, the Rivers State Government issued several warnings to Caverton and other operators to ensure that their pilots and passengers are tested by Rivers State health authorities. Caverton Helicopters disregarded the warnings…
> At the last count, Caverton Helicopters ferried over 220 passengers into the state without allowing health professionals of the Rivers State Government ascertain their coronavirus status. They also refused to avail the state government their contacts, so they can be traced and tested.[124]

In responding to Governor Wike's style of handling the Caverton Helicopters' matter, the Federal Government accused him of ignorance of the fact that aviation issues belong to the Exclusive List of the Constitution. The Federal Government through the Honourable Minister of Aviation, Alhaji Hadi Sirika explained that it granted the authorisation to the company to make the flight to Rivers State in the national interest.

---

[124] Okocha, Chuks, *et al (2020)*: 'We arrested Pilots, Passengers for refusing COVID-19 checks, Says Rivers Government', *THISDAYLIVE,* April 12. https://www.thisdaylive.com /index.php/2020/04/12/we-arrested-pilots-passengers-for-refusing-covid-19-checks-says-rivers-government/

The minister also explained that the *PTF on COVID-19* exempted workers in the oil and gas sector from the lockdown restriction order. This clarification was in order but it failed to recognise that there was a Chief Security Officer called a Governor who needed to be informed and taken into confidence at a period when airports were closed. So the Federal Government was wrong for not doing this.

In this respect, Nigerians need governors such as Barrister Wike to be able to assert the rights of state governments when matters of unnecessary and avoidable jurisdictional conflicts arise. Although, one may not like his style, Governor Wike was right in the way he handled the Caverton Helicopters case. As he sarcastically put it: "you can fly, but as you fly and land, don't enter our territory." He might have been overzealous in the way he went about it, no one would fault his goal of protecting people of his state in dangerous times like the COVID-19 pandemic emergency.

The second notable case of Governor Wike's overzealous style of punishing violators of the lockdown restrictions was the arrest of 22 ExxonMobil staff. Entering the state from the neighbouring Akwa Ibom State without permission, and violating the Executive Order (as was the case of the Caverton Helicopters), the governor ordered their arrest. He explained that since their coronavirus status was unknown, they constituted health risk to the people of the state. The governor remained uncompromising too. According to him:

> ...even though security agencies advised that they be allowed to go back to Akwa Ibom State, I insisted that the law must take its course...This is because nobody is above the law...As a responsive government, we have quarantined them in line with the relevant health protocols and they will be charged to court.[125]

The third notable case of acting overzealously and in a draconian manner was the demolition of two hotels whose owners also flouted the Executive Order banning the operation of hotels for the time being.

---

[125] See Ukpong Cletus (2020): 'Why I ordered arrest of 22 ExxonMobil workers – Gov. Wike', *Premium Times*, April, 17, via https://www.premiumtimesng.com/news/top-news/388415-why-i-ordered-arrest-of-exxonmobil-workers-gov-wike.html

Chapter Twenty five | Isaac Nnamdi Obasi

Although, the governor took great pains in the media to explain the true story and to justify his actions, he however, came under heavy criticisms for acting with a high dose of despotism. His army of critics compared him with his Lagos State counterpart, who faced with the same situation, simply closed down the hotels rather than demolishing them. Governor Babajide Sanwo-Olu of Lagos State was consequently called a democrat, while Governor Wike was called a despot, by critics.

In this particular case of demolition, it is our humble opinion that governor Wike's overzealousness (defended earlier in the two cases) sadly crept into despotism. The governor violated the rule of law himself never-minding his highly commendable legacy statement that nobody is above the law. Although, his action was meant to check flagrant acts of impunity in both government and in the wider society, he nevertheless crossed the line. Nobody doubts the fact that many Nigerians are lawless and enjoy disobeying government directives knowing from experience that they would get away with such misbehaviour. So there has to be an effective way to check such reckless acts of impunity and lawlessness. The problem is how?

We share the view that to fight impunity in this country, there has to be some dose of high-handedness but this should not be at the expense of the rule of law. The use of draconian style and measures has no place in a democracy. We however, support instant dispensation of justice that acts as good deterrent measures for reckless acts of impunity that have messed up this country for a very long time. Does this justify Governor Wike's style?

In an earlier Chapter, Governor Wike's style of fighting impunity in governance and in the wider society was applauded. Specifically, we said that a prompt dispensation of justice (like the hot-stove theory of discipline) usually sends the message loud and clear, and that offenders of lockdown violation should be given instant justice and not the usual refrain that they will be brought to justice, a promise or assurance people have come to know hardly gets implemented. We also recall that the governor had on certain occasions meted out 'mild' or 'moderate' instant justice against violators of lockdown restrictions. For instance, he sent violators to quarantine centres for two weeks.

Elsewhere in this country (FCT inclusive), offenders were ordered by mobile courts to carry out some form of public works that were highly useful to the wider society. These are alternative commendable measures than draconian or extreme measures. The governor had within the framework of this approach, suspended (and rightly too) few Local Government chairmen and ceased their allowances because violators were residing in their domains. He had earlier warmed them against allowing such to happen. The promptness of these mild punitive measures was within the ambit of the law and also within his powers.

Crossing the Line by Adopting Draconian Measures

His adoption of draconian measures which ran against the spirit of the rule of law was improper. We cite some cases here where his good intentions and actions went too far. In this first illustration, the *Businessday* reported that Gov. Wike arrested several violators and impounded some cars. He also arrested some very important persons (VIPS), who were not on essential duties, but were allegedly moving around with their police escorts. Again at the Elekahia Isolation Centre, over 200 persons were arrested and over 20 vehicles impounded by different teams enforcing the lockdown. All these people would face the full weight of the law.[126] It is our considered view here that the governor's commitment to the enforcement of the law and his usual statement and insistence that 'nobody is above the law' is very commendable. This statement to us is acceptable even with his overzealous style, as it is still within the confines of the law, after all there should be no impunity. However, the governor crossed the line when he further announced and insisted that the 20 impounded vehicles must be auctioned. In fact, he directed the State Attorney General to advertise the auctioning of the vehicles the next day.[127] Such a decision in our view was a draconian measure and an act of despotism devoid of democratic credentials.

---

[126] See Ignatius Chukwu (2020): *"Gov. Wike takes over the streets as Port Harcourt moves into 'extreme lockdown'", BusinessDay,* May, 7.
[127] See Chukwu Ignatius (2020): "Gov. Wike takes over the streets as Port Harcourt moves into 'extreme lockdown'"
BusinessDay, May 7, via https://businessday.ng/coronavirus/article/gov-wike-takes-over-the-streets-as-port-harcourt-moves-into-extreme-lockdown/

Chapter Twenty five | Isaac Nnamdi Obasi

The second illustration reported in *Sundiata Post*[128] revealed that the Governor impounded two trailer loads of cows for violating the lockdown restrictions. The governor also arrested 14 persons in the two trailers conveying the cattle and then directed the State Ministry of Health to conduct tests on them to ascertain their coronavirus status. The governor's high level of vigilance was typical of his zeal and the action still fell within his powers. In fact, he demonstrated that he ranked very high among the *action governors* in Nigeria, but an act of dictatorship came in when he directed that the cows and the trailers should be auctioned. This was simply a draconian measure which was unnecessary.

The last illustrative case in this Chapter was the arrest of 20 dockworkers who were on their way from essential duties in the Port Harcourt port. In the *Vanguard* news report of May 13 & 14, 2020, it was revealed that the affected workers were returning from essential service operations to BUA/PTOL terminal in Port Harcourt and were unlawfully and forcefully arrested, and detained even after presenting duly signed 'Essential Duty Port Pass' issued by the Nigerian Ports Authority, (NPA). This was another case of crossing the line more so when it was further revealed that it took the prompt response and intervention of the Presidency, the Executive Secretary of Shippers Council, President of NLC, Managing Director of the NPA, Director-General of NIMASA, Chairman, Seaports Terminal Operators Associations of Nigeria, the IGP, and other well-meaning Nigerians, to facilitate the release of the incarcerated dockworkers. One may ask: what was actually their offence if they were exempted from being on lockdown as workers on essential services? Was there anything that the governor knew in this matter that the rest of the people did not know?

Conclusion

There are two lessons (one for, and another against) to be learnt from the governor's style of enforcing laws. On the one hand, to be an action governor (with a little dose of overzealousness) is good for governance in

---

[128] Sundiata Post (2020): '*Wike impounds 2 trailer loads of cows for violating lockdown*. May 8, via https://sundiatapost.com/wike-impounds-2-trailer-loads-of-cows-for-violating-lockdown/.

Nigeria where many of those in power as well as the citizens themselves, behave in lawless manners. Governor Wike's style enabled him to check impunity which has been a major governance disease in Nigeria. His style also enabled him to make great strides in his developmental efforts more so when there was no (publicly known) political 'God-father' to distract him or hijack state resources. On the other hand, overzealousness (or just zealousness) has to be exercised within the confines of the law. An overzealous style needs moderation to check the attendant excesses that might unknowingly creep into dictatorship. Draconian measures that may make one to be perceived rightly or wrongly as a despot should have been avoided.

CHAPTER TWENTY SIX

COVID-19 and the Gentle Fighting Style of Governor Babajide Sanwo-Olu

Since the Federal Ministry of Health confirmed the first case of coronavirus (COVID-19) in Nigeria on Thursday, February 27, 2020, through the entry of an Italian citizen working in Nigeria, the Lagos State Government provided effective and exemplary leadership in containing the spread of the deadly disease in the state. Unfortunately, the increasing number of cases recorded daily in Lagos State, appeared to be overshadowing the tremendous and commendable efforts made also on a daily basis by the Lagos State Government and the Nigeria Centre for Disease Control (NCDC), to stop the spread of this very stubborn virus.

Governor Sanwo-Olu as a dogged Incident Commander

The seriousness attached to the fight against the spread of COVID-19 made the Lagos State Governor, Babajide Sanwo-Olu, to take the title of an Incident Commander. According to the Wikipedia,[129] the concept of an Incident Command System was first used in a meeting of Fire Chiefs in Southern California, USA, for the purpose of fighting off wildfires. It has since then evolved as a system used in fighting all-hazards (disaster management) situations. The system offers a standardised approach to command, control and coordination of emergency response. A major feature of its operation is the existence of unity of command driven by management by objectives. Since adopting the title by the Governor of Lagos State, he had made tremendous efforts to live up to the expectation, working tirelessly with his able lieutenants (such as the Honourable Commissioner for Health, Prof. Akin Abayomi) to stop the spread of the coronavirus.

---

[129] See *The Wikipedia*. https://en.wikipedia.org/wiki/Incident_Command_System.

Writing about the performance of the Governor as an Incident Commander, Segun (2020) had this to say:

> As the Chief Incident Commander on the COVID-19 pandemic in the state, Sanwo-Olu took the battle against the disease head on. At the beginning of the pandemic in the country, only Lagos was ready with a standard facility to house victims. Since the outbreak, he has increased the number of isolation centres in the state to eight, each with no less than 100 bed capacity. He updated the people daily on what is happening and what efforts the government is taking to manage it. For his efforts, corporate organisations, individuals and the federal government have donated cash and medical materials to the government, all in appreciation of how Sanwo-Olu has handled the situation.
>
> He has since become a role model for other Governors in the country.[130]

In this role model spirit of comparison, the Editorial Board of the *BusinessDay*[131] had earlier on commented on the governor's fighting effort against COVID-19 as follows:

> To be fair, the performance of the governors of Ogun and Oyo States in managing the pandemic has also been commendable. However, Sanwo-Olu stands above all others in empathetic leadership, practical organization and effective communication of the dangers posed by a virus...

The editorial also contrasted Sanwo-Olu's performance 'with the shambolic handling of the pandemic' by a particular Northern governor who lived in denial of the ravaging effects of the virus in his state.

---

[130] Segun James (2020): *THISDAY*, May 6, via *https://www.thisdaylive.com/index.php/2020/05/06/the-making-of-an-action-governor/*

[131] Editorial Board of the *BusinessDay* (2020), via *https://businessday.ng/editorial/article/sanwo-olus-leadership-skills-come-under-covid-19-test/).*

Strong forces against Governor's efforts

In spite of all the efforts of the government, the rising cases of infection recorded in Lagos State appeared very embarrassing. As at 17 May 2020, the number of cases in Lagos stood at 2,550, with 556 recoveries/discharged and 36 deaths.[132] Lagos State remained the epicentre of COVID-19 pandemic in Nigeria, as it retained 42% share of the total number of cases in Nigeria which was 5,959 (May 17, 2020).[133]

The rising cases in Lagos brought a lot of pressure on the State government's efforts to contain the spread of the virus. At this particular point in time, Lagos State was reported to be running out of bed spaces. Given the Mega City population of Lagos, and also recording the index case in Nigeria, the rising numbers, are understandable. Some critics may be wondering if the gentle, persuasive and 'democratic' style of the Incident Commander was very effective in reducing the rising numbers. Although, it is not deniable that the governor displayed some aggressiveness in a gentle manner, and also had demonstrated commendable level of activism in fighting the virus, one could still question whether the governor's gentle style was actually very effective in stopping the high level of non-compliance by Lagos residents to the lockdown restrictions and the social distancing protocols.

Given the high level of impunity displayed in the violation of lockdown restrictions by Lagos residents, it could have been advisable for Governor Sanwo-Olu to add a bit of Governor Nyesom Wike's overzealousness (within the confines of the law) to curb the high level of impunity in Lagos. Wike's overzealous style (though with some objectionable doses of draconian measures) succeeded considerably to keep the number of COVID-19 infections in the state very low (ie total cases stood at 51, with three deaths, as at 17 May 2020).

Yet, admirers of Governor Sanwo-Olu called him a democrat, and then called Wike a despot. This reactions followed the flouting of the restriction order in Lagos State by two hotels which the governor reacted by closing them down. The case of Rivers State had already been

---

[132] NCDC daily update May 17, 2020, via https://covid19.ncdc.gov.ng/.
[133] Ibid

discussed earlier. In other words, faced with the same situations where two hotels flouted the lockdown restrictions in their different domains, Governor Sanwo-Olu shut them down, while Governor Wike adopted an extreme measure of demolishing them.

In conclusion, one lesson here is that although Governor Sanwo-Olu's gentle, persuasive, and democratic style remains commendable, but it was not as effective as it should have been given the magnitude of the problem. It becomes obvious therefore that a little dose of overzealousness within the limits of the law, should have been applied to curb the flagrant violation of the lockdown restrictions, and the social distancing etiquette by Lagos residents. Evidence around us (for example lawless driving culture everywhere) shows that Nigeria is majorly a lawless society. However, the level of lawlessness in Lagos State, appears to be unimaginably high, and therefore needed some doses of Governor Wike's overzealousness within the ambit of the law.

CHAPTER TWENTY SEVEN

COVID-19 Pandemic and Bad Politics

This chapter discusses the negative impact of politics generally and more particularly on the efforts to control the spread of COVID-19 pandemic. The chapter was inspired by happenings at both the national and international levels with respect to the negative influence of politics on the fight against the pandemic. We do not assume in this chapter a common or general understanding of what politics means, and as such would go ahead to provide the meaning of politics from an academic point of view.

The concept of Politics

According to Nnoli[134], politics refers to "all those activities which are directly or indirectly associated with the seizure of state power, the consolidation of state power, and the use of state power". As he rightly pointed out, "politics is power, but not all power is politics", hence it is state power that is of interest to political scientists. It is in this context therefore that some other distinguished political scientists much earlier defined politics. Easton for example defined politics "as the authoritative allocation of values for a society,"[135] while Lasswell defined it as the science and art of "Who gets What, When and How."[136]

Political Scientists by these definitions did not however neglect the struggle for power within non-state actors, or the centrality of conflict in the struggle for power either by state or non-state actors. Going further on this, Obasi[137] while discussing the scope and methods of political science research underscored the ubiquity of conflict in the struggle, acquisition and exercise of power by either the state or non-state actors.

---

[134] Nnoli, Okwudiba, (1986): *Introduction to Politics*, London: Longman.
[135] Easton, David (1965): *A Framework for Political Analysis*, N. J.: Prentice Hall.
[136] Lasswell, Harold, (1958): *Politics: Who Gets What, When and How*, New York: Meridian Books.
[137] Obasi, I. N, (1999): '*Research Methodology in Political Science*, Enugu: Academic Publishing Company.

Conflict he argued, is largely present in the struggle to acquire power and also in the exercise of power or simply in sharing the benefits accruing from power so acquired. All said and done, politics Obasi pointed out is "the process of acquiring and exercising power by state and non-state actors for utilitarian purposes." With respect to politics within non-state actors specifically, examples include student's union politics, religious politics, ethnic politics, church politics, politics among actors in the entertainment industry, politics within sports (football, athletics,) federations, trade union politics, and boardroom politics in private sector organisations.

The concept of bad politics

With respect to the concept of bad politics, Tyagi's postulation is helpful here. Adopting a contrasting approach, his slightly modified articulation reads:

- ✓ Good politics tries to empower citizens. Bad politics tries to empower politicians.
- ✓ Good politics improves system and institutions. Bad politics tries to concentrate power in individuals and criticize individuals for problems.
- ✓ Good politics tries to find out permanent solutions of the problems. Bad politics tries to divert attention from the real problems.
- ✓ Good politics believes in Unity is Strength. Bad politics believes in Divide and Rule.
- ✓ Good politics promotes logic and scientific temper. Bad politics promotes blind faith and superstitions.
- ✓ Good politics believes in love and respect for all people irrespective of their religion, caste, race, place of birth and any difference created by chance. Bad politics believes in creating hatred among people on the basis of these differences.[138]

---

[138] Tyagi, D. (2019): What is difference between good politics and bad politics? Available at: https://www.quora.com/What-is-difference-between-good-politics-and-bad-politics.

For us here, our operational definition of bad politics, means politics which centres around: (a) the advancement of selfish interest rather than the common good, (b) domination rather than justice and equity, and (c) divide and rule rather than promotion of unity and strength.

This picture represents a typical case of an illegal movement in a period of *inter-state lockdown*. Source: *Sundiata Post,* May 22, 2020.

Illegal movements during the period of lockdown

Proceeding from these theoretical and operational viewpoints, we can now properly understand why the illegal movements of people from the North (suspected to be Almajirai, Herdsmen or members of Boko Haram) represented simple act of not just politics but bad politics in a COVID-19 emergency period in Nigeria. The illegal movements (as illustrated in the picture above) were in pursuit of advantageous power or economic gains over others in the domain of non-state actors. People involved in these illegal movements were allegedly having links and protection with state actors for certain selfish gains. For example, there was no reason whatsoever for people to be concealed in truck load of cows or trucks conveying cement, if they did not have less than noble intensions. As we noted in an earlier chapter, the perpetrators even went to the extent of forging the signature of the Rivers State Governor Nyesom Wike. They also confessed that they paid money to security personnel (among other fraudulent things) for them to be able to get through to Port Harcourt. In Abia State for instance, as many as 40 persons in this category were intercepted at a time. Many more were reported in other states across the country. These fraudulent acts characterized the violation of the ban on inter-state movements which we discussed in an earlier chapter.

Bad politics as a driver of bad governance

Furthermore, when politics is used instrumentally for domination of one group over another, and for self-enrichment, it becomes more destructive to collective efforts towards development than corruption. This is why we also argue that bad politics killing Nigeria more than even corruption. How? It is bad politics that turns everything upside down in our country and engenders bad governance. Only few things work appropriately and predictably in Nigeria.

Few examples here will illustrate our point more. First, It is bad politics that has been the main driver of grand corruption in Nigeria. The psychology of political appointees (across states and geo-political zones) appears to be that they have been given the opportunity to enrich themselves and not to serve. Those who appointed them appear to understand this interpretation in the same way. This is why corruption thrives regardless of the political party in power.

Secondly, it was bad politics that was behind the way COVID-19 palliatives[139] were distributed lopsidedly without any remorse. Thirdly, it was bad politics that determined how the conditional cash transfer was allegedly distributed lopsidedly in the country. Fourthly, it was bad politics that sustained the existence of unfair revenue allocation system in the country for a very long time. For the fifth example, it was indeed bad politics that was behind the unfair (lopsided) creation of local government areas in the country. The sixth example, it was bad politics that sustained the continued marginalization of the people of the South-

---

[139] The issue of the brouhaha over COVID-19 palliatives will be discussed later.

east geo-political zone with an air of impunity, satisfaction and self-congratulations by perpetrators for a long period of time.

The seventh example, it was bad politics that sustained the existence of unfair implementation of the federal character principle without qualms. Lastly, it was out-rightly bad politics that sees nothing wrong with provincialism and nepotism in federal government appointments under the Buhari administration. Politics has come into everything, and unfortunately, it has been killing everything and constituting a cog in the wheel of national developmental progress. Bad politics has for a very long time been killing the best in all of us. Unfortunately, and in an unintended manner, every section of this country suffers its debilitating effects, and everyone becomes a loser.

This was what distinguished Professor Gabriel Olusanya many years ago called 'poverty of imagination and creativity'[140] with specific reference to the implementation of the federal character principle. This is similar to what Brian Stelter (an Anchor of the CNN's *Reliable Sources)* called collective failure of imagination.[141] There is hardly any sphere of our national lives that the Buhari administration has not completely ran down due to provincialism – name it: education, economy, aviation, security, insecurity-induced agricultural failure, unity of the country, - and countless others.

Good Politics through the right leadership can build as well as rebuild a battered nation. Good political leadership has actually built great nations, while bad politics can destroy a nation so badly beyond redemption. Think of what has happened in Syria, Afghanistan, Iraqi, South Sudan, Somalia, among many other places. It is good politics (through great leadership) that built the United States of America and made it GREAT, and it is the other side of politics (the bad side) that brought America to its knees under the administration of former President Donald Trump. Under his leadership for example, the US left a huge leadership gap on the global scene (particularly in multilateral

---

[140] Olusanya, G. O. (1986): *Attempts at Nation-Building in Nigeria: a study in the poverty of imagination and creativity,* Social Science Council of Nigeria Annual Lecture Series, No. 3. Ijebu-Ode: Nire Press.
[141] Brian Stelter of CNN's *Reliable Sources* made this statement in 2020 while anchoring his programme.

Chapter Twenty seven | Isaac Nnamdi Obasi

organisations) which China and Russia gladly tried to fill or take advantage of the gap.

Bad politics under President Trump for example, was systematically eroding (within just four years) America's greatness achieved the over centuries. He tried to destroy America's hard won democratic credentials including stopping a smooth transfer of power after a democratically conducted election. In the area of appointment for example, Trump was sacking professionals/technocrats in the American bureaucracy because of his political interests. He created an unenviable record of having the highest turnover rate of political and administrative staff in American history. He was interfering with the work of scientists and professionals in the fight against COVID-19. He made politics rather than science to drive the fight against COVID-19 in his country, and he was still blaming China for the failure of his wrong choices (bad politics).

Furthermore, as a result of bad politics, President Trump tried reopening the economy (when the lockdown was highly necessary) in a manner that led to an unprecedented rise in the number of cases of COVID-19 infection. In spite of the fact that the numbers of COVID-19 infections were still very high with many people dying daily, the president stubbornly decided to intensify his political campaign. His wrong political choices affected lives outside the US particularly among COVID-19 sceptics. For example, such sceptics in many countries were citing his actions to disregard COVID-19 safety protocols.

In conclusion, it was very regrettable and bad that in Nigeria some people were spreading COVID-19 in the name of transporting cows, agricultural products and cement. The effects of such spread were very palpable especially in Rivers State where the number rose sharply[142] thereafter, in spite of the spirited efforts of Governor Wike to stop the spread of the virus. Bad politics contributed to the spread of the COVID-19 pandemic in Nigeria, but it also did across the world, as the example of the United States under Donald Trump demonstrated.[143]

---

[142] The issue would be discussed further later.
[143] The case of the United States of America would be discussed further later.

CHAPTER TWENTY EIGHT

COVID-19 War and the Verve of Inter-Governmental Cooperation

Federations all over the world (and there are not very many of them anyway) thrive well on the verve, of inter-governmental cooperation and collaboration. The Nigerian federation, despite its imperfect and wobbling nature, is not different. The verve of inter-governmental cooperation and collaboration is maintained through good inter-governmental relations management. Inter-governmental relations in a federal system could be on federal-state relations, federal-state-local relations, state-local relations, all at the vertical level of relationship. But the relationship could also be horizontal at the sub-national levels. It could for instance be state-state relations, or local-local relations.

With respect to the COVID-19 pandemic, it could be for instance state-state relations in the area of enforcing COVID-19-induced inter-state lockdown restrictions at the border of two states. Consequently, at no time was the verve of good inter-governmental relations management desperately needed, than in a life-threatening period of COVID-19 pandemic emergency. Good inter-governmental relations management therefore could not have been over-emphasised in the fight to contain the community transmission of the devastating virus.

Dynamics of inter-governmental cooperation under COVID-19

Many reasons inspired this discussion arising from the enforcement of the lockdown order, but chief among them was the hostile attitude of the Kogi State Government towards the officials of the Federal Ministry of Health and the Nigeria Centre for Disease Control (NCDC). At that time, the verve of inter-governmental cooperation and collaboration between the Kogi State Government and the federal government in the war against the ravaging COVID-19, was at its lowest ebb. Genuine critics of Nigeria's imperfect federal system (who rightly would blame the federal government most of the times) were disheartened to see some states pulling the federal government back in the fight against the COVID-19 war. Analysis of the situation then reveals that some states cooperated very well with the federal government, while some others did not.

It is proper to start this discussion with Lagos State where coronavirus was first discovered in Nigeria. Following the recording of the index case through Lagos as port of entry, the immediate challenge posed by the COVID-19 pandemic then, was first and foremost inter-governmental in nature. Since a pandemic requires every nation in the world to provide concerted and collective national policy response, no one expected the Lagos State government to face the COVID-19 challenge on behalf of Nigeria alone. Expectedly too, the Federal Government appreciated this fact very well and then responded immediately with a very encouraging financial support to the Lagos State Government.

In a nationwide address on March 26, 2020, President Muhammadu Buhari announced his approval of the immediate release of N10bn grant to Lagos, the epicentre of the COVID-19 outbreak in Nigeria. According to the President, the grant would enable Lagos Sate increase its capacity to control and contain the outbreak, while also supporting other States with capacity- building. Furthermore, the president approved the immediate release of N5bn special intervention fund to the Nigeria Centre for Disease Control (NCDC) to equip, expand and provide personnel to its facilities and laboratories across the country.[144]

Since health issue is in the concurrent list of the 1999 Constitution (as amended), both the federal and state governments are expected to cooperate and collaborate in tackling any serious health problem that arises in any state of the federation. Fortunately enough, the federal government (through the NCDC) was already providing the necessary leadership and support in the fight against the COVID-19 scourge.

As at April 14, 2020, barely two months after the index case, the NCDC established capacity for COVID-19 testing in its National Reference and in 11 other molecular laboratories. While updating these numbers during the Presidential Task Force on COVID-19 National Briefing on May 21, 2020, the Minister of Health Dr. Osagie Ehanire, announced that there were already 26 laboratories in 17 states of the

---

[144] See: https://statehouse.gov.ng/wp-content/uploads/2020/04/Presidential-Update-on-Covid-19-Response-March-26-2020.pdf.pdf.

federation. Without doubt this development demonstrated the needed leadership by the federal government in the management of COVID-19 pandemic emergency. The state governments were therefore expected to give a commensurate level of cooperation for effective containment of the spread of the virus. How did some state governments cooperate with the federal government in this regard?

With respect to Lagos State (the epicentre of the virus), the State government responded very well. Ever since this experiment in inter-governmental relations management of COVID-19 began in Lagos, the two sides also collaborated and cooperated very well. First, there was no overt conflict or reported cases of intrigues and squabbles between the two sides. Secondly, at the level of inter-agency collaboration, there were no visible frictions that attracted serious media attention. It appeared that professionals were fully in control and that politics was given a back stage. Perhaps the Ebola experience, where both sides cooperated excellently well also, helped to bring about what we could rightly describe as cordial, cooperative and collaborative inter-governmental relations management in the COVID-19 emergency operation.

However, the efforts of the Federal Government towards effective collaboration with some other states witnessed a mixed bag of successes and disappointments. For example, at the Presidential Task Force on COVID-19 national Press Briefing held on May 7, 2020, the Minister of Health, Dr. Osagie Ehanire disclosed that a team of the Federal Ministry of Health left for Kogi State to ensure that the State received adequate testing capacity. The team, he said, would also advocate for the engagement of traditional rulers and community leaders in surveillance efforts on COVID-19 in the state. The minister equally revealed that a similar team would depart Abuja for Cross River State. These two states during that period were showing exceptional signs of non-cooperation and had at that time not reported any case of COVID-19 infection. What was the outcome of these visits?

Engagement with Kogi State proved problematic, while that with Cross River State progressed from being initially problematic to being very constructive and encouragingly fruitful. Although these states were COVID-19 free, there were however serious doubt about their infection-free record, especially given the initial hostile attitude of their governors.

A further background analysis revealed that the infection-free record of Cross River State could be understandable. The state needed to be given the benefit of doubt for certain reasons. First, the governor, Prof.

Ben Ayade was operating from a point of view and strength of knowledge as an expert in environmental microbiology. This explanatory factor could not just be dismissed with a wave of the hand, if we recall that one of the reasons why the Republic of Germany was reported to have performed better than other European countries in combating the COVID-19 disease was because the then leader Chancellor Angela Merkel a scientist, was acting a scientist- in-chief.[145]

According to the *Homeland Security News Wire* (2020) Chancellor Merkel was acting as a Scientist-in-Chief. She was an effective leader who was relying on science and evidence-based reasoning in the fight against COVID-19. Again, she was rigorous in collating information, honest in stating what is not yet known, and maintaining good composure, all of which paid off. In addition to this and for the purpose of our discussion here, the Republic of Germany is a strong federation, where inter-governmental cooperation and collaboration are well institutionalised. This fact also enhanced the verve of inter-governmental relations management towards the containment of COVID-19 pandemic across the Republic of Germany at that time.

Like Chancellor Merkel, Prof. Ayade as a scientist and as an expert had been deploying knowledge to its correct and full use right from the commencement of the fight against the coronavirus. His approach at that material time demonstrated the power of pro-active measures (preparedness and prevention) in the fight against COVID-19. More details on this thesis will drive the point home.

First, Governor Ayade in his proactive approach was among the few governors that ordered the closure of their state borders earlier enough to prevent the transmission of the virus in their domain. We recall that the governor as early as the month of March 2020, prevented 35 Americans from entering into the state (through an Air Peace flight) in line with his ban on cross-border movements on land, air and sea.[146]

---

[145] The Homeland Security News Wire (2020): 'The Secret to Germany's COVID-19 Success: Angela Merkel is a Scientist'. Available at: http://www.homelandsecuritynewswire.com/dr202 00421-the-secret-to-germany-s-covid19-success-angela-merkel-is-a-scientist.

[146] See https://www.vanguardngr.com/2020/03/covid-19-why-we-refused-35-americans-entry-into-calabar-%E2%80%95-ayades-aide/.

Secondly, ahead of other governors also, the governor on April 1, 2020, declared that 'no resident of the state would be allowed to leave home without a face mask'. The order took effect on Wednesday April 3, 2020. As the Vanguard newspaper reported it: *COVID-19: Ayade goes tough on residents, says no nose mask, no movement.*[147] In order to demonstrate the seriousness of his policy of no-mask, no-movement, the governor imposed a fine of N300,000 against any driver who carried passengers without wearing face masks. The driver's vehicle would only be released after the fine was paid and after being quarantined for 14 days. Encouragingly, to give the policy a human face, the governor ordered that face masks should be distributed free of charge to everyone in the state, having brilliantly and commendably converted his government-established Garment factory in Calabar into a mask-making industry. There was definitely therefore no reason for anyone to refuse wearing a face mask in Cross River State. This again demonstrated the power of prevention in the fight against COVID-19, and more than anything else, exemplified the full deployment of knowledge in fighting COVID-19.

Thirdly, after setting up the COVID-19 Response Team (State Task Force on COVID-19), Governor Ayade released the sum of N500,000 and 20 vehicles to enable the team perform its task effectively. It is on record that the Response Team lived up to expectation thereafter.

Fourthly, in the area where many critics thought the governor was not doing well, the governor subsequently made amends. This was because as critics began to appreciate his knowledge-driven style (though initially misunderstood and seen as out-rightly uncooperative and hostile towards the federal government health officials), the governor too adjusted his style of responding to criticisms on the management of COVID-19 in his state. For instance, in the area of lack of testing, samples were subsequently sent out as required. His initial uncooperative and hostile attitude towards officials of NCDC who he had threatened to quarantine for 14 days if they visited the state for their official duties was rescinded. The officials actually visited and left the state satisfied with what they saw.

---

[147] See https://www.vanguardngr.com/2020/04/breaking-covid-19-ayade-goes-tough-on-residents-says-no-nose-mask-no-movement/.

As the governor's efforts appeared to have yielded good results, the federal government through the Minister of Health in turn commended the governor. At the PTF on COVID-19 National Briefing on 21 May 2020, the minister announced that the fact finding team to Calabar was back and that a report had been submitted. He commended Governor Ben Ayade for his proactive approach, and promised to work with the state teams to ensure a scale-up surveillance and contact tracing in the state. He also promised to explore the possibility of upgrading laboratories in the state to ensure ease of testing when suspected cases are identified.[148]

Reporting further, the leader of the NCDC delegation to Cross River State, Dr. Omobolanle Olowu, said that they had every reason to believe that COVID-19 had not spread to the state as a result of the swift response and proactive measures put in place by the state governor, Prof. Ben Ayade. She further said that they were surprised at the level of work put in place by the state government. Finally, she said that all the people they saw were on face masks with different teams at various points in the state.[149] Following all these, it turned out that the federal and Cross River state governments were on the same page with respect to cooperation and collaboration in the management of COVID-19.

Governor Ayade's style of non-cooperation and non-collaboration with the federal government initially on the strength of knowledge and strategy, was quite different from what happened in some other states where there was ignorance and sometimes arrogance, outright deceit and self-delusion. With hindsight thereafter, critics of Prof. Ayade would now forgive the exuberance with which he initially handled his relationship with the federal government on the containment of COVID-19.

Kogi State and its notorious denial of COVID-19

With respect to some other states, one notable area of states' lack of cooperation with the federal government in the fight against COVID-19

---

[148] See https://statehouse.gov.ng/covid19/2020/05/21/national-briefing-may-21-2020-remarks-by-minister-of-health/

[149] See report by Bassey Inyang of *THISDY* newspaper, via https://allafrica.com/stories/202005190279.html

was through the denial of the existence of the virus. Kano State was guilty of this at a period in time, but Kogi State was notoriously guilty in this regard. Officially, Kogi State (before Wednesday May 27, 2020) did not record any case of infection of COVID-19. However, the way the state defended the COVID-19-free record raised serious suspicion. When the federal government sent a delegation to the state to validate the claim that no case of coronavirus had been recorded, the officials met both hostility and outright lack of cooperation from the state government.

The Governor, Yahaya Bello had earlier on ordered that the officials of the Nigeria Centre for Disease Control (NCDC) should be quarantined for 14 days and also be tested for the coronavirus before they could be allowed to carry out their assignment in the state. The officials eventually left the state without accomplishing their mission. Reacting to this, the Minister of Health, Dr. Osagie Ehanire regrettably announced that the efforts of the federal government to support the state in its response to the coronavirus pandemic, was a failure. There was allegation that deaths suspected to be caused by COVID-19, were being covered up by officials of the state government. One of the allegations reported in *The Nation* newspaper revealed that "no less than six people infected by the coronavirus disease had died at the Federal Medical Centre (FMC), Lokoja."[150] The nurse who revealed this to *The Nation* alleged that "an aide to the governor warned members of staff of dire consequences should the news leak."[151]

The second allegation and a more disturbing one came from doctors at the same FMC, Lokoja. According to the Association of Resident Doctors, (FMC chapter), the state government had been frustrating their efforts to test patients suspected to be suffering from COVID-19, which they complained exposed health workers to high risk of infections that are transmissible to members of their families and other unsuspecting patients.[152] To compound the matter, the state government claimed that it had tested 111 patients in the state and all of which came out negative.

[150] The Nation newspaper, (2020): 'Controversy over Kogi's COVID-19 status,' May 12, via https://thenationonlineng.net/controversy-over-kogis-covid-19-status/
[151] Ibid.
[152] For details of the doctors' lamentation, see: http://www.linderikesblog.com.

Chapter Twenty eight | Isaac Nnamdi Obasi

The NCDC, however, revealed that only one test had taken place in the state. Perhaps, the tests were carried out with what was called the COVID-19 App of Kogi state, which was not part of the NCDC testing facility.

However, a new development emerged during that period. The NCDC on Wednesday, May 27, 2020, announced that Kogi state had now recorded two index cases. In a characteristic manner, the state government rejected the result. The State Commissioner for Health, Dr. Saka Haruna Audu declared the result 'as a fallacy'. According to him, Kogi State till this very moment was COVID-19 free. We have developed full testing capacity and have conducted hundreds of tests so far which have returned negative. We have also continued to insist that we will not be a party to any fictitious COVID-19 claims which is why we do not recognise any COVID-19 test conducted by any Kogite outside the boundaries of the State except those initiated by us. Any attempt to force us to announce a case of COVID-19 will be vehemently rejected.[153]

One might wonder why the Kogi State Government was out rightly defensive on this matter. What was indeed responsible for the Kogi State Government's attitude of defending at all cost its claimed COVID-19-free record? Eniola Bello a notable indigene of Kogi State (and Managing Director of *THISDAY* newspaper) was of the opinion that incompetence was at the centre of it all. According to him, the state government was hiding its incompetence as it could not face the challenges of fighting the COVID-19 disease.[154] Mr. Eniola Bello spoke the minds of many on this matter.

Experience of poor inter-governmental cooperation with other states

With respect to some other states, denial and lack of cooperation were at play. First, in some northern states, the case of many deaths suspected to

---

[153] The *Punch* newspaper (2020), Thursday, May 8 via https://punchng.com/covid-19-kogi-rejects-ncdc-result-insists-state-still-free/.
[154] Mr. Eniola Bello (Managing Director of *THISDAY* newspaper) expressed this opinion on *ARISE NEWS TV, Morning Show*, May 25, 2020.

be COVID-19-related were unconvincingly attributed to other diseases. Kano State was notorious in this regard. Other states like Jigawa, Bauchi and Yobe experienced also many of such so-called 'mysterious' deaths. The good thing though was that they did not adopt hostile and uncooperative attitude (like Kogi) towards the federal government health officials, which would have impeded both cooperation and collaboration with the federal government in fighting the virus in their states.

Secondly, couple of Northern governors prematurely eased the lockdown restrictions to allow risky mass gathering for religious activities. They ignored the *PTF on COVID-19* advisory against lifting the ban on religious gathering especially during the Eid-el-Fitr celebration within the period. These states also ignored the pleading by President Muhammad Buhari and the Sultan of Sokoto that people should pray at home or in their neighbourhood. The irony of all these was that these states that did not care about the consequences of such risky gatherings, would also turn-round to expect the federal government to provide financial assistance when there were increases in the number of COVID-19 infections in their states.

Thirdly, some states did not do well in building the 300-bed isolation centres which the federal government encouraged all the states to build. This was one major area where some states failed to cooperate with the federal government in the fight against COVID-19.

In conclusion, with the exception of very few states, many others failed to cooperate well with the federal authorities in the fight against COVID-19. It was as if the fight against the virus was for the federal government alone to execute, as some of them were in subtle denial of the devastating effects of the virus, while some others prematurely eased the lockdown restrictions to allow risky mass gathering of people for religious activities. On the whole, the Nigerian wobbling federal system, revealed its very uncooperative nature as the federal and some of the state governments, were not on the same page in the fight against the virus.

CHAPTER TWENTY NINE

COVID-19 and Nigeria's Fight at the Sub-National Levels

The Background

Across much of the world, the war against coronavirus (COVID-19) pandemic has been frontally led and coordinated at the national level. This has also been the case with Nigeria where the Presidential Task Force on COVID-19 has been in charge in order to ensure a coordination of a 'single set of national strategic objectives', as required by its mandate. Three months into its existence, the PTF on COVID-19 was implementing the various guidelines under the Phase 1 of Easing of Lockdown which was first extended for two weeks (May 18 – June 1, 2020), and then extended for the second time for one month (June 2 – June 29, 2020). As the PTF looked ahead in its crucial fight against COVID-19, its chairman, Boss Mustapha, during a national briefing on 2 June 2020, re-emphasised the fact that 'as the PTF focuses on community engagement and risk communication…State Governments now have the responsibility to shape and drive the process'. He had earlier urged all sub-national entities (state and local governments) which had been collaborating with the PTF "to expeditiously factor the guidelines on the easing of the lockdown into their decisions and resultant protocols that would be agreed to."[155]

The PTF Chairman also urged governments at sub-national levels "to strengthen their enforcement and monitoring mechanisms so as to ensure that the desired results are achieved."[156] In all of these admonitions, the federal government had a major role of assisting the states and local governments through the PTF and the Nigeria Centre for Disease Control (NCDC). This task was in consonance with the mandate of the PTF which we discussed in an earlier chapter. For example, as at June 2020, the Nigeria Centre for Disease Control (NCDC) had activated a total number of 30 laboratories for the testing of COVID-19 across the

---

[155] PTF on COVID-19 (2020): 'National Briefing, June 2, 2020 – Remarks by SGF/Chairman of PTF'.
[156] Ibid

states in Nigeria. This was a major achievement against the background of a few number of laboratories that existed at the time the COVID-19 index case was recorded in Lagos on 27 February 2020.

Furthermore, during the same national briefing on June 2, the Minister of Health Dr. Osagie Ehanire, while elaborating on further collaboration with sub-national governments, revealed that his Ministry was working with the National Primary Healthcare Development Agency, to finalise plans on engagement of existing community volunteers and agents to conduct house-to-house sensitisation on COVID-19 at community level. The main targets were the high burden Local Government areas where about 20 LGAs contributed nearly 60% of Nigeria's COVID-19 positive cases. He said that "states are at varying levels of readiness and it is important to re-strategize to meet all citizens at their points of need. This includes the decentralisation that requires making a minimum of 300 Isolation beds ready..."[157]

More importantly, the minister rightly captured the expectations of concerned Nigerians at this stage of the easing of the lockdown restrictions when he said: "as we move into the next phase of easing of the lockdown", everyone is expected to urgently "take responsibility for ensuring that we actively play our role in ensuring that COVID-19 does not spike or bounce up, as has been observed in many countries where lockdown was relaxed." It is important, he further said, "...that this phase, more than the lockdown itself, is in the hands of the people, more than in the hand of government. We must fight the spread of the disease by adhering more strictly than ever, to the various social guidelines...announced, published and publicised."[158]

So far, the efforts of the federal government to provide support to sub-national level governments in the fight against COVID-19, had been very encouraging. But what about the efforts made at the sub-national levels, particularly at the state government level?

---

[157] PTF on COVID-19 (2020): Remarks by the Minister of Health at the National Briefing, June 2, 2020.
[158] Ibid.

The lack of sense of urgency by some State governments at the early stage

We start with the issue of how serious the states were in the fight against COVID-19 after the index case was reported in Nigeria. First, historical facts reveal that many of the state governors did not react (after the index was announced) with the expected sense of urgency. Many continued their activities with business-as-usual mentality. This mind set demonstrated a complete lack of seriousness in understanding the devastating nature of the virus. In some other states, the governors displayed a brazen attitude of living in denial of the virus. In one or two states, a combination of these behavioural reactions subsisted even for a long time.

Starting with the lack of a sense of urgency and a continuation of a business-as-usual mentality, it is necessary to recall that the first three weeks in the month of March 2020, were very critical in the efforts to stop the early and further spread of the virus in Nigeria. That month was a missed and painful opportunity at the sub-national levels. With the establishment of the Presidential Task Force on COVID-19 (PTF on COVID-19) on March 9, 2020, the danger of the coronavirus was brought home to everyone. In actual fact, the PTF through its regular national briefings went straight into action by creating the awareness needed for all the states to begin to take preventive measures. The Nigeria Centre for Disease Control (NCDC) commenced aggressive public enlightenment campaigns in print, electronic and on social media platforms, but a good number of state governors failed to fully appreciate the seriousness of the situation during that month of March.

In Oyo State for instance, our amiable Governor Seyi Makinde on 18 March organised a mega rally of the Peoples Democratic Party (PDP) in Ibadan. This was at a time the World Health Organization (WHO) had earlier on 31 January 2020 listed Nigeria (among 13 other African countries) as high-risk areas for the spread of COVID-19. It was not surprising that the same governor later tested positive for the virus. However, he later apologised for hosting the mega rally and described his action as a product of bad judgment. Two days earlier, on 16 March 2020, 16 governors from the All Progressive Congress (APC) held a meeting in Abuja. All these were happening at a time when more cases of infection were being recorded in Lagos. On March 18 for example, five new cases were recorded. There was no indication that the governors had come to terms with the reality of the situation even though they were the ones expected to lead the fight against the spread of the virus in their various states. Many still operated as if the coronavirus pandemic was not a public health emergency.

The Big Mistake of March 2020

Unfortunately, perhaps unknown to many of them, it was within this period that certain unpleasant developments started unfolding. On 24 March, the Chief of Staff to President Muhammad Buhari, Malam Abba Kyari tested positive the same day that Bauchi State governor Malam Bala Mohammed also tested positive for the virus. Another display of lack of seriousness was exhibited by many of the governors. By this time, it was expected that all governors who had interacted with Malam Abba Kyari during the Abuja meeting, should have self-isolated as required by the safety protocols of the WHO and the NCDC. Only few of them did, and also presented themselves for testing. This was a very big mistake by such governors who interacted with the late Chief of staff. It was much later that they started presenting themselves for testing but then it was already late. It was a big mistake because the month of March was critical in containing the spread of the virus because Nigeria was yet to enter the stage of community transmission of the virus, which is usually most difficult to contain. The dreaded community transmission however came, as was announced by the Minister of Health Dr. Ehanire on April 14, 2020, at the briefing of the PTF on COVID-19.

Noteworthy serious efforts by some Governors

It was heartening, however, that some governors showed seriousness in responding earlier to the demands of the situation. For instance, governors in North-west geo-political zone took good proactive measure of shutting down schools with effect from 23 March 2020. Many other governors also ordered that their junior public servants should stay at home and work from there until further notice. This directive was equally given around this critical period in March. Another good proactive measure taken by some state governors around the same month of March was the lockdown of their states. Governor Nyesom Wike of

Rivers State, Governor Nasir El-Rufai of Kaduna State and Governor Ben Ayade of Cross River State, among some others did this as early as 23 March. Regrettably, by this date Governor Nasir El-Rufai had not gone into self-isolation given his high profile interactions in Abuja. Unfortunately, by 28 March he tested positive for the coronavirus and then announced that he had gone into self-isolation in line with the guidelines of the NCDC for an asymptomatic person. It was a good action however, but it was taken too late.

Scandalous case of denial of the virus by some Governors

With respect to the issue of denial, a handful of governors by their words and actions lived in denial of the dreaded virus in that crucial month of March. First, Kogi State continued to live in denial even after the NCDC recorded few cases of infection in the state. This was in spite of the alleged COVID-19-related deaths at the Federal Medical Centre (FMC), Lokoja, for which doctors and nurses working there drew the attention of the federal government. The Nigerian Medical Association (NMA) openly complained to the federal government about how the uncooperative attitude of the Kogi State Government towards the management of the virus posed a grave risk to health personnel in the state. The NMA then asked the federal government to call the Kogi State governor to order.

The second issue of denial relates to the high number of unexplained deaths that occurred in some of the states. Although, informed opinion linked these deaths to COVID-19, the official positions in the affected states differed. The deaths were therefore described as mysterious deaths and these complicated and delayed efforts to contain the spread of the virus. Such mysterious or unexplained deaths occurred in Kano, Jigawa and Yobe states, among other places, but the case of Kano State was terrifically disturbing. Fortunately, the PTF on COVID-19 put the controversy surrounding the mysterious deaths in Kano State to rest. The Minister of Health Dr. Ehanire at the PTF briefing on Monday, 8 June 2020, revealed that 50-60% of the 979 deaths that occurred in Kano state during the months of April and May 2020 may have been triggered by or due to COVID-19.

Effects of the Big Mistakes of March 2020

As already noted, mistakes were made in March 2020 when the various states ought to have waged the war more energetically against the spread of COVID-19. Ever since those mistakes, the number of infections continued to rise with an unprecedented number of 663 cases reported for Tuesday, June 9, 2020. This highest number recorded within 24 hours brought the total number of infections in Nigeria to 13,464 as of that date. A disaggregation of this total figure (as of that date) reveals that Lagos State with 6,065 and FCT with 1,012, (totalling 7,077) contributed 53% of the total (13,464) number of cases of infection. This disproportionate figure from two sub-national level governments was understandable as many people came into Nigeria from overseas through the two major airports in Lagos and Abuja, before the closure of airports all over the country then.

Commendable efforts of Lagos, FCT, and Noteworthy efforts of Rivers, Kaduna and Cross River States

Nevertheless, public policy measures to contain the spread of the virus in both Lagos State and the FCT were very swift, and the fighting spirit remained very high over time. For example, both Lagos and the FTC responded swiftly with the establishment of mobile courts to try offenders of the lockdown restriction order. We have had reason in earlier chapters to commend the Lagos state governor and his team of health professionals in confronting the daunting challenge of this virus. The same commendation should go to the entire FCT administration particularly the FCT Ministerial Task Team on COVID-19 lockdown enforcement for the verve and passion it exhibited in carrying out its assignment even at great risk. The Chairman of the Ministerial Task Team, Ikharo Attah was exceptionally active and so were some other officials.

One may wonder why two areas with the highest number of infections should be commended. What is of interest to us here is the verve and passion in fighting the virus and not just the rising figures, as it could have been more overwhelming and ultimately worse without such a verve or high fighting spirit. The case of New York State (the epicentre of COVID-19) in the United States (US) readily comes to mind. In spite of the fact that New York State former Governor Andrew Cuomo more than any other governor in the US waged the war against the virus excellently well, his state nevertheless recorded the highest number of infections and fatality in the US at the peak of COVID-19 outbreak. The sustained high fighting spirit and the resources deployed in this case were very important, as both clearly demonstrate the priority a government attached to this matter of serious public health concern and emergency.

It is in this respect also that we recognise (apart from Lagos) all other governors who exhibited such verve in Nigeria. There were quite a good number of them that were outstanding, but three (for our purpose here), were very outstanding and they were those of Rivers, Kaduna and Cross River States. We did a study of activities of the governors in this regard very closely over time to arrive at this conclusion. For those who were monitoring the fight against the virus at the state level, these three governors put their lives on the line even at difficult times of the night to make sure that things were rightly done to control the spread of the virus. If there are some others we failed to identify, it means their actions were not well publicised nationally and we can safely absolve ourselves from any blames.

The link between the mistakes of March 2020 and the pattern of spread of the Virus in States

The issue of commendation apart, a further look at the disaggregation of the total number of infections on state basis (as of Tuesday, June 9, 2020), also reveals that many states whose governors had high profile interactions in Abuja around the mid-month of March were also among the highest contributors to the total figure as of that date. As we earlier noted, 16 APC governors under the Progressives Governors Forum held a meeting in Abuja on 16 March 2020 with President Muhammadu Buhari and his late Chief of Staff, Abba Kyari, in attendance. As we also noted earlier, many of them returned to their states and continued with a business-as-usual mentality. They therefore failed to recognise COVID-19 pandemic as an emergency. Regrettably, many of these states were among the highest contributors to the total figure of 13,464 infections.[159]

---

[159] This is part of a discussion of another chapter later.

Next to these negligent states and highest contributors to the total COVID-19 figures, was Oyo State whose governor as earlier observed hosted a mega rally in Ibadan. It is also noteworthy that Bauchi State whose governor also had interactions with the late Chief of Staff around the same mid-March, and who later tested positive, recorded a moderately high figure like Oyo and these other states.

Surprisingly and regrettably, Rivers State was among states with a very high number of infections, in spite of the commendable early efforts of Governor Nyesom Wike to check the spread of the virus in the state. For those who care to know, Governor Wike literally cried out loud that his efforts were being sabotaged by those who flouted the inter-state lockdown to enter into his state illegally.

Closer look at the NCDC total statistics for each state as of Tuesday, June 9, 2020 revealed how the earlier mistakes in March contributed in putting Nigeria into the community transmission stage. The statistics support the argument being made here that there was a link between actions or inactions in mid-March, and the pattern of the spread of the virus subsequently. This is also why it is therefore incomprehensible that Kogi State Government continued to claim that the state was COVID-19 free. The claim were not helpful in the national efforts to contain the spread of the virus and that was perhaps why the PTF On COVID-19 at a time reported the governor to President Buhari.

Furthermore, going by what happened in mid-March and thereabout, the attitude of Kano State Government is also regrettable as the governor neither had the early conviction to fight the virus nor exhibited any verve when the state was going through an unprecedented debacle in the history of this virus. As *The Africa Report*[160] aptly put it, the state government was criticised for being neither proactive nor reactive. It took President Buhari to impose a total lockdown of Kano State.

With respect to level of cooperation by state governments, the noticeable lack of verve on the part of some of them, affected their level of cooperation with the federal authorities in the fight against the virus. For example, some states were still struggling to build the 300-bed

---

[160] The Africa Report, (2020) via https://www.theafricareport.com/27773/coronavirus-nigerias-varied-responses-to-controlling-covid-19/

isolation centres as requested by the PTF. The PTF at a time expressed disappointment over this development. Furthermore, some states were not able to make enough funds available to support effective operation of the State Emergency Operation Centres which were crucial in the containment of the virus at community-level transmission. They appeared to be expecting the federal government to provide every important thing needed.

The second area of lack of cooperation was the reluctance by some states to impose a lockdown at a time when it was considered very necessary. In fact, some governors openly declared that it would not be possible to impose a lockdown in their states. Fortunately enough, the Nigeria Governors Forum (NGF) proposed to President Buhari a nation-wide inter-state lockdown of movements. This proposal was accepted by the president which he subsequently included in his nation-wide address on COVID-19. Unfortunately however, the lockdown restrictions were widely violated across the states. Some governors in the southern part of the country arrested many violators of the order who were concealed in trucks carrying Cattles and cement.

The last area of lack of cooperation which was already noted in an earlier chapter was the premature relaxation of lockdown restrictions to allow mass gathering of people for religious activities, in spite of the advisory by the PTF on COVID-19 against lifting the ban on religious gathering especially during the festivities. Regrettably, the large gathering of worshipers ignored social distancing and other safety protocols thereby creating more problems.

In conclusion, it was cheering to hear later from the Minister of Health, Dr. Ehanire at the National Briefing on Thursday, June 11, 2020, that a good number of states were cooperating well with the federal government in the fight against the virus. We commend the states that turned a new leaf in this regard. This commendation is however, not without prejudice to the conclusion we made earlier in Chapter 28 about the existence of the poor level of cooperation.

CHAPTER THIRTY

COVID-19 War: Kogi State in Focus

As we noted in chapter 28, the verve of inter-governmental cooperation and collaboration between the Kogi state government and the federal government in the war against COVID-19, was at the lowest ebb. The hostile attitude adopted by the Kogi State Government towards the fight against the COVID-19 dated back to the inception of the national response to the COVID-19 pandemic. The State Government consistently rebuffed all national combined efforts directed at curbing the spread of COVID-19 by the Presidential Task Force (PTF) on COVID-19, Federal Ministry of Health (FMH), and the Nigeria Centre for Disease Control (NCDC).

PTF's declaration of Kogi State as a High Risk State amidst growing hostility

The hostility reached its crescendo when the Presidential Task Force on COVID-19 declared Kogi State a 'high risk state'[161] and urged people to avoid visiting the state. In a very combative reaction, the Kogi State Government accused federal authorities of using the war against the virus, as a self-enrichment project. The PTF on COVID-19 had accused the Kogi State Government of refusing to acknowledge the existence of the COVID-19. Aside from that, the state refused to report testing results, and failed to establish isolation centres. It should be recalled that Governor Yahaya Bello's government refused NCDC officials entry into the state unless they quarantined for 14 days after arriving in the state. The condition made it impossible for the NCDC officials to carry out their legitimate public health duties in the state.

Facts further revealed that first, the governor himself refused to wear face mask. Secondly, the government denied COVID-19-related deaths

---

[161] See *Vanguard* newspaper, (2021): 'PTF Declares Kogi High risk State, warms Nigeria not to visit', February 2, (report by Lawal Sherifat). This news item was widely reported by the mass media.

of citizens and claimed that they should be counted as deaths that occurred in FCT even while the sick people contacted the virus in Kogi. Thirdly, the governor himself again declared that COVID-19 vaccines were meant to kill all of us hence advised people against taking the jab.[162] The position of the Kogi state government defied logic given the locational centrality of the State (bordering a good number of other states) with the capital hosting many travellers on transit between the Northern and Southern parts of the country every single day. With no NCDC recognized testing going on in the state, there was no way of establishing the veracity of the claim by the state.

The Kogi State Government's accusation against PTF on COVID-19 and Reactions

In spite of the fact against Kogi State's denial of COVID-19, the State's Commissioner for Information and Communication, Kingsley Fanwo, accused the PTF on COVID-19 of trying to raise alarm in the state and drive investors away. He then claimed that the PTF attacked the state because of its stance that the COVID-19 pandemic should not be turned into a money-making venture to the detriment of Nigerians.[163]

According to the Commissioner, Kogi State was the first state to procure face masks in thousands and distributed them to all the councils, as well as the first to set up a team to combat the spread of the virus. Continuing, he said that the state "set up isolation centres with state-of-the-art equipment", and that the state had "done sensitisation more than any other state". He then erroneously added: "so if we don't believe that COVID-19 exists, we won't be doing all we are doing to ensure it doesn't ravage our state". He then concluded that "what we said and still saying is that COVID-19 is not worth all the marketing going on just for a few to make billions; that we do not have to suffer innocent Nigerians while a few smile to the banks."[164]

---

[162] The Sun newspaper (2021): 'COVID-19 vaccines meant to kill us – Gov. Bello'. January 20, (report by Emma Njoku, *et all*).
[163] See International Centre for Investigative Reporting (ICIR) (2021): 'COVID-19 travel alert: Kogi accuses NCDC, PTF of scaring away investors from state'. February 3, Available at: http://www.icirnigeria.org.
[164] Ibid

How does one assess the commissioner's reactions? One can simply say that the commissioner apparently performed his public relations job well, but what he refused to tell concerned Nigerians was why in spite of the existence of the "isolation centres with state-of-the-art equipment", the government was not transparent enough to allow NCDC officials to carry out their duties in the state. Secondly, the commissioner did not explain why the state refused to carry out COVID-19 tests or send results of tests (if any), to the NCDC.

Thirdly, if the commissioner's claims were to be correct, why would there be many condemnatory statements against his governor? For example, why would the Nigeria Governor's Forum (NGF) through its chairman, Governor Kayode Fayemi issue a disclaimer to Governor Bello Yahaya's unscientific claim that vaccines are meant to kill us in Nigeria? If the Commissioner's claims were to be true, why would there be a COVID-19 war of words between PTF on COVID-19 and the State government? More importantly, was the commissioner aware that some Nigerians, who were embarrassed by his governor's false claims and inactions, had called on the federal government to sanction him?

Elder statesman, Edwin Clark, in a news report[165], while narrating his terrible experience with COVID-19, called on the Federal Government to sanction Governor Yahaya Bello over his claims that the pandemic was not real. He was reported to have said that the governor should be ashamed of himself and that "this is a man parading himself that he wants to be president of Nigeria. It's all nonsense. Some of them feel because they are very close to Mr. President, they can do anything". Lastly, was the Commissioner aware that some Nigerians in and outside the state, had this kind of harsh words for his governor?

Historically speaking, Kogi State Government's confrontation with the COVID-19 national response team (broadly comprising the PTF, FMH and NCDC) started very early in the national fight against the virus. As we pointed out much earlier, it all started like a drama when notably two states namely Cross River and Kogi were reported not to

---

[165] See *The Nation* (2021): 'Clark: My battle with COVID-19', Wednesday, February 10, via https://www.thenationonlineng.net/clark-my-battle-with-covid-19/

have recorded any COVID-19 cases. It appeared as if that positive record represented a political mileage gained by the governors of the two states. Perhaps to keep their positive image intact, the two governors started to protect their records. Both of them also prevented the NCDC officials from visiting their states on the grounds that they would bring in the virus into their states. This sounded plausible particularly for Cross River State whose governor had taken proactive measures against COVID-19 based on his scientific and professional knowledge as a professor in a related field. This could not be said of his Kogi State counterpart, who was simply grandstanding.

Over time, officials of federal health authorities reached understanding with the Cross River State Government and both moved on from there with little hiccups here and there. However, the relationship with Kogi State Government got bad and kept on degenerating. It was as if the federal authorities allowed the governor to have his way, and were no more concerned about the state's intransigence. In fact, it appears that the NCDC officials and indeed those of the PTF and Federal Ministry of Health were too soft on Kogi by taking cover under the fact that health is on the Concurrent List of the 1999 Constitution (as amended). The fact that the federal government was giving out funds to the states to help control the spread of the virus, demanded more supervisory actions against the state than was witnessed.

Policy Lessons from the Federal Government's soft treatment given to Kogi State

The apparent soft treatment given to Kogi state should not have been so, for an issue that posed serious danger to public health. If the federal authorities had leveraged on their legitimate power of setting national health minimum standards, and also applied the carrot and stick policy to get the states to fall into line, Kogi state would have had no choice but to fall into line earlier enough to avert arriving at the high risk appellation that it later acquired.

There are few lessons for effective inter-governmental relations management in the interest of public health. First, the federal health authorities should not be too soft in such similar situations in the future. Secondly, this softness in itself was a disservice to good and effective public health management in Nigeria. Lastly, national health standards should always be enforced across the states regardless of how governors feel. Our public health management is too important to be sacrificed on the altar of palpable intransigence of any particular governor.

CHAPTER THIRTY ONE

COVID-19 Numbers and the 10 Leading States
(February 2020-February 2021)

After one year of COVID-19 pandemic in Nigeria, the analysis of the cases of infection and death across some selected states revealed a trend which emanated from mistakes made by the governors of those states during the early period of the pandemic. The analysis was based on the argument made in an earlier chapter that the mistakes made in the month of March 2020 (when the various states in Nigeria ought to have waged the war more energetically against the spread of the virus) was the major cause of the continued rise in the number of infections and deaths. The discussion in this chapter is an amplification of this thesis. By COVID-19 numbers, we mean (a) the number of cases of infection confirmed, (b) number of cases on admission, (c) number discharged, and (d) number of deaths recorded.

What the Numbers Reveal

In June 2020, the total number of COVID-19 cases recorded in Nigeria was 13,464. A disaggregation of this number on state basis showed that Lagos State had 6,065 and FCT had 1,012, both of which (7,077) contributed 53% of the total number of COVID-19 infections in Nigeria then. This disproportionate figure from two sub-national level governments was understandable as many people came into Nigeria through the two major airports in Lagos and Abuja, before the closure of airports all over the country thereafter.

A further disaggregation of the total number of infections on state basis also revealed that many states whose governors had high profile interactions in Abuja around the mid-month of March were also among the highest contributors to the total figure as of that date. As we observed in an earlier Chapter, 16 APC governors under the Progressives Governors Forum held a meeting in Abuja on 16 March 2020 with President Muhammadu Buhari and his late Chief of Staff, Abba Kyari in attendance. As earlier noted also, many of these governors returned to their states and continued with a business-as-usual mentality and failed to recognize COVID-19 pandemic as a public health emergency.

A close look at the table below reveals that after one year of COVID-19 in Nigeria, all the states whose governors participated in the March 2020 meeting in Abuja were still among the 10 leading states with COVID-19 numbers in February 2021. Oyo and Rivers states are exceptions as their governors were not in the Abuja meeting. As we noted earlier, Oyo state governor hosted a PDP mega rally in Ibadan around the same time and this led to spread of the virus with the governor himself, getting infected. Regrettably, Rivers State whose governor was not in the Abuja meeting later joined in recording a very high number of infections like many of these other states, in spite of the early commendable efforts of Governor Nyesom Wike to check the spread of the virus in his state.

Ten leading States with COVID-19 numbers (Thursday, 9.40pm February, 25, 2021)

States Affected	No. of Cases Confirmed	No. of Cases on Admission	No. Discharged	No. of Deaths
Lagos	55,122	2,128	52,591	403
FCT	19,115	7,145	11,827	143
Plateau	8,854	109	8,688	57
Kaduna	8,422	217	8,143	62
Oyo	6,708	1,012	5,586	110
Rivers	6,398	316	5,990	92
Edo	4,491	589	3,740	162
Ogun	4,277	728	3,503	46
Kano	3,716	208	3,405	103
Ondo	2,944	807	2,080	57

Source: Extracted from NCDC via https://covid19.ncdc.gov.ng/

The Aftermath of March 2020 Mistakes

It is also argued here that the March 2020 mistakes contributed indirectly in leading Nigeria into the community transmission stage of COVID-19 spread. The statistics support the argument that there was a link between actions or inactions of many governors in mid-March 2020, and the pattern of the spread of the virus subsequently.

In terms of the total number of deaths recorded across states within the same period, the table further shows that a couple of other states outside the 10 leading ones whose governors attended the meeting were Osun with 50 deaths, Kwara with 49 deaths, Gombe with 43 deaths, and Borno with 38 deaths. However, one state whose governor was not at the Abuja meeting but which recorded a very high number of deaths comparable to the 10 leading states was Delta with 65 deaths. In terms of the total number of cases confirmed which was used to rank the states in the table above, Delta (not listed in the table above) ranks number 12, with Kwara State ranks number 11.

Useful Policy Lesson

There is one major lesson from this analysis for the future response to any pandemic or even epidemic. The experience from some of the states closely studied, demonstrates that failure to take early actions (preventive, enforcement and therapeutic, testing and contact tracing) against the spread of the COVID-19 after the index case was confirmed, invariably put the virus ahead of those fighting against it. It is a fact that the virus was always running faster than those fighting it.

Although Nigeria's national policy response was on average noteworthy and commendable, the lack of preparedness and the initial delays experienced in March and April 2020 before the lockdown, led to the spread of the virus. The late closure of two of Nigeria's major international airports namely Lagos and FCT made it possible for travellers into Nigeria to bring in the virus. This point was underscored in an earlier Chapter on the temporizing style of President Buhari. Although Lagos and FCT swiftly confronted the virus, however, the virus was already ahead of them. Experience from the United States also shows that the failure of former President Donald Trump to take proactive measures to fight the virus put the US continuously behind it. As of 25 February 2021 (2.23pm East Coast American time), the US had the unenviable record of having the highest number of confirmed cases of over 28 million (i.e. 28,336,566), as well as the highest number of deaths 505,899.[166] The trend continued under former President Trump and only got reversed during President Joe Biden administration.

---

[166] See https:/coronavirus.jhu.edu/.

Part Five
Private Sector Policy Response (CACOVID), and Citizens' Uncooperative Behaviour to COVID-19 Policy Interventions

CHAPTER THIRTY TWO

CACOVID and the Fight against COVID-19 in Nigeria

Nigeria on Saturday June 6, 2020 marked the 100 days since the index case of COVID-19 was recorded in Lagos on 27 February 2020. At the national briefing on Monday June 8, 2020, Boss Mustapha, the chairman of the Presidential Task Force on COVID-19 (PTF on COVID-19), rightly said in his remarks that, "there are several on-going infrastructure interventions being made by government, development partners and the private sector nationwide". The last hundred days, he equally noted, have "brought out the best in the spirit of Nigerians. There has been tremendous private sector and corporate mobilisation". This very apropos recognition by the PTF chairman, of the contributions made by the private sector on the war against COVID-19 in Nigeria deserves further attention and elaboration in this chapter. This is because the *private sector* Coalition Against COVID-19 (CACOVID), is in our view, a brilliant and innovative initiative formed to support the fight against COVID-19 in Nigeria.

Origin, Goal and Objectives of CACOVID

With the establishment of the PTF on COVID-19 by President Mohammad Buhari on 9 March 2020, the private sector in its wisdom shortly afterwards, formed CACOVID on 26 March 2020 as its own task force to partner "with the Federal Government, the Nigeria Centre for Disease Control (NCDC) and the World Health Organisation (WHO), with the sole aim of combating Coronavirus (COVID-19) in Nigeria." In order to achieve this, CACOVID tasked itself with "pulling resources across industries to provide technical and operational support while providing funding and building advocacy through aggressive awareness drives." This innovative and commendable initiative was "spearheaded by Aliko Dangote, Herbert Wigwe, and other private sector leaders."[167]

---

[167] Private Sector Coalition Against COVID-19 (CACOVID) (2020): 'About Us', via https://www.cacovid.org/#aboutUs.

The announcement of the formation of this task force was, however, made by Godwin Emefiele, the Governor of the Central Bank of Nigeria (CBN).

Primarily inspired by its motto of 'Staying Alive Together', the goal of CACOVID was 'to have as many organisations (companies, philanthropists, donors) join this effort to effectively complement Government's efforts to combat Covid-19'. And its objectives were to: (a) support the Nigerian Government in its efforts to combat Coronavirus in Nigeria; (b) mobilise private sector thought leadership; (c) utilise the resources of the private sector; (d) provide direct support to private and public healthcare's ability to respond to this crisis; and (e) increase general public awareness of the existence of Coronavirus (COVID-19).[168]

In its first Press Release, CACOVID made one of the most outstandingly powerful statements about the need to form a united front to fight COVID-19 in Nigeria. The statement reads:

> From China to Chile, Mexico to Italy, and from Switzerland to South Africa, the World is being dragged through a tunnel of despair, doom and uncertainty, with the collective fear of the unknown putting civilization and economies at great risk.COVID-19 may be the most powerful adversary Nigeria has ever faced, but with our unity of purpose it can be defeated. Now is the time to draw from our wellspring of courage to challenge the virus and conquer it. It is time to take responsibility for one another and truly be our brother and sister's keeper with overall support across all ages, races, tribes, political and religious affiliations. Out of this collective desire to protect and preserve humanity, the Coalition Against COVID-19 (CACOVID) was born, to fight the spread of the virus in Nigeria; a singular mission worth fighting for. With sustained focus on putting in place all the measures needed to flatten the curve in the shortest possible time, the members of this coalition have no doubt in the will and their capacity to overcome COVID-19 and preserve this country for future generations yet unborn. Together we can, Together we will.[169]

---

[168] Ibid.
[169] Ibid

This was a courageous commitment and undertaking judged against the fact that at the time of its release, COVID was killing people in great numbers across the world and was the most single dreaded phenomenon on earth. It was at this time that CACOVID rolled up its sleeves to fight the virus.

In its second press release (also very powerful) supporting the first, CACOVID rightly said again:

> There is a time for everything in life. This is the time to rise up and fight as one against a scourge that is currently ravaging countries and laying entire economies to waste.
>
> This is the moment for all corporate organizations to unite against a common enemy, the coronavirus (COVID- 19), and tackle it before it takes all of us down the path of recession and ruin. The current daily statistics of COVID-19 infections, emerges only from tests conducted. There may be other infections out there and we need not live in ignorance. This calls for a concerted effort geared towards ensuring that our beloved country, Nigeria, is saved from this ravaging plague.
>
> It is therefore essential to build synergy among all stakeholders for a better stronger and bigger coalition which can harness pulled resources and commonwealth to sustain and eventually win this battle. This is the time for Team CACOVID (Private Sector Coalition Against COVID- 19} to make a historical change and help humanity. This is the time for other peers to join the action.
>
> Delay is dangerous, the time to act one is now! Join Us.[170]

Management of CA-COVID

With respect to management of CACOVID's activities, there are three committees with each responsible for funding, intellectual leadership and operations. The *Funding Committee* is responsible for funding and raising funds for all activities. This committee is made up of the following people: Godwin Emefiele, Aliko Dangote, Herbert Wigwe, Abdulsamad Rabiu, Femi Otedola, Folorunso Alakija, Jim Ovia, John Coumantaros, Raj Gupta, Segun Agbaje, Tony Elumelu and Modupe Alakija.

---

[170] Ibid

The *Technical Committee* is responsible for intellectual leadership around testing issues, treatment protocols, isolation centres, amongst others. Members of this committee are: Prof. Akin Abayomi (Lagos State Commissioner for health), Dhamari Naidoo (WHO), Dr. Christian Happy, Dr. Phillip Onyebujo, Chikwe Ihekweazu (NCDC), Paulin Basing (Bill and Melinda Gates Foundation), Zouera Youssoufou (Aliko Dangote Foundation), Omobolanle Victor-Laniyan (Access Bank).

Lastly, the *Operational Committee* is responsible for project management, logistics and communication. The members of this committee are: Amaechi Okobi (Access Bank), Tony Chiejina (Dangote Group), Osayi Alile (ACT Foundation), representatives of Zenith Bank, GT Bank, First Bank, Stanbic IBTC, Ecobank, Fidelity Bank, Unity Bank, Nigerian Breweries Plc.[171]

Achievements

CACOVID had after short period of its existence in 2020 achieved its lofty goal and objectives. First, with respect to its goal of mobilising many organisations (companies, philanthropists and donors), CACOVID was able to mobilise many private sector organisations within and outside the country as members. As its website showed then, there were 109 partnering members as of Saturday, June 13, 2020. It is impressive that its membership cuts across all industry trade groups in the private sector. There were also individual donors whose names were listed as contributors to CACOVID relief funds. It is even more impressive that CACOVID was able to mobilise some notable organisations outside the country such as CNN and other multinational companies.

Part of the remarkable achievement of CACOVID was the provision and equipping of medical facilities in the six geopolitical zones in Nigeria. This involved the creation of testing, isolation and treatment centres (*see pictures below showing two of such centres located in Kano and Port-Harcourt*), as well as the provision of Intensive Care Units (ICUs) and molecular testing laboratories across the country.

---

[171] CACOVID (2020): 'About Us"via https://www.cacovid.org/#aboutUs.

As a task force, CACOVID swiftly commenced operations in an emergency responsive manner. For example, in line with its motto of 'Staying Alive Together', it wasted no time embarking on massive distribution of palliatives to mitigate the hardship caused by the lockdown restrictions imposed to stop the spread of COVID-19. This was done across the country without discrimination.

Source: CACOVID (2020): 'About Us" via https://www.cacovid.org/#aboutUs.

In line with the swift manner of carrying out its operations, CACOVID started work immediately with the provision of facilities in Lagos (1,000 beds), Kano (500 beds), Rivers (210 beds), Abuja (200 beds), Enugu (200 beds) and Borno (200 beds). It also started working on setting up facilities in Katsina, Ogun, Bayelsa, Anambra, Bauchi and Plateau states. It delivered these projects in the various states.

The progress recorded then (from just two laboratories at the commencement of the war against COVID-19, to 33) with the establishment of Molecular Testing Laboratories by the NCDC across the states at its earlier and most difficult stages, was very impressive within a limited period of time. It was unimaginable to think that this would have been possible without the active support of CACOVID. This was a major and commendable achievement.

Furthermore, a look at the CACOVID's Fundraising Thermometer shows that its target was to raise N120 billion in support of the fight against COVID-19 in Nigeria. However for the year 2020, CACOVID total expenditure was N38,594,085,824.97 (nearly N39 billion). A breakdown of CACOVID's items of expenditure is presented in table 2 below:

Table 2*: CACOVID Items of Expenditure by Category for the Year 2020

S/No	Category of Expenditure	Amount in Naira	Percentage (%)
1.	Welfare	22,215,669,287.40	57.56
2.	Case Management	8,569,031,064.21	22.2
3	IPC	3,443,583,896.5	8.92
4	Laboratory	2,568,993,134.61	6.66
5	Logistics	904,704,931.07	2.34
6	Branding & Communication	772,762,991.18	2.00
7	Surveillance	119,340,520.00	0.31
Total		38,594,085,824.97	

Source: CACOVID (2020): 'About Us"via https://www.cacovid.org/#aboutUs.
*This was put in a Tabular form by the Author

The priority given to welfare (taking about 58% of the expenditure) reflected the major and pressing needs of the people during the COVID-19 lockdown. During that particular period, what was called *hunger-virus* constituted equally a big problem to the generality of the people particularly those who depended on daily wages to make a living. The spending of 22% of the total expenditure to case management again reflected the prevailing need of managing COVID infections and providing the necessary support.

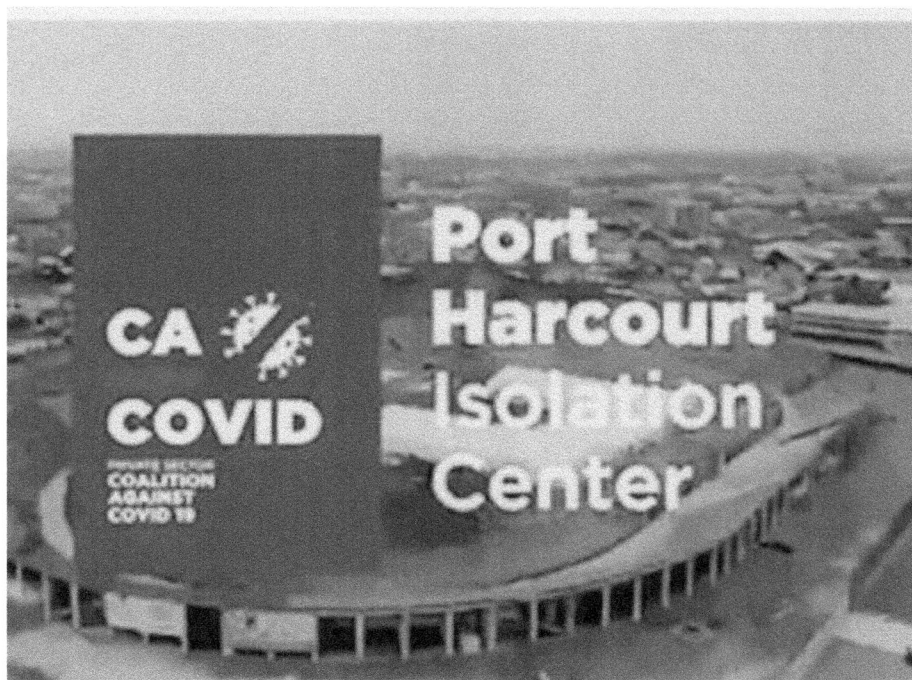

Source: CACOVID (2020): 'About Us" via https://www.cacovid.org/#aboutUs.

Generally therefore, we can itemise CACOVID's major areas of achievements to include (a) food relief palliatives targeting 1.67 million households (with 10 million vulnerable Nigerians in all the 774 LGAs); (b) purchase and distribution of ventilators, PPEs, and testing kits. For example, it ordered 400,000 test kits for distribution; (c) funding part of the Surveillance Outbreak Response Management and Analysis System (SORMAS); (d) providing for logistics cost of ambulances and movement of patients in the enormous contact tracing exercises across the states; and (e) carrying out aggressive advocacy and public enlightenment campaigns.[172] It is on this note that CACOVID is commended for its excellent service to humanity during the fight against COVID-19 pandemic in Nigeria.

---

[172] See https://nairametrics.com/2020/05/12...

CHAPTER THIRTY THREE

Mega Rallies and Protests under COVID-19

During the most risky period of COVID-19 pandemic, the crowding of people (whether indoors or out-doors) was prohibited. This is why the keeping of social distancing was one of the most important non-pharmaceutical safety measures under COVID-19. Holding of mega political rallies during such risky period, was therefore considered dangerous and unacceptable. Unfortunately, politicians appeared not to care about such serious safety protocol, the breach of which had some unintended consequences on the youths who came to believe that COVID-19 was no longer a major problem in the country. Be that as it may, this chapter examines one of the unintended consequences of the mega political rallies on the behaviour of the youths.

Mage Political Rallies in Edo and Ondo States and their Aftermath

When politicians campaigned during the Edo and Ondo governorship elections held on 19 September 19, and October 10, 2020 respectively, little regard was given to the observance of the non-pharmaceutical guidelines and protocols issued by the Nigeria Centre for Disease Control (NCDC) for stopping the spread of the coronavirus pandemic. For instance, the issue of crowd management during the rallies was entirely neglected even when the politicians had promised to organize their rallies in compliance with the NCDC guidelines. As the first two pictures of campaign rallies below reveal, the politicians, at best paid lip service to the NCDC guidelines. Little did it occur to them then that our youths who formed part of the mammoth crowd at many of the campaign rallies held in different parts of the two states, were watching keenly.

•Mammoth crowd at PDP political rally in Edo State, 2020 (Source: Nairaland Forum & Picture by eseosa77 (m)

There is little doubt that the youths must have gone away with the wrong impression that the fight against COVID-19 was no longer an issue to worry about. Even if it was, there was neither enforcement nor penalty for non-compliance by the politicians who operated in their business-as-usual-mentality. Regrettably, the risk communication messages regularly sent out by the Presidential Task Force on COVID-19 and the NCDC during the period of the campaign appeared not to have yielded the desired attitudinal and behavioural changes.

•**Mammoth Crowd at APC Political Rally in Edo, 2020 (Source: NaijaNews.com)**

The Effects of the big gathering at the 60th Independence Anniversary

When the Federal Government of Nigeria celebrated the 60th Independence anniversary on 1st October 2020, our youths watched the crowd that gathered at the Eagle Square, Abuja, the venue of the colourful event. Although, the organizers observed the COVID-19 guidelines and protocols with respect to all the VIPs that sat at the arena, but such could not be said entirely of the large crowd of other people at the event. There was a large crowd made up of security forces that took part in the parade, some people who performed cultural dances and displays at the ceremony, as well as others like journalists who covered the event in a crowded vantage position. Even though on balance, the event was not a complete violation of the COVID-19 guidelines, the youths who were watching it would likely go away with the impression that things had become normal with respect to gathering of large people in public.

•**Cultural Troupe on display (with large crowd at the background) during the 60th Independence anniversary on October 1, 2020, at the Eagle Square, Abuja (Source: thisdaylive.com...)**

The *#EndSARS* Protests and its Effects on the Second Wave of COVID-19 in Nigeria

Based on these two cited events that occurred between the months of September and October 2020, it was not surprising to see a mammoth crowd of youths under the #EndSARS protest, showing a total disregard for the COVID-19 guidelines and protocols. Looking at the two pictures below, they gave the impression that Nigeria was no longer fighting the battle against COVID-19 pandemic which was then still killing thousands of people in the United States of America, Brazil and India, among many other places. Europe for example, was at that particular time witnessing its second wave which was not only devastating their economies, but also causing tensions between the people and their governments with respect to the imposition of more restrictions to curb the spread of the virus. This goes to demonstrate that a total disregard for the COVID-19 social distancing protocol by the #EndSARs protesters, in pursuit of their constitutionally guaranteed rights of peaceful protest, was a dangerous risk that eventually caused the second wave of the virus in Nigeria thereafter.

•EndSARS protesters at the Murtala Muhammed Airport, Ikeja, (Source: https://www.aljazeera.com/… Benson Ibeabuchi/AFP)

#EndSARS Protesters at the Lekki Toll Gate, Lagos (Source: Quartz Africa via qz.com/africa…

It was in this regard that Boss Mustapha, Chairman of the Presidential Task Force (PTF) on COVID-19, while reminding the nation of the negative health impact of the #EndSARS protests, warned of the danger ahead as the protests would likely lead to a resurgence of the virus. He warned that the youths protest would lead to rising cases of infections.

As the PTF Chairman put it:

> I can say it authoritatively that with the ongoing protest across the country, in the next two weeks the cases of COVID-19 would have increased. Each and every one that attended the protest and did not put up any form of protection, is likely going to spread the virus. When people contract the virus during the protest gathering, they will go back home and spread it.[173]

He rightly called the *End SARS* protects 'a super spreader event'. Although the super spreader event was worrisome, but more worrisome was the fact that the youths in such a huge number showed a total disregard for the guidelines and protocols meant to keep them alive. Put differently, why would the youths show far greater interest in their #EndSARS cause, than in respecting the NCDC guidelines meant to protect their precious lives? One possible and plausible reason is their state of hopelessness.

Arresting Youth Restlessness

For too long, the youths had found life meaningless, helpless and more regrettably hopeless. If hope at least existed, many of them would show caution and patience. In the absence of hope (and in midst of more hostile policies, it became difficult to dissuade them from participating in such risky protests under COVID-19. This is a serious psychological issue which should give any responsive government a food for thought. There is no gainsaying the fact that the youths need meaningful jobs where they can make their careers and start meaningful lives. Although such stop-gap job opportunities as SURE-P, N-Power, public works in 774 Local Government Areas (LGAs) by the federal government, are good as temporary interventions, the need for sustainable and well-

---

[173] National Briefing on COVID-19 held on Monday, October 19, 2020.

paying jobs to enable the youths live fulfilling lives, cannot be over-emphasized.

Lastly, the federal government as a matter of urgency should democratise job opportunities in all its agencies than what presently obtains where people secure employment through privileged connections. As it became clear, the #EndSARS protests was a metaphor for the governance injustice plaguing the country. If it is a fact that many of our meaningfully employed youths did not participate in the #EndSARS protests even when they identified with its CAUSE, it then goes to confirm the saying therefore that *an idle mind is devil's workshop*.

CHAPTER THIRTY FOUR

COVID-19 Crisis Management Amid Protests,
Looting and Chaos

The aftermath of the condemnable shooting at the #EndSARS peaceful protesters at the Lekki Toll Gate in Lagos on Tuesday, October 20, 2020 expanded and compounded the negative effects of mega rallies by politicians and youth protests generally, and particularly on the super-spreading of COVID-19 in Nigeria. As we argued in chapter 33, the mammoth crowds of people at the Edo and Ondo governorship campaign rallies as well as those at the #EndSARS protests, were complete violation of COVID-19 safety guidelines and non-pharmaceutical protocols. Such flagrant violations sent the wrong message that the fight against COVID-19 crisis had either been won already or was not taken seriously by the generality of the people.

Unintended Consequences of the #EndSARS Protests

Although the large crowds of people at the #EndSARS peaceful protests was already a threat to the effective containment of the virus, the take-over of the protests by hoodlums was like pouring fuel in an already raging fire. The #EndSARS protests across the country, took a turn for the worst when very hungry and angry hoodlums turned it into an anarchical situation and started looting public properties and setting them on fire. They also did the same to private businesses and properties. Picture 1 below which shows BRT buses on fire, is just one of the many Lagos State government properties burnt or vandalized. The huge negative impact of such lawless acts on Nigeria's ailing and struggling economy (already devastated by COVID-19 pandemic) became very palpable and highly regrettable for a country which had already acquired the appellation then as the poverty capital of the world.

•Picture 1: Oyingbo Bus Rapid Transport (BRT) terminus set on fire by hoodlums in Lagos (Source: Premium Times, Wednesday, October 21, 2020.)

Unknowingly to these miscreants, their unsavoury acts further made the effective management of COVID-19 scourge very difficult for many states particularly Lagos which was for long time the epicentre of the virus in Nigeria. This was indeed unfortunate for a state which had all along maintained a commendable record of a dogged and focused fight against the virus from DAY ONE. For example, the records revealed then that Lagos State and the Federal Capital Territory Administration (FCTA) so far, were the only sub-national governments that had met the requirement of testing up to 1% of their population for COVID-19. The massive destruction in Lagos therefore constituted a major drawback in the management of COVID-19 crisis.

Sadly enough, the hoodlums also extended their looting spree to many other states and continued in the same pattern of looting public and private properties and burning them down. In Plateau State for example, the war and tension between hunger and coronavirus reached a crescendo when the hoodlums climbed to the roof of a warehouse to loot COVID-19 palliatives. Picture 2 below shows how a massive crowd of people totally disregarded the social distancing safety guidelines on COVID-19 in search of palliatives.

•**Picture 2: Looters attacking from both the ground and the roof of the COVID-19 Palliatives Warehouse in Bukuru, Jos, Plateau State, October 24, 2020** *(Source: Screenshot of a social media circulated video).*

Looting of Medical Stores as great damage to Public Health

Regrettably again, in a couple of states, medical stores (pharmaceutical warehouses) serving strategic interest were looted, vandalised or burnt down. In Cross River State for example, hoodlums went to the Infectious Disease Hospital, Calabar and stole COVID-19 testing machines. Worst still, the hoodlums visited and looted one of the offices of the World Health Organisation (WHO). According to its African Regional Director, Dr. Matshidiso Moeti, the hoodlums looted one of its offices making away with Personal Protective Equipment (PPT) and other items used in tackling the COVID-19 pandemic in the country.[174] This was indeed a great national embarrassment. It appeared confusing

---

[174] See Punch newspaper Thursday, October 29, 2020, via https://punchng.com/endsars-hoodlums-stole-covid-19-equipment-says-who/.

Chapter Thirty four | Isaac Nnamdi Obasi

235

to unravel the motive for stealing COVID-19 equipment and materials by looters. Was it hunger for example, as a result of poverty? Was it ignorance as a result of lack of proper education? Was it deep-seated anger against those in government? Furthermore, was it sheer wickedness as a result of lack of patriotism or all of the above? Whatever the answer was, the hoodlums were simply causing great damage to the public health system and to themselves particularly, as these heinous acts were counter-productive to the COVID-19 crisis management. For those riotous looters, the Nigeria Centre for Disease Control (NCDC) safety guidelines on physical distancing were meaningless, as none of them observed the guidelines in their actions. This again was a real danger to public health as such riotous large gatherings without physical distancing, constituted a big threat to even those who were not in physical contact with them.

Coronavirus Vs Hunger-virus

One very noticeable behaviour of the looters was their total disregard for the NCDC safety guidelines. The looters appeared not to be afraid of COVID-19 any longer, rather more afraid of *hunger-virus* given the nature of their ferocious struggle to loot warehouses of COVID-19 palliatives. At the Bukuru warehouse in Jos, Plateau State for instance, one of the looters attributed their action to hunger. According to him, everybody is here (Christians and Moslems) looking for what to eat, rather than fighting one another; - we are no more fighting - 'suffer too much for Nigeria'[175]. Picture 3 below shows the desperation of looters in search of food items.

---

[175] AIT News report, October 24 & 25, 2020.

•**Picture 3: 'Hunger-virus' Vs Coronavirus: Looters on rooftop of a food warehouse** *(Source: Linda Ikeji's Blog via https://www.lindaikejisblog.com/2020/10/residents-break-into-warehouse-in-plateau-state-loot-covid-19-palliatives.html.*

Again in Abuja, a disappointed looter who was talking to AIT reporter spoke of coronavirus in the past tense as if the scourge was already over (i.e. probably referring to the lockdown period). This disappointed looter was among those prevented by armed policemen and soldiers from gaining access to the Cyprian Ekwensi Centre, Garki[176] in search of palliatives previously stored in the compound during the lockdown. According to him, "during that coronavirus time, we saw trailers carrying many-many things gala, indomie, rice..."[177]

Lastly, during the period of the #EndSARS protests and the anarchy subsequently created by the hoodlums looting everything they could lay their hands on, testing for COVID-19 by the states were either slowed down or completely abandoned, due to unsafe conditions for carrying out the testing

---

[176] Formerly called National Council for Arts and Culture, Garki
[177] Also in AIT News report, October, 24 & 25, 2020.

activities. The result has been the low testing numbers reported by the NCDC over this period. For example, on the 24th of October, 48 new cases were reported from only six states. On October 25, it was 62 new cases, and on October 26, it was 119 new cases. Then on October 27, it was 113, and lastly on October 28, the number was 147 new cases. These numbers did not in any way reflect the reality in the population, as it only reflected low testing capacity of the states within the period. This was another major setback in the COVID-19 crisis management. No one was surprised much later that Nigeria went into the second wave of COVID-19 shortly after the period of riotous protests across the country.

CHAPTER THIRTY FIVE

Premature vanishing of fear of COVID-19
in Nigeria and its Consequences

Since the period of mammoth political rallies in both Edo and Ondo states (September and October, 2020), and followed closely by the #EndSARS protests and its aftermath, Nigerians degenerated further to abysmal level in their observance of the non-pharmaceutical protocols. Prior to this, the citizens' non-compliance level to COVID-19 safety rules were very poor. A close observation of how Nigerians were behaving would have made one to conclude right away that the war against the virus was over. The world (including Nigeria) was "still in the middle of this pandemic" as Boss Mustapha (Chairman of PTF on COVID-19) would always put it when making passionate appeal to Nigerians to obey the non-pharmaceutical protocols and guidelines during that most risky period of the pandemic.

Dynamics of Compliance to Safety Rules amidst Global Surge

During the early period of the pandemic (when the virus was raging and ravaging lives across the world), people were very cautious to perverse their lives. As time progressed, people started getting weary about being very careful. For example, towards the last quarter of 2020, Nigerians started behaving as if the pandemic was over, even when records of deaths were still high. This was reflected in their low level of compliance to the risk communication messages by the PTF on COVID-19 and the NCDC. But the fast vanishing fears of the virus were premature. Records of what was happening then in some parts of the world such as Europe, United States of America, South America, India, and Australia, showed that the virus had even become deadlier since its first wave in China and Europe. At this point in time too (i.e. November 19, 2020 (at 3.45 pm Eastern Time) the Johns Hopkins University records showed that the world had recorded a total number of 56.7 million COVID-19 cases and about 1.4 million deaths.

The statistics in five countries with the highest number of infections and fatalities clearly demonstrate that COVID-19 pandemic was still very dangerous as it was in China about a year ago at this last quarter of 2020. The statistics released by Johns Hopkins University as at the same date and time above, revealed that the United States of America had 11,647,930 total number of cases of infections, and 251,756 deaths. This was followed by India with 8,958,483 total number of cases and 131,578 deaths; and then Brazil 5,945,849 cases and 167,455 deaths; France with 2,087,196 cases and 46,795 deaths; and lastly Russia with 1,998,966 cases and 34,525 deaths.

At this time too, there were a number of countries, however, that recorded total number of deaths much higher than either France or Russia among the first five countries above. Such countries were Mexico with 99,528 deaths; United Kingdom with 53,755 deaths; Italy with 47,870 deaths; Iran 43,417 deaths; Spain with 42,291 deaths; Peru with 35,317 deaths; and lastly Colombia with 34,563 deaths. In terms of the total number of deaths recorded alone, Mexico ranks fourth after France. The United Kingdom with 53,755 deaths had higher figure than France and Russia listed among the five countries above.

The central message here then was that the fact that many countries had recorded very high number of deaths should ordinarily put fear into the minds of people across the world. This was not the case in some countries, as many people did not seem to care much about respecting or observing the non-pharmaceutical protocols. For example, former President Donald Trump of the United States, had made such safety measures (like wearing of masks) a huge political issue. Surprisingly, many people in some countries of the world were even protesting against the observance of safety measures introduced by their governments.

In Nigeria, the lower number of cases and deaths in relation to other nations reported above could be contributing to making people not to be afraid of COVID-19 any longer. Nigeria then had recorded 65,693 total number of infections and 1,163 deaths (as at the same 3.45 pm Eastern Time reported by the Johns Hopkins University). Nigeria no doubt and other African countries, were enjoying God's mercy otherwise millions of people would have died had the virus been ravaging the country like it was doing in USA, Europe, India and Latin America among other places. Why should Nigerians be taking this divine favour for granted? As the saying goes, heaven helps those who help themselves. The consequences for taking things for granted by abandoning the observance of the non-pharmaceutical protocols were very catastrophic.

Consequences of Poor Compliance

First, economically, Nigeria was too weak to experience another wave of the virus. It experienced this later at grave consequences. The various governments across the three tiers were struggling to meet their enormous financial obligations. The execution of both the capital and recurrent expenditures were seriously challenged by paucity of funds.

Secondly, Nigeria's health system was equally too weak to withstand any further stress of its infrastructure and facilities. In human terms, the health professionals and allied workers who had been working very hard and making enormous sacrifice since the outbreak of the virus were already experiencing serious fatigue to face such a new scaring challenge. These patriotic Nigerians had been working under poor conditions of service, as some previous chapters revealed. Hence the observance of the non-pharmaceutical protocols, would help them a lot.

Lastly, the level of poverty in Nigeria was unprecedentedly high as the poverty capital of the world. In such economic situation, it would be catastrophic to experience a second wave. Nigeria still experienced a second wave at a very high cost as many more people died. At this period of the pandemic then, millions of people were struggling to eat, as unemployment was very high that those working were basically sharing their salaries at the end of the month among the endless list of requests from relatives, friends, well-wishers, or even acquaintances and unknown people whom they came into contact with in the course of daily activities. Burial ceremonies requiring assistance from those working had become endless. Indeed things had become harder than they were before the pandemic. The reality of it was that many people were literarily begging at the end of the month but in a disguised manner.

Then it was surprising that with all these challenges, people were still not ready to help themselves by preventing a more calamitous health situation. All that was required of them was simply the wearing of face masks and observing other less difficult or burdensome non-pharmaceutical protocols. This contradiction in behaviour appeared to be a mystery which social psychologists could help to unravel.

CHAPTER THIRTY SIX

PTF on COVID-19 Handling of Non-Compliant International Air Passengers

The end of December 2020 marked the expiration of the extension granted to the Presidential Task Force on COVID-19 (PTF on COVID-19) by President Buhari. The three-month extension of the end-date of the PTF by the president was made in September, 2020. The PTF was established on the 9th of March 2020 to "coordinate and oversee Nigeria's multi-sectoral inter-governmental efforts to contain the spread and mitigate the impact of COVID-19 pandemic in Nigeria." One major aspect of its task, was focused on managing international air passengers whose movements across nations posed a significant threat to national efforts to contain the spread of the virus. This chapter discusses the PTF's handling of non-compliant international air travellers.

PTF as a Task Force: Some background issues

As we pointed out in an earlier chapter, a task force generally is a *special-purpose-vehicle* for executing a time-bound important project requiring urgent attention. A project by its very nature has a completion date after which its management team gets disbanded or simply ceases to exist. As an *ad hoc* body therefore, the *PTF on COVID-19* was not an exception, but with respect to the PTF, the uncertain nature of COVID-19 made its own life span uncertain also.

After one year of COVID-19, its resurgence (by way of second, third or more waves) in countries it had ravaged earlier, created a dilemma on the end-date of the PTF on COVID-19. This uncertainty also imposed additional burden on the PTF to achieve its primary purpose as fast as possible. Here comes a dilemma as well as a burden.

Following the gradual easing of Phases Two and Three lockdown restrictions (which allowed among other things the reopening of markets, churches, schools, offices, and airports), the job of the PTF on COVID-19 and more specifically that of the Nigeria Centre for Disease Control (NCDC), had become even more enormous. This was because more than ever before, they were expected to keep their eyes constantly on the ball to contain the further spread of the virus amid the high risk associated with large crowds in the reopened places. In addition, the PTF and NCDC had even bigger task to fight for the containment of the spread of the virus during the festive season involving increased domestic and international travels.

Reopening of International Air Travels and High level of Non-Compliance with PCR Test

The reopening of international air travels with passengers sometimes from countries still suffering very high rate of infections and deaths, posed one of the greatest challenges to the success story of both the PTF on COVID-19 and NCDC during that period in time. There was palpable fear that passengers coming from high risk countries during the festive season (particularly the Christmas period) may be super spreaders of the virus. The possibility of this could lead to higher level of community infections in the country. This possibility was even more dreadful with the revelation by the Chairman of the PTF on COVID-19, Boss Mustapha, that a huge number of 39,070 international travellers have so far shunned the mandatory coronavirus test.[178] This in our view, was both scaring and scandalous, as it constituted a national embarrassment.

According to this startling revelation by Mustapha, some of those who paid for post-arrival test had failed to show up for the tests. Secondly, some of the travellers indulged in presenting fake documents. Elaborating further, Mustapha said that as of November 9, 2020, statistics showed that the total number of bookings was 91,522; total number of passengers exempted (diplomats and some others), 5,470 (6%); children, 1,248 (1.36 per cent); diplomats, 3,392 (3.7 per cent); and evacuees, 830 (0.9 per cent). Again, he said that while the total passengers expected to pay were 86,052 (94 per cent), those that paid were 46,982 (54.6 per cent) and those that had not paid were 39,070 (45.45 per cent).

---

[178] This was during a national briefing on Monday, 23 November 2020. See for example Punch, November 24, 2020) in its report titled: 'FG threatens sanctions as 39,070 travellers shun coronavirus test', or Transport Day newspaper with same title via https://transportday.com.ng/covid-ptf-sanctions-passengers-test/.

Finally, Mustapha announced that the PTF was concluding steps to work with relevant institutions and legal authorities to impose appropriate sanctions on those that defaulted on the protocols.

The proposal to sanction defaulters whose actions posed serious danger to public health was in order, as their actions constituted a betrayal of trust and a serious act of irresponsibility. It would be recalled that this was not the first time that the PTF on COVID-19 threatened sanctions against international passengers on the issue of their non-compliance with COVID-19 safety protocols. In early November 2020 for example, Mustapha revealed that the level of non-compliance by international passengers for compulsory (COVID-19) PCR test was very high.[179]

Consequent upon this observed high level of non-compliance, the PTF threatened to prevent travellers who refused to make themselves available for compulsory PCR test, seven days after arriving the country from using their international passports for a minimum of six months. The PTF revealed that this non-compliance by defaulters had reached a 65 per cent level. Furthermore, the PTF regretted that statistics from record indicated that only one out of three passengers, who arrived from abroad, were presenting themselves for the mandatory in-country test, which they signed up to and paid before arrival. To demonstrate further how serious the matter was, the National Coordinator of PTF on COVID-19, Dr. Sani Aliyu, vowed that the PTF would publish the list of the first 100 persons to be suspended for defaulting on the compulsory test and suspend their passport for six months.

Enforcement as Key to Achieving Results

In policy management, implementation (and in this case enforcement) is key to achieving desired goals, and this is particularly important for a COVOD-19 risky issue which poses great danger to public health. The urgent enforcement of sanctions against defaulters by the PTF was the

---

[179] See a news report by THISDAY titled 'FG Considers Passport Ban for Passengers Breaching COVID-19 Test', November 4, 2020 via: https://www.thisdaylive.com/index.php /2020/11/04/fg-considers-passport-ban-for-passengers-breaching-covid-19-test/.

way to go. If this was not done, the defaulters would continue to operate with their business-as-usual mentality of high level of non-compliance. It was right that impunity of such irresponsible actions should be checked always. It is unthinkable that none of the defaulters would ever shun the mandatory tests in their places of residence abroad. This is because they knew that they would suffer severe consequences. The same culture of enforcement should be obtainable in Nigeria. Nobody should be given the opportunity to continue to take Nigeria for granted. Enforcement remained one of the effective measures for preventing the spread of the virus in communities that were relatively free of infections.

CHAPTER THIRTY SEVEN

The Challenge of Adjusting to New Normal
Under COVID-19

The phrase new normal is not as new as many in Nigeria and in other parts of the world would think. Actually, the use of the phrase predates the period of COVID-19 pandemic. However, its frequent usage has become popularized and even polarized under COVID-19. Simply put, the phrase 'new normal' encapsulates all that is generally known now as the non-pharmaceutical protocols in the war against the spread of COVID-19 pandemic.

•*The New Normal: with face mask and physical distancing:* *Governor El-Rufai and CAN President Reverend Supo Ayokunle flanked by some other officials. (Source: Kaduna State Government Media (KDSG) August 18, 2020, via https://www.thenewsnigeria.com.ng/2020/08/18/photos-governor-el-rufai-receives-can-leadership/.*

History and definition of the phrase 'New Normal'

History has it that as far back as 1966, an American author, Robert A. Heinlein, used the phrase 'new normal' in his novel titled *The Moon is a harsh Mistress,* to describe a life situation "free of the Authority, free of guards, free of troops stationed on us, free of passports and searches and arbitrary arrests."[180] In later years, the phrase was used in America, China and other places particularly by the powerful media across the world. As an American phrase, 'new normal' is used very aptly to mean a "previously unfamiliar or atypical situation that has become standard, usual, or expected."[181]

In the context of COVID-19 pandemic (with no vaccine then), the concept of 'new normal' operationally refers to the expected new ways of behaviour that promote social and physical distancing among people, regular washing of hands with soap under a running water, avoidance of handshaking and hugging, use of alcohol-based sanitiser to clean the hands after touching surfaces, sneezing into one's elbows or with tissue paper, and a host of other new behavioural practices aimed at stopping the spread of the deadly COVID-19. 'New normal' emerges when people adopt new ways of interaction and abandon an existing or old ways of interaction. When such new ways are practised for a long period of time, such new ways of interaction will also become culturally ingrained or habitual to the extent that they would in turn become normal practice and the word 'new' would be removed from normal.

As a never-ending or evolving phenomenon, a new normal behaviour today may become so deeply and culturally ingrained that it becomes normal tomorrow, and in which case, it losses the title 'new' attached to it. This means that the expected new normal behaviour under COVID-19 may vanish so quickly with the discovery of a vaccine. Had COVID-19 lasted longer without a vaccine, the new normal behaviour would gradually become culturally ingrained and also become difficult to change. This is why a consistent, persuasive, passionate and spirited appeal or message was needed under COVID-19 to change existing

---

[180] See https://en.wikipedia.org/wiki/New_normal.
[181] See https://www.lexico.com/definition/the_new_normal

behaviour to a desired new normal. This persuasive approach for behavioural adjustment to the new normal is also needed because *old habits die hard*, as the saying goes.

The Challenge of adjusting to 'New Normal'

There was a big challenge for people in Nigeria adjusting to the expected new normal behaviour necessary for stopping the spread of the COVID-19. Nigerians generally were finding it difficult to follow the passionate appeal regularly made by the Presidential Task Force on COVID-19 to wear face mask always and to maintain physical distancing when in a large group. Unfortunately, the compliance level were low even among those expected to be role models and who should lead by personal example.

Experience demonstrated that there was no one best way of fighting the war against COVID-19 as there are both pharmaceutical and non-pharmaceutical approaches. The pharmaceutical protocols which are curative or treatment-based are administered by health experts, professionals and workers to fight the war on people's behalf. The non-pharmaceutical protocols which are preventive or deterrent-based are to be observed by everyone else excluding no one whether big or small, rulers or ruled, high/mighty or the lowly. All in this category are expected to join in fighting the war through the strict observance of the non-pharmaceutical protocols.

Although, these non-pharmaceutical protocols are very simple in nature, they however demand a high degree of discipline and personal responsibility on the part of everyone to observe them. And above all, the observance requires some sacrifices or inconveniences, financial cost (expenses incurred in buying face mask or sanitiser for example), as well as attitudinal and behavioural modification or changes to one's life. Embarrassingly, many in authority (both secular and religious) behaved as if they were exempted from complying with the non-pharmaceutical protocols. There were many examples to support this claim but very few examples are used here.

•*Source: Kaduna State Government Media (KDSG) August 18, 2020,
via https://www.thenewsnigeria.com.ng/2020/08/18/photos-governor-el-rufai-receives-can-leadership/*

The picture above showing Governor Nasir el-Rufai of Kaduna State with officials of the Christian Association of Nigeria (CAN) who paid him a visit in Kaduna on Monday, August 17, 2020, did not comply with the expected new normal behaviour, as there was absence of physical distancing and many on the right side of the picture were not wearing face masks. Interestingly, this picture was full of people who ought to know better and show exemplary leadership no matter the situation. Taking the group picture was good for record purposes but it was not more important than preserving life through complying with the COVID-19 new normal behaviour. Incidentally, those in both secular and religious authorities were always appealing to the people to follow the protocols, but some of them did not follow it here.

The picture above can also be interpreted as a clear case of state protocol officials failing in their duty to enforce COVID-19 protocols. This they would have respectfully done with a gentle humour reminding the big officials about the COVID-19 protocols. This author attended a workshop in Abuja with a minister in attendance and where many (while taking a group picture) also violated both the physical distancing and wearing of face marks. When this author gently reminded everyone, the reaction was that everyone laughed it away without complying. This particular picture would have been included here but for the fact that it was not made available to participants and also was not in the public domain unlike the two pictures included above that were in the newspapers.

Furthermore, an embarrassing example of a flagrant violation of COVID-19 protocols happened at a religious service in a very large Pentecostal worship centre of Winners Chapel in Ogun State where religious activities had just been lifted by the state government. This service was the first church service following the lifting of the ban by the Ogun State Government. One therefore expected a high level of compliance with the COVID-19 protocols by religious bodies that had been clamouring for the lifting of the ban. During the service, (as seen later on television), the officiating bishop was characteristically moving around preaching to his large congregation but with people in front (possibly pastors and other senior officials) without wearing face masks just like himself also. Another case of violation was that the bishop, who was moving freely was touching people while demonstrating on his excellent sermon though. He was speaking closely to them and also raising the hands of some of them up (in such demonstration) without a face mask on either his face or those he was closely talking to and demonstrating with their hands.

Another example of open and flagrant violation of COVID-19 protocols was during the Edo 2020 electioneering campaigns where both the Peoples Democratic Party (PDP) and the All Progressives Congress (APC) (the two biggest parties) attracted large crowd of people who totally disregarded the COVID-19 protocols. This was in spite of the fact that the both political parties promised to obey strictly the protocols before the commencement of the campaigns. The last example for our purpose here, was the ENDSARS protests across the country.

Conclusion

Some critics would accuse this author of always using religious and government officials more in citing cases of violation of COVID-19 protocols. Such critics are right as the use of such examples were deliberate to make the point that those in authority must show good examples to encourage or even motivate a critical mass of people to follow and obey the protocols.

One sad lesson that came from the two years of our study of Nigeria's response to COVID-19 pandemic, is that leadership-by-example is very scarce in Nigeria. It is seriously in short supply not only in Nigeria anyway, but also in sizeable number in other places across the world. This is a major hindrance to good governance, as leaders can hardly offer what they do not have.

Part Six

Transformation of PTF to PSC on COVID-19, and WHO's
Positive Verdict on Nigeria's Policy Response

CHAPTER THIRTY EIGHT

From PTF to PSC on COVID-19: A Smart Move to Retain the Tenure of a Task Force

Prior to April 1, 2021, Nigeria's coordinating institutional response to the coronavirus (COVID-19) pandemic was through the Presidential Task Force on COVID-19 (PTF on COVID-19). We recall that the PTF on COVID-19 was established on March 9, 2020 by President Muhammadu Buhari 'to coordinate and oversee Nigeria's multi-sectoral inter-governmental efforts to contain the spread and mitigate the impact of the Covid-19 pandemic'. The Secretary to the Government of the Federation (SGF), Boss Mustapha, was appointed chairman of the 12-member body drawn from various ministerial and disciplinary backgrounds as well as from a development partner.

Boss Mustapha, Chairman of PTF turned PSC on COVID-19 *(Source: https://statehouse.gov.ng/covid19/members/).*

Elaborate Mandate of the PTF

By its operational design, the PTF was created "as a scalable structure with various Working Groups assisting it at the operational level." Its three-fold major objectives were to: (a) advise the President on the national response to the pandemic; (b) assess the needs of State and Federal Governments, and liaising with the private sector and multilateral partners to mobilise needed resources; and (c) carry out accreditation of Isolation and Treatment Centres nationwide. And to refresh our minds, its elaborate mandates were as follows:

- ✓ Provide overall policy direction, guidance, and continuous support to the National Emergency Operations Center (EOC) at the NCDC, and other Ministries and Government Agencies involved in response activities, and ensure their coordination towards a single set of national strategic objectives.
- ✓ Enable the delivery of national and state-level outbreak control priorities which include;
- ✓ Effective and safe treatment centres to ensure capacity to manage outbreaks
- ✓ Coordination of National and State Emergency Operation Centres
- ✓ Response commodities for case management, infection prevention and control, diagnostics, etc
- ✓ Sensitization and awareness campaigns for the general public on prevention measures and response activities
- ✓ Diagnostic laboratories and deployment strategies
- ✓ Review and make approval recommendations for implementing country-wide or regional non-pharmaceutical interventions if and when needed; such as school closures, suspension of large gatherings, implementation of social distancing, flight limitations etc.
- ✓ Provide recommendations for the provision of direct funding and technical support to states and local governments to strengthen their preparedness capacity and mobilise human, material and financial resources from within and outside the country for effective national and state-level preparedness.
- ✓ Define targets and monitor the progress in the delivery of these targets to meet the minimum requirements for a satisfactory performance and use this to advise the Presidency on the overall national response to COVID-19.
- ✓ Coordinate Nigeria's engagement with other countries' bilateral and multilateral bodies, international organisations to share lessons, best practices, and technical assistance.
- ✓ Keep the public abreast of strategic progress with Nigeria's

response, and emerging developments regarding preparedness and response.[182]

Overview of PTF Achievements

The PTF started its work with intense passion and drive holding daily briefings to update the nation on the national response to the COVID-19 pandemic. Although, it gradually scaled its briefings down to twice a week, it remained focused with strong energetic drive. It is a fact that the nature and operation of a task force are not meant to last for a very long time if it is to accomplish its task effectively with passion and drive.

During the one year period of its existence (March 2020 – March 2021), the PTF discharged its assigned task with a sense of urgency, passion and drive. Since an earlier chapter had assessed its performance in the past, it suffices to say that under its guidance, Nigeria was able to build molecular laboratories in 52 federal medical centres and teaching hospitals across the country. Other accomplishments include provision of isolation centres, provision of personal protective equipment, supporting key agencies in the fight against COVID-19, provision of 10 ICI beds in each of the 52 federal medical centres and teaching hospitals, supporting states and the Federal Capital Territory with the sum of one billion naira each to help fight COVID-19 with the exception of Lagos and Kano states that got N10 billion and N5 billion respectively.[183]

The Emergence of PSC

As an ad hoc body, the PTF was created to last for six months. However, as we all know, the ravaging effects of COVID-19 made it to exist for about one year, enjoying two presidential extensions of three months each, first from end of September 2020 to end of December 2020, and subsequently from December 2020 to March 31, 2021. However, during the first week of April, 2021, Boss Mustapha announced that following approval by the President, the PTF on COVID-19 has been transformed

---

[182] About the PTF via https://statehouse.gov.ng/covid19/.
[183] (See for example Vanguard newspaper, Thursday, April 22, 2021 via https://www.vanguardngr.com/2021/04/how-we-spent-covid-19-funds-so-far-fg/.

into a Presidential Steering Committee (PSC) on COVID-19 (PSC on COVID-19).

He also said that after considering its report, the President approved the following:

✓   That the PTF will transition to a Presidential Steering Committee on COVID-19, effective from April 1, 2021, with a modified mandate to reflect the non-emergent status of COVID-19 as a potentially long-term pandemic;

✓   That the structure of the PSC shall reflect the new focus of the response with a targeted approach on vaccine oversight, risk communication, international travel quarantine processes and sub-national engagement; and

✓   That the tenure of the Presidential Steering Committee shall last till 31st December, 2021.

Furthermore, he said that the Presidential Steering Committee (PSC) would:

✓   maintain the present constitution, functions and strategies of the PTF;

✓   be supported by a slim technical and administrative structure; and that

✓   the current National Incident Manager (Dr Mukhtar Mohammed) shall formally take over from the National Coordinator and function as the Head (Technical Secretariat) and member of the PSC.[184]

One major question raised by analysts following the announcement of the transformation of PTF to PSC, is on whether there is a difference between the two coordinating institutional frameworks in the fight against COVID-19 to warrant such a change of name. Put differently, in what ways would the PSC on COVID-19 operate differently from its predecessor PTF? Is the change in nomenclature from PTF to PSC

---

[184] See Punch newspaper, 6 April, 2021 via https://punchng.com/covid-19-ptf-transforms-to-presidential-steering-committee/.

merely cosmetic in nature? Again, is there really a good reason for the change in name? These are questions that need to be examined further in this chapter.

Is there any substantial difference between the PTF and PSC?

First, it is pertinent to discuss the question as to whether there is really a good reason for the change of name from PTF to PSC. Theoretically speaking, the change of name is justified for the simple reason that a task force by its very nature is not meant to exist for a long period of time. In actual fact, the PTF had long over-stayed its short-term nature which characterizes a task force. It was on the basis of this that it was granted an extension twice. As a close observer of the PTF since its establishment, this author had wondered towards the end of March 2021 (i.e. end of its second extension) what would happen to the body against the backdrop that its tenure had already been extended twice. Candidly speaking, it was a pleasant surprise to see the smart move of changing its name to PSC.

Secondly, with respect to whether the nomenclatural change was merely cosmetic in nature or not, the answer is that the change was simply cosmetic and not substantial as some people may think. This answer addresses the first and second questions altogether as raised above. The truth is that there is actually no substantial difference (in both theory and practice) between the functions of a task force and those of a steering committee. The simple difference is that a task force is ad hoc in nature, while a steering committee can last as long as an assigned project which it is 'steering' continues to exist. The PTF itself admitted the fact that the PSC would 'maintain the present constitution, functions and strategies of the PTF', as we pointed out earlier. This statement itself also is an admission that there is no substantive change in both name and in its operation.

More importantly, the functions of a steering committee in theoretical terms are also not substantially different from those of the PTF on COVID-19 in its operation. For example, the first elaborate mandate of PTF as presented earlier is to provide overall policy direction, guidance, and continuous support to the National Emergency Operations Center (EOC) at the NCDC, and other Ministries and

Government Agencies involved in response activities, and ensure their coordination towards a single set of national strategic objectives.

If therefore we compare this mandate side by side with that of a steering committee, the similarity becomes obvious. For example, according to MyManagementGuide.com a steering committee 'provides support, guidance and oversight of progress.' This Guide further defines a project steering committee as "a decision-making body within the project governance structure that consists of top managers and decision makers" who provide, review and monitor strategic direction and policy guidance to the project team and other stakeholders. If for instance we compare PTF's functions and role during the lockdown in 2020 (such as issuing periodical guidelines among others) with what is said above about a steering committee, we will discover that there is little or no difference between two of them.

Furthermore, whether it is a task force or a steering committee, the essential role is to 'provide advice, ensure delivery of the project outputs and the achievement of project outcomes'. Some other functions of a steering committee that relate also to a task force include:

- Providing input to the development of a project, including the evaluation strategy;
- Providing advice on the budget;
- Defining and helping to achieve project outcomes;
- Identifying the priorities in a project;
- Identifying potential risks;
- Monitoring risks;
- Monitoring timelines;
- Monitoring the quality of a project as it develops;
- Providing advice (and sometimes making decisions) about changes to a project as it develops.[185]

All the enumerated functions were in one way or the other listed in the mandate of PTF as we also documented above. As we can see clearly, the PTF represented what MyManagementGuide.com describes as "a

---

[185] See https://mymanagementguide.com/project-governance-structure-the-project-steering-committee/

framework for governing a project' within the overall "project governance structure". Generally, a project governance structure is defined as a "project management framework that includes a number of committees and their roles with agreed responsibilities and decision-making rules."[186] From this, we can rightly deduce that the PTF was at the top of COVID-19 project governance structure which had other bodies such as the National Emergency Operations Center (EOC) at the NCDC, and other Ministries and Government Agencies involved in response activities on COVID-19.

Consequently, the cosmetic (but appropriate) change of name guaranteed the relevance of a coordinating institutional framework (PSC in this case) in continuing the fight against COVID-19 pandemic until the virus no longer poses a serious threat to Nigerians. The appropriate choice of a new name was imperative to take care of the continuing existence of COVID-19. So the relevance of the same body (though with an appropriate new name) was a smart way to keep the fight against COVID-19 going without major disruption to its functional and operational modalities, as well as the rich experience gathered so far.

The issue of the Tenure of PSC

Lastly, with respect to how long a steering committee should last, we can say that by its very nature, a steering committee exists to oversee a project from its beginning to its completion. This simply means that a steering committee ceases to exist after the completion of a project. However, President Muhammadu Buhari had given 31st December, 2021 as the lifespan of the Presidential Steering Committee (PSC). This means that the PSC was given 9 months to discharge its functions. This was perhaps in anticipation that by this end-date (December 31, 2021), COVID-19 would have ceased to pose a serious threat in Nigeria. It is important to restate that what determines the lifespan of a steering committee is the completion of a project it is overseeing, (and in this case the end of COVID-19) in Nigeria (or more appropriately the considerable reduction of the risks it poses).

---

[186] https://MyManagementGuide.com.

The Gradual Fading away of the PSC

Obviously, the December 31, 2021 given to the PSC as end-date by the president had come and gone with the PSC still in existence. This was primarily because the ravaging effects of COVID-19 were still on as at that date, though on a declining trend. The steady declining trend of COVID-19 as at the first quarter of 2022, was an indication that the PSC would be gradually fading away. Consequently, the relevance of PSC as a coordinating mechanism in the fight against COVID-19 would be diminishing gradually with the passage of time. From all indications, the PSC's actions in March and April 2022, suggested that it was fully aware that its days were numbered. For example, it had practically removed the major restrictions it imposed on movement, curfew, social gathering, as well as on some non-pharmaceutical interventions such as wearing of face mask. It had among others removed the compulsory requirement for the PCR test for passengers traveling overseas. This development is an indication that the PSC would probably be leaving the remaining fight against the virus for the Nigeria Centre for Disease Control (NCDC) to handle as a routine task, just like other diseases within its mandate.

CHAPTER THIRTY NINE

The Global Verdict on Nigeria's Policy
Response to COVID-19

The news report[187] on August 14, 2021 that the World Health Organization (WHO) had ranked Nigeria's response to COVID-19 as the fourth most successful in the world, came as a very cheering one. The news of this positive rating was announced by the country representative of WHO in Nigeria, Dr. Walter Kazadi Mulombo at the "event to mark the arrival of the first batch of 177,600 doses of the Johnson and Johnson COVID-19 vaccine." According to Dr. Mulombo, "Nigeria was ranked fourth among the top ten most successful responses to COVID-19."[188] This cheering news report passed virtually uncelebrated, except for the Buhari Support Organization (a partisan political body) that made political capital out of it, but the success story goes beyond politics and partisan political celebration. The fact is that on balance Nigeria did well in the fight against COVID-19 pandemic and such positive rating and commendation, were well-deserved.

WHO clarification of its earlier Statement

In a corrected version of this cheering news on August 16, 2021, the same Dr. Walter Mulombo however made a clarification on his earlier statement. We reproduce here how the Premium Times reported it based on Agency report:

> The World Health Organization (WHO) Country Representative, Walter Mulombo, has clarified that the organization has not ranked countries on the basis of their response to the COVID-19 pandemic. Mr Mulombo made the clarification in an interview with the News Agency of Nigeria (NAN) on the sidelines of the commencement of

---

[187]The Cable (2021), via https://www.thecable.ng/who-nigerias-covid-response-ranked-fourth-most-successful-worldwide
[188] Ibid.

Nigeria's second phase of the COVID-19 vaccines programme, held at the Federal Medical Centre (FMC), Jabi Abuja, on Monday.

He however, noted that Nigeria had mounted one of the most effective responses to COVID-19, putting in place courageous measures and helping to avert the spread that was predicted. According to him, some independent media analysis had previously presented a ranking for top 10 countries, with Nigeria appearing in 4th position. It should be noted, however, that this is not a WHO ranking.[189]

Based on the News Agency of Nigeria (NANS) report, the Premium Times reported further that it was *The Global Normalcy Index* that ranked Nigeria 4th position in the Economist's Global Normalcy Index, out of 50 countries. We do not know what changed that made the WHO Country Representative to make the clarification because he did not say that he was misrepresented by the media. In any case, in spite of his clarification, he equally confirmed the indisputable fact that "Nigeria had mounted one of the most effective responses to COVID-19, putting in place courageous measures and helping to avert the spread that was predicted," as reported above. Since this author followed closely Nigeria's policy response for close to two years through his column, it is necessary therefore to provide evidence to confirm the global verdict on Nigeria's policy response to COVID-19.

The Evidence Supporting the Verdict

For a period of one year and five months (17 months precisely), this author through his column in *Sundiata Post Online* newspaper, ran a commentary on Nigeria's policy response to the COVID-19 pandemic and other related issues. The column had without break followed the dynamics of Nigeria's policy response – exposing its good, bad and ugly sides. The column also covered the citizens' attitude and behaviour towards the policy response. It is against this background therefore that

---

[189] Mulombo W. (2021): 'COVID-19: Nigeria's 4th place response ranking not ours – WHO'. See *Premium Times*, August 16, 2021 via https://www.premiumtimesng.com/news/top-news/479631-covid-19-nigerias-4th-place-response-ranking-not-ours-who-country-rep.html

this author is well positioned to provide evidence in support of the verdict on Nigeria's response to COVID-19 pandemic. What follows now is a presentation of some of the positive comments the column made on how Nigeria's coordinating agency for the policy response to COVID-19 (PTF-turned PSC) discharged its functions during the period. We start by presenting relevant aspects of the different articles published in May, June, October and December 2020, as well as in April and May 2021.

Dr Osagie Ehanire, Hon. Minister of Health *(Source: https://statehouse.gov.ng/covid19/members/).*

First, on May 4, 2020 while writing on "Task Force Model on COVID-19 emergency management," this author said:

With regards to the deployment of expertise to fight COVID-19, PTF has confronted this enemy with an extra-ordinary sense of commitment expected of task force members anywhere. Members have been visible even to a point of exhaustion and putting their lives at great risk. For those with a good sense of understanding of the PTF's work, there is enormous intellectual and physical energy involved.

It takes people who possess both qualities to execute the equally enormous tasks involved. It is highly commendable that the members of the Task Force have been able to discharge their functions in a sustained manner for nearly two

months now.[190]

Secondly, in the third instalment of the same article on May 6, 2020, this author then commended the "PTF and other health bodies (Federal Ministry of Health, NCDC, WHO etc) for their remarkable demonstration of rare courage and professionalism in the war against COVID-19 in Kano State." The combined intervention by these mentioned bodies (under the PTF) was in reaction to the health crisis that engulfed Kano state (with massive mysterious deaths) amid the claim by the Kano state government that the 'mysterious deaths' were not COVID-19-related. These health professionals risked their lives to do the needful and arrest the situation subsequently.

Thirdly, writing on 'COVID-19 and Nigeria's fight at the sub-national level' on June 8, 2020, this author then observed that:

The PTF on COVID-19 which was established on 9 March 2020 is now three months old, and to its credit, It is still operating with strong drive, verve and commitment.

In May while celebrating the two months existence of PTF (in a three-part series), this column made the point that a task force by its nature and design, stands the risk of losing its initial drive and verve if it exists for too long. It is gladdening to note that the PTF on COVID-19 is still operating with its initial verve and commitment since three months ago.

---

[190] Sundiata Post (2020) via https://sundiatapost.com/task-force-model-for-covid-19-emergency-management-2-by-isaac-n-obasi/, May 4.

The article then added that "so far, the efforts of the Federal Government to provide support to governments at sub-national levels in the fight against COVID-19, is very encouraging and only needs to be sustained."[191]

Furthermore, in continuation of the June 8 article, this author on June 12, commended specifically the efforts of the Lagos State Government and the FCT Administration for displaying commendable verve and passion in fighting the virus without which the situation would have been worse within their areas. The efforts of other state governments (e.g. Rivers and Kaduna) were also recognized then by this author.

Fourthly, writing on 'COVID-19 and implementation of Nigeria's Phase 3 ease of lockdown' on October 2, 2020, this author then wrote:

> The establishment of the PTF on COVID-19 was a milestone on the journey of Nigeria's national response to COVID-19 pandemic. The PTF has maintained a steady, strong and commendable verve in the discharge of its duties since its creation. As a task force, it exceeded the expectation that it would likely suffer fatigue, lose focus and ultimately lose commitment if it exists for too long.
> However, the PTF has lasted over six months (and still counting) given the three months presidential extension to last to till December, 2020.

The article further observed then that:

> Another milestone in Nigeria's early national response to COVID-19 pandemic was the announcement by President Muhammadu Buhari of the immediate release of a N10 billion grant to Lagos State, which was then (and for a long time) epicentre of the COVID-19 outbreak in Nigeria to enable it increase its capacity to control and contain the outbreak. Also, the President announced the immediate release of a N5 billion special intervention fund to the Nigeria Centre for Disease Control (NCDC) to equip, expand and provide personnel to its facilities and laboratories across the country. The Federal Government equally gave N5 billion to Kano State following the mysterious and

---

[191] Sundiata Post (2020) via https://sundiatapost.com/covid-19-and-nigerias-fight-at-the-sub-national-levels-1-by-isaac-n-obasi/, June 8.

alarming deaths that occurred thereafter. Furthermore, the Federal Government gave N1 billion each to over 30 states to help them fight the COVID-19 scourge. By these and other numerous policy measures, the Federal Government of Nigeria, clearly demonstrated some level of seriousness in fighting COVID-19.[192]

Fifthly, writing on 'COVID-19 and 'a week-like-no-other' in Nigeria' on December 18, 2020 this author (while commenting on the performance of the PTF for the period of its 9th months of existence) then observed that:

> For those who have been monitoring closely the coordination of the national policy response to COVID-19, the Chairman of the Presidential Task Force, Mr. Mustapha, has been exemplary in leading from the front. He was always urging Nigerians to comply with the non-pharmaceutical protocols and he demonstrated his appeal through leadership by example. Although Nigeria performed less than satisfactory on testing, history will, however, be kind to Mr. Boss Mustapha and members of the Task Force for putting a good and courageous fight against COVID-19. Again…despite the fact that comparatively speaking, Nigeria's low numbers on infections and deaths do not necessarily reflect reality, Nigeria COVID-19 policy response is on balance commendable. The Task Force on COVID-19 executed its duties with verve, enthusiasm, humility, simplicity, and honesty of purpose (as could be observed from the outside) as against lethargy, fatigue, and arrogance for which task forces are known in theory to easily fall into after a long period of existence. This is an informed humble opinion of this column but as they say, the jury is still out there to interrogate the objectivity of this opinion.[193]

With hindsight now, one of such verdicts from the outside on this opinion, is the Global Verdict on Nigeria's policy response which ranked it as the 4tt most successful in the world.

---

[192] Sundiata Post (2020) via https://sundiatapost.com/covid-19-and-implementation-of-nigerias-phase-3-ease-of-lockdown-by-isaac-n-obasi/, October 2.

[193] Sundiata Post (2020) via https://sundiatapost.com/covid-19-and-a-week-like-no-other-in-nigeria-by-isaac-n-obasi/, December 18.

Sixthly, writing on 'From PTF to PSC: Nigeria's COVID-19 coordinating policy response revisited (1)' on April 23, 2021 (a year after the PTF was established), this author then wrote:

> The PTF started its work with intense passion and drive holding daily briefings to update the nation on the national response to the COVID-19 pandemic. Although, it gradually scaled its briefings down to twice a week, it remained focused with strong energetic drive. Those who are familiar with the nature and operation of a task force generally know that such a body is not meant to last for a very long time if it is to accomplish its task effectively with passion and drive. During its existence, the PTF discharged its assigned task with a sense of urgency, passion and drive. Nigeria was able to build molecular laboratories in 52 federal medical centres and teaching hospitals across the country.[194]

Finally, writing on 'Sustaining PTF's dogged spirit in PSC on COVID-19', this author then said:

> Apart from financial matters on the running of PTF (which this column has no capacity to interrogate), the body throughout its existence performed (on balance) creditably well with zeal, energy and commitment. For example, it performed its risk communication function with precision and clarity.[195]

Conclusion

Given this dynamic monitoring assessment of the PTF/PSC and the consistent positive rating of it by this author, it did not come as a surprise that the Global Verdict would rank Nigeria's policy response to COVID-19 very high or successful.

The truth is that this author did not have any contact or relationship with PTF/PSC's chairman or any other member of the Task Force or its secretariat. Finally, it is important to note that there were many articles in

---

[194] Sundiatapost (2021) via https://sundiatapost.com/from-ptf-to-psc-nigerias-covid-19-coordinating-policy-response-revisited-1-by-isaac-n-obasi/. April, 23.

[195] Sundiatapost (2021) via https://sundiatapost.com/sustaining-ptfs-dogged-spirit-in-psc-on-covid-19-by-isaac-n-obasi/, May 21.

this author's column during the period it covered that were critical of the government's management of COVID-19 pandemic issues. On balance however, available evidence support the verdict that Nigeria's performance in the management of COVID-19 was above average if rated along such a continuum.

CHAPTER FORTY

Dr. Chikwe Ihekweazu: Nigeria's COVID-19 Dogged Fighter

In chapter 39, we celebrated the ranking of Nigeria's COVID-19 response as the fourth most successful in the world. In that chapter, this author agreed totally with the positive ranking of Nigeria's COVID-19 policy response as consistent with his own assessment. The Presidential Task Force on COVID-19 (now turned Presidential Steering Committee on COVID19) was specially commended for its courageous fight against the COVID-19 pandemic in Nigeria. The author also recognized the Nigeria Centre for Disease Control (NCDC) as a strong and effective member of the Task Force that made its enormous responsibilities easy to accomplish. Specifically, the Director-General (DG) of the NCDC, Dr. Chikwe Ihekweazu, distinguished himself as a dogged fighter in the war against the COVID-19 pandemic.

Dr. Chikwe Ihekweazu (Former Director-General of NCDC) & now Assistant Director-General of WHO *(Source:https://en.wikipedia.org/wiki/Chikwe_Ihekweazu).*

The Elevation of Dr. Chikwe Ihekweazu as WHO Assistant Director General

The appointment by WHO of Dr. Chikwe Ihekweazu as its Assistant Director-General for Health Emergency Intelligence with effect from November 1, 2021 did not come to many discerning minds as a surprise. The announcement of the appointment said that Ihekweazu "will lead the work on strengthening pandemic and epidemic intelligence globally, including heading the WHO Hub for Pandemic and Epidemic Intelligence in Berlin."[196] The fact that his appointment by WHO was specifically in the area of 'strengthening pandemic and epidemic intelligence globally', is a clear demonstration that Ihekweazu's accomplishments in the war against COVID-19 pandemic in Nigeria was extra-ordinarily noteworthy. In actual fact, he fought the war with a high sense of patriotism without minding the risk to his life. His appointment is further evidence that the positive rating of Nigeria's policy response to COVID-19, was objectively done.

Reactions to WHO's Elevation of Dr. Ihekweazu

The news of Dr. Ihekweazu's well-deserved elevation to this global health body was also well received by the Federal Government and other well-meaning Nigerians and organizations. The federal government paid him glowing tribute for leading "the NCDC through period of remarkable transformation". As the Minister of Health, Dr. Osagie Ehanire, said in a statement signed by Mamman Mahmuda the ministry's permanent secretary, Ihekweazu's new appointment by the WHO is in recognition of his excellence and professionalism. The statement further said that "Dr Ihekweazu joined NCDC as a nascent institution and has led the agency through a period of remarkable transformation and global recognition. Under his leadership, Nigeria's health security capacity has improved, evidenced by the improved capabilities and resources for infectious disease control."[197]

---

[196] Sundiata Post (2021) via https://sundiatapost.com/dg-ncdc-chikwe-ihekweazu-appointed-who-asst-dg-%ef%bb%bf/, September 1.

[197] The Cable (2021) via https://www.thecable.ng/he-led-ncdc-through-period-of-remarkable-transformation-fg-commends-ihekweazu. News report was based on the original report by the News Agency of Nigeria (NAN).

On her part, Dr. Ngozi Okonjo-Iweala (Director General, World Trade Organization) said very aptly that Dr. Ihekweazu's appointment was "a great choice" but "a big loss to Nigeria." Dr. Okonjo-Iweala's statement was a very apt one, because Nigeria indeed lost her COVID-19 dogged fighter who put his life on the front line when it mattered most. In the same manner, the Good Morning Show of the *ARISE News Television* (led by Dr. Reuben Abati) celebrated Dr. Ihekweazu's appointment for his accomplishment in the fight against COVID-19 pandemic. Furthermore, the Premium Times[198] reported also that "many Nigerians have continued to shower encomiums on the director-general of the Nigeria Centre for Disease Control (NCDC), Chikwe Ihekweazu, over his appointment as an assistant director-general of the global health body - World Health Organisation (WHO)". It specifically reported that 'a former deputy governor of the Central Bank of Nigeria (CBN) and former presidential candidate during the 2019 general election, Kingsley Moghalu, spoke glowingly' of Dr. Ihekweazu, describing his appointment "as a reward for hard work."[199]

It was indeed a "reward for hard work". The saying that "the reward for hard work is more work" (ie. additional higher responsibilities and more recognition) aptly applies to Dr. Ihekweazu's meritorious elevation. For example, during the 17 months (i.e. a year and five months) that this author (though his column) monitored and chronicled Nigeria's policy response to COVID-19 (of which Dr. Ihekweazu was a key player in both policy formulation and implementation), ample evidence abound that Dr. Ihewkeazu demonstrated by his numerous actions that he is quintessentially an exceptional and exemplary public servant. This contrasts with many 'accidental public servants' (apology to Governor Nasir Ahmad El-Rufai) who preoccupy themselves with looking for ways to loot the treasury leaving no remarkable achievements before some of them also 'accidentally' exit the service.

---

[198] Premium Times (2021): 'Encomiums as NCDC boss, Ihekweazu gets WHO job', September 1, via https://www.premiumtimesng.com/news/more-news/482420-encomiums-as-ncdc-boss-ihekweazu-gets-who-job.html
[199] Ibid.

Dr. Ihekweazu's Persuasive and Non-controversial Demeanour

One thing that went well for Ihekweazu was his mien in public while performing his duties. In particular, his mien which epitomized unbounded humility smartly clothed with confidence, made the fight against COVID-19 to go on unhindered in spite of the huge risk. This appearance was particularly helpful during the lockdown period when the whole nation was living in great fear. During that time for example when many others in his position would shout at Nigerians who were violating the non-pharmaceutical protocols with impunity, Ihekweazu would respectfully and with a persuasive tone remind Nigerians that wearing a mask is better than being on a ventilator. Wearing a mask, he repeatedly said, might seem cumbersome, but it is less cumbersome than being on a ventilator.

He repeatedly appealed to them to bear the inconveniences of the mask than suffer the precarious condition in the Intensive Care Unit (ICU). In the same spirit, he appealed to Nigerians to "take responsibility" for their actions with respect to observing the safety protocols of COVID-19. He reminded them that anyone who is not taking the virus seriously has himself or herself to blame. Furthermore, he appealed to them to do their best to protect one another, never to throw caution to the wind and to take responsibility so that together Nigerians can collectively win the war against COVID-19. His risk communication messages either at the PTF briefings or in the social media platforms, were endearing and commendable. This is something that other public servants who do similar work, should emulate.

Looking at the secret of his success and staying power on the various aspects of his risky job, Dr Ihekweazu was known to repeatedly emphasize, that health professionals and workers need to continuously focus their eyes on the ball without distractions that nevertheless abound. That was the philosophy that kept him and many of his staff working courageously irrespective of the dangerous nature of their jobs in the infectious disease world. Under his watch, the number of molecular laboratories built increased from about two or so at the emergence of COVID-19, to 52 in federal medical centres and teaching hospitals across the country. He was a man great vision who worked tirelessly to see this dream come through. Watching him from outside, he was not known to be hypocritical in the discharge of his duties, and like the

Chairman of the PTF/PSC on COVID-19, Boss Mustapha, he worked the talk, and as leaders, both men led from the front. These are the special breed of public servants that Nigeria needs in order to get out of her current cyclic trap of underdevelopment.

In conclusion, Dr. Ihekweazu accomplished much more than is reported here. In fact, he has accomplished a lot more in other areas of infectious disease control which formed part of his mandate as the DG of NCDC. As a man not given to too much controversy (in his public appearances), Dr. Ihekweazu stands tall and remains properly and well equipped to face the challenges of his new office in Berlin, Germany.

Part Seven
COVID-19 Vaccine and its Controversies

CHAPTER FORTY ONE

COVID-19 Vaccine and its Associated Controversies

The world was in great need of a vaccine to win the war against the ravaging COVID-19 pandemic. When one was eventually discovered, the expectation was that people across the world would express overwhelming relief and outright joy. Although such expression of relief reverberated across the world, but surprisingly some people did not welcome the arrival of a vaccine. They staged protests against the vaccine and its use in midst of a ravaging pandemic. The arrival and administration of vaccines across the world generated one form of controversy or the other within countries and even across nations particularly between developed and developing countries.

The Vaccine and Lockdown Resistance: A reflection of growing level of Distrust in Governance

A growing level of distrust in governance was recorded across the world during the most dangerous period of COVID-19 pandemic. During that period governance systems around the globe witnessed a growing distrust (mistrust or trust-deficit) of governments by sizeable number of citizens. And with particular reference to the war against COVID-19, a growing number of people did not trust their governments and scientists well enough to guide them in taking preventive measures against the rapid spread of the deadly disease. In many countries, people protested openly against the lockdown or restriction measures (including the wearing of face masks) meant to stop the further spread of the virus.

In a report by *Metro* UK,[200] thousands of protesters opposed the lockdown measures, and went further to object to a potential mandatory vaccines on the people. These protesters called for an end to what they referred to as 'Government lies', and they called for the restoration of 'all freedoms'. Some among the large crowd of protesters in London carried

---

[200] Metro UK (2020): '10,000 anti-lockdown protesters gather in London to claim coronavirus is 'a hoax', August 29.

placards referring to COVID as 'CONVID HOAX' and some others reading 'No more lies, No more masks, No more lockdown'.

For many people in developing countries, the messages by the protesters in developed countries, appeared strange in an enlightened society where respect for science should be taken for granted. It did appear that science was itself a victim of trust-deficit in the governance system. The anger of the people against their governments was transferred to the other age-long, time-honoured and well-respected scientific institutions and values of the state that constituted the foundation of modern civilisation and advancement of humanity. The example of protesters in London was just one out of the many demonstrations against the lockdown restrictions and mandatory vaccines by people across the world.

The case of Germany – a country long and well-known for its scientific achievements – was not different and was even embarrassing. If these demonstrations were limited to developing countries where there exists high level of ignorance and superstition, perhaps it could have been understandable. Its occurrence in highly developed countries was a reflection of the increasing level of people's distrust of their governments around the globe.

While what happened in Europe was shocking, that of the USA was both shocking and embarrassing as a result of a two-pronged problem of distrust of science (politically engineered by former President Donald Trump) and its concomitant distrust and resistance of governments' lockdown measures imposed by states controlled by the Democratic Party. With President Trump disparaging and disregarding science, his supporters also did the same thing. Like in Europe, the protesters called for the restoration of liberty the denial of which was perceived as enslaving them.

Some protesters described COVID-19 measures as tyranny and were protesting to protect their liberty. These protests and distrust dovetailed into high level of non-compliance and in some cases outright disobedience to the COVID-19 safety guidelines in many developed and developing countries. The world paid dearly for such high level of non-compliance as more and more people got infected and many also died, following the outbreaks of different waves.

In Nigeria, the protest against the lockdown measures started first in

Lagos by those the media called hoodlums. The protests later spread to other states with Delta State recording fatalities among the protesters.

Some aggrieved youths in Lagos started rioting in areas such as Shasha, Orisunbare, Idimu, and Ejigbo. Source: UGC *(See https://www.legit.ng/1320709-covid-19-hoodlums-rampage-protesting-president-buharis-lockdown-extension.html*

In Nigeria again, the aftermath of the #EndSARS protest which saw hoodlums taking over the streets looting public and private properties, as well as vandalising or burning them out rightly, was a clear demonstration of trust-deficit in action. The protests were carried out with resoluteness and anger. Although many were hungry and angry, the burning of courts, properties of the Federal Roads Safety Commission (FRSC), among others in Lagos, demonstrated a high level of distrust of anything which has link with the government at the various levels.

The real #EndSARS protest also registered a strong message that demonstrated a total loss of faith by the youths in governance. The fact that the protesters continued their protests even after their five-point demands were on the table for consideration by the government (with some of them already acceded), further demonstrated their lack of trust on the government.

We need a trust-deficit 'vaccine' which is a metaphor for effective solutions towards rebuilding trust in governance. The use of the word signifies that the problem is like an epidemic or even a pandemic which requires urgent vaccine-like antidote for a cure. If we are to search for a trust-deficit 'vaccine', the first thing is to focus on the governance system that generates the mistrust. It has to be improved radically before it can rebuild trust. This will require the various levels of government to embark on a soul-searching retreat on how to proceed. Although there is no one best way on how to proceed, but one worst way on how not to proceed is to embark on harassment of those who take part in peaceful protest which is an exercise of their fundamental rights, as they were completely different from hoodlums.

CHAPTER FORTY TWO

The Vexed Question of Local Production of COVID-19 Vaccine and Other Issues in Nigeria

It is ridiculous that when the serious scientific people of the world started the race for the COVID-19 vaccine shortly after the outbreak of the pandemic, Nigeria to the best of our knowledge did not join the race, but very much later started considering the idea of embarking on a local production of the vaccines developed by others. It was a noble decision that Nigeria did not enter the race for a vaccine as it did not make sense to enter a race one would certainly be among the losers at the end. This is because the countries that embarked on the race for a vaccine deployed their 'Ben-Johnsons' (excellent scientific talents supported by enabling environment) into the race, and in less than a year, the 'first three finishers' emerged to the delight of the anxiously waiting world. The first to be announced was Pfizer-BoiNTech with a 95% efficacy; then followed by Moderna with a 94.5% efficacy; and the third was Oxford- AstraZeneca with 62-90% efficacy depending on dosage.[201]

Apart from these three top vaccine discoverers, Russia and China in non-transparent manners, announced the development of vaccines in their countries. As at January, 2021, the three top vaccines were presently in use in different parts of the world including the United States of America (USA), Europe, India, Israel, Mexico, just to name a few. It is important to note that as at January 2021 researchers were testing 62 coronavirus vaccines in clinical trials on humans.[202]

Nigeria's interest in local production of COVID-19 Vaccine

At the time different countries of the world were focusing on how to procure and distribute the already produced vaccine, the Nigerian federal government announced that it was making money available for local

---

[201]The New York Times (2021) via https://www.nytimes.com/interactive/2021/health/how-covid-19-vaccines-work.html.
[202] Ibid.

production of a vaccine. The government announced that it was proposing to spend Four Hundred Billion Naira (N400 billion) to procure vaccines.

At the national briefing of the Presidential Task Force on COVID-19 (PTF COVID-19) held on Monday, 18 January 2021, the Minister of Health, Dr. Osagie Ehanire disclosed that the sum of N10 billion had been approved by the Federal Government to support local production of the COVID-19 vaccine. Giving further details, the minister said that:

> …the Federal Ministry of Finance has released N10 billion to support domestic vaccine production. While we are working to develop our own vaccines, Nigeria is exploring options for licensed production in collaboration with recognised institutions. We are also exploring the option of local production of the vaccines in-country and have had discussions with a producer.[203]

One was wondering why Nigeria started very late to decide to develop its own vaccines after the race was almost over. Why for example, should Nigeria at that late hour be 'exploring options for licensed production in collaboration with recognized institutions'? One was worried because this late decision gave the impression that Nigeria is only good at consuming the knowledge or intellectual ingenuity of other people. It also gave the impression that Nigeria is perpetually a knowledge consumer nation. On the contrary, Nigeria has rich intellectual endowment capable of discovering and producing any vaccine if the enabling environment is created. Nigerian scientists in diaspora are among the celebrated brains that produced the vaccines and other COVID-19 drugs at the time it mattered most.

Although, there is nothing inherently wrong for the government to focus on local efforts towards producing a vaccine, yet it is wrong to throw non-existent funds around for such a planned licensed production of vaccines in collaboration with foreign recognized institutions. In the COVID-19 vaccine race, Nigeria did not position itself well for a meaningful accomplishment. In any case, at the time the race started,

---

[203] Sundiata Post (2021) via https://sundiatapost.com/fg-releases-n10bn-to-support-local-production-of-covid-19-vaccine/

Nigeria's intellectual power house was in disarray as a result of the prolonged strike by the Academic Staff Union of Universities (ASUU) whose members should have been involved in the race for a vaccine. Bsides, Nigeria's relevant research institutes were not well-funded to embark on such an expensive vaccine production then.

Bill Gates' and other Competing Advice on Acquisition of Vaccine

The preceding discussion brings us to the well-reasoned advice given by Bill Gates that "Nigeria does not need to spend too much on acquiring COVID-19 vaccines but should rather focus more on revitalising the weak and underfunded health sector especially the primary health care centre", and that "Nigeria should not divert the very limited money that it has for health into trying to pay a high price for COVID vaccines."[204]

It is important to separate Bill Gates' view from some others such as the Kogi State governor Yahaya Bello who, while discouraging the use of COVID-19 vaccines said that the "vaccines are meant to kill all us."[205] Gates' view was also different from that of the Sultan of Sokoto, Alhaji Sa'ad Abubakar 111, who in what appears to be doubting tone, said that 'we can't force Nigerians to take COVID-19 vaccine', because "there are myths, people talk of conspiracy theories."[206]

It is important to point out that Nigeria has all it takes to develop and produce a vaccine for a future disease if it makes available the required resources for such a project. Nigeria's present level of funding research undertakings is too low to accomplish such a huge project. Were it not to be so, the signs would be there to see in the available research infrastructure and facilities in the universities. Nonetheless, the universities still have the required brains that can carry out any research if provided with adequate funding and the right environment.

---

[204] Sundiata Post (2021) via https://sundiatapost.com/fixing-health-sector-more-important-than-buying-covid-19-vaccines-bill-gates-tells-fg/.

[205] Sahara Reporters (2021) via http://saharareporters.com/2021/01/19/covid-19-vaccines-meant-kill-us-%E2%80%93-kogi-governor-yahaya-bello. January.

[206] Punch, Thursday, January, 28.

Chapter Forty two │ Isaac Nnamdi Obasi

Politics of Vaccine Distribution

Although there were initial controversies surrounding the proposed list of vaccine distribution after its acquisition, the matter was finally resolved satisfactorily. But the discussion here is to point out what an earlier chapter called bad politics which creeped into the exercise. Announcing its distribution plan for the COVID-19 vaccine in Nigeria, the National Primary Health Care Development Agency, said that the rate of infection in each state was the criterion for allocating vaccines to the states. It consequently released the following distribution list of the COVID-19 vaccine: Kano State would receive 3,557; Lagos, 3,131; Katsina, 2,361; Kaduna, 2,074; Bauchi, 1,900; Oyo, 1,848; Rivers, 1,766; Jigawa, 1,712; Niger, 1,558; Ogun, 1,473; Sokoto, 1,468; Benue, 1,423; Borno, 1,416; Anambra, 1,379; Zamfara, 1,336; Delta, 1,306; Others are Kebbi, 1,268; Imo, 1,267; Ondo, 1,228; Akwa Ibom, 1,161.Adamawa, 1,129; Edo, 1,104; Plateau, 1,089; Enugu, 1,088; Osun, 1,032; Kogi, 1,030; Cross River, 1,023; Abia, 955; Gombe, 908; Yobe, 842; Ekiti, 830; Taraba, 830; Kwara, 815; Ebonyi, 747; Bayelsa, 589; FCT, 695; Nasarawa, 661.[207]

This distribution list above shows that like in many things in Nigeria, politics was unnecessarily brought into vaccine distribution or else how could one explain that Kogi State which was practically not carrying out any testing would be allocated 1,030, while the Federal Capital Territory (FCT) Abuja, the second most badly affected 'state' after Lagos would be allocated only 695. Lagos state which remained the epicentre of COVID-19 disease in Nigeria was allocated only 3,131, while Kano State which 'downgraded' COVID-19 related deaths to mysterious deaths and was not testing enough like Lagos in spite of many laboratories that were set-up there, was allocated as high as 3,557. This confirms our argument much earlier that one of Nigeria's worst governance diseases is bad politics. The criterion used for allocating the yet-to arrive vaccines appeared not to be clear at all.

---

[207]Sundiata Post via https://sundiatapost.com/how-the-covid-19-vaccines-will-be-distributed-to-states-in-nigeria-nphcda-reveals/.

Chapter Forty two | Isaac Nnamdi Obasi

For sure, COVID-19 vaccines whether in national or international circles, became a big and vexed question. Underlining the vexed nature of the question is the issue of distributional equity. The issue of fair distribution of vaccines to those who need them most (namely the frontline health workers, the aged, and other vulnerable groups serving humanity in the period of COVID-19 pandemic), as against the politically powerful and connected, the rich and other members of the privileged class, became very controversial and vexatious. It should not have been so.

CHAPTER FORTY THREE

COVID-19 Vaccine Euphoria in Nigeria and its Critics

Euphoria over the discovery, approval, distribution and administration of the COVID-19 vaccines was a worldwide phenomenon and not limited to specific countries in the Southern Hemisphere like Nigeria, where the arrival of vaccines appeared to be over-celebrated. The euphoria accompanying the arrival of vaccines attracted criticisms from those who felt it was unnecessary. Needed to say that the euphoria was perfectly understandable as the ingenious discovery of COVID-19 vaccines (that immediately reduced the severity of the disease) was a great miracle even in medical circles. This author salutes all the scientists who worked tirelessly to invent the COVID-19 vaccines that are being distributed and administered all over the world today. And above all, we give God the glory for making it possible for COVID-19 vaccine to be discovered within a short period of time.

Vaccine euphoria in Nigeria

Why would anyone in the first place not be euphoric over the discovery and the eventual administration of a vaccine when at the time of its discovery over two million deaths (precisely 2,621,986) were recorded globally due to the pandemic?[208] Why would anyone in Nigeria not be over-excited with the arrival of a vaccine when the total number of confirmed cases was 159,646, with nearly 2,000 (precisely 1,993) lives lost to the virus as at the time in question.[209] The situation was not different in other countries. For example, in Brazil, hospitals were overwhelmed with a daily fatality reaching a record high of nearly 2,000 (i.e. 1,972 deaths) on Tuesday, March 10, 2021. The situation got so alarming that France24 reported that on March 10, 2021, Brazil was facing a dire

---

[208] Johns Hopkins University Coronavirus Tracker (2021) via https://coronavirus.jhu.edu/map.html, as of Thursday, March 11, at 12:25pm.
[209] NCDC (2021) via https://covid19.ncdc.gov.ng/, as of Thursday, March, 11, at 1.09pm.

situation with intensive care units with more than 80 percent occupied in 25 of Brazil's 27 capital cities.[210] It is against this background that the euphoria over the arrival of vaccine in Nigeria was justifiable.

Nigeria's euphoria over the expected arrival of the COVID-19 vaccine started long before its arrival with the PTF on COVID-19 making the vaccine issue a major one (and rightly too) during its national briefing in the preceding months. The PTF rightly reminded Nigerians that the arrival of the vaccine was not the end of the pandemic as we still needed to be vigilant by obeying the COVID-19 safety protocols and guidelines. The chairman of the PTF, Boss Mustapha, was never tired of giving out this appropriate and timely warning.

When the nearly four million (3.94 million precisely) doses of the AstraZeneca/Oxford vaccines shipped by COVAX eventually arrived, there was palpable excitement in the air. The COVAX facility that shipped the vaccine from the Serum Institute of India (SII) was and still working in partnership with CEPI, Gavi, UNICEF and WHO – the organizations that made the free vaccines possible for developing countries like Nigeria to have them.

Furthermore, local and international media made the arrival of the vaccine an exciting event more so when all relevant Federal Government officials and agencies displayed a high level of euphoria. The news of the euphoria that heralded of a vaccine arriving in Nigeria was all over the world. Aljazeera described it as a 'fantastic step forward' noting that "Nigeria was the third country in Africa to get the shots through COVAX, a global scheme formed to ensure fair access to inoculations for low-and middle-income states." An excited Dr. Tedros Ghebreyesus, Director-General of the WHO tweeted: "Congratulations to #Nigeria and our #COVAX partners on making the third delivery of #COVID19 vaccines in Africa."

Also, WHO Regional Office (WHO Africa) excitedly said that "the arrival marked a historic step towards the goal to ensure equitable distribution of COVID-19 vaccines globally, in what will be the largest vaccine procurement and supply operation in history."[211] In the same

---

[210] France24 (2021) via https://www.france24.com/en/americas/20210310-hospitals-overwhelmed-as-brazil-reaches-new-daily-covid-19-death-record, March 10.

[211] WHO Africa (2021) via https://www.afro.who.int/news/covid-19-vaccines-shipped-covax-

vein, Thabani Maphosa, Managing Director for Country Programmes at Gavi, (the Vaccine Alliance) said 'this is a landmark moment for the country and the COVAX Facility's mission to help end the acute phase of the pandemic by enabling equitable access to these vaccines across the world. We are glad to see Nigeria is amongst the first receiving the doses from COVAX, thanks to the excellent level of preparedness put in place by the Government of Nigeria'. He added that 'Gavi looks forward to these vaccines being made available to the people most at risk, as soon as possible, and to ensuring that routine immunization services for other life-threatening infections are also delivered to avoid other disease outbreaks."[212]

The chairman of PTF Boss Mustapha must be one of the fulfilled government officials overseeing this project, simply because the Federal Government's promise to get the vaccines eventually materialized without issues. Consequently and expectedly, he said excitedly that "the successful development of vaccines and the accelerated process for emergency authorization has brought hope to humanity all over the world." According to him, the government planned to start by vaccinating frontline healthcare workers, the highest-priority recipients, in Abuja on March 5, 2021 followed by strategic leaders on March 8, 2021. Lastly, he said the government expected to receive 84 million doses of the Oxford/AstraZeneca vaccine from COVAX in 2021, enough to inoculate 20% of the population.[213]

The Minister of Health, Dr Osagie Ehanire, could also not hide his excitement when he said that "it is a feeling of relief and elation that at last we are joining the community of nations who can vaccinate their citizens against COVID-19 disease which has been raging across the world. We have to some extent lagged but are relieved that we can now start vaccinating our citizens."[214]

Dr. Faisal Shuaibu the ED/CEO of the National Primary Health Care Development Agency (NPHCDA) expressed excitement through a

---

[212] Ibid.
[213] As reported by Reuters (2021), via https://www.reuters.com/article/us-health-coronavirus-nigeria-vaccines-idUSKBN2AU125.
[214] WHO Africa (2021) via https://www.afro.who.int/news/public-health-experts-elated-covid-19-vaccine-delivery-assure-nigerians-vaccine-effectiveness.

tweet. At exactly 4.45pm (March 2, 2021) Dr. Shuaibu announced through his official twitter handle that:

> Today, we had a reception ceremony – an activity that allowed a multi-sectoral delegation to inspect and receive the vaccines at the airport.
> This was followed with a press briefing. This is a key part of our commitment to the Nigerian people to ensure full transparency, as we distribute and introduce safe and effective COVID-19 vaccines.

Dr. Shuaibu's tweet evoked further excitements and even criticisms from vaccine critics. Critics wondered why there should be a reception ceremony and also a press briefing. The reactions generated by Dr. Shuaibu's tweet particularly the concomitant criticisms it generated among vaccine sceptics were also captured by this author. On the excitement side, shortly after Dr. Shuaibu's tweet, an excited citizen tweeted: 'We @AbujaFhis want to identify with @NphcdaNG, @NCDCgov, @Fmohnigeria, #PTFCOVID19 and all stakeholders for this milestone step in the fight against Covid 19.' Then a critic asked 'was the reception ceremony of any use?' Another critic replied 'Bros you no understand the celebration. It's time to cash out. Do you know how many millionaires that'll start calling in to buy the vaccines for their families and perhaps staff at any price? Abegi make dem celebrate. Free money don land.' Apart from critics in the social media, there were many others who used the mainstream media to take exception to the airport ceremonies and press briefing.

As we argued earlier, the euphoria over the arrival of the vaccine is understandable and is in order. Even the former President Donald Trump, who was undoubtedly the number one global worst manager of COVID-19 as well as its virulent sceptic, encouraged millions of his Republican Party supporters to take the vaccine, which according to him is good. His appeal was against the news that many Republicans said that they would not take the vaccine.

However, a point that one of the critics made which should not be over-looked is the perception of the motive behind the euphoria. The perception that some officials would become millionaires out of the vaccine business mirrors the thinking of many Nigerians about the prevailing systemic and pervasive corruption in the land, a perception that erodes trust in governance. As we pointed out in earlier chapters, public trust in governance is very low. This is a big challenge as those in government need to go extra mile to demonstrate their integrity by being more transparent and accountable in the discharge of their duties. Nigerians would be happy to see that there is continued transparency in the whole process of vaccine distribution and administration.

Issues beyond Vaccine Euphoria and its Critics

First, during the early period of the distribution and administration of the vaccines, some government officials started reacting prematurely on the issue of vaccine hesitancy. For example, some of them said that the taking of the vaccine was mandatory. One state governor for instance threatened that 'no vaccination, no attendance to the Executive Council meeting'. This kind of statement and proposed action was inappropriate at that point in time as the vaccines were not there to go round. The statement had the unintended effect of making some powerful politicians and other people of means to start looking for the vaccine desperately thereby denying those who are most at risk, from receiving inoculation. There is no doubt that intensified risk communication messages to the citizens on the importance of taking the vaccine (in line with the laid down plan for administering it to the various categories of citizens) was absolutely necessary and in order. However, this should not warrant threatening people at a time when the vaccines were limited in quantity.

Secondly, with respect to the distribution of the vaccine among the states, there was evidence that to a very large extent, there was distributional equity in the quantities given to the various states. This was against the background of the figures released previously before the arrival of the vaccine, which we had reacted in an earlier chapter as bad politics. This eventual correction was good politics which is highly commendable. For example, under the Phase 1 Rollout Plan which targeted frontline and essential personnel, the allocation to Lagos (507,000), FCT (219,800 and Kano (209,520) all making up 936,320 and representing 23% of the received quantity, which reflected distributional equity. This is because Lagos and FCT had the highest number of COVID-19 cases and even deaths. Apart from few states that received more out of the proportion of their contributions to the confirmed cases, there was distributional equity which should be maintained in the subsequent phases of the vaccine distribution. This author commends the efforts and sacrifice of the staff of National Primary Health Care Development Agency (NPHCDA), as well as those of the Primary Healthcare Centres that were administering the vaccines.

Recognizing the Generosity of Donors

The generosity of vaccine donors should not be taken for granted given the barrage of criticisms against vaccines and vaccination by critics. First, vaccine sceptics do not even recognize the fact that vaccines are not cheap to produce, distribute and administer. Secondly, many vaccine critics do not also recognize the enormous sacrifice made by some thoughtful individuals, countries, and donors in making vaccines available to poor countries and even to richly endowed but poorly governed countries like Nigeria. Consequently, it is appropriate to say few things about the thoughtful acts of vaccine donors.

There is a number of generous donors that make the COVAX Facility-delivered vaccines reach the poor countries of the world, and a realization which could reset the mind set of vaccine critics. Most of these donations indirectly come from hard earned incomes of tax payers in the developed world and some other less developed countries.

According to COVAX Facility, these donors include governments, foundations, the European Commission, countries of the European Union, Japan, the United Kingdom and the United States. From the list of vaccine donors, there are 15 countries under the Donor Governments category that include such other countries as Australia, Bhutan, Canada, Colombia, Japan, Korea, Kuwait, Monaco, New Zealand, Qatar, Saudi Arabia, Singapore and Switzerland. Secondly, there are 16 Donors under Team Europe category. Thirdly, there are 12 Donors under the category **of** Foundations, Corporations and Organizations. In addition to all these donors that focused on vaccine purchases, some countries notably Canada, Germany and the United States, also made generous donations towards vaccine delivery and/or logistics, covering 2021 and 2022.[215]
According to COVAX, these partners

---

[215] WHO Africa (2021) via https://www.afro.who.int/news/covid-19-vaccines-shipped-covax-arrive-nigeria.

have been especially active in working with some of the world's poorest countries: those that will benefit from the Advance Market Commitment (AMC), an innovative financial mechanism to help secure global and equitable access for COVID-19 vaccines. This includes assisting with the development of national vaccination plans, support for cold chain infrastructure, as well as stockpiling of half a billion syringes and safety boxes for their disposal, masks, gloves and other equipment to ensure that there was enough equipment for health workers to start vaccinating priority groups as soon as possible.[216]

As said earlier, vaccines do not come cheap. The relevant authorities are commended for administering the acquired vaccines with the utmost level of transparency and care. Fortunately, there were no eye-catching scandals associated with the administration of the various vaccines in the first phase roll out plan and subsequent phases.

[216] Ibid.

CHAPTER FORTY FOUR

COVID-19 Vaccine Nationalism Vs Equity

N ational policy responses to the containment of the ravaging COVID-19 pandemic across the world in 2020, varied across nations particularly more markedly between what can be called the high capacity performing governments and those of low capacity performance. Even at this, there were some exceptions. For example, the United States under former President Donald Trump was one such exception. Although the US belongs to the category of high capacity performing countries, its COVID-19 national policy response under Trump was a disaster. However, Trump invested hugely in the search and race for a vaccine which ultimately paid off. The emergence of President Joe Biden consolidated the achievement of Trump in the area of vaccine investment and production. Joe Biden's administration was effective in the procurement, logistics and administration of vaccines to US citizens. The history of COVID-19 devastation of the US changed for the better, as US restored its capacity to effectively address the challenges posed by the pandemic. The COVID-19 numbers (infection, hospitalization and fatality) steadily went down under President Biden.

Accusation of Vaccine Nationalism

One common feature characterizing all high capacity performing nations is their effective response to the pandemic particularly in the area of COVID-19 vaccine discovery, production, acquisition and its effective administration to their citizens. Serious (i.e. productive) leaders of some developed nations invested heavily in the race for the development of a vaccine. They followed this up with the signing of pre-purchase agreements with pharmaceutical companies to supply millions of vaccines for administration to their citizens. Meanwhile, many (less serious) leaders of low capacity performing nations were helplessly watching and did practically nothing to invest in vaccine discovery and production. As the success of vaccine acquisition and administration by developed countries became manifest, critics started accusing serious leaders of high capacity performing nations of cornering all the vaccines for their citizens to the exclusion of citizens of low capacity performing nations. Another accusation that emerged was that these serious leaders were hoarding the vaccines for their citizens only. From this accusation, one popular concept that emerged was vaccine nationalism.

According to Amir Khan,[217] vaccine nationalism "occurs when governments sign agreements with pharmaceutical manufacturers to supply their own populations with vaccines ahead of them becoming available for other countries". And as Globalcitizens.com says, "the term has essentially been coined in the wake of dozens of governments in wealthy countries scrambling to sign deals with pharmaceutical companies directly, to secure vaccines for their own populations — limiting the stock available for others." Seen in this light, vaccine nationalism is used in a pejorative sense.

This pejorative connotation neglects the fact that any serious leader of a country would endeavour to prevent the death of his/her citizens from the ravaging virus first before thinking of other countries. This is a natural law of survival which in itself is not bad. It appears that the concept of vaccine nationalism was hastily used at a time when high performing governments were nationalistically and commendably struggling to do everything within their powers to prevent the alarmingly high COVID-19-related deaths among their citizens. Seen in this perspective therefore, their actions were justifiable in prioritizing their national health problem first before going international.

The Call for Vaccine Equity

From the criticisms of vaccine nationalism and its concomitant vaccine inequality, the call for vaccine equity emerged with even greater force and passion. According to *Concern.org.uk* [218] vaccine equity means "distributing vaccines based on need first, regardless of someone's nationality or

---

[217] Aljazeera's Doctors Note (2021) via https://www.aljazeera.com/features/2021/2/7/what-is-vaccine-nationalism-and-why-is-it-so-harmful.

[218] Concern.org.uk via https://www.concern.org.uk/news/vaccine-equity-what-does-it-mean-and-how-can-it-be-achieved.

wealth." It goes to argue that "the pandemic will only end when everyone across the globe is protected." It added that "we know that no one is safe until everyone is safe." Vaccinating those on the frontline and the most vulnerable everywhere – irrespective of their wealth or nationality – is not a choice but a necessity. It is the only way back to 'normality'.[219] With this new concept in place, the World Health Organization (WHO) began to champion vigorously for vaccine equity. Its director-general, Dr Tedros Adhanom Ghebreyesus, decried the 'Me First' attitude to vaccine distribution describing it as 'catastrophic moral failure'. WHO then warned that the world faces 'catastrophic moral failure' because of unequal vaccine policies.

Intensifying its campaign, the WHO released the *Call to Action: Vaccine Equity* Declaration which specifically calls for:

➤ *World leaders* to increase contributions to the COVAX facility and to share doses with COVAX in parallel with national vaccine rollout.
➤ *Vaccine manufacturers* to share know-how with C-TAP to scale up vaccine manufacturing and dramatically increase the global supply of vaccines for the coming years. Furthermore, we ask for leaders to prioritize supplying to COVAX over new bilateral deals.
➤ *Regulatory bodies* to accelerate approval processes in a safe and deliberate way.
➤ *Ministries of Health* to work with WHO and others to invest in and prepare their primary health care systems for distribution of COVID-19 vaccines to their health workers and to develop data systems on vaccine supply, distribution and uptake, including sex-and age-disaggregated sub-national data, to drive delivery, equality and impact.
➤ *All governments* to ensure that COVID-19 vaccines are distributed free at the point of care and without risk of financial hardship, starting with health workers and those people at greatest risk of COVID-19, to prioritize affected communities and the voices of essential workers in decision-making and ensure gender equality is central to all actions.

---

[219] Ibid.

> ➤ Furthermore, it says that 'distributing COVID-19 vaccines quickly and equitably is essential to end this pandemic, restart our economies...[220]

As we pointed out earlier, the accusation of vaccine nationalism and hoarding of vaccines appeared to be somewhat premature at the time it was being made. We say so because those accused of vaccine nationalism were the ones who were also in partnership with COVAX - a 'global scheme formed to ensure fair access to inoculations for low-and middle-income states'. The global partnership also includes CEPI, Gavi, UNICEF and WHO – champions of vaccine equity. The point is that the countries accused of vaccine nationalism were not oblivious of the fact that any COVID-19 infection in any part of the world is a threat to the entire world – the basis upon which vaccine equity is being canvassed.

In conclusion, while we agree with the Director-General of WHO, Dr Tedros Ghebreyesus, that in as much as vaccine nationalism and its concomitant inequality may be a 'catastrophic moral failure', we also stress the fact that political leaders in developing countries should wake up to their responsibilities of strengthening their weak health systems. They should stop being complacent or wait for serious leaders in developed countries to do the investment in vaccines for them. The worst is that after this, these unproductive leaders in developing countries, would hide under the convenient slogan of vaccine equity to demand for the vaccines as if it is part of their natural right to enjoy the fruits of such investment. The bitter truth is that the huge investment in vaccine research and its eventual discovery, is funded mainly by tax payers' money in some high capacity performing nations. Unfortunately such resources in developing countries are frittered away through corruption by their unproductive political leaders.

---

[220] Who (2021) via https://www.who.int/campaigns/annual-theme/year-of-health-and-care-workers-2021/vaccine-equity-declaration.

CHAPTER FORTY FIVE

Resistance to Enforcement of Compulsory COVID-19 Vaccination Policy

COVID-19 pandemic has since its emergence remained very controversial, divisive and manifestly a conflict-ridden phenomenon. Right from its emergence in Wuhan, China in 2019, not a few people across the world doubted its reality. This phenomenal and disturbing doubt of COVID-19 existence prompted international and national health authorities to adopt the well-known risk communication catch-phrase COVID-19 is real. Even at this, some notable political leaders (like Donald Trump, former president of the United States of America; Brazilian President Jair Bolsonaro, Mexican President Andres Manuel Lopez Obrador, late president of Tanzania John Magufuli, and late president of Burundi Pierre Nkurunziza to mention just a few), doubted its existence for sheer political and selfish reasons. As a result, there emerged many irrational sceptics of COVID-19 around the world. Many have remained so regardless of the high fatalities recorded globally.

COVID-19 as a divisive Phenomenon

Apart from its early controversy, COVID-19 pandemic has also created and continued to create divisions, acrimony and manifest conflict between citizens and their governments around the world. The division and acrimony started with the adoption of different forms of non-pharmaceutical safety interventions such as lockdowns, wearing of face masks, prohibition of large social gatherings and in-door crowding of people, and maintenance of social distancing among others. Many people were seen in public not complying with these safety measures that were introduced by their governments. Meanwhile, there emerged a constant stream of protests and demonstrations against these measures in some countries, as we discussed in an earlier chapter.

The policy on compulsory wearing of face masks in public places became one of the most controversial of these non-pharmaceutical safety interventions in some countries. In the United States for instance, many people (particularly in the Republican Party) vehemently opposed the wearing of face masks. Some people with their young children even went to the extent of burning their face masks publicly, arguing that it was a violation of their constitutionally guaranteed fundamental human rights to liberty. To them, their personal freedom was paramount, regardless of the risk the exercise of such freedom, poses to public health.

The discovery of vaccines generated even more controversies, divisions and outright conflict in many countries as well. Many vaccine critics emerged in both the developed and developing countries. This again became a major challenge and concern to many governments across the world. The vaccine critics were not swayed by the glaring fact of the high fatality rate of the ravaging virus. For example, as of September 23, 2021 (at 13:21), the world recorded a total number of 230,189,529 cases of infections, and 4,721,127 deaths.[221] With over 230 million cases of infections globally, and close to five million deaths, many people were still not persuaded that vaccination was imperative. Their insensitivity to the danger which non-vaccination poses to public health became a very worrisome issue. It was at this point that various governments around the world responded to vaccine obstinacy by adopting one policy measure or the other in the interest of public health. Some countries made vaccination compulsory for their citizens generally or just for their public servants. Some other governments went further to make vaccination as a condition for entering public offices and for accessing government services.

Compulsory COVID-19 Vaccination Policy and its Resistance

On October 13, 2021, the Federal Government (FG) of Nigeria announced, through the PSC on COVID-19, that it would make vaccination compulsory for its employees with effect from December 1, 2021. By this announcement, it gave adequate notice to its employees before the implementation of this policy. Prior to the announcement, the government was adopting moral persuasion strategy to appeal to those it

---

[221] John Hopkins Coronavirus Resource Centre,
via https://coronavirus.jhu.edu/map.html.

called vaccine 'hesitants' and critics to get vaccinated in the interest of public health. At the same period, some state governments went ahead to make vaccination compulsory for their workers and for others who want to access services provided by them. They were compelled to do so because their appeal to the conscience of the people was not yielding the desired results.

Edo state was the first state government to announce the adoption of a compulsory vaccination policy. This was closely followed by Ondo State and later by Osun State. A couple of other states also announced their intention to adopt the policy. The policy in Edo State stated that those "who have not taken COVID-19 vaccines will be prevented from accessing churches, mosques, banks, event centres and other public places from the middle of September" in 2021. The Ondo State Government also adopted a similar policy of barring people entering churches, mosques and other public places if they fail to take the vaccines on or before 14 September 2021.

In Edo State, the implementation of the policy generated a lot of controversies. First, there was a huge demonstration by people in the state. Secondly, the Nigerian Medical Association (NMA) and the health workers in the state under the umbrella of the Joint Health Sector Unions (JOHESU) criticized the adoption of the policy. The NMA for instance argued that the "people have the right to reject vaccines the same way they can reject medical treatment". Thirdly, JOHESU on its part harshly called the adoption of the policy senseless. Fourthly, the Federal High Court, Port Harcourt, Rivers State granted an order restraining the Edo State Government from enforcing the policy. The Court order was unfortunate, as it was wrong for anyone to play with such an issue that involves life and death. However, regardless of these, the Edo State government commenced the enforcement of the policy. The enforcement of the policy actually progressed well and unhindered. The implementation was seen as the right way to go, more so when the five deaths that were reported on September 21, 2021 in the state, were among the unvaccinated. These deaths could have been prevented if those affected were vaccinated.

Appropriateness of FG's Compulsory COVID-19 vaccination policy

With the bold implementation of the compulsory COVID-19

vaccination policy by the Edo State Government (policy pathfinder) and later by Ondo State Government (co-policy pathfinder), the PSC on COVID-19 rolled out the federal government compulsory vaccination policy that took effect from December 1, 2021. The policy provided that federal government employees were required to "show proof of COVID-19 vaccination or present a negative COVID-19 PCR test result done within 72 hours, to gain access to their offices, in all locations within Nigeria and our Missions."[222] The announcement of this policy was made by the Chairman of the PSC on COVID-19 and Secretary to the Government of the Federation, Mr. Boss Mustapha.

Immediately after the announcement, some critics raised objections to the compulsory character of the policy. They felt that it breached the liberty of individuals who were not willing to take the COVID-19 vaccines. They forgot that the policy was not 100% compulsory, as there was an option for those who out rightly refused to take the vaccine. However, the option itself has a compulsory requirement that an unvaccinated person must present "a negative COVID-19 PCR test result done within 72 hours."

Some people may ask: what is this PCR test that must be compulsorily presented as an alternative to remaining unvaccinated? According to the Cleveland Clinic:

> ...the polymerase chain reaction (PCR) test for COVID-19 is a molecular test that analyses your upper respiratory specimen, looking for genetic material (ribonucleic acid or RNA) of SARS-CoV-2, the virus that causes COVID-19. Scientists use the PCR technology to amplify small amounts of RNA from specimens into deoxyribonucleic acid (DNA), which is replicated until SARS-CoV-2 is detectable if present. The PCR test has been the gold standard test for diagnosing COVID-19 since authorised for use in February 2020. It's accurate and reliable.[223]

---

[222] See for instance Obasi, I. N. (2021): 'Enforcing FG's 'Compulsory' COVID-19 vaccination policy'. Sundiata Post via https://sundiatapost.com/enforcing-fgs-compulsory-covid-19-vaccination-policy-by-isaac-n-obasi/, October 22.

[223] Cleveland Clinic via https://my.clevelandclinic.org/health/diagnostics/21462-covid-19-and-pcr-testing.

Seen in this light therefore, the policy gave option for a person to remain unvaccinated but makes it compulsory for that person to present a negative PCR test result within 72 hours. The choice is freely within the power of the individual to decide to remain unvaccinated. However that choice, must NOT (emphasis ours) endanger public health which is what a negative PCR test result within 72 hours compulsorily demands. Critics of the compulsory vaccination policy who say that it restricts the liberty of an individual have, therefore, no case to make as the policy has expressly given an individual the freedom to select from the two options namely (a) get vaccinated or (b) show a negative PCR test result.

The Federal Government was on a right path to enforce the mandatory vaccination policy as announced. There were many good reasons to enforce the implementation. First, the protection of public health is paramount not only in Nigeria but all over the world. The aviation industry as well as its tourist counterpart became the worst economically hit under the pandemic because of measures taken by many countries to protect public health. In fact, priority was placed on public health than on pursuit of money. This goes to show that in the public space, the exercise of freedom (liberty) is allowed to the extent that it would not endanger public health namely the health of the generality of the population.

Secondly, since COVID-19 pandemic kills people on a large scale or on an unimaginable proportion, everything within the realm of civility must be made to mitigate its devastating effects. Although WHO reported that global record of cases and death showed a declining trend as at October 2021, Nigerians should not forget that the pandemic was still ravaging the world. The Moscow Times, Russia (on Monday, October 18, 2021), reported a new record high number of "34,325 cases and 998 deaths over the last 24 hours." It revealed further that on Tuesday, 19 October 2021, Russia reported 33,740 new cases and 1,015 deaths, showing an increase in the number of deaths.[224] Since Nigerians (including our public servants) travel a lot all over the world, the Federal

---

[224] The Moscow Times (2021) via https://www.themoscowtimes.com/2021/10/19/coronavirus-in-russia-the-latest-news-oct-19-a69117, October 19.

Government was on the right path of taking the compulsory vaccination measure to protect her citizens.

Thirdly, in many countries, a good number of people have not been obeying the COVID-19 safety protocols thereby endangering the health of many in society. This is also the case with Nigeria, as many people in social and religious gatherings violated the COVID-19 non-pharmaceutical protocols with impunity, thereby taking God's mercy for granted. In spite of all the risk communication messages from the Nigeria Centre for Disease Control (NCDC) and from other agencies of the federal and state governments, many Nigerians were moving in the public spaces with the business-as-usual mentality. Such a mentality requires the implementation of a compulsory vaccination policy to check the spread of the virus.

Finally, for critics who argue that full vaccination is not really the antidote against COVID-19 infection by citing cases of some people who took the vaccination and still died, these critics appear to be ignorant of how science works. Some critics even cite the case of a high profile American General and distinguished diplomat, Colin Powell, who died in spite of being fully vaccinated. Such an isolated example further demonstrate that these critics have limited understanding of science, as few deviations from the mean do not invalidate a confirmed hypothesis (proven fact). A man who died at the age of 84 years following complications from COVID-19 with an underlying condition (namely cancer and Parkinson's disease), did not just die because of COVID-19. The man had even done pretty well in managing his health.

In conclusion, with availability of vaccines in the country, a policy on compulsory vaccination makes sense and has to be sustained. This is the way to go in the interest of public health. In any case, the policy became a global best practice as no one could travel to some countries then without showing evidence of having been vaccinated. Across the world, many COVID-19-related recorded deaths, were predominantly among the unvaccinated. This being the case, compulsory vaccination is the way to go.

306

CHAPTER FORTY SIX

Averting the 'Pandemic of the Unvaccinated'

This brief chapter is to demonstrate that COVID-19 vaccination remains the most effective means to reduce the severity of COVID-19 and possibly get out of the ravaging pandemic. This is because overwhelming evidence show that it is within the group of the unvaccinated that COVID-19 infection has been mainly reported across the world around 2021.

The Evidence

On 1st September 2021, the Associated Press (AP) in a news report said that "this summer's coronavirus resurgence has been labelled a 'pandemic of the unvaccinated' by government officials from President Joe Biden on down". The report revealed that 'the glaring reality' is "that unvaccinated people overwhelmingly account for new cases and serious infections, with a recent study of government data showing that hospitalisation rates among unvaccinated adults were 17 times higher than among those fully vaccinated." According to President Joe Biden "the pandemic of the unvaccinated is a tragedy that is preventable."[225] Then on 3rd November 2021, the CNN reported that:

> Germany's Health Minister Jens Spahn said the country was experiencing a "massive" pandemic of the unvaccinated as authorities raised the alarm on rising infections and increased pressure on hospitals due to Covid-19 admissions. The number of infections is increasing, as well as the number of deaths from Covid and especially the number of patients in intensive care units in some regions of Germany, regions where vaccination rates are not as high as in other regions.[226]

---

[225] Associated Press (AP) (2021): "Questioning a catchphrase: 'Pandemic of the Unvaccinated'" via https://apnews.com/article/health-pandemics-coronavirus-pandemic-9845c7257300ff6546c20489e642a1ea). September 1. (Report by Ricardo Alonso-Saldivar).

[226] CNN (2021) via https://edition.cnn.com/2021/11/03/europe/germany-fourth-wave-unvaccinated-intl/index.html).

Furthermore, it reported the German minister as saying that 'the truth is that there would be far fewer Covid-19 patients in [intensive care] if everyone who could do it got a vaccination'. The minister then called for measures to "strengthen checks at public venues where only those with proof of vaccination or a Covid-19 recovery certificate will be granted entry."

It cannot be overemphasized that Nigerians who are yet unvaccinated should do so in the on-going vaccination exercise across the country. The fact is that as long as COVID-19 subsists even at a very low rate of infection, the need for vaccination is still there and some aspects of the observance of non-pharmaceutical safety measures should also subsist.

Although, the massive vaccination programme of governments across the country is progressing well, many Nigerians are yet to go for their vaccination in spite of the enlightenment campaigns and persuasive efforts going on across the country. The low or slow response accounts for why more state governments have joined in making the presentation of vaccination certificate or negative COVID-19 test result, a condition for entry into their work places. This is the minimum that can be tolerated in the interest and promotion of public health, meanwhile, some other countries are already implementing a more stringent policy in this regard.

In the United States for example, the ABC news of September 30, 2021 reported that "hundreds of health care workers across the country are being fired or suspended in droves for not complying with COVID-19 vaccine mandates. President Joe Biden announced earlier this month a vaccine mandate for health care facilities that receive Medicare and Medicaid reimbursement, impacting some 17 million health care workers in the nation. States including New York, California, Rhode Island and Connecticut also set vaccine mandates for health care workers that take effect this week."[227]

---

[227] ABC news (2021) via https://abcnews.go.com/US/hundreds-hospital-staffers-fired-suspended-refusing-covid-19/story?id=80303408.

Specifically again, ABC news also reported that:

> …in North Carolina, the Novant Health hospital system, which has over 35,000 employees across 15 hospitals and over 800 clinics, fired around 175 of its workers for failing to get vaccinated…In Texas, Houston Methodist Hospital, which has some 26,000 employees, saw 153 employees quit or fired over the vaccine requirement after the June 7 deadline to get the shots. Of those, 26 were nurses…In Delaware, 150 employees left ChristianaCare, a major hospital system in the state, after they failed to meet the Sept. 21 deadline to get vaccinated…In New York, hundreds of staffers have been suspended this week and risk losing their jobs as the statewide vaccine mandate for health workers reached its first dose deadline…In New York City, about 500 nurses for NYC Health + Hospitals are not at work and have been preemptively replaced. Unvaccinated workers have been placed on unpaid leave but can return once they get their shot.[228]

Furthermore, in the United Kingdom, the inews of November 3, 2021 reported that, "all NHS staff in England will have to get both Covid-19 and flu vaccines or risk losing their job as the Government prepares to crackdown on those who still refuse to get protected." It went on further to say that "although the vast majority of the health service's 1.4 million employees have already been vaccinated against Covid, around 100,000 people have yet to do so."[229] It was widely reported in the press that these 100,000 NHS staff were directed to get vaccinated or lose their job. It is either you get a jab or lose your job. If this is the harsh reality in some other countries, Nigerians who are yet to go for vaccination and still kicking against federal and some state governments' vaccine mandate policy (which even offers them the 'luxury' of an option) need to reconsider their stand.

In conclusion, the truth is that as President Joe Biden rightly stated above, "the pandemic of the unvaccinated is a tragedy that is preventable." This wise and instructive statement should inspire other

---

[228] Ibid.
[229] https://inews.co.uk/news/health/all-nhs-staff-in-england-will-need-mandatory-covid-and-flu-vaccines-or-risk-losing-their-jobs-1281852.

Chapter Forty six | Isaac Nnamdi Obasi

countries such as Nigeria, to continue to take proactive measures to avert this preventable scourge. Nigeria therefore needs to keep our eyes fixed on the ball to make sure that the unvaccinated do not pose serious risk to our public health. The statistics of Nigerians vaccinated as at the second week of April 2022, was only about 13 million people representing about 12% of the population. However, data from *Our World in Data*[230] as of 22 August 2022 reveal a significant improvement. The data show that as of that date, 61.6 million doses had been given, with 28.2 million people fully vaccinated. The percentage of population fully vaccinated was 13.7%. Although, this is commendable, the saying however that to be fore-warmed is to be fore-arned (forewarned is forearmed) is a reminder that proactive measures should continue to be taken by federal and state governments against the spread or resurgence of COVID-19. However, the greater focus of such proactive measures should be on the unvaccinated section of the population. From available evidence on the vaccination efforts, the government appears to be on track.

---

[230] Our World in Data (2022): Nigeria: COVID-19 vaccine, via https://www.google.com /search?q=coronavirus+vaccine+nigeria&rlz=1C1RLNS_enNG815NG817&oq=Statistics+of +Nigerians+vaccinated+against+COVID-19...

Part Eight
COVID-19 Pandemic: Cross-cutting and General Issues

CHAPTER FORTY SEVEN

The Spiritual Dimension of COVID-19 Pandemic

Across the world, the policy response to COVID-19 pandemic was not strictly limited to pharmaceutical and non-pharmaceutical interventions, as some countries adopted a spiritual approach to the problem. In Nigeria, the Federal Government at a point in 2020 resorted to a spiritual intervention calling on God to stem the tide of the then rising cases of infections and deaths. Seen against the fact that there is an omniscient and omnipotent God, this spiritual approach was not bad in itself when done with a sincere heart and also following science. However, in two African countries (Tanzania and Burundi), this approach was taken too far and it lead to the avoidable death of their presidents. In Nigeria, where the approach was combined with science, the action still generated controversies among critics who accused the government of running out of ideas of how to handle the COVID-19 crisis. This chapter underscores the importance of the spiritual dimension of COVID-19 when the approach is combined with science.

Different Interpretations of Government's call for Prayers

In July 2020, the Federal Government said that it had become necessary to call on all Nigerians to seek the face of God in order to stop the spread of COVID-19 pandemic. The Chairman of PTF on COVID-19, Mr. Boss Mustapha said this during the National Briefing on COVID-19 on Thursday, 2 July 2020. Continuing, he said that:

> …in furtherance of the synergy being built, the Co-Chairmen of the Nigerian Inter-religious Council NIREC, His Eminence Alhaji Mohammed Sa'ad Abubakar, CFR, the Sultan of Sokoto/President General of the Nigerian Supreme Council for Islamic Affairs, and His Eminence Rev. Dr. Samson O. A. Ayokunle, President of the Christian Association of Nigeria, CAN, would be directing Muslim and Christian adherents all over the country to go in for a period of fasting and prayer. The NIREC will announce the details and we urge all Nigerians

to participate in this effort to seek divine intervention.[231]

This call for prayers and fasting was subject to different interpretations, and three of which are examined here. First, some people could rightly see the call as a sincere and humble resignation to the Almighty God to intervene in a novel pandemic that was then incomprehensible to world's greatest scientists, God and only God alone is omniscient. Seen from this spiritual lens therefore, the call was in order. Any right thinking nation should be humble enough to do this, for as the saying goes: "when you are in crisis, your strongest position is on your knees."[232]

Relatedly, as Michel (2020)[233] rightly said "as COVID-19 sends the globe into a crisis, it also sends us to our knees", and again as "prayer is never the last resort of God's people. It is our first point of action." With respect to Nigeria, there was every reason for all right thinking and humble hearts to pray fervently to God to come to her aid and to the entire sinful world, to take this plague away. Indeed, for men of humble hearts, worldly knowledge and wisdom alone might not defeat this pandemic scourge. For those who believe, science and faith are needed to work together to remove the scourge of a novel pandemic.

The resort to prayers had long been in use since the outbreak of COVID-19 pandemic. Anyone who went on the Internet then would be surprised to see multiplicity of prayers adopted by groups and religious organisations throughout the world including Nigeria. The Catholic Archdiocese of Lagos for example, had its own prayer against the pandemic since its outbreak. This prayer was recited in its Holy Masses every day and also transmitted live on the Lumen Christi Television (Channel 350 on DSTV). Many of the prayers (in and outside Nigeria) were started as early as the months of March, through April and May. The bottom line, therefore, is that the adoption of prayers against the COVID-19 was in practice since the outbreak of the virus.

---

[231] Vanguard (2020): "COVID-19: FG goes spiritual, partners religious leaders on Prayers, Fasting', July 3, via https://www.vanguardngr.com/2020/07/covid-19-fg-goes-spiritual-partners-religious-leaders-on-prayers-fasting/.

[232] Fritz Chery (2020): 'Plagues', *Bible Verses About*, May 9, via http://www.Biblereason.com.

[233] Michel, J. P. (2020): *Christianity Today International*, March 18.

The second possible interpretation of the call for prayers and fasting is that the PTF on COVID-19 might was running out of ideas and steam in its efforts to contain the increasing and equally embarrassing spread of the virus in our dear country. Critics, therefore, saw the call as a sign of failure of the Government to effectively confront the deadly disease. The critics were asking for effective policy interventions to stop the spread rather than the easy recourse to prayers and fasting by the people. Such critics would likely cite the delay in paying the allowances of medical personnel (who were fighting both at the front line of attack and at the last line of defence against this virus), as a demonstration of lack of seriousness on the part of the government.

The third angle of interpretation of the call was given by some critics who felt that religion should be separated from the State, and that the PTF on COVID-19 therefore had no business in the first place calling for a spiritual intervention by the two main religions in Nigeria, since religion is a private affair. Late Dr. Obadia Mailafia (former Deputy Governor of the Central Bank of Nigeria), was among those who strongly shared this view. Appearing on *The Morning Show* of ARISE NEWS Television (Monday, July 6, 2020), Dr. Mailafia criticised the introduction of religion to COVID-19 pandemic in Nigeria, on the basis that there is too much hypocrisy. For him, the government should keep religion out of it. He recommended, however, that people should pray privately against the scourge.

One would no doubt agree with Dr. Mailafia that there has been too much hypocrisy and manipulation of religion in Nigeria which might reduce the efficacy of such prayers and fasting. The Scripture is clear about this when it says 'righteousness exalts a nation, but sin is a reproach to any people' (Proverbs 14:34). It needs to be added however, that a call for prayers and fasting was still necessary as a challenge to such hypocrites. The presence of Hypocrisy should not discourage the Saints since Jesus Christ himself spoke extensively against hypocrisy of leaders (which applies to both the Spiritual and Temporal in our case here) in the whole of Chapter 23 of the Gospel of Matthew. And in spite of the existence of hypocrisy, Jesus urged his Believers to do what the leaders tell them to do, but not to imitate their actions, because they don't practise what they preach. So calling for prayers and fasting was still a good idea.

It is strongly argued that while the Federal Government made the initial mistake of delaying to take some proactive measures during the first and second weeks of the month of March 2020, it however demonstrated some level of seriousness through the PTF on COVID-19, and the Nigeria Centre for Disease Control (NCDC) under the Federal Ministry of Health, in fighting the spread of the virus. The ever-presence of verve and steam on their part, was a measure of the federal government's strength when benchmarked with some other countries like the United States under Trump for instance. Nigeria deployed science effectively in the management of COVID-19. And its resort to spiritual intervention was not misplaced. It is against this backdrop that one can say that the accusation that the government was running out of ideas and steam by critics appeared to hold no water or to a large extent over-exaggerated.

The Spiritual Root of COVID-19

The spiritual root of COVID-19 pandemic is a controversial one. Although one does not claim any expertise to discuss this matter authoritatively, but one feels that there is a spiritual dimension to the pandemic. The Holy Scriptures have 50 major verses about plagues.[234] The plagues are about human beings and some of them had actually taken place in the past, while some others are yet to happen. Plagues therefore have a biblical root and they exist to achieve different purposes. As Chery rightly mentioned: (a) God uses plagues for His glory, e.g. 2 Samuel 24:13, Habakkuk 3:5-6, Psalm 91:5-6; (b) God used plagues to demonstrate his great power in punishing the stubborn Pharaoh of Egypt in the Ten Plagues (See Exodus Chapters 7-12); (c) In the Book of Revelation, seven plagues that will occur in the Tribulation Period are well revealed. These plagues demonstrate the wrath of God.[235]

There are many instances where plagues, pestilence, scourge, and famine were talked about in the Holy Scriptures. Over the centuries in

---

[234] Chery F. (2020): 'Plagues', *Bible Verses About*, May 9, via http://www.Biblereason.com
[235] Ibid.

history, plagues in the form of pandemics have been recurring events at least once or more than once in a century. The 1918 Flu pandemic regarded as one of the deadliest pandemic in human history infected 500 million people and killed between 17 million and 50 million plus people.[236]

In conclusion, the lesson for all of us (big and small, rich and poor, strong and weak) is to know always that the mercy and wrath (justice) of God are both a reality. Human beings who truly seek God do understand that God's words always come to fulfilment. And as Packer aptly concluded "to know that nothing happens in God's world apart from God's will may frighten the godless, but it stabilizes the Saints."[237]

---

[236] Wikipedia, The Free Encyclopedia via http://www.en.m.wikipedia.org
[237] Packer, J. I.: "Is the coronavirus a Plague from Revelation, 50 Important Bible Verses About Plagues".

CHAPTER FORTY EIGHT

World Mask Week amidst Opposition against Face Mask

The Week of Friday, August 7 to Friday, August 14, 2020 was a period of a globally-organised public awareness campaign on wearing of face mask tagged *World Mask Week*. The aim of the World Mask Week was "to inspire global movement to wear face coverings in public". In fact, the week long campaign was an initiative of many partner organisations such as the Pandemic Action Network, the World Health Organisation (WHO), the US CDC, Africa CDC, the CDC Foundation, the Federation of American Scientists (FAS), Facebook, Google, Global Citizen, and over 40 other partner organisations.[238]

Opposition against wearing of Face Mask

The World Mask Week campaign was a compelling-awareness and enlightenment exercise, given the controversy surrounding the wearing of mask in some parts of the world. The politicisation and jettisoning of the wearing of face mask in some countries was a big and troubling challenge in curbing the spread of COVID-19 pandemic across the world. In a very well propagated, notorious, embarrassing and unscientific manner, three world leaders namely the then President of the United States of America, Donald Trump; President of Brazil, Jair Bolsonaro; and the President of Mexico, Andrés Manuel López Obrador, dismissed the wearing of mark in ways that also discouraged many of their citizens from wearing such. Yet, the wearing of mask was proven and recognised globally as a potent means of stopping the spread of COVID-19. Unfortunately, a sizeable number of people across the world did not see it so.

In Nigeria, the reluctance to wear face/nose mask in public places and in large gathering of people was a big challenge militating against the efforts of both the federal and state governments to stop the further

---

[238] Africa CDC (2020) via https://africacdc.org/news-item/world-mask-week-aims-to-inspire-global-movement-to-wear-face-coverings-in-public/

spread of the deadly coronavirus. Incidentally, Nigeria is not alone in this low level of compliance with the wearing of face mask, as some other countries of the world were also experiencing the same challenge. The low level of compliance consequently became a source of global concern, hence the imperative of 'World Mask Week'.

In the United States of America for example, there were some states and counties where the wearing of mask was not made mandatory. The governors and mayors of such areas remained adamant over calls to make the wearing of mask mandatory amidst the high number of daily deaths recorded. Although, such high number of deaths amply demonstrated the reality of COVID-19, some people stubbornly refused to wear mask, seeing the wearing of such mask as infringing on their democratic rights. This was an act of taking their freedom or liberty too far, thereby crossing the red line in the exercise of such freedom. This is because their excesses (non-compliance) posed serious danger to other people's right to life – a non-negotiable issue. Unfortunately, many of these people (in US and elsewhere) had to suffer severely from the deadly virus before accepting its reality. Some had to apologise for downplaying the deadly nature of the virus, while some did not have the opportunity to be alive to regret their action of doubting the ravaging disease.

Significance of the World Mask Week in Nigeria

It is against the background of all these that one could appreciate the significance of the World Mask Week. Nigeria joined the rest of the world to mark the World Mask Week using the #MaskOnNaija. Two separate statements from the honourable Minister of Health, Dr. Osagie Ehanire, and the Director-General of the Nigeria Centre for Disease Control (NCDC), Dr. Chikwe Ihekweazu, were released to encourage Nigerians to always wear their marks. The minister's statement reads, "the appropriate use of face masks is one of the most comprehensive non-pharmaceutical preventive and control measures adopted to limit the spread of COVID-19." The then Director-General of NCDC restated his often quoted apt statement that "wearing a mask is less cumbersome than being on a ventilator."[239] If you think a mask is inconveniencing, as he also always said, try a ventilator.

Although, the week-long campaign received media attention, it was doubtful if the expected level of behaviour modification and compliance of Nigerians was appreciable. Prior to the World Mask Week, the NCDC was already sending out appropriate text messages to Nigerians. Two of such messages read: "Wearing a mask helps protect us from the droplets that carry the COVID-19 virus. Please Take Responsibility for your health and for your loved ones;" and the second: "Ease of lockdown does NOT mean that COVID-19 is over. Take Responsibility. Cover your nose/mouth with a mask..."

The Issue of Low Level of Compliance

In spite of these messages, a lot of Nigerians moved about without any mask even when entering public transport such as buses and taxis that carry other passengers. The level of abuse in the use of mask by a number of users was high. It was irritating. Some just pretended to be complying by putting it under their chin (jaw). Some others just covered their mouth leaving the nose. Unfortunately, some who wore the mask appropriately, removed it when they want to speak to people standing very close to them. This meant that people very close to them could get the droplets in such a situation. This therefore defeated the essence of wearing the mask. Many politicians, some government officials, as well as choristers in many Churches or worship centres were equally guilty of this practice. For Church choristers, the use of plastic-like face shield should have been a good alternative to avoid the situation of the mask pulling off the mouth while singing.

The low level of compliance was embarrassing when it was found to be common even in the House of God. These were people who ought to obey easily or were expected to obey easily for fear of God. However, many were observed entering the Church with their masks on, but quickly put it under their chin as soon as they settled down for worship.

---

[239] See,https://web.facebook.com/NCDCgov/photos/pcb.3492858200777178/34928578041105 51/?type=3&theater

A case in point was what happened in one of the worship centres which was very disgraceful. As the service was going on, the officiating minister who is an Archbishop made a passionate appeal to members of his congregation to make sure that they wear their masks properly by covering their mouth and nose. Right there standing before the Archbishop were two men (one elderly and the other middle aged), who never adjusted their wrongly placed masks even in front of a television camera covering the service for viewers across the entire world. The two men kept participating in the worship as if they were exempted from the directive of the Archbishop. By the way, if the elderly man felt inconvenienced wearing a mask, why bother to come to the place when people of his age were asked to worship from home. There was however no reason why the Church wardens did not enforce the directive of the Archbishop with some measure of authority.

If this type of behaviour with impunity was observed before a highly placed minister of God, it is doubtful if this type of people will ever obey any government directive or act in ways to promote the public goods. Their concern would always be self and self alone. It is even worse when there is a high level of trust-deficit between the rulers and the ruled in our society.

In conclusion, the World Mask Week (August 7-14, 2020) was meant to improve the attitude of people towards the wearing of face mask across the world significantly. However, opposition and reluctance to the wearing of mask persisted across the world with some people in Republican party-controlled states in the US publicly burning their face masks with those of their children. As revealed above, the low level of compliance was prevalent in Nigeria throughout the active period of COVID-19. The World Mask Week therefore appeared not to have made appreciable impact in Nigeria. Nevertheless, it was a useful public awareness campaign.

CHAPTER FORTY NINE

Nigeria Economic Sustainability Plan under COVID-19

The Background: Recalling the Effects of COVID-9 on Livelihood

The outbreak of the Coronavirus (COVID-19) pandemic was an emergency that created serious health and economic crises across the globe. In order to stop the spread of the virus, many nations responded (among other policy interventions) by imposing a lockdown that restricted the movement of people, goods and services except for very essential activities. However, the lockdown in turn seriously threatened economic livelihood in both the formal and informal sectors of the economy. For instance, international trade suffered and economies of many nations experienced deeper crisis than ever imagined. In the informal sector also, many of those in self-employment became more vulnerable to threat to their livelihood.

In Nigeria, there were numerous and vociferous complaints that the lockdown was generating unintended consequences such as hunger-virus, increased number of reported rape cases, and other forms of domestic violence. Many who depended on daily economic activities for survival became poorer as their lives were threatened. The concept of hunger-virus emerged. The some people argued that hunger-virus itself was claiming more lives than the dreaded and ravaging coronavirus. In Lagos, Ogun and Delta states, among others, there were reported cases of youth restiveness manifesting in protests, violent demonstrations and armed robbery attacks in some neighbourhoods.

In some sectors, jobs were lost as employers could not afford to pay their workers. In some other sectors retention of jobs became seriously threatened, as the devastating impact of COVID-19 was high. Some sectors were forced to remain on lockdown much longer than others, while some witnessed partial re-opening of activities. The sectors that were badly affected include the entertainment industry, the private education sub-sector, the aviation industry, the hospitality and service industry (including event planning, catering and restaurants). Many organisations in these industries suffered incalculable economic losses as a result of the lockdown. The need for a stimulus package to get them out of the impending doom and gloom became urgent. This informed the intervention programme of giving strong financial support to these endangered sectors. Consequently, the Economic Sustainability Plan of the Buhari administration was conceived.

The adoption of the Economic Sustainability Plan

Amidst this bold idea, the Nigeria's economy plummeted with the price of crude oil falling as low as $18 a barrel. This was against the $57 used as benchmark in the 2020 budget. This notwithstanding, President Muhammadu Buhari promptly responded by setting up the Economic Sustainability Committee (ESC) on 30 March 2020. The ESC was headed by the Vice-President, Prof. Yemi Osinbajo with five ministers as well as the Governor of the Central Bank of Nigeria (CBN), and Group Managing Director of Nigerian National Petroleum Corporation (NNPC) as members. The Permanent Secretary, Cabinet Office served as the Secretary to the Committee. In addition, nine other ministers whose activities were relevant to the work of the Committee were co-opted.

It is important to examine how the Nigeria Economic Sustainability Plan[240] (developed by the ESC) proposed to address the economic problems generated by the COVID-19 pandemic as identified earlier. In looking at this, some relevant questions need to be addressed. First, are the terms of reference given to the ESC adequate enough to address the identified economic problems? Secondly, did the Economic Sustainability Plan developed by the ESC replace the existing Economic Recovery and Growth Plan (ERGP)? Thirdly, was the 9-Point Agenda announced by President Buhari (as his priority plan in the remaining three years of his administration) different from the Economic Sustainability Plan? Fourth question, what were the general objectives and pillars of the Economic Sustainability Plan? Fifth question, what were the key projects proposed in the Economic Sustainability Plan, and could these projects be realistically accomplished within the 12 month lifespan of the Plan? Sixth question, were the needs and fears of the higher education sub-sector

---

[240] See Federal Republic of Nigeria (2020): Bouncing Back: Nigeria Economic Sustainability Plan 2020.

adequately taken care of, in the Plan given the perennial crisis in the sub-sector? These and some other questions are examined in this chapter.

Terms of Reference (TOR) of the ESC

The ESC was given the following terms of reference:

(i) Develop a clear Economic Sustainability Plan in response to challenges posed by the COVID-19 Pandemic;

(ii) (ii) Identify fiscal measures for enhancing distributable oil and gas revenue, increasing non-oil revenues and reducing non-essential spending, towards securing sufficient resources to fund the plan;

(iii) (iii) Propose monetary policy measures in support of the Plan;

(iv) (iv) Provide a Fiscal/Monetary Stimulus Package, including support to private businesses (with emphasis on strategic sectors most affected by the pandemic) and vulnerable segments of the population;

(v) (v) Articulate specific measures to support the States and FCT; and

(vi) (vi) Propose a clear-cut strategy to keep existing jobs and create opportunities for new ones; and (vii) Identify measures that may require legislative support to deliver the plan.[241]

The TOR as outlined above had a mixture of thematic areas that could comprehensively and adequately address the economic problems identified earlier. This was because the TOR touched on measures that could address the COVID-19 generated problems in both the formal and informal sectors.

The Link between the Sustainability Plan and the ERGP

The question of whether the Economic Sustainability Plan replaced the then existing Economic Recovery and Growth Plan (ERGP) was a genuine one. Actually there appeared to be confusion between the two Plans, but looking closely, the confusion was apparent than real. The Sustainability Plan drew a lot from the ERGP and as the ESC rightly

---

[241] Ibid.

pointed out, the ERGP was one of the four existing documents that were incorporated into the Sustainability Plan. The other ones were (i) Report of the Economic Crisis Committee (headed by the Hon. Minister of Finance, Budget & National Planning); (ii) The Finance Act 2019; and (iii) Central Bank of Nigeria (CBN) Proposals.

The Sustainability Plan and President Buhari's 9-Point Agenda

The announcement by President Buhari that his remaining three years in office would focus on nine key areas, raised some questions as to whether the 9-Point Agenda had also replaced the Sustainability Plan. Some analysts were wondering why the president who had been struggling to achieve his three areas of priority focus (security, economy and anti-corruption) since five years would suddenly announce a 9-Point Agenda for the next three years. However, looking closely at the Sustainability Plan, one would discover that the 9-Point Agenda were drawn directly from the key proposed projects in the Sustainability Plan. There was actually no confusion but if there was any at all, it was as a result of the lack of clarity in the announcement of the nine key areas of focus.

   What follows now is a discussion of some specific aspects of the Plan. Before presenting and examining the key proposed projects of the Plan, the general objectives as well as the three pillars of the Plan have to be examined. It is important to point out again that the Sustainability Plan was designed to be executed in 12 months and hence both the general objectives and the three pillars were also meant to cover 12 months. All these meant that the Sustainability Plan was an emergency intervention which implied that time was of essence in achieving the various projects.

General Objectives of the Plan

The general objectives of the plan were:

   (i) to stimulate the economy by preventing business collapse and ensuring liquidity; (ii) retain or create jobs using labour intensive methods in key areas like agriculture, facility maintenance, housing and direct labour interventions;

(iii)undertake growth enhancing and job creating infrastructural investments in roads, bridges, solar power, and communications technologies; (iv) promote manufacturing and local production at all levels and advocate the use of Made-in-Nigeria goods and services, as a way of creating job opportunities, achieving self-sufficiency in critical sectors of our economy and curbing unnecessary demand for foreign exchange which might put pressure on the exchange rate; and (v) extend protection to the very poor and other vulnerable groups – including women and persons living with disabilities – through pro-poor spending.[242]

These general objectives were consistent with the Terms of Reference and therefore covered adequately a wide-range of economic issues and problems generated/or exacerbated by the COVID-19 pandemic. This consistency or clarity of purpose would no doubt facilitate implementation of proposed projects in so far as the corresponding political will and spirit of selfless service were present.

Three pillars of the Plan

The pillars of the Plan were (a) real sector measures, (b) fiscal and monetary measures, and (c) implementation. The aim of the Real Sector Measures was "to safeguard existing micro, small and medium scale businesses while ramping up local productive capacity by encouraging opportunities for innovation in the various sectors". The aim of the Fiscal and Monetary Measures was to "maximise government revenue, optimise expenditure and enshrine a regime of prudence with an emphasis on achieving value for money." Its overriding objective was to "keep the economy active…and boost investments in strategic sectors affected by the COVID-19 pandemic, while supporting the financial viability of State Governments." Under the third pillar (i.e. Implementation) each minister was assigned the responsibility of supervising the implementation of plans situated in their Ministry through a ministerial implementation Committee chaired by the Minister.

---

[242] Ibid.

Proposed Key Projects

The Economic Sustainability Plan provided for a stimulus package of N2.3 trillion to be spent in 12 months. Each of the proposed key projects was allocated a specified amount of money based on the estimates. The Plan proposed many projects in various sectors in the areas of (a) mass agricultural programme, (b) extensive public works and road construction programme (focusing on both major and rural roads), (c) mass housing programme, (d) Installation of Solar Home Systems, (e) strengthening the Social Safety Net, (f) support for micro, small & medium enterprises, (g) reduction in NAFDAC registration fees, (h) Survival Fund, (i) promotion of domestic gas utilisation, and (j) digital technology. There were also provision made for cross-cutting imperatives.

Concluding Observations

First, the proposed key projects were comprehensive and adequate to address the COVID-19-induced economic problems. However, concerning the universities, the provision under the cross-cutting imperatives as provided by the plan, were not enough, as they needed a separate and more targeted package. Universities constitute huge but neglected business areas or centres that would have required their own separate COVID-19 stimulus package to generate huge multiplier effects given their mammoth student and staff population. This was a huge opportunity that was missed for revitalizing the universities thereby stemming the tide of perennial ASUU strikes.

Secondly, the implementation of the Plan was, threatened by the slow wheel of the bureaucracy which did not significantly operate differently under the COVID-19 pandemic emergency. The dominant reliance on the ministries for the implementation of the various key projects in the Plan, was a major drawback.

Thirdly and lastly, the 12 month period for implementing the projects was unrealistic. It is doubtful if the Plan actually turned the economy around given the level of hardship in the land as a result of the increased millions who became poor thereafter. The Nigeria Economic Sustainability Plan offered a good opportunity for the revitalization of the economy. But it seemed not to have achieved much. This is an area for research by others on the impact of the Plan.

CHAPTER FIFTY

The Safe Schools Declaration under COVID-19 Pandemic

The abduction of 276 schoolgirls by members of the Boko Haram terrorist group from Chibok Secondary School in Borno State, Nigeria in 2014 was one frightening event that has remained fresh in the minds of peace-loving Nigerians and indeed the whole world. Since that sad event, the education of secondary school students in Chibok was disrupted and for many of Chibok youthful generation, the dream of being educated in a school environment in the community remained unrealized. However, it was a cheering news that the West African Examination Council (WAEC) had successfully conducted the 2020 Senior School Certificate Examination (WASSCE) in Chibok for the first time (six years after that closure)[243] under protection of the military. This achievement brought to mind the issue of safe schools in Nigeria.

The Importance of Safe Schools Declaration

The successful conduct of WASSCE underscores the importance of the Safe Schools Declaration whose International Day is celebrated on September 9 of every year. In fact, it was on May 29, 2020 that the United Nations General Assembly proclaimed September 9 every year as the International Day to Protect Education from Attack, and mobilising action to safeguard education in armed conflict.

According to the Global Coalition to Protect Education from Attack (GCPEA), the Safe Schools Declaration (SSD) is 'an inter-governmental political commitment to protect students, teachers, schools, and universities from the worst effects of armed conflict.'[244] Put briefly, the SSD says that:

---

[243] Sundiata Post (2020) via http://www.Sundiatapost.com, September 10.
[244] Safe School Declaration, via https://ssd.protectingeducation.org/

Every teacher, professor, and school administrator should be able to teach and research in conditions of safety, security, and dignity. Every school should be a protected space for students to learn, and fulfil their potential, even during war. Every boy and girl has the right to an education without fear of violence or attack. Every university should be a safe place for students and academics and to foster critical and independent thinking, and to harness knowledge.[245]

The Second declaration above (ie *Every school should be a protected space…even during war*) reminds one of what happened during the Nigeria-Biafra war (1967-1970) when schools were suddenly shut in the then Biafran area, dashing the hope of school children. Fortunately enough, good leadership quickly adapted to the emergency war situation. Not long, schools were opened in hidden make-shift or temporary shelters to shield them from bombardments by Nigerian Air Force planes. Good leadership understands that in times of emergencies, education of children should go on even in set-up temporary schools as the one shown in the picture below.

Children playing outside a UNICEF set-up temporary school during a mid-day break in Kasai region of the Democratic Republic of Congo (DRC), *(Source: unicef/tremeau, 2018 via https://ssd.protectingeducation.org/)*

---

[245] Ibid.

This again reminds us of the commendable efforts of school proprietors and relevant stakeholders who championed the continuation of learning by Nigerian children using many innovative and adaptable learning platforms during the period of COVID-19 lockdown. More importantly, thanks to many in various spheres of life who championed the need to courageously but cautiously go ahead with the conduct of the 2020 WASSCE. Although, this is now history, it will always be remembered with great joy by parents and students who would have been adversely affected had the examination not taken place. Many thanks also go to WAEC authorities for displaying uncommon courage and confidence that made the conduct of the examinations possible and successful. WAEC officials even went extra-miles to make sure that some students who got the coronavirus disease before or while taking the examinations were well taken care of in Isolation Centres. History will definitely be kind to all those who made the sacrifice for the successful conduct of the examinations in 2020 when it was risky to execute such a task.

Origin of, and Reasons for, the adoption of the Safe Schools Declaration

The idea of the Safe Schools Declaration started in 2015, when:

> ...the governments of Norway and Argentina led a process among United Nations (UN) Member States to develop the Safe Schools Declaration...The Safe Schools Declaration...outlines a set of commitments to strengthen the protection of education from attack and restrict use of schools and universities for military purposes. It seeks to ensure the continuity of safe education during armed conflict. The Declaration was opened for countries to endorse at the First International Conference on Safe Schools in Oslo, Norway, in May 2015. In March 2017, the government of the Argentine Republic hosted the Second International Conference on Safe Schools, further building upon the development of a global community dedicated to protecting education in armed conflict. As at that date, 105 states around the world had joined this international political agreement.[246]

---

[246] Safe School Declaration, via https://ssd.protectingeducation.org/.

It is also necessary to add that "the government of Spain hosted the Third International Conference on Safe Schools, which took place on 28-29 May 2019 in Palma de Mallorca, Spain."[247]

With respect to the reasons for the adoption of the Safe Schools Declaration, the following provides a brief summary:

> The impact of armed conflict on education presents urgent humanitarian, development and wider social challenges. Worldwide, schools and universities have been bombed, shelled and burned, and children, students, teachers and academics have been killed, maimed, abducted or arbitrarily detained. Educational facilities have been used by parties to armed conflict as, inter alia, bases, barracks or detention centres… Attacks on schools and universities have been used to promote intolerance and exclusion – to further gender discrimination, for example by preventing the education of girls, to perpetuate conflict between certain communities, to restrict cultural diversity, and to deny academic freedom or the right of association.[248]

Nigeria's efforts at implementing the Safe Schools Declaration (SSD)

Although COVID-19 is not a physical war, but however, it has been a war against lives and livelihood disrupting schooling at almost all levels since March 2020 in Nigeria and elsewhere. About the same month March 20, 2020 Nigeria became the 37th country to endorse (i.e. ratify) the Safe Schools Declaration. By this endorsement, Nigeria, like the others, committed herself to undertake to protect students, teachers, schools, and universities from attack and military use, by taking the following steps:

> (a) Implement the Guidelines for Protecting Schools and Universities from Military Use during Armed Conflict, and bring them into domestic policy and operational frameworks as far as possible and appropriate;

---

[247] Ibid.
[248] Ibid.

(b) Collect reliable data on attacks and military use of schools and universities, including through existing monitoring and reporting mechanisms;

(c) Provide assistance to victims of attacks, in a non-discriminatory manner;

(d) Investigate allegations of violations of national and international law and prosecute perpetrators where appropriate;

(e) Develop and promote "conflict-sensitive" approaches to education;

(f) Seek to continue safe education during armed conflict and restore access to safe education after attacks;

(g) Support the UN's work on the children and armed conflict agenda; and lastly,

(h) Meet on a regular basis, inviting relevant international organizations and civil society, to review implementation of the Declaration and use of the Guidelines.[249]

As earlier pointed out, the SSD is co-championed by the Governments of Norway and Argentina. However, the Global Coalition to Protect Education from Attack (GCPEA) coordinates advocacy for endorsement, and monitors implementation, of the SSD. The GCPEA publishes Newsletters that provide updates on implementation (among other things) of the SSD in the endorsing countries around the world.

With respect to Nigeria, the GCPEA reports that the "process of domestic ratification was led by the Education in Emergencies Working Group in Nigeria, which is co-led by the Federal Ministry of Education, UNICEF and Save the Children and consists of over 50 active local and international NGOs, government agencies and departments."[250] Subsequent discussion will draw from the GCPEA reports on Nigeria with respect to its declared commitment to the SSD.

In the first edition of its Safe Schools Declaration Newsletter in 2017, the GCPEA revealed that Nigeria announced, at the Buenos Aires Conference on Safe Schools, its plans to formulate a national policy on Safe Schools to bring all stakeholders on board to implement the SSD Guidelines. The policy, the report said, would outline the roles and

---

[249] Ibid.

[250] GCPEA Newsletter Nos. 1, 2017, & 5, 2019, via https://protectingeducation.org/news/…

responsibilities of all stakeholders, including the Ministry of Defence, Federal Ministry of Education, and the Ministry of Foreign Affairs, in protecting education from attack. Nigeria also announced that plans were underway by the Ministry of Defence and state governments to revise the decision to use or occupy schools as military or operational bases with a view to finding available alternatives.

This GCPEA report showed that Nigeria demonstrated an early commitment (i.e. 2017) even before endorsing the Declaration. In fact, by attending the Buenos Aires Conference, and making a commitment to formulate a national policy on Safe Schools, Nigeria had started implementing steps (a) and (h) of the eight steps listed above. This was very encouraging given the fact that Nigeria had experienced painful disruption of the education of many school children following the abduction of secondary schoolgirls by Boko Haram terrorists in Chibok, Borno State, in 2014 and at the Government Girls' Science and Technical College, Dapchi in Yobe State in 2018, among other disruptive activities. For example, as the Minister of Education, Adamu Adamu, revealed in 2018, the Boko Haram and other insurgents in the northeast had killed 2,295 teachers since 2009, with approximately 1,500 schools destroyed since 2014. The minister's statement showed that Nigeria needs to double her efforts at implementing the Safe Schools Declaration to reverse the destructive impact of insurgency.

However, it appeared that the gains of the early declaration of initiative of rolling out a policy by Nigeria was not matched effectively by concrete actions at least at the sub-national levels of government. This was against the background that the United Nations (UN) had asked Nigerian states in September 2020 to domesticate policy on Safe Schools. In an interview[251], Dr. Judith Giwa-Amu, (UNICEF Education Officer) called on "Nigerian states to fast-track the domestication of the policies on Safe Schools in line with the Safe Schools Declaration which Nigeria endorsed." It is important to point out also that Dr. Giwa-Amu commended Nigeria for showing commitment towards ensuring that schools were kept safe and protected for children to learn in them. She specifically commended the military for showing understanding of

---

[251] News Agency of Nigeria (NANS) on Wednesday, September 9, 2020.

children-related issues and without whose efforts no learning would have taken place in some parts of the North-east.

Some other areas where Nigeria had done well which the GCPEA Newsletter No. 1 (2017) highlighted include the collaboration among the Federal Ministries of Education and Finance, the National Emergency Management Agency, and state-level authorities to relocate students and teachers from high-risk zones in the Adamawa, Borno, and Yobe States to secondary schools in safe zones. The Ministry of Defence reported that the pilot phase of the program saw 2,400 students (800 from each state) transferred to 43 Federal Unity Colleges across the northern part of the country. In our view, this transfer was a very successful and commendable initiative. The second area involved the implementation of many other measures to enhance school security to facilitate the continued provision of education. Such measures include the constructing ditches around school perimeter fences; installing security lighting throughout school compounds; using sand bags to deter intruders; deploying armed military personnel to carry out vehicular and foot patrols; stationing security personnel at school gates; and setting up roadblocks on access roads.

Enough funds need to be provided at the sub-national levels to carry out more works in this area. Many of our schools and tertiary institutions, are in serious need of protection from attacks by terrorists, bandits, kidnappers, and herdsmen. However, it is gratifying to note that the Federal Government approved N400m for the building of the perimeter fence around the University of Abuja which had in recent times been attacked a number of times by bandits and kidnappers.[252] It would be recalled that the Vice Chancellor of the University of Abuja, Prof. Abdul- Rasheed Na'Allah, had lamented over the menace posed by bandits who had been encroaching on the university land due to its unprotected nature.

In its overall assessment of Nigeria's efforts, the GCPEA Newsletter No. 3 (2018) reported that the Safe School Declaration Sub-Committee of the Education in Emergencies Working Group in Nigeria hosted a

---

[252] See for example: https://tribuneonlineng.com/fg-approves-n400-million-to-fence-university-of-abuja/.

Chapter Fifty | Isaac Nnamdi Obasi

multi-stakeholder workshop in Abuja, to launch a review of the legal framework on the protection of education in Nigeria. Participants included the Federal Ministries of Defence and Education, members of the armed forces, the Presidential Committee on the Northeast Initiative, and a wide range of protection, education, legal, and policy experts. This activity further demonstrates the commitment of Nigeria in deepening its activities as required in the eight earlier listed commitments.

Lastly, the GCPEA Newsletter No. 5, (2019) reported that as part of implementing the Declaration, Nigeria's armed forces had ordered military teachers to stop carrying weapons openly in schools. It equally reported that:

> ...the Education in Emergencies Working Group is finalising a draft National School Safety and Security Policy and is advocating for an amendment to the Armed Forces Act which would legally ban the military use of schools by the armed forces. Such a ban would help to prevent attacks on education by opposing armed groups, and limit disruptions to students' learning.

The stoppage of open carrying of weapons by military teachers as well as the finalisation of a draft National School Safety and Security Policy is a welcome development.

Commending the Efforts of the Education in Emergencies Working Group Nigeria (EiEWGN)

We commend the advocacy efforts of the Education in Emergencies Working Group Nigeria (EiEWGN) which is:

> ...a coordination structure that serves as a pressure group to facilitate the provision of quality education that meet the physical protection, psychosocial, developmental and cognitive needs of people affected by emergencies. The aim is to enable structured learning to continue in times of acute crisis or long-term instability.[253]

---

[253] See https://www.humanitarianresponse.info/sites/www.humanitarianresponse.info/files/doc uments/files/25062018_nga_eiewg_ssd_advocacy_brief.pdf.

The principal drivers of EiEWGN which are the Federal Ministry of Education (lead), UNICEF (co-lead), Save the Children (Co-lead), Riplington Education Initiative (Sub-Committee Chair), Ministry of Defence (Education Corps), Plan International Nigeria, Talents in Children Promotions, and United Kingdom Department for International Development (DFID), have demonstrated commendable commitment that needs the support of the sub-national levels of government (i.e. States & Local Governments) in whose domains many of the schools are located. EiEWGN needs the support of all in its efforts to keep our schools protected and safe.

Finally, from all that have been said so far on SSD, it is clear that stopping schooling for too long under COVID-19 pandemic is inadvisable, as it disrupts the education of generations of our children. As Prof. Tijjani Muhammad Bande, then President of the United Nations General Assembly (UNGA), revealed, 463 million school children, mostly from developing countries lack access to remote learning. This figure from a UN report, represents nearly a third of the world's 1.5 billion school children forced to stay at home following the closure of their schools due to COVID-19.[254] The lesson is that learning should not stop because physical schools are closed due to a pandemic.

In conclusion, COVID-19 pandemic is like a war emergency and requires that leaders devise smart ways of not disrupting schooling for so long. Call it virtual classroom & learning, e-schooling, or simply e-learning etc, the governments and education authorities at all levels should see it as the new normal, with blended e-learning. We should all remember that if not for the courage shown by WAEC authorities and other stakeholders, the 2020 conducted examinations would not have taken place. The Nigerian federal government was reluctant to re-open schools because of the pandemic emergency. Here lies the challenge and at the same time, the wisdom which the SSD offers in the period of COVID-19 pandemic.

---

[254] See https://www.vanguardngr.com/2020/09/what-covid-19-has-taught-us-unga-president-reveals/.

Chapter Fifty | Isaac Nnamdi Obasi

CHAPTER FIFTY ONE

COVID-19 Data on Infections and Deaths in Nigeria

A close look at the COVID-19 global data as at December 9, 2020, across countries as tracked by the Johns Hopkins University Coronavirus Resources Centre,[255] would draw the conclusion that Nigeria which had 70,669 confirmed cases, with 1,189 deaths was not doing badly at all. Using five most affected countries for such comparison with Nigeria, statistics on cases of infection and deaths (as at December 9, 2020) reveal a stunning difference. The United States of America for example had over 15.4m cases, with 290,992 deaths; India had over 9.7m cases, with 141,772 deaths; Brazil had over 6.7m cases, with 178,995 deaths; Russia had over 2.5m cases, with 44,769 deaths; and France had over 2.3m cases, with 57,043 deaths.

Note that as of 24 August 2022, the new figures for these countries stood at: Nigeria over 263,000 confirmed cases with over 3,000 deaths; USA over 93m cases and over 1m deaths; India over 44m cases and over 527,000 deaths; Brazil over 34m cases and over 682,000 deaths; Russia over 18m cases and over 375,000 deaths; and France had over 34m cases and over 154,000 deaths.[256]

In this order of ranking (i.e. the first five countries), the criterion used for the December 9, 2020 comparison, was the number of cases of infection rather than the number of deaths. If the number of deaths were to be used, the order would slightly change regarding the first five countries, as the USA with 290,992 deaths; Brazil 178,995 deaths; India 141,772 deaths; Mexico 111,655 deaths (note this new entrant into the first five with respect to the number of deaths); and then United Kingdom with 63,179 deaths. If these were compared with Nigeria's

---

[255]Johns Hopkins University Coronavirus Resources Centre, December 9, 2020 via https://coronavirus.jhu.edu/map.html.
[256] Ibid, August 24, 2022.

figure of 1,189 deaths (as at the same December 9, 2020), then Nigeria appeared to be doing well. Was Nigeria really doing well?[257]

Reasons why Nigeria's COVID-19 Data were not a true reflection of reality

Perhaps, the logical question should focus on whether Nigeria's coronavirus (COVID-19) data are robust and reliable enough to warrant the conclusion that Nigeria was doing well. It is a considered opinion that Nigeria's COVID-19 data on infections and deaths were not necessarily a true reflection of reality. One can start from the fact that Nigeria was not testing enough. With an estimated population of slightly over 200 million people (December 2020 figure released by the National Population Commission was about 206 million), Nigeria had not yet tested up to 1% of her population. As of December 9, 2020, Nigeria had been able to test only a total number of 817,913 people. The truth is that COVID-19 testing was a huge problem for many African countries and not just Nigeria. What were the reasons for this? one would focus only on two issues to show that Nigeria's COVID-19 data did not fully reflect actual numbers of infections and deaths in the society.

First, as Dr. Matshidiso Moeti of the World Health Organisation (WHO) observed[258], although the COVID-19 cases in Africa are a small fraction of the global count but low testing in many African countries means infections have been under-reported. According to Dr. Moeti, while testing facilities increased in some countries compared to when the outbreak began, Africa still fell behind the global benchmark. Therefore, Dr. Moeti's point is very important as it challenged the robustness and reality of Nigeria's COVID-19 data. Governments at the sub-national level were not testing enough in spite of appeals by federal authorities. Evidence revealed at a time that only two sub-national governments namely Lagos State and the Federal Capital Territory (FCT)

---

257 The earlier newspaper article from which this chapter originated was primarily motivated by the issues which Prof. Ladipo Adamolekun raised on the authenticity of Nigeria's COVID-19 data. His helpful comments helped the author to research further on the issue. I am very grateful to him.

258 Interview with Bukola Adebayo of CNN, August 2020.

were able to meet the expectation of testing up to 1% of their population. Some states, did not made testing or even the fight against COVID-19 a priority and failed therefore to cooperate with the federal government in this regard. As revealed in an earlier chapter, one particular state governor dismissed COVID-19 as a hoax and refused to cooperate with NCDC officials.

At a particular time again, the then Director-General of NCDC, Dr. Chikwe Ihekweazu expressed regrets that seven states were not testing enough and these were Cross River, Jigawa, Kogi, Osun, Ebonyi, Adamawa and Zanfara. He revealed this during the national briefing of the Presidential Task Force on COVID-19 on December 10, 2020 despite the fact that the federal government had built molecular laboratories in states of the federation and had on number of times given financial assistance to state governments to enable them manage the COVID-19 effectively. In addition, the private sector-led Coalition Against COVID-19 (CACOVID) had also rendered tremendous assistance to the states to help them manage COVID-19. CACOVID built isolation centres, procured private protective equipment (PPE) and bought and supplied large quantity of food items and other materials worth billions of naira as an earlier chapter documented.

Apart from lack of cooperation from some state governments, testing (though free in government-owned laboratories) became a big issue in Nigeria. Testing was not easy to come by particularly when people voluntarily wanted to be tested to know their status. Furthermore, it took a very long time for the result to be out after undergoing the test. Many people experienced different levels of anxiety or frustration regarding testing and results of their tests. To be candid, testing for the coronavirus was one particular area where Nigeria's response to COVID-19 pandemic was less than satisfactory.

Given this fact therefore, the overall NCDC announced figures of infections and deaths could not accurately reflect the reality out there in the society. The conclusion therefore is that Nigeria's COVID-19 data on infections and deaths are not robust enough for the comparison made earlier as it was like comparing apples and oranges.

The second major reason that supports the thesis that COVID-19 infections and related deaths in Nigeria were not true reflections of reality, is that actual causes of many deaths were unknown. Some deaths that appeared obvious to be COVID-19-related in some states were called mysterious deaths, thereby resulting to gross under-estimation and under-reporting of figures. Across states, there was a good number of deaths that appeared to be COVID-19-related and officially they were not regarded as such. Above all, many of us lost either relations, friends, colleagues, acquaintances or even (street) neighbours that died in COVID-19-related circumstances that were not reported as one. It was as if people did not want to tolerate the stigma associated with COVID-19 related deaths of their loved ones.

One indicator that deaths were under-reported (not deliberately though) was that the mortuaries were unusually filled to capacity in some parts of the country where people do not bury the dead immediately. For a long time after the lockdown restrictions were lifted, burial ceremonies were going on in some parts of the country every single day except on Sundays. For instance, burial dates were fixed by the churches during the month of December 2020 and even parts of January 2021. The officiating priests did not have any free days as people had to queue up to obtain dates in order to bury their loved ones.

In conclusion, given all these and the fact that COVID-19 testing was a weak link in the chain of effective national policy response, Nigeria's reported low cases of infections and deaths in comparison to other countries appeared not to have reflected fully the reality. The numbers were more likely to be higher than reported. Going by evidence therefore, the obvious conclusion is that the national data on infections and deaths were not robust enough to say that Nigeria did well in relation to other countries where the numbers were much higher.

CHAPTER FIFTY TWO

COVID-19 and 'A Week-Like-No-Other' in Nigeria

During the nearly two years of COVID-19 pandemic, some weeks/months witnessed more devastating occurrences with respect to infections and deaths. The month of December 2020, for instance was the most devastating. Specifically, the week of 7th (Monday) to 13th (Sunday) December, 2020 was an unforgettable period of sad news. Prior to this remarkably sad week, the Nigeria Centre for Disease Control (NCDC) observed then that since the beginning of September to the end of November 2020, Nigeria had recorded a gradual increase in the number of confirmed COVID-19 cases. It continued, that in the last week (30th of November to the 6th of December) our surveillance system had recorded a sharp increase in cases. The average number of daily cases recorded in the last week was higher than was recorded between September–November.[259] This chapter reflects on the issues that happened around this period.

The Period of Unusually High Numbers

In fact, records from the NCDC website showed that in the week of 30th November to 6th December (i.e. NCDC's Epidemiological week 49) the number of new confirmed cases increased rapidly from 1,029 to 1,843 (i.e. previous week 48). Then came the NCDC's Epidemiological week 50 when the number started climbing much more rapidly. For example, on Monday, 7 December, new confirmed cases rose from the previous day's figure of 318 (i.e. December 6) to 390, and then to 550 on Tuesday, 8 December. Subsequently, on Wednesday, 9 December, it went down to 474 and then moved sharply to 675 on Thursday, 10 December. On Friday, 11 December, which was a record breaking day with 796 new confirmed cases. This all-time high figure raised an alarm that Nigeria could be in its threshold of experiencing a second wave of COVID-19. However, this sharp increase came down

---

[259] NCDC, (2020) via http://ncdc.gov.ng/news/237/update-on-covid-19-in-nigeria.

to 617 on Saturday, 12 December, and then to 418 on December 13. As a footnote, the figure for the new week remained on this declining trend recording 199 on December 14, and surprisingly rose rapidly again to 930 on Wednesday, 16 December which was another record breaking number, highest ever in a single day, until the unusually very high number 1,145 figure recorded on a single day on December 17. This figure (930) in week of 14th to 20th (i.e. NCDC's epidemiological week 51) is outside the focus of this discussion.

Reasons why December 7-13, 2020 was 'a Week like no other.'

The week of focus (7-13 December, 2020) with very high rising cases of infection is described here as *'a week like no other.'* The very high cases of infection, was not the only reason for this appellation, as there were many other remarkably sad things that happened. First, Nigeria lost Major-General Johnson Olu Irefin, who was the General Officer Commanding (GOC) the 6th Division of the Nigerian Army in Port Harcourt, Rivers State. Major-Gen Irefin reportedly died of complications associated with COVID-19.[260] This officer was among the participants who were attending the 2020 Chief of Army Staff Annual Conference in Abuja, at the time he took ill.

Secondly, this sad news did not stop there, as many as 26 Nigerian Army Generals (who were attending the conference) were reported to have tested positive for COVID-19. The initial news report gave the figure as 18. However, according to the Acting Director, Army Public Relations, Brigadier-General Sagir Musa, the 26 confirmed cases were among the 417 personnel who were tested for the virus.[261] All the officers who attended the conference were directed to go into self-isolation. This development was no doubt a trying time for the Nigerian Army and the nation at large given the dangerous level of insecurity in the land.

Thirdly, there was the unsettling news that Governor Babajide Sanwo-Olu of Lagos State had gone into self-isolation after one of his close aids tested positive for COVID-19 on December 10, 2020.[262] Few

---

[260] The Nation, December 10, 2020 via http://thenationonlineng.net)
[261] THIS DAY, December 15, 2020.
[262] Vanguard newspaper, December 11, 2020.

days after, disconcerting news came that the governor himself had tested positive for the virus.[263] It is important to put this news within a context. Lagos State was the epicentre of COVID-19 in Nigeria and Governor Sanwo-Olu was one of the most effective fighters of the war against COVID-19. In an earlier chapter, he was described him as "an action governor" with respect to the fight against COVID-19. He and his Commissioner for Health, Prof. Akin Abayomi, consistently led-by-example in the fight against COVID-19 as much as could be observed throughout that most risky period of the virus. The governor had done pretty well in staying safe since the announcement of the index case in Lagos on 27th of February, 2020.

Fourthly, and relatedly too, the week had another dogged fighter against the COVID-19 war, Governor Nasir El-Rufai, going into self-isolation because as he reportedly said "he has been notified of more positive COVID-19 test results of persons close to him, including an immediate family member and senior officials of the Kaduna State Government".[264] Governor El-rufai was one of the governors that took the fight against COVID-19 very seriously. He had previously contracted the virus and this therefore was the second time he would go into isolation in compliance with COVID-19 protocols. This is also leading by example.

The fifth shocking news of the 'week-like-no-other' was the abduction of about 333 students of the Government Science Secondary School (GSSS), Kankara, Katsina State on Friday, 11 December, 2020 by gunmen. Few days later, the Boko Haran terrorist group claimed responsibility for the abduction. This abduction was a complete slap on the face of the Safe School Declaration (SSD) which as pointed earlier is championed by the *Global Coalition to Protect Education from Attack (GCPEA),* working as "an inter-governmental political commitment to protect students, teachers, schools, and universities from the worst effects of armed conflict." The SSD says that: "Every boy and girl has the right to an education without fear of violence or attack."

---

[263] Vanguard newspaper, December 12, 2020.
[264] Premium Times, December 12, 2020.

Chapter Fifty two | Isaac Nnamdi Obasi

As pointed out in an earlier chapter, the SSD is a relevant initiative in a coronavirus pandemic period as both physical and health protection measures need to be adopted and effectively implemented. Luckily Nigeria was the 37th country to endorse (i.e. ratify) the SSD on 20 March 2020. With this kind of easy abduction, it appears that Nigeria's endorsement of the SSD and its accompanying domestication policy, were not taken seriously at the sub-national levels where majority of the schools are situated and managed. It is however important to point out that the abducted schoolboys regained their freedom on December 17, 2020.

The last of the sad occurrence in the 'week like no other' was the news that the Chairman of the Presidential Task Force on COVID-19 and Secretary to the Government of the Federation (SGF), Mr. Boss Mustapha (who was courageously leading the coordination of the national response to COVID-19 since March 2020) was going into self-isolation because some members of his household tested positive for COVID-19.

The statement released by the chairman himself, read as follows:

> I would like to inform the general public that some members of my household tested positive for COVID-19 yesterday (Saturday) evening…My wife and I tested negative, but will remain in self-isolation and work from home according to protocols by the health authorities. I would like to remind all Nigerians that COVID-19 is real…Please stay self and protect yourself. Adhere to all public health and safety measures so that we do not lose the gains we have made in the fight against COVID-19…Please take responsibility for yourself and to protect our country.[265]

This was another excellent case of leadership-by-example which was the hallmark of his style as Chairman of PTF on COVID-19.

In conclusion, the "week-like-no-other" demonstrated beyond doubt that COVID-19 was no respecter of persons and class. It also demonstrated the importance of respecting the COVID-19 safety

---

[265] Vanguard newspaper, December 13, 2020.

measures regardless of one's position in society. Lastly, the exemplary leadership of some top government officials, is both noteworthy and commendable.

Part Nine:
COVID-19 Policy Response in some Countries

CHAPTER FIFTY THREE

COVID-19 'War': New York State as Most Dreaded Battle Ground

It is natural for people to forget easily their unpleasant or even sad experience and its concomitant lessons in the name of moving on with their lives. The same thing is likely to happen with respect to the COVID-19 pandemic. This is because many people appear to be in hurry to do away with the non-pharmaceutical protocols even before the pandemic goes away. This chapter therefore is meant to remind us of the COVID-19 experience of the people of New York State (USA) during the peak period of the pandemic. It is hoped that the lessons would serve as a guide for the management of public health problem in the future.

COVID-19 Pandemic as a War

With the outbreak of COVID-19 pandemic, the entire world was confronted with a state of 'war'. This was a war against an 'invisible enemy' which medical personnel were mainly fighting. Within few months of its outbreak, over three million people (3,234,836) had been infected, with 228,597 fatalities[266] across the entire world, - a figure which a physical war could hardly cause in short a period of time. Expectedly then, many world leaders rightly called COVID-19 a war which should be waged forcefully. The use of this war imagery to describe COVID-19 was apt, which resonates well with Yasmeen Serhans who captured an article as "The case against waging 'war' on the coronavirus."[267]

It is not by sheer coincidence that former President Donald Trump of the United States called himself "a war president". The US then was the new epicentre of the coronavirus after China, Italy and Spain. As at 30 April 2020 (10.59GMT), the US had recorded over one million cases (precisely 1,064,572), and 61,669 deaths. Embarrassingly, New York

---

[266] This was as at April 30, 2020 as monitored by Worldometer via https://www.worldometers.in fo/coronavirus/

[267] Yasmeen Serhans (2020): "The case against waging 'war' on the coronavirus." *The Atlantic*, London, March.

State (with its New York City as the political capital of the world) was the epicentre of the virus in the US. And as at the same date, the New York State had recorded 299,691 cases of infection with 18,000 deaths. By this number of infection, New York State alone, represented 28% of the total number cases in the US. Its number of death represented 29% of the total number deaths in the US. The state then could be viewed as the dreaded battleground of the COVID-19 war not only in the US, but in the whole world then.

The COVID-19 Horrifying Experience in New York

On 28 April 2020), the BBC World News released the shocking news that a top New York doctor had taken her own life. According to the report, Dr. Lorna Breen, a medical director at the New York-Presbyterian Allen Hospital died on self-inflicted injuries on Sunday, 27 April 2020. This unfortunate incident amply demonstrated the frustration of those in the battleground of the COVID-19 war. This was particularly so in the dreaded battleground of New York State where health personnel had been overwhelmed physically and psychologically.

We recall that on 11 April 2020, the BBC in another report titled: Coronavirus in New York: a paramedic's diary carried an eyewitness account by Anthony Almojera a senior paramedic's in New York City[268] who gave a shocking 'minute-by-minute' story of his physical and psychological ordeals while working for 16 hours daily trying to save lives across the City. According to Almojera, though he had always been close to death by the nature of his work, nothing in his 17-year career could have prepared him for the outbreak of the coronavirus. With New York State recording more diagnosed Coronavirus cases than any single country in the world, Almojera regrettably stated that the state had the grim distinction of being at the forefront of a global health crisis.[269]

Describing what he called the toughest day in his career, he painted the war-like imagery of his experience in these words:

---

[268] BBC Report (2020) via https://www.bbc.com/news/world-us-canada-52196815.
[269] Ibid.

I put on my uniform, grab my radio and start the process of decontaminating my equipment. We have to wipe down all the radios, keys, trucks, bags and the rest of the gear. This virus can stay alive on everything. Nothing is safe – even your co-workers. In wars you see the bullet, you know who your enemy is. This is a war with an invisible bullet – everyone you come into contact with is a bullet who could get you.[270]

Describing further the ordeal, Almojera said that they got well over 6,500 calls from distressed patients a day. Continuing, he said,

...we noticed the spike in cases around March 20, and by the 22nd it was like a bomb. Right now about 20% of the emergency medical services (EMS) of the workforce is out sick. We have a lot of members who have contacted COVID-19, we have members who are in the ICU and over 700 people who are being monitored with the symptoms.[271]

Finally, for our purpose here he said,

I'm single and have no kids. This is the only time in my life that I've ever been happy that I'm single because I don't bring it home. But so many people are worried about this...Right now, I have guys who sleep in their car because they do not want to bring it home to their families.[272]

Almojera's personal account was very pathetic to hear and the world sympathized with all the affected frontline health workers.

---

[270] Ibid. I had wished then that Nigerians in our big cities could pick this message clearly in order to actually take the observance of the social and physical distancing protocols seriously. But to my dismay, many did not do so as they kept moving in their business-as-usual-mentality.

[271] Ibid.

[272] Ibid.

Why should anyone, be bothered about what happened in New York under a Pandemic?

New York City of New York State is arguably the 'political capital of the world' hosting the United Nations Organization (UNO). By this fact therefore, it is the home of nationals of every nation in the world. This implies that through international travels, diplomats and members of their families in New York could easily transmit the virus from there to their home country

Finally, what happened in New York was a timely reminder to all Nigerians that COVID-19 was a war and a matter of life and death. This fact was underscored then by the President in one of his COVID-19 nation-wide speeches.[273] As at the time New York was undergoing such a sad experience, not a few Nigerians were still living in denial of the deadly virus. The fact is that at times, government can do its best under this type of pandemic, but the best results can only be achieved if people take the NCDC appeal for personal responsibility seriously.

---

[273] Attached in the Appendix section.

CHAPTER FIFTY FOUR

COVID-19 Global Politics

Since the outbreak of coronavirus (COVID-19) in Wuhan, Hubei Province China on December 31, 2019 and its declaration as a pandemic by the World Health Organisation (WHO) on March 11, 2020, the world had never been the same again. Politically, COVID-19 brought world leaders to their knees, scampering for solutions on how to contain the spread of the virus in their different national jurisdictions. Economically, the means of livelihood of vast numbers of people across the world were disrupted, making the International Monetary Fund (IMF) to declare a global recession, signalling *doom and gloom* for many countries. In fact, many countries had already requested for emergency financial assistance from IMF as early as March 2020.

Trump's Misplaced Anger against China

The United States of America, which had recorded the highest number of deaths (70,272 as of May 6, 2020), was bearing the heaviest burden then. It was a political embarrassment for Trump as that was an election year, with its feared negative impact on Trump's re-election bid. Strangely, this raised the COVID-19 controversy and its politics to a high fever level. Consequently, President Trump started using all manner of Machiavellian strategies to fight for his political survival.

In spite of his praising China at the early period of the outbreak of the virus for measures taken to contain the spread of virus, Trump turned round to blame China repeatedly for lack of transparency with information on the origins of the virus. He consequently insisted that the virus originated from a Wuhan laboratory as against China's claim that it originated from Wuhan seafood market.[274] Later on, Trump turned his anger also on the World Health Organisation (WHO) blaming it for

---

[274] We note here that China was not actually transparent with its information on the origin of the virus. So Trump's accusation was valid, but we note however that the issue here is not about the origin of the virus but on the Machiavellian tactics of Trump.

negligent of duties and "for being too 'China-centric' in its tackling of the coronavirus pandemic."[275] In his characteristic trade mark of cutting funding to some multilateral organisations (UNESCO among others for example), Trump directed his administration to halt funding of WHO, while reviewing its role in severely mismanaging and covering up the spread of the coronavirus.

CNN Report of May 5, 2020[276] revealed that Trump officials were trying "to enlist foreign allies in pressure campaign against China over coronavirus response." This revelation took what started originally as a controversy in international politics to another level we can rightly call *global politics of COVID-19*. Trump's further move towards forming an anti-Chinese alliance arose from his accusation that China was working against his re-election because of what China considered a hurtful trade deal with the US under Trump.

Truly, the controversy over the origins of the COVID-19 lasted for many months but Trump deliberately and consistently kept it on the agenda of global politics. He was cleverly using it to cover up for his temporizing shortcomings in handling the COVID-19 since its entry into the US. Although Trump was not alone in accusing China for lack of transparency regarding the source of the virus, he in particular made it a big issue in global political discourse. He then planned to influence many more US allies to join in criticising China thereby diverting attention from his failure to control the virus at home. Without doubt western critics joined him to accuse China of "silencing dissent", being "extremely secretive", of "manipulation of information", and of "muzzling criticisms."[277]

Reeling under heavy criticisms at home on his administration's poor policy response to the COVID-19 pandemic, Trump adopted the use of any available alibi as a cover for his failure. He hoped to employ his latest Machiavellian manoeuvres as a weapon to manipulate and influence the psychology of voters in his favour.

---

[275] BBC via https://www.bbc.com/news/world-us-canada-52213439.

[276] This report was by the trio of Vivian Salama, Jeremy Diamond and Kevin Liptak.

[277] This point was well noted by Xu Sicong of CGTN, March 18, 2020 via https://news.cgtn.com/news/2020-03-18/....

China's ill-Advised Aggressive and Defensive Reaction

China which had since January 2020 remained the focus of some critics was largely defensive and also aggressive in attacking critics particularly Trump's administration. China repeatedly defended its actions in containing the spread of the virus and blamed Trump for not effectively attacking the spread of the virus in his country given the ample time available for doing so.

As earlier noted, Trump was not alone in attacking China for bringing the ravaging virus to the entire world. In Nigeria, Dr. Oby Ezekwezili in an opinion piece in *Washington Post* asked China to "demonstrate world leadership by acknowledging its failures to be transparent on covid-19." She then asked China to pay reparation to Africa for the incalculable damages the Wuhan-originated virus had done to African economies. According to her, "China must pay reparations to Africa for its coronavirus failures."

Specifically and more concretely, Dr. Ezekwesili said that:

> China should immediately announce a complete write-off of the more than $140 billion that its government, banks and contractors extended to countries in Africa between 2000 and 2017… Beijing's leadership should then commit to an independent expert panel evaluation of its pandemic response. China and the rest of the Group of 20 countries should engage with the African Union and countries to design a reparations mechanism.[278]

In a reaction, China went for an over-kill. In a statement issued by its Embassy in Nigeria, China absolved itself of all blames, saying that 'the virus was the enemy here and not China', declaring further that 'the demand for hundreds of billions of dollars in compensation, made no sense.'[279]

---

[278] Obiageli Oby Ezekwesili (2020): "China must pay reparations to Africa for its coronavirus failures", Global Opinions, *Washington Post*, April 16, via http://www.washingtonpost.com . Dr. Ezekwesili's call was widely reported in Nigerian newspapers.

[279] See The Interview via https://theinterview.ng/2020/05/04.

The Chinese Embassy through its press secretary Mr. Sun Saixiong stated further that since the outbreak of COVID-19, China had taken the most comprehensive, rigorous and thorough measures to contain its spread and conduct international cooperation. According to Saixiong, China had made tremendous sacrifices, accumulated valuable experience, and made significant contributions to the global response.[280] Dr. Ezekwesili in a reaction to China's aggressive and defensive posture fired back and said: "Yes, I insist That #ChinaMustPay Africa Damages for COVID-19."[281]

China's non-conciliatory approach in responding to Dr. Ezekwesili was not helpful at all. One wondered how far China could go with such aggressive and defensive approach. The US State of Missouri had actually sued China claiming damages for her failure to prevent the spread of coronavirus. Some other bodies threatened to sue China also.

More importantly, across the globe, there was one form of discontent or the other against China as a result of COVID-19. This happened even in Nigeria and some other African countries. For instance, according to Steven Erianger,[282] "as calls for inquiries and reparations spread, Beijing has responded aggressively, mixing threats with aid and adding to a growing mistrust of China." This he said "has only added momentum to the blowback and the growing mistrust of China in Europe and Africa, undermining China's desired image as a generous global actor."

As Erianger rightly observed also:

> ...in the past several weeks, at least seven Chinese ambassadors — to France, Kazakhstan, Nigeria, Kenya, Uganda, Ghana and the African Union — have been summoned by their hosts to answer accusations ranging from spreading misinformation to the 'racist mistreatment' of Africans in Guangzhou."

---

[280] Ibid.

[281] Oby Ezekwesili (2020: "Yes, I insist That #ChinaMustPay Africa Damages for COVID-19." *The Africa Report*, Sunday, 10 May.

[282] Steven Erianger (2020): 'Global backlash builds against China over coronavirus', *New York Times*, May 3, https://www.nytimes.com/2020/05/03/....

In conclusion, it is my well-considered view that considering the incalculable human and economic damages that the COVID-19 has caused and continues to cause to humanity, China should be remorseful and conciliatory rather than aggressive and defensive. China cannot run away completely from paying some 'damages', call it reparation, compensation, debt forgiveness, debt cancellation or debt rescheduling to poor African victims of COVID-19. Such a demand is admissible if China wants to retain her friendship with African leaders especially of the future who may be more nationalistically aggressive in asserting and protecting their interests. China can play its power politics on COVID-19 with the US, but for Africa, her tone should sound conciliatory.

CHAPTER FIFTY FIVE

COVID-19 Pandemic and China's New Conciliatory
Tone on Africa

In Chapter 54, the hostile reaction of the spokesman of the Chinese Embassy in Nigeria was frowned at over the statement by Dr. Oby Ezekwezili that China must pay reparations to Africa for the incalculable damages the coronavirus had done to African economies. As a former Vice President of the World Bank, (Africa Region), and also former Minister of the Federal Republic of Nigeria, Dr. Ezekwesili knew what she was demanding from the People's Republic of China. In an angry tone, China absolved herself of all blames, saying that the demand by Dr. Ezekwesili for hundreds of billions of dollars in compensation, made no sense.

In that chapter, China's non-conciliatory approach in responding to Dr. Ezekwesili's call was viewed as not helpful. One wondered how far China could go with such defensive and antagonistic approach. Consequently, It was concluded among other things that China should be remorseful and conciliatory rather than aggressively defensive.[283] However, after about two weeks, China changed its aggressive rhetoric and this forms the subject of discussion in this chapter.

From Aggressive to Conciliatory Rhetoric

To the delight of many, China within a space of less than two weeks changed her aggressive and defensive rhetoric to that of a conciliatory tone. It all happened at the Virtual Event of the 73rd World Health Assembly on Monday, 18 May 2020 when the Chinese President Xi Jinping struck the right chord.

---

[283] Please note that Chapter 54 appeared as an opinion piece on May 8, 2020, while this chapter appeared later on May 20, 2020 nearly two weeks after during which China changed her aggressive and defensive rhetoric.

In his address at the Virtual Event's Opening ceremony, His Excellency, President Xi Jinping, said to the joyful delight (we assume) of delegates that:

> We must provide greater support for Africa. Developing countries, African countries in particular, have weaker public health systems. Helping them build capacity must be our top priority in COVID-19 response. The world needs to provide more material, technological and personnel support for African countries. China has sent a tremendous amount of medical supplies and assistance to over 50 African countries and the African Union…At present, 46 resident Chinese medical teams are in Africa helping with COVID-19 containment efforts locally.[284]

Consequently, he finally announced *inter alia* that:

> China will provide US$2 billion over two years to help with COVID-19 response and with economic and social development in affected countries, especially developing countries. China will establish a cooperation mechanism for its hospitals to pair up with 30 African hospitals and accelerate the building of the Africa CDC headquarters to help the continent ramp up its disease preparedness and control capacity. COVID-19 vaccine development and deployment in China, when available, will be made a global public good. This will be China's contribution to ensuring vaccine accessibility and affordability in developing countries. China will work with other G20 members to implement the Debt Service Suspension Initiative for the poorest countries. China is also ready to work with the international community to bolster support for the hardest-hit countries under the greatest strain of debt service, so that they could tide over the current difficulties.

Again, President Xi Jinping made an incontrovertible statement to the Assembly when he said that *solidarity and cooperation is our most powerful weapon for defeating the virus.* It is also instructive that the theme of President Xi's address was appropriately titled: *Fighting COVID-19*

---

[284]Beijing Review for full text   via: http://www.bjreview.com/Documents/202005/t20200518_8 00205038.html)

through Solidarity and Cooperation: Building a Global Community of Health for All, which presumably struck the right chord.

It is against this background, that one wonders why the Chinese Embassy in Nigeria adopted such a belligerent undiplomatic approach in responding to Dr. Oby Ezekwesili. One also wonders whether diplomats go out of their way to be overzealous in defending their countries even at the risk of contradicting the fundamental tenets of their foreign policies. Unless, President Xi changed his mind of late on his government's aggressive attitude towards those who were criticizing China since the outbreak of COVID-19, One would be constrained to think that the Chinese Embassy was overzealous and undiplomatic in the way it responded to Dr. Ezekwesili. It should be assumed that the Chinese president had just changed the mind of his government and in which case, one should proceed to sympathize with the Embassy in Nigeria and perhaps overlook China's overzealousness.

From another viewpoint, perhaps, one can understand the controversial political circumstances that Chinese diplomats found themselves against the often unwarranted serial nature of antagonism by the Trump administration, as well as his global mobilisation of hostility against China then. For example, Trump was consistently blaming China and using the pandemic as an excuse for his failures at home. Even his self-inflicted problems were also blamed on China. One can therefore understand the aggressive and defensive reactions of the Chinese Embassy to criticisms even outside the US perhaps thinking that all were the same.

In conclusion, against the COVID-19 pandemic-induced problems of African nations, China's conciliatory initiatives are welcome. This should however be deepened or expanded to include more China-specific debt-related relief outside the G20 members' Debt Service Suspension Initiative. It is hoped that African countries are holding China responsible for these promises and are also following-up to see that they are fully implemented.

CHAPTER FIFTY SIX

Andrew Cuomo's Victorious Battle Against COVID-19 in New York State

The fight against the ravaging scourge of COVID-19 across the world, unmistakably exposed on the one hand, the poverty of leadership of some world leaders, while on the other hand, it also brought out the outstanding leadership prowess of some other leaders. One prominent name in the former category is undoubtedly former President Donald Trump of the United States of America, who unpardonably failed to fight COVID-19 in his country. However, to the rescue of the US, one prominent name in the latter category of leaders is unquestionably Andrew Cuomo former governor of New York State, who was perceived to be a perfect gentleman and an exceptionally humane character in the US governance system with badly damaged image under Donald Trump.

There were many other world leaders who demonstrated strong leadership in the fight against COVID-19 and notable among them were the former German Chancellor, Angela Merkel, Prime Minister of New Zealand. Jacinda Ardern, and Prime Minister of Australia, Scott Morrison. History will definitely be kind to these leaders and others of their likes who fought against the deadly pandemic by separating destructive politics of self-aggrandizement from the pursuit of the national interest and good public health of their citizens, and humanity in general. No doubt, there were some other leaders like the President of Brazil Jair Bolsonaro, President of Mexico, Andres Manuel Lopez Obrador, late President of Tanzania, John Magufuli, and late President of Burundi, Pierre Nkurunziza, who played politics with COVID-19 in their countries, with catastrophic consequences.

New York State as COVID-19 Battle Ground

For as long as the outbreak and spread of COVID-19 in the US lasted, the State of New York was for long the epicenter of the disease. New York State was for long under the heavy burden of COVID-19 regardless of its known resource-endowment. The COVID-19 induced fatality in the state at a time surpassed that of Italy or Spain, which were the worst affected then across the world. For example, on 6 April, 2020, New York State alone reported 731 deaths under 24 hours which were at that time, the highest fatality recorded in a single day. At that period, New York State recorded a total number of 5,487 deaths, with New York City alone recording 3,544 deaths. The State had at the time in April also recorded a total number of 138,863 cases which was the highest number recorded in any other State in the US. Relatedly, New York City alone recorded 74,601 cases.

By 30th April 2020, the entire US had recorded over one million cases of COVID-19 infections with 61,669 deaths. At that time too, New York State had recorded 299,691 total cases of infections, with 18,000 deaths. In terms of percentage share, New York State's share of total number of cases in the US was 28%, while its share of total number of deaths was 29%. Worst still, at a particular period in the management of COVID-19, there were practically no-where to keep dead bodies in New York City, prompting the use refrigerator trucks to store the dead bodies. This was graphically the war which former Governor Cuomo was relentlessly battling with.

After closely following the efforts made by the indefatigable former governor to reduce the number of cases of infections, number of hospitalisation, as well as the number deaths, one could infer that Andrew Cuomo was indeed one of the most gallant fighters against COVID-19 around the world.

The Winning stage of Cuomo's Battle against COVID-19

After over two months of hard-hitting battle, then Governor Cuomo entered the winning stage of the war in the month of June 2020. The numbers were beginning to reduce drastically in terms of total number of infections, hospitalizations and death. According to the Governor, as reported by CBS New York, "New York has tamed the beast of coronavirus", as it recorded the lowest number of deaths and hospitalizations since the start of the pandemic.[285] It is on record that

---

[285] As reported by the CBS New York, June 13, 2020 via https://newyork.cbslocal.com/2020/06/13/...).

Cuomo was consistently knowledge-driven in fighting the virus, as against Trump who abandoned science and allowed politics to becloud his judgement.

The Governor in the same CBS New York, excitedly acknowledged that the news was very, very good, as New York had its lowest level of COVID-19 hospitalizations since "this nightmare began" on March 20 in the US. He said further that we've done it. We've tamed the beast. We are now 180 degrees on the other side. There were 32 additional deaths – the lowest number since the beginning of the pandemic. The people of the state, by their actions, saved thousands of lives. That is not overly dramatic. That is not rhetorical. That is not metaphorical. It is factual. They saved thousands and thousands of lives.[286] On 15 June 2020, the Governor again reported excitedly that New York was at the lowest daily number of COVID-19 deaths and hospitalisation since the pandemic started, as there were 25 COVID-19 related deaths.

One shared in the governor's excitement, and had wished that the same success would happen in Lagos State, Nigeria's epicentre of the virus. This expectation was based on the fact that the Lagos State Governor also fought a gallant battle against the virus, but unfortunately, the numbers kept rising embarrassingly at that particular time. What was the difference between Governor Cuomo's effort and that of Governor Sanwo-Olu? Both Governors fought gallantly but the cooperation of the citizens made much difference. Governor Cuomo acknowledged that "the people of the state, by their actions, saved thousands of lives." The same could not be said of the people of Lagos State who were violating COVID-19 safety measures with impunity as observed in some earlier chapters.

On the basis of his knowledge-driven policy response to COVID-19, Governor Cuomo in response to the decreasing numbers started the gradual easing of the lockdown of the State. As a lesson for Nigeria, his advice to the people of New York State and his direct action in warning violators is worth reproducing here. According to the CBS New York (June 15, 2020) the governor:

---

[286] CBS New York, Ibid.

...urged New Yorkers to continue to follow state-wide guidance on social distancing and other practices because he said it is working. So local governments, I say do your job. We know the alternative. You're seeing all across the nation the virus actually increasing.

We have 22 states where the virus is increasing. It's a dramatic national turnaround. We are the exception here in New York. We don't want the same plight of these other states. The governor said he has called a few restaurant and bar owners personally and told them that, according to photos he's seen, they're in violation. He said the state controls liquor licenses and those restaurants may be in jeopardy of losing theirs. Cuomo said some of those restaurant and bar owners couldn't believe he was the one calling.[287]

In conclusion, Nigeria has a lot to learn from Governor Cuomo's effective and courageous leadership. The personal monitoring efforts of the governor made a lot of difference in helping to bring the huge number of infections, hospitalizations and deaths down. Cuomo provided leadership-by-example and that made a lot of difference in the fight against COVID-19 in the US generally, and in New York State in particular. With such a quality, the people cooperated in helping to stem the spread of the virus.

---

[287]CBS New York (2020) via https://newyork.cbslocal.com/2020/06/15/coronavirus-new-york-lowest-deaths-and-hospitalizations/

CHAPTER FIFTY SEVEN

COVID-19 Policy Response in Brazil: Irrational Scepticism and its Repercussions

Scepticism is all about doubt, a philosophical concept and school of thought that 'questions the possibility of certainty in knowledge'. It is not inherently bad. Science itself thrives on scepticism and intellectual curiosity. In actual fact, scepticism and inquisitiveness are major drivers of scientific discoveries or inventions. The problem of scepticism therefore depends on its type and not just scepticism in general terms. There is little or no problem with rational scepticism but there are problems with irrational scepticism. This chapter therefore, discusses how irrational scepticism of one man and his followers wreaked havoc in Brazil.

Rational Vs Irrational Scepticism

As observed above, two forms of scepticism can be identified. On the one hand, a rational sceptic will stop doubting when there is overwhelming evidence that clears such doubt. Scepticism in this form is "an outlook which does not deny assent but withholds it until justification is given."[288] This is why Professor B. J. Dudley described scepticism as a political virtue in his Inaugural Lecture at the University of Ibadan in 1975.

On the other hand, an irrational sceptic will maintain his/her doubt over an existence of something even when the evidence is very clear. An irrational sceptic is not evidence-driven in his/her approach to issues, unlike his/her rational counterpart. Sometimes driven by ignorance (knowingly or unknowingly), an irrational sceptic continues doubting in a bid (perhaps) to maintain his/her ego.

---

[288] B.J. Dudley (1975): *Scepticism and Political Virtue*, Inaugural Lecture at the University of Ibadan, 1975-76. Ibadan: Ibadan University Press.

Irrational Scepticism in Action in Brazil

For avoidance of doubt, the topic of the original write-up of this Chapter had already been selected before the President of Brazil, Mr. Jair Bolsonaro tested positive for coronavirus (COVID-19) on Tuesday, 7 July 2020. It was his prior irrational scepticism over COVID-19 pandemic, (amply demonstrated by his attitude, loud statements and behaviour) that inspired the choice of the topic.

It was a fact that President Bolsonaro (like Donald Trump of the United States) lived in denial of the existence of COVID-19 pandemic and downplayed its ravaging impact since its outbreak in China. He was widely reported for calling the coronavirus 'a little flu'. Afterwards, he began to have problems with his health professionals over the management of COVID-19 pandemic.

On 16 April 2020, President Bolsonaro sacked his health minister following disagreement over social isolation measures which he dismissed as unnecessary. In less than a month (May, 2020), a second minister (the successor of the sacked minister) voluntarily resigned following a disagreement with the president over the management of COVID-19 issues. This was at a time when Brazil recorded 844 new deaths in 24 hours (total death toll at 13,993 then), and a total number of infections at 202,918. At this time too, Brazil was the sixth most infected country in the world.[289] With the exit of two health ministers (who were health professionals) and the appointment of non-health professional (with a military background), Brazil began to witness the worst in total number of infections and fatalities as statistics would show later. Despite the rising number of cases and fatalities, President Bolsonaro was still going ahead with a business-as-usual mentality.

He carried on his public duties without wearing a face mask, even after a court ordered him to be wearing one. He joined the American Ambassador in the 4 July 2020 Independence Celebration activities without a face mask and took a photographer with selected guests without wearing masks. His penchant for disregarding the social

---

[289] See http://www.theguardian.com.

distancing and hygiene protocols as well as the lockdown guidelines was unparalleled and only comparable to that of Donald Trump.

With President Bolsonaro's defiant attitude and not-well-thought out statements about the coronavirus, it was not surprising that Brazil began to face calamitous repercussions. Based on the Johns Hopkins University global records, as of 9 July 2020, (7:35pm), Brazil had a total number of 1,713,160 infections, with a total death toll of 67,964. This fatality figure ranked second to the United States' figure of 132, 803 deaths, which was the highest figure recorded globally by a single country. It was on the basis of this unenviable and embarrassing record of Brazil that Uri Friedman[290], aptly said that "the coronavirus-denial movement officially has a leader, and it's Brazilian President Jair Bolsonaro." Well said, but one could state that Bolsonaro was only a deputy leader of this movement while Donald Trump was the real and undisputed global leader. It was a fact, that Bolsonaro was a good political student of Trump in everything of which coronavirus denials (or 'denialism'), was just one aspect.

Of all of President Bolsonaro's denials and a do-nothing mentality, the one that was most scandalous and totally unacceptable, was his statement that "I'm sorry, some people will die, they will die, that's life…You can't stop a car factory because of traffic deaths."[291] It is the height of unpardonable insensitivity and laziness for a president who was elected to protect life (among other things), to make such a callous statement. Still he was taking practically no preventive measures to fight the deadly virus. In fact, he was busy fighting sub-national level governments that were adopting lockdown measures to stop the spread of the virus. As earlier noted, he once described coronavirus as a 'little flu', which he later contacted denying its ravaging impact.

As Uri Friedman rightly reported, President Bolsonaro:

---

[290] See Uri Friedman (2020): *The Atlantic*, March 27, via https://www.theatlantic.com/politics/arc hive/2020/03/bolsonaro-coronavirus-denial-brazil-trump/608926/.

[291] The president made this statement in a Television Interview. See The Hindu (2020): "'Sorry some will die': President Jair Bolsonaro on Brazilian Coronavirus death toll". Available at: https://www.thehindu.com/news/international/brazils-bolsonaro-questions-coronavirus-deaths-says-sorry-some-will-die/article61957321.ece.

...railed against lockdowns; closures of businesses, schools, and public transport; anything that strays far from normalcy. He has lashed out at governors and mayors who have implemented these policies, alleging that they're committing crimes and 'destroying Brazil,' and actively sought to block some of these measures.[292]

In deed like President Trump, he has been more obsessed with opening up the economy, thereby disregarding cautious measures to balance life and livelihood, which many serious leaders were battling with all over the world.

Given Bolsonaro's defiant behaviour, which was considered dangerous to humanity, perhaps the time has come for the world to initiate conversations around the appropriate punishment to be meted out to such leaders. The International Criminal Court (ICC) should consider as crime against humanity leaders who through wilful negligence failed to protect their citizens in a pandemic such as this. The irrational scepticism of such leaders in a period of novel pandemic, should no longer be tolerated. The avoidable repercussions are very huge to bear, as witnessed in both the United States of America and Brazil. Initiating trial of such leaders at the ICC will make others like them respect science and keep irrational and unpardonable scepticism and ignorance out of science.

In conclusion, as Uri Friedman noted "if there's one lesson from the global responses to COVID-19, it's this: The countries that have had the most success 'flattening the curve' acted quickly and aggressively to contain the virus, rather than downplaying the threat it posed. Bolsonaro has had months to absorb this lesson, yet has chosen to take the opposite tack". One can only add that his behaviour was a clear case of irrational scepticism in action, and as would be seen later, this irrational scepticism claimed the lives of two African leaders.

---

[292] Uri Friedman, *op cit.*

CHAPTER FIFTY EIGHT

US Policy Response to COVID-19 Pandemic under the Trump Administration

Although the United States of America's (US) population of 330,970,517 constituted 4.2% of the world's population of 7.8 billion, it contributed disproportionately 25.3% (i.e. 2,381,361) of total number of coronavirus (COVID-19) infections (i.e. 9.4m), and also 25.3% (i.e. 121,979) of deaths globally (i.e. 482,000), all as of June 25, 2020.[293] These frightening statistics in this supposedly most powerful nation on earth, should have caused its president sleepless nights. But that was not the case for President Donald Trump. Unfortunately, he behaved as if there was no public health crisis in his country. He proved beyond doubt that he (like Jair Bolsonaro of Brazil) was an irrational sceptic without regrets

It was argued that Trump's behaviour was dangerous not only to the US, but to the rest of the world. The climbing number of cases of infection in the US at a time when there was a move towards opening up the airspaces around the world was potentially very catastrophic to global public health. The thought by the European Union (EU) then to consider banning visitors from the US when it opened its land and air borders was quite in order. This chapter discusses in details the management of COVID-19 in the US under the Trump administration.

Trump's response to COVID-19 pandemic

Historically speaking, what do we know about the way the Trump administration responded to the containment of the spread of the COVID-19 pandemic in the US? Did he as president temporise initially in responding to the public health emergency of COVID-19 pandemic? If he did not initially delay, why then did he change his attitude and verve in fighting the war against the deadly virus unlike state governors (like

---

[293] See Johns Hopkins University Mortality Analyses for total number of infections and deaths only via https://coronavirus.jhu.edu/data/mortality.

Andrew Cuomo of New York State) and others who actually understood the deadly nature of the disease? How did Donald Trump's political calculations over his re-election bid affect his attitude, pronouncements, zeal and commitment to fight COVID-19?

A review of the timeline of Trump's response to the COVID-19 pandemic as chronicled by both *The Washington Post* (21 April 2020); and *Vox* media (8 June 2020), reveals a mixture of erratic reactions consisting of both inconsistent pronouncements and what appeared to be purposeful policy response. Put differently, the timeline revealed not only the inconsistent behaviour of a president who was not sure of the knowledge-content of what he was saying and doing, but also that of one who was certainly sure of his intension to use the management of COVID-19 pandemic to advance his political interest of re-election in the November 2020 Presidential election.

As Cameron Peters[294] rightly put it:

> ...there are many reasons the US death toll is so high, including a national response plagued by delays at the federal level, wishful thinking by President Trump, the side-lining of experts, a pointed White House campaign to place the blame for the Trump administration's shortcomings on others, and time wasted chasing down false hopes based on poor science.

As Cameron further reports, although President Trump was (as early as January 2020) warmed about the global danger of the novel virus in daily intelligence briefings by the US national security officials (a fact revealed by the *Washington Post* in March 2020), he:

> nonetheless in public comments and tweets...consistently played down the fledgling pandemic even as the first US case was reported in Washington State. He also applauded China's handling of the virus at several points in January 2020, before taking action to protect the US in the form of a limited travel ban from China on January 31."[295]

---

[294] Vox Media via https://www.vox.com/2020/6/8/21242003/trump-failed-coronavirus-response.
[295] Ibid.

It is very important to take note of his commendation of China's handling of the virus, an opinion which he later changed.

In that same month of January Trump declared in an interview with CNBC that the COVID-19 was totally under control. According to him, "It's one person coming in from China, and we have it under control. It's going to be just fine". In the same January, Trump tweeted that his administration would continue monitoring the ongoing development in China. He added that America "has the best experts anywhere in the world, and they are on top of it."[296]

Based on hindsight, if Trump had practised what he acknowledged by allowing the US experts who should be on top of the situation to professionally manage the containment of the virus, perhaps the then prevailing COVID-19 trajectory in the US would have been significantly different. Instead, Trump side-lined the experts, and continued to politicise the COVID-19 pandemic within and outside his country. For as John Kerry (former US Secretary of State under the Obama administration) pointedly said, Trump's coronavirus response was a "denial of science, experts and facts."[297]

President Trump entered February 2020 with his false and deceptive mind-set that coronavirus was under control in the US, and on 26 February 2020 the first case of community transmission was reported by the US Centres for Disease Control (CDC). It was during the same day that the reality of the devastating impact of what he said was under control came to the fore. In reaction, he appointed Vice-President, Michael Pence Chairman of the relatively non-active White House Coronavirus Task Force which he had established earlier on January 29, 2020 following the recording of the index case in the US on 20 January 2020.

In his erratic manner, after appointing a Task Force Chairman, Trump announced shortly that the virus would disappear like a miracle. Not long after this statement, he described the coronavirus "as a

---

[296] See http://www.alternet.org.
[297] As reported by CNBC, June 10, 2020, via https://www.cnbc.com/2020/06/10/trumps-coronavirus-response-a-denial-of-science-and-facts-john-kerry.html.

Democrats' new hoax". Yet it did not occur to President Trump that something he denied its existence (a hoax) cannot be expected to disappear like a miracle. Something must exist, before disappearing. This is a clear case of mixed messaging driven by his inordinate (a do or die) political ambition of remaining in power.

How did President Trump handle the fight against COVID-19 pandemic after these two months of serious blunder? Did he continue to live in denial even as the State of New York then became overwhelmed by the catastrophic manifestation of COVID-19 pandemic?

Just like in Nigeria, where the month of March 2020 was a missed opportunity in the early fight against the COVID-19 pandemic (as pointed out in earlier chapters), the month February 2020 was described as 'a lost month' in the early fight against virus in the United States. This verdict on US was given by the trio of CNN's Marshall Cohen, Tara Subramaniam and Christopher Hickey.[298] In spite of this unfavourable but objective characterisation, President Trump had in a calculated manner tried to use propaganda to re-write history of his dismal record of fighting COVID-19. The White House Coronavirus Task Force chaired by his Vice Mr. Pence had remained dormant for about two months since Trump stopped the White House briefing on coronavirus angrily because he could not take the heat any longer from highly perceptive journalists.

Going back to the chronological narrative of the continued blunders committed by Trump in fighting against the virus, the month of March started with a mixed bag of other blunders and targeted policy response. First, on the side of blunders, Trump diverted attention on 2 March 2020 when he said that a vaccine "could come earlier than anticipated"[299] even when Dr. Anthony Fauci (US top most infectious disease expert) had earlier told him that testing of a vaccine would require a year or more. It appeared that the president was just raising a false hope to make people believe that he was working very hard to solve the problem.

In his characteristic attempt to downplay the seriousness of the coronavirus, Trump "compared it to the common flu, a comparison which at that time had already been debunked by experts including Dr.

---

[298] CNN of 18 April 2020 via https://edition.cnn.com/interactive/2020/04/politics/trump-covid-response-annotation/.

[299] Report by Aaron Blake of The Washington Post, 21 April 2020.

Anthony Fauci."[300] On March 10, Trump still insisted that the virus would go away, but as history records, the virus did not go away, as the numbers were still climbing embarrassingly higher and higher in such big states as Texas, California, Florida, etc.

Trump's mixed-bag of good policy response and bad conduct

On the good side of actions taken in the month of March, the president announced (on March 11) the suspension of travels from most European countries as the World Health Organisation (WHO) declared the coronavirus a global pandemic. Subsequently, the president also declared a national emergency on March 13. Even with this, he still slipped into his denial mode when reminded by journalists of what he said about the virus being "under control". As Blake captured his mind, Trump said "if you're talking about the virus, no, that's not under control for any place in the world. ... I was talking about what we're doing is under control, but I'm not talking about the virus."[301]

Other targeted policy responses in March include the (a) release of federal funding to fight the virus; (b) release of new guidelines on social distancing to stop the spread of the virus, and states followed by announcing their lockdown, which later got extended to April 30; (c) mutual agreement with the Canadian Prime Minister Justin Trudeau to close the US-Canada border; (d) official invoking of the Defense Production Act (DPA) in order to push domestic manufacturing industries to produce badly needed medical supplies, (e) closing of the US-Mexico border, (f) the signing of $2.2 trillion stimulus package considered to be the largest in US history comprising direct cash payments to Americans, additional funding for hospitals, and some $500 billion in loans for companies.[302]

This relief package was the most single important policy response by the Trump administration as it became a standard for other countries to

---

[300] As reported by *Vox* Media, June 8, 2020.
[301] Aaron Blake of the Washington Post, *op cit*.
[302] *Vox* Media, 8 June 2020.

gauge (or benchmark) their policy response. Despite these positive policy responses, Trump was still involved in mixed messages during this month because of his political calculations. For example, worried about the economic impact of the lockdown, he proposed an early lifting of the lockdown on April 12, Easter Sunday. He pressed hard for this, but the reality on ground made him to see reason against implementing his proposal.

Trump's aggressive mind-set and actions

As the number of cases of infection (1 million cases by April, 28) and deaths (50,000 by April 24) kept rising and hurting his political calculations, Trump in the month of April adopted an aggressive mind-set and blame-game propaganda against China, the World Health Organisation (WHO) and his main Democratic political rival Joe Biden. His aggressive mind-set and blame-game tactic were a well-orchestrated political propaganda and survival strategy. The Peoples Republic of China which he praised to high heavens few months earlier (as pointed out above) then turned into his worst enemy as he started blaming the same China for not being transparent in both the origin/sources of the virus and the manner the virus was handled. The WHO then was accused (couple of times) of covering up the handling of the virus with China and this led Trump to announce his administration's stoppage of funding to WHO, a policy that was widely criticised around the world.

The month of April also saw Trump pushing for an early opening up of the economy even when restrictions were still in place until the end of April. This led him to announce his administration's reopening guidelines which the various states were allowed the freedom to decide how to implement it. However, as a result of lack of firmness by Trump in handing the management of the virus, eight States governed by Republican governors namely Arkansas, Iowa, Nebraska, North Dakota, Oklahoma, South Dakota, Utah and Wyoming resisted issuing a state-wide lockdown. By the end of April, the Federal Stay-at-Home Guidelines expired and as it was not extended, the states were therefore allowed to take charge of the lockdown issues.

How did President Trump react to the continued rising of the coronavirus infections and death during the months of May and June, 2020, following the failure of his denial and blame-game tactics? It later became obvious that Trump's denial and blame-game tactics failed to help him gain political mileage. He was more interested in scoring cheap political goals than in fighting the COVID-19 pandemic.

The months of May and June 2020, were tough ones for President Trump as he continued floundering in his failed management of the COVID-19 pandemic. To his utmost embarrassment, the US had recorded 75,000 COVID-19 deaths as of 7 May 2020. Given this embarrassing situation, he began to attack anything considered to be a stumbling block to his re-election bid. For instance, he entered the month of May replacing "a top official at the Department of Health and Human Services who angered him with a report…highlighting supply shortages and testing delays at hospitals during the coronavirus pandemic". The top official was Christi A. Grimm, the principal deputy inspector-general who exposed hospital equipment shortages.[303] He had earlier on also fired Glenn A. Fine, the acting inspector-general for the Defence Department, a "pandemic spending Watchdog known for independence."[304]

Any reasonable person would wonder why President Trump would oust Glenn Fine, who according to Savage and Baker was "the leader of a new watchdog panel charged with overseeing how his administration spends trillions of taxpayer dollars in coronavirus pandemic relief." Recall that a $2.2 trillion Coronavirus Aid, Relief and Economic Security (CARES) Act was no small amount of money to be spent without financial oversight which was part of the functions of inspectors-general. Indeed, as Savage and Baker put it, inspectors-general "are meant to be semi-autonomous watchdogs ferreting out waste, fraud and corruption in executive agencies."[305]

---

[303] See Peter Baker, The New York Times, May 1, 2020, via: https://www.nytimes.com/2020/05/01/us/politics/trump-health-department-watchdog.html?…).

[304] Charlie Savage and Peter Baker, The New York Times, April 7, 2020 via: https://www.nytimes.com/2020/04/07/us/politics/trump-coronavirus-watchdog-glenn-fine.html?….

[305] Ibid.

It was on record that during the coronavirus pandemic, Trump removed four inspectors-general. The only reason therefore why President Trump was attacking these officials was to weaken their authority thereby enabling him to advance his political ambition unhindered – an ambition he had put over and above public health, integrity, transparency and efficiency.

Trump in the whole month of May, used lies, diversionary tactics, and raising of false hope as political survival strategies. Following *Vox* Media (8 June 2020) chronology, Trump made a lot of false claims. First, he claimed that the US was the world leader in responding to the coronavirus.[306] In one sense, his stimulus package was a path-setting policy intervention, but beyond that, he failed in fighting the virus.

Secondly, "Trump attributed his decision to limit travel from China as the major factor in avoiding a death toll numbering in the millions". Thirdly, though many states were yet to meet the minimum requirements for reopening based on the White House's guidelines, yet Trump continued to push for the reopening of non-essential businesses, using the slogan 'TRANSITION TO GREATNESS!.' This was a deceptive slogan to divert the attention of the people away from his failure in tackling the ravaging virus. Fourthly, in a diversionary manner, he went after the Obama administration for the handling of the 2009 swine flu pandemic which of course had no bearing to the issue facing the US at that period in time.

He falsely claimed again that the US had had prevailed in responding to the coronavirus. He equally claimed (falsely) that he was earlier than anybody thought in fighting the virus. He labelled churches as 'essential' and called for governors to allow their reopening, as well as threatening – without authority – to 'override' any governors who failed to do so. Lastly, Trump falsely claimed in a tweet that "if I hadn't done my job well, & early, we would have lost 1 1/2 to 2 Million People." This was a time the death toll was 100,000. Trump in a clever way, was just trying to divert concerns away from the rising number of deaths.

---

[306] Vox Media (8 June 2020) chronology.

Chapter Fifty eight | Isaac Nnamdi Obasi

Trump's ill-advised political campaigns amidst COVID-19 rising cases

Trump entered the month of June 2020 determined to damn the consequences of his failure in managing COVID-19 and by enmeshing himself unabashed into his political campaigns. Nothing worried him any longer than politics. This was after the shameful killing of George Floyd in Minneapolis on 25 May 2020. He used the hostile moment created by the Black Lives Matter protests to boldly come out fully to confront his political opponents. The planning of his scheduled political campaign rally in Tulsa, Oklahoma dominated discussion around him, but his opponents were worried about holding such a rally without observing the social distancing protocols. Many of his supporters attended the rally with and without face masks, although attendance was not to his expectations as he had boasted earlier. To worsen matters, he made the wearing of face mask a non-issue and even said that those who wear mask are "trying to hurt him politically,"[307] and that "masking up is intrinsically weak, liberal and un-American."[308]

Following the Tulsa rally was another rally in Arizona where his largely unmasked indoor crowd also did not observe the social distancing guidelines. It was reported that Trump's campaign workers removed the social distancing stickers (Do-not-sit-stickers) that would have disallowed people to sit closely. Trump's behaviour and statements at the rally were very disturbing. As Stephen Collinson and Caitlin Hu in another article observed, Trump resorted to his a familiar strategy which is a "divisive cultural and racial rhetoric – in his quest for a second term…The left-wing mob is trying to demolish our heritage so they can replace it with a new, oppressive regimes that they alone can control."[309]

Along with his pro-media outlets, Trump's most negative impact on the fight against the COVID-19 pandemic was his downplaying the dangers of the virus, thereby keeping millions of Americans misinformed and making many more to become victims of the virus. The right-wing

---

[307] Stephen Collinson and Caitlin Hu (2020): CNN's *Meanwhile in America*, 23 June.
[308] Ibid.
[309] Stephen Collinson and Caitlin Hu (202): CNN's *Meanwhile in America*, 25 June.

media such as Fox kept millions away from knowing the dangers of the virus. Secondly, Trump's speeches downplayed the dangers of the virus and devoted more time to other issues.[310] Indeed, his re-election bid was everything.

In conclusion, except for the diehard supporters of President Trump, there is consensus that Trump failed in his fight against the COVID-19 pandemic in the US. His former security adviser, John Bolton, said as much when he appeared on CNN's *The Situation Room* anchored by Wolf Blitzer on 24 June 2020. Bolton accused Trump of showing no strong leadership in fighting the virus. Secondly, he turned a blind eye to COVID-19 pandemic at the initial period. Thirdly, he politicised every move he made on the fight against COVID-19, as political calculations went into every decision and policy made on the virus. Lastly, he was erratic in the way he was reacting to the pandemic, as he had no comprehensive strategy to fight it.

One can therefore say that the issue of fighting COVID-19 occupied a lesser position in the priority list of Trump's actions. And given the fact that Americans travel a lot all over the world, Trump's actions and inactions might have helped to keep the virus circulating across the world. Here comes the danger posed by Trump's manner of fighting the virus to the rest of the world. This was perhaps the wisdom behind the EU's decision to exclude US travellers from entering the European Union territory then with effect from July 2020.

---

[310] Brian Stelter (2020): *Reliable Sources*, CNN 28 June.

CHAPTER FIFTY NINE

COVID-19 and Donald Trump's Total Disregard for Science

At the heart of Trump's abysmal mismanagement of COVID-19, was his total disregard for science in preference for the politicization of the virus for self-serving purposes and gains. Right from the time of the outbreak of the virus and up to the time Trump tested positive for the virus, he unrepentantly used lies, denial, scapegoating, buck-passing, mixed-messaging, outright misinformation, and deceit, to keep his politicization strategy alive and apparently effective. He was involved in a supremacy battle between science and politics, the height of which manifested during his hospitalisation at the Walter Reed National Medical Centre in Maryland where he was receiving treatment for his COVID-19 infection. To the surprise of everyone, Trump unilaterally left the hospital (while still on admission and treatment) to go on a show in a motorcade and waving to his supporters. By this action, Trump simply mocked science. This chapter discusses the details and dangers of Trump's mocking of science.

Trump's consistency in mocking Science

As revealed in Chapter 58, Trump behaved throughout the period of the pandemic as if there was no public health crisis in his country. For example, it should be recalled that he moved from his state of denial of the coronavirus, to a stage of holding dangerous indoor political rallies with large crowds many of whose members were neither observing physical distancing protocols, nor wearing protective masks. Unfortunately, he politicized the wearing of mask and regrettably encouraged his supporters to jettison such. It was therefore not surprising that he and his wife tested positive for the virus.

Throughout the period of the pandemic, Trump failed to listen to globally respected health experts and scientific institutions in his country. He even pulled the US out from the World Health Organization (WHO). Due to his disregard for science, *Nature* (one of the most authoritative, prestigious and long standing scientific journals with over 150 years of existence) had good reasons to lament. According to *Nature*, Trump administration had undermined, suppressed and censored government scientists working to study the virus and reduce its harm. His appointees have made political tools out of the US Centers for Disease Control and Prevention (CDC) and the Food and Drug Administration (FDA), ordering the agencies to put out inaccurate information, issue ill-advised health guidance, and tout unproven and potentially harmful treatments for COVID-19.[311]

Trump's misbehaviour after his COVID-19 infection became even more disdainful of science than his pre-COVID-19 state. For example, while still undergoing treatment in the hospital, he advised Americans in a tweet (among other statements) not to be afraid of COVID-19 and not to let it dominate their lives. This wrong advice was consistent with his manner of downplaying the seriousness of the virus and perhaps inadvertently putting many more Americans at great risk. However, it was only the ignorant person or the irrational sceptic that would listen or follow his advice after seeing the deaths of over 200,000 Americans as a result of COVID-19. Even if Trump survived as a result of the preferential attention and treatment he received as Mr. President then, would other lesser mortals without access to such treatment and drugs be lucky to survive?

His leaving the hospital (while still on treatment) to acknowledge cheers from supporters along the streets and endangering the lives of his driver, security staff etc, was another act of recklessness. Furthermore, he continued his assaults on science by insisting that he should be discharged after staying only three days in the hospital. Indeed, he had his way and after getting back to the White House he broke another protocol by removing his mask. The worst aspect of his misbehaviour was when he insisted that he would be leaving his isolation room (from where he was being treated) to the Oval Office to continue discharging his presidential duties. He actually went into the Oval Office for duties putting his staff at great risk.

---

[311] Nature (2020): 'How Trump damaged Science – and why it could take decades to recover', October 5, & Updated on October 7.

Chapter Fifty nine | Isaac Nnamdi Obasi

Trump's Ill-advised Actions and their risk to public health

As we argued much earlier, Trump's misbehaviour was dangerous not only to the US, but to the rest of the world. First, he was putting a lot of people at risk. For example, Fiana Tulip (daughter of a COVID-19 victim) narrated to CNN how her mother got infected and died. According to her, the mother died because she came in contact with someone in a hospital where she worked and who refused to wear mask. When requested to do so, she replied that she does not have to wear mask because the president does not wear one. Mr. Trump's bad example was certainly sending many people to avoidable early graves. It could be recalled that he mocked Joe Biden wearing mask during their last presidential debate.

Secondly, through his misbehaviour and bad example also, as many as 34 people connected to White House (more than previously known) were infected by coronavirus,[312] while the Trump administration sought to downplay the spread.

Thirdly, using God's name to justify his bad behaviour thereby misleading some people and sending them to their early grave remains objectionable and condemnable. It was wrong for Trump to have said that COVID-19 illness was a blessing from God. Although, while it is true that COVID-19 can be a plague or scourge from God to demonstrate his wrath, it is wrong for Trump who was receiving preferential VIP treatment to tell poor folks (who have no such privilege or benefit) that COVID-19 illness was a blessing from God. By the way, why did Trump go for such preferential treatment at the Walter Reed Hospital in Maryland where there were expert medical hands to take care of him? Why did he not remain in the White House and refuse being flown to the hospital that particular day? By the way again, would Trump have been bold enough to say publicly that COVID-19 was a blessing if any of his children or close family member died as a result of it? We suspect that he would not have been bold enough to say so.

---

[312] As reported by ABC News, October 8, 2020, via https://abcnews.go.com/Politics/34-people-connected-white-house-previously-infected-coronavirus/story?id=73487381

Chapter Fifty nine | Isaac Nnamdi Obasi

In conclusion, it was good that Americans rescued science from Trump's political machine of destruction by voting him out of office in the November 3, 2020 presidential election. That was a good way to oust him for mismanaging the COVID-19 pandemic and desecrating all known and respected US scientific institutions. That was an effective way to stop him from influencing or supporting the emergence of Trump-like leaders across the world like in Brazil, Mexico and some other places where their leaders were jettisoning science as well as misusing the name of God to deny the reality of COVID-19. Indeed, it was good that science was rescued from Trump's repugnant style of politics.

CHAPTER SIXTY

COVID-19 War and Joe Biden's Golden Opportunity

Saturday, 7 November 2020 was a great and remarkable day in the annals of the political history of the United States of America. Regardless of the political inclinations and preferences of people in different parts of the world, individuals reacted in an idiosyncratic manner to the outcome of the 3 November 2020 presidential election between former President Donald Trump of the Republican Party and Joe Biden of the Democratic Party. While some people were rejoicing, dancing, and shouting at the top of their voices in merriment over the victory of Joe Biden, some were dumbfounded and of course speechless over the loss of Trump. The victory of Biden was a golden opportunity to restore the lost glory of science under the Trump administration. This chapter therefore discusses the contrast between Trump's disdain for science and Biden's restoration of the primacy of science.

Triumph of politics over science under Trump

Some people might be wondering why this author is very critical of Trump's handling of COVID-19 pandemic, when he should be focusing more on Nigeria. The answer is very simple and which is that fighting the war against coronavirus in the US is of interest to the whole world because what America does has a lot of impact on the rest of the world either directly or indirectly. The mishandling of COVID-19 by the Trump administration was at the root of the devastating impact of the virus in the US and indirectly in some other parts of the world (Brazil, Mexico for example) where their leaders followed the footsteps of Trump.

At the root of the mishandling of the virus, was the total disregard for science by Trump himself. Several examples support this thesis. Throughout the long period of the US presidential campaign, Trump organised his rallies in total defiance of COVID-19 safety protocols and guidelines. He held rallies without wearing face masks and by his action discouraged his supporters from wearing masks. A number of times,

Trump and his supporters mocked those who wore masks. Trump himself mocked his Democratic Party counterpart, Mr. Joe Biden for wearing mask at one of the presidential debates.

Furthermore, Trump's rallies observed no physical distancing and his crowd of supporters behaved as if COVID-19 was not real. Indeed Trump called coronavirus a hoax. President Trump mocked science in every considerable way. First, he politicised every aspect of the war against the virus by disregarding the advice of US top infectious disease experts such as Dr. Anthony Fauci, among others.

Secondly, he openly mocked Dr. Anthony Fauci for doing his work professionally accusing him of being there forever and protecting his career. Thirdly, he made his Coronavirus Taskforce a political body that did only what he wished. Fourthly, he sometimes disregarded or even encouraged the modification of guidelines released by the relevant disease control agencies like the US Centres for Disease Control and Prevention (CDC). The intension was to issue a 'politically correct' version of such guidelines. His politically (rather than professionally) driven Taskforce was completely rendered ineffective in its operation. The Task Force was even disbanded at a period when the virus was still raging and ravaging the country. Fifthly, Trump mismanaged as well as subverted the lockdown measures meant to control the spread of the virus, even at a time when New York State was still under the debilitating effect of the virus. The mishandling of the lockdown restrictions by Trump was one of the factors that frustrated the war against the virus in the US.

Sixthly, Trump's organised couple of events in the White House constituted a super-spreader of the virus. It was no news therefore that he, his wife, Melania Trump, and one of his sons eventually tested positive for the virus. The worst of his culture of disregard for science was when he violated the treatment protocols by first driving outside the hospital to acknowledge cheers from his supporters along the street. Furthermore, he broke the protocols by requesting to be discharged from the hospital prematurely, and while back into the White House he also broke the quarantine regulation. He stayed only few days in his isolation room and in defiance to all protocols started work at the Oval Office thereby putting a good number of his staff at great health risk. It was not surprising therefore that many staff in the White House later tested positive for the virus including his Vice-President, Mike Pence, his Chief of Staff, Mark Meadows and some aides. This is the story of Trump's lost battle in the war against COVID-19 in the US because of his total disregard for science.

Biden's golden opportunity: Victory of Science over Politics

All this became a sharp contrast to Joe Biden's COVID-19 safety compliant political campaign. A man who showed in words and deeds that he had great respect for science, his campaign was strictly guided by COVID-19 safety rules and protocols. Mr. Joe Biden wore his face masks and encouraged his supporters to do the same. He organized his campaigns in the most COVID-19 compliant manner including using Virtual platforms to put his messages across to his teaming supporters.

Biden innovatively and successfully organised drive-in campaign rallies not minding its perceived harmful effects on loss of crowd of supporters. The use of car horns by his supporters to cheer him (as against clapping and shouting by Trump supporters), was a triumph of smart and compliant behaviour over COVID-19 super-spreading behaviour of Trump's supporters. Joe Biden's campaign promise of waging a serious war against COVID-19 started immediately after his election when he inaugurated a 13 member COVID-19 Task Force on Monday, November 9, 2020. The measure was a sharp contrast to that of Trump who found such a Task Force of no use under him.

In conclusion, a golden opportunity to fight a successful war against COVID-19 presented itself with the election of Joe Biden. There is no reason whatsoever to doubt his sincerity, courage, and political will to wage a serious war against COVID-19. By his various policy actions taken so far on mask mandate, vaccination and others, Biden has been effective in fighting the virus thereby bringing the numbers down in area of infections, deaths and hospitalizations. By his policy response, Biden has been able to demonstrate that America can do better than many other countries in fighting the pandemic, given her past spectacular achievements in the field of medicine, science and technology.

CHAPTER SIXTY ONE

COVID-19 and Fate of Sceptical Political Leaders

The untimely and shocking death of two East African controversial political leaders one at 61 and the other at 55, is an unforgettable lesson in the misuse of Godly faith as well as a total disdain for science. The death of coronavirus (COVID-19) sceptic President John Magufuli of Tanzania on 17 March 2021 at the age of 61 years, and the earlier death of another COVID-19 sceptic President Pierre Nkurunziza of Burundi on 8 June 2020 at the age of 55 years (both of which were shrouded in controversial circumstances) demonstrated a clear case of pushing scepticism beyond limit.

Scepticism, as pointed out earlier is all about doubt, and as a philosophical concept and a school of thought, it is not inherently bad. Science itself thrives on scepticism and intellectual curiosity. In actual fact, scepticism and inquisitiveness are major drivers of scientific discoveries or inventions. The problem of scepticism therefore depends on its type and not just scepticism in general. On the one hand, rational scepticism is healthy and supportive of human development, while on the other hand, irrational scepticism does the opposite. We have seen cases of irrational scepticism over coronavirus (COVID-19) across the world.

The Trio of Trump, Bolsonaro and Obrador

Former President Donald Trump of the US led the way of such irrational scepticism, while the President of Brazil Jair Bolsonaro, and President of Mexico Andres Manuel Lopez Obrador, (both of South America) were his notable disciples. In Africa, late Burundian President Pierre Nkurunziza and late Tanzanian President John Magufuli were the two notable COVID-19 sceptics. All these five leaders share one brand of political ideology and practice in common and that is 'reactionary populism' borrowing from Jeffrey Sachs and Roberto Unger's concept in their Lecture Series titled: "The Turn: From Reactionary Populism to a

Progressive Alternative."[313] All of them were infected by COVID-19 disease, with three surviving and two others dead.

The mismanagement of the COVID-19 pandemic by the Trump administration and his Brazilian counterpart President Bolsonaro, are already a familiar story. The Brazilian president was on record to have appointed the fifth Minister of Health in an attempt to have his way. Like Trump, the Brazilian president not only demonstrated a disdain for science and allowed political considerations to drive his actions, he was also unperturbed by the soaring COVID-19 fatality figures in his country. His actions and inactions made Brazil to have an unenviable record of 3,780 deaths in a single day (i.e. Tuesday, 30 March 2021). On the same date, Brazil recorded a total number of 84,494 new cases. The health system became over-overstretched if not completely overwhelmed. Here was a president who called coronavirus a "little flu", a "media trick" and said in 2020 that "strong measures" were "unnecessary", and thereby leading many of his country men and women to their untimely death.

As for the Mexican president, Andres Obrador, he told Mexicans in 2020 that "they shouldn't fear COVID-19". Despite warnings from global health officials, he continued to hold political rallies, kiss supporters, requested that Mexicans go out shopping to prop up the country's spurting economy during a global slowdown. He told them "Live life as usual", and "if you're able and have the means to do so, continue taking your family out to eat", which according to him "strengthens the economy". President Obrador's comments made Alex Ward to warm as early as 28 March 2020 that "Mexico's Coronavirus-sceptical president is setting up his country for a health crisis."[314] That predicted health crisis actually came to pass a year later in 2021.

Following Obrador's actions and inactions, Mexico was one of the most COVID-19 devastated countries with details showing that it recorded 4,683 new cases as of 30 March 2021 with a seven-day average of 4,267 cases. Details also showed that it recorded a single day's death of 801 as of 30 March 2021 and also a seven-day average of 512.[315]

---

[313] SGD Academy Library, Available at:https://sdgacademylibrary.mediaspace.kaltura.com/categ ory/By+Series%3ET%3EThe+Turn%3A+From+Reactionary+Populism+to+a+Progressive +Alternative/207206793

[314] See www.vox.com.cdn.

[315] John Hopkins Global Update on COVID-19.

However, the situation was even worse as Mexico later published revised figures indicating that the number of deaths caused by coronavirus was 60% higher than previously reported. More than 321,000 people are believed to have died from COVID-19 thereby placing Mexico with the second highest number of COVID-related deaths in the world after the US.[316] This is the fate of Mexicans caused by one man's total disregard for science and driven by his stubborn and irrational scepticism. Like Trump and Bolsonaro, president Obrador is alive after carelessly leading others to their untimely death. The late Burundian President Pierre Nkurunziza and late President John Magufuli of Tanzania were not lucky to be alive like the trio mentioned above. All of them jettisoned science in their management of the coronavirus, and were brazenly driven by their selfish political and economic interests in the management of COVID-19.

For three of these leaders, their countries broke some unenviable records as of April 2021. The US for example, served for a very long time, as the world's epicenter of the pandemic, and had the highest number of COVID-19 infections as well as deaths (i.e. 555,000 as of 7 April 2021[317] in the world. Brazil followed the US with the second-highest number of infections as well as deaths (i.e. 332,000 as of 7 April 2021) in the world. As at that same time, Brazil served as the new epicentre of the pandemic in the world.[318] At the same time too, Brazil had recorded over 4,000 deaths within 24-hours for the first time.[319] Mexico was then the third highest number of deaths (i.e. 204,000) as of 7 April 2021.[320] For those who followed closely these three countries since the pandemic, they would have no doubt observed that most of the infections and deaths were avoidable as they were products of huge and costly mistakes by their leaders. We shall now devote the rest part of this chapter discussing late president of Burundi and that of Tanzania.

---

[316] BBC News in a report titled 'Covid-19: Mexico revises coronavirus death toll up by 60%', 28 March 2021.
[317] John Hopkins Global Update on COVID-19.
[318] ABC News via https://abcnews.go.com.
[319] BBC News via https://www.bbc.com.
[320] John Hopkins, *Op cit.*

Chapter Sixty one | Isaac Nnamdi Obasi

Nkurunziza of Burundu and Magufuli of Tanzania

As a serving president in 2020, Pierre Nkurunziza while unconcerned about managing the coronavirus, said that the pandemic was "transmitted by air" and that God has "cleared the coronavirus from Burundian skies."[321] Among other wrong actions he took was the expulsion of four officials of the World Health Organization (WHO) from his country by 15 May 2020, and declared them persona non grata.[322] He held political campaigns involving large crowds of supporters in total violation of the safety protocols of COVID-19. His government did not make any serious arrangements for testing of citizens against the virus, as it paid lip service to the testing problem. Furthermore, there was under-reporting of cases of infections and deaths, many got infected after attending huge crowds of political rallies.

Above all, Nkurunziza was using the name of God to rationalise his COVID-19 wrong policy actions and inactions, an act that constituted a glaring abuse of the exercise of faith. It was ironical that this authoritarian leader invoked faith in God as only the means of fighting the pandemic rather than adopting concrete actions or at best combining faith with concrete actions. His contradictory actions were blatantly an act of deception. Here was a political leader who was involved in wide scale repression of political opponents and clampdown of popular protests by citizens opposed to his third term bid, calling God as if he was a sincere and devout follower. Granted that God is so merciful to all, He is also a God of justice as no one has a licence to misuse His name deliberately and hypocritically for selfish interests. It was not surprising that the same virus he claimed God had cleared in the skies touched the ground and took his life.

His behaviour was typical of politicians belonging to the school of 'reactionary populism'. These days they are found in many countries of the world deceiving their people for political gains. Religion has steadily and increasingly become an instrument for the promotion of selfish and sectional political interests, as well as expansion of political empire and domination of competing ethnic and religious groups.

---

[321] Anadolu Agency via www.aa.com.tv.
[322] VOA News, May 14, 2020 via https://www.voanews.com.

The case of the late president of Tanzania, John Magufuli, was not quite different. Here was a president who also 'downplayed the severity of the virus.' He was very suspicious of COVID-19 testing results, and at a time said "that people were getting false positive results."[323] Furthermore, he did not order a lockdown when other countries considered it necessary to do so, but rather he declared:

> ...that Tanzania would remain open for business", saying that "we Tanzanians have not locked ourselves down, and I don't expect to announce even a single day that we are implementing a lockdown because our God is still alive, and he will continue protecting us Tanzanians.[324]

Yes correctly said: God is alive and will continue to be alive, but we must do our own part of the work He gave us authority to do.

It was on record that the WHO pleaded with him to allow the reporting of COVID-19 cases but to no avail. To show how wrong he was, Aljazeera News reported that his successor, President Samia Suluhu Hassan, had said that it was not proper to ignore the coronavirus pandemic. This, Aljazeera rightly said signals "a shift in approach from the COVID-scepticism of her late predecessor John Magufuli", who downplayed the disease.[325] Before he died Magufuli warmed Tanzanians against COVID-19 vaccines thereby following the path of late Burundian president who was the first leader in Africa to repudiate coronavirus vaccines. Today both of them are no more. What lesson(s) can we learn from the irrational scepticism of both leaders?

The first lesson is from the Holy Scripture itself as some of these politicians who use the name of God know very little about His Word. At creation, God gave man power to continue His work of creation and to conquer and dominate the Earth. As Psalm 8: 1, 4-6 went further to elucidate:

---

[323] Chrispin Mwakideu, Deutsche Welle DW, March 17, 2021, via www.dw.com.
[324] From www.dw.com.
[325] Aljazeera News, 6 April 2021 via http://.www.aljazeera.com.cdn.amproject.org.

How great is your name, O Lord our God through all the earth!
What is man that you should keep him in mind, mortal man that you care for him?
Yet you have made him little less than a god; with glory and honour you crowned him, gave him power over the works of your hand, and put all things under his feet.

Those who invoke the name of God on anything (like our two late African leaders with respect to coronavirus) should always trust God that He has given man the knowledge and power to develop useful things including COVID-19 vaccine to free man from such pandemic scourge. In fact, many faithful children of God prayed seriously for a vaccine to be developed and when it came they thanked and glorified God. That is the right attitude and it is the appropriate use of Godly faith.

Secondly, the controversy between faith and science (as to whether they are compatible) has been settled long ago. Both are mutually-re-enforcing. God Himself is the greatest scientist. So, no man should be grandstanding with the name of God in a hypocritical manner of invoking His name and at the same time rejecting His creation through man who was made in His image and likeness.

The last lesson is that political leaders, influencers in society and indeed all men and women, should apply wisdom in using the name of God in their pursuit of good things of life. Like Babatunde Fashola (Nigeria's Honourable Minister of Works and Housing) rightly observed in a Channels programme Hard Copy in 2019 *"there is too much God in our daily conversation"* in Nigeria, which is an abuse of the name of God. As he also aptly said, "most people want God to do everything for them without playing their own part. There is enough work for God to do". God says, 'Work and pray'. But do we do the work? God didn't make money, it is people who make money. So, you need to go and work for money."[326] This was well said.

In conclusion, how I wish late Pierre Nkurunziza and late John Magufuli applied Honourable Minister Fashola's advice in fighting COVID-19. Irrational scepticism driven by reactionary populism is not

---

[326] See for example: https://phenomenal.com.ng/2019/10/there-is-too-much-god-in-our-daily-discussions-fashola/.

helpful to the development of human society and political leaders who follow this path do no one any good. People (both leaders and citizens) should use God's name in the most appropriate and reverential manner, and not for selfish reasons. Nigerians unfortunately, are guilty of this misuse and regrettably they do it with impunity.

CHAPTER SIXTY TWO

COVID-19'S Delta Variant

Despite the impressive and highly commendable efforts made by the WHO, scientists and many governments across the world to stop the spread and ravaging effects of the COVID-19 pandemic, the virus simply remained unyielding. The virus' mutative power gave rise to the emergence of different variants. These variants made many countries to experience different waves that led to the re-introduction of lockdowns in the affected countries. The emergence of variants therefore posed big threats to global efforts to arrest early the ravaging effects of the virus. It is against this background that this chapter discusses the emergence of the Delta variant and the few things we know about it in the history of the coronavirus pandemic.

The Principle behind WHO's Naming of Variants

As we all know, the virus originated in Wuhan, China. It was then followed by a new variant that originated in the United Kingdom (UK). This was followed by another that originated in South Africa, another in Brazil, and yet another in India, among others. In order to avoid reference to a variant's country of origin or geographical location, the World Health Organization (WHO) responded wisely to name the different variants with Greek letters starting with Alpha, to Beta, Gamma, and Delta etc. Consequently, the WHO named the variant discovered in the UK as Alpha, then that of South Africa as Beta, Brazil as Gamma and India as Delta. The Delta variant emerged as a more dangerous virus than earlier ones, hence its focus here.

There is a complementary classification announced by the Centre for Disease Control and Prevention (CDC) of the United States of America (US). This US-based classification provides clearer understanding of the level of ravaging effects of each variant on human beings, its power of transmission, expected therapeutic response and efficacy, and lastly, the level of hospitalisation. Accordingly, the CDC's three-fold classifications are: (a) Variant of Interest (VOI), (b) Variant of Concern (VOC), and (c) Variant of High Consequence (VOHC).[327]

The CDC's Variant of Interest is associated "with …reduced neutralisation by antibodies generated against previous infection or vaccination, reduced efficacy of treatments, potential diagnostic impact, or predicted increase in transmissibility or disease severity."
Then, a Variant of Concern is one where

> …there is evidence of an increase in transmissibility, more severe disease (e.g., increased hospitalisation or deaths), significant reduction in neutralisation by antibodies generated during previous infection or vaccination, reduced effectiveness of treatments or vaccines, or diagnostic detection failures.

Lastly, a Variant of High Consequence is one which "has clear evidence that prevention measures or medical countermeasures have significantly reduced effectiveness relative to previously circulating variants."[328]
Our focus in this piece is on the WHO's Delta Variant which is the same as the CDC's Variant of Concern, though it has a minor mutation called delta plus. Simply put, a delta variant of COVID-19 is more dangerous than the previous Alpha and Beta variants. In fact, Emily Anthes[329] called it a 'super-contagious' variant because of its high rate of transmission. The delta variant is known so far to be characterised by five features.[330]

First, delta variant spreads rapidly around the world. For example, as of 14 June, 2021, it was already in 74 countries worldwide according to the WHO but as of 29 June 2021 (about two weeks later) it had spread to 96 countries. Secondly, delta variant appears to be more transmissible. The UK government estimate said that it was 40% more transmissible than the Alpha variant and it accounted for more than 91% of UK COVID-19 cases. Thirdly, delta variant may be associated with different

[327] CDC via https://www.cdc.gov/coronavirus/2019-ncov/variants/variant-info.html.
[328] Ibid.
[329] In New York Times, June 2021.
[330] See Linda Geddes' summary via https://www.gavi.org/vaccineswork/five-things-we-know-about-delta-coronavirus-variant-and-two-things-we-still-need.

symptoms, with headache, sore throat, running nose and fever as major features, while cough and loss of sense of smell which were major features of earlier variants becoming rare. Fourthly, delta variant may cause more hospitalisation compared with the Alpha variant as it may "double the risk of hospitalisation." Lastly, with delta variant, one vaccine dose is less effective, but with two doses are still strongly protective.

Faced with all these frightening features, how was Nigeria affected, and what was Nigeria's policy response then? According to the Nigeria Centre for Disease Control (NCDC), so far (as at late June, 2021) there was no delta variant in Nigeria. This was good news which did not, however, call for complacency. This was because, according to the African Regional Office of the World Health Organization (WHO) in its announcement on 24 June 2021, the delta variant was in 14 African countries.[331] More worrying was that Ghana and South Africa which have high level of air travel contacts with Nigeria were already having the delta variant. This places Nigeria in a dangerous situation if nothing seriously was done by way of restriction of movement particularly with Ghana.

On Nigeria's policy response, the Presidential Steering Committee had much earlier placed travel ban on India, South Africa and Brazil that had the delta, beta and gamma variants respectively. This earlier proactive policy response saved Nigeria from the embarrassment that its health system would have had if the ban had not been imposed. Nigeria was also right to shift the searchlight to air travel and land border movements between Nigeria and Ghana. It was equally cheering that Nigeria placed itself on high alert monitoring what was happening in African countries where the delta variant had been reported. According to the health minister, Dr. Osagie Ehanire, Nigeria had scaled up surveillance at all border entry points to prevent the importation of the delta variant in the country. All these proactive measures were commendable.

In conclusion, spite of all these re-assuring policy measures, the Delta variant still entered Nigeria though not in any catastrophic proportion. It

---

[331] See https://www.cidrap.umn.edu/news-perspective/2021/06/delta-covid-variant-fuels-global-surges-complicates-reopenings.

entered because at that period in time, Nigerians were still notorious at flouting the COVID-19 safety protocols in public. For example, a close look at social interactions revealed that observance had become a thing of the past. At event centres where wedding ceremonies were held on weekly basis, people did not care to observe the social distancing safety rule. To make matters worse, they also did not care to put their face marks on, even when the 'No Mask, No Entry Notice' was conspicuously placed at the entrance to the arena. With respect to religious groups, some actually tried their best, but some others had gone back to their business-as-usual behaviour. The situation was not better at burial ceremonies and other potential super-spreading arenas of the virus. All these point to the fact that a pandemic is controlled more effectively by proactive measures than taking actions when it has already infected people, because as the saying goes, 'a stitch in time saves nine'.

CHAPTER SIXTY THREE

COVID-19 Omicron Variant and its Needless Controversies

OVID-19 pandemic as we observed much earlier is a controversial and divisive phenomenon. As the world struggles to combat its devastating effects, it continues to unleash its unwholesome characteristic even with the emergence of new variants. Indeed, COVID-19 pandemic generated controversial outcomes and not only created divisions across (between, and among) countries, but also regrettably created serious conflicts between governments and their citizens in many countries. This chapter discusses in details these controversies in general and omicron variant in particular.

COVID-19 as a driver of controversies

A quick recap shows that since the outbreak of COVID-19 pandemic, controversies emerged between China (origin of the virus) and other countries particularly (the United States of America under President Donald Trump). Following this was the controversial imposition of travel restrictions across the world and shortly after, some developed countries imposed discriminatory safety protocols against citizens of some other countries particularly the developing ones. The aviation and tourism industries in many of these affected countries suffered serious damage.

The emergence of different variants of the virus brought another controversy surrounding the profiling of it by the country of origin. The World Health Organization (WHO) in its wisdom quickly resolved this by naming variants by Greek Alphabets. This quick intervention saved the world from needless controversies of profiling countries and diverting attention from confronting the common enemy (the pandemic).

Yet after this, controversies raged within countries and in this case between governments and their citizens. Some citizens were vociferously protesting against their government-imposed safety measures of wearing face masks and obeying other safety protocols. The discovery and eventual arrival of vaccines as antidotes against the virus generated yet another controversy and further divided governments and their citizens.

The adoption and implementation of a vaccine mandate policy by many countries became a controversial and divisive issue across the world. In Nigeria, for example, the adoption of the Federal Government policy of "no vaccination, no entry into its offices," on 1 December 2021, was also controversial.

Furthermore, the distribution of vaccines at the international level was equally controversial. The problem of vaccine nationalism or hoarding (by developed countries) and vaccine equity being advocated for, by developing countries, became a big issue. Many argued for instance, that the lack of vaccine equity has been responsible for the emergence of new variants like the Omicron variant first dictated in the month of November, 2021.

According to vaccine equity advocates, no country is safe until everyone in the world is vaccinated. Although their argument was plausible, the fact is that governments in developing countries should wake up from their slumber and begin to invest in vaccine production rather than lazily calling for vaccine equity as if it is an entitlement or a right. They forget that all reasonable governments across the world take care of the health needs of their own citizens first, before extending their generosity to citizens of other countries, for as the saying goes, charity begins at home.

The controversy surrounding the Omicron variant

The emergence of Omicron variant in November 2021 which was said to have originated in South Africa accentuated the controversies surrounding COVID-19 pandemic. This also brought back in a controversial manner the economic damage caused to the aviation and tourism industries in a country like South Africa for instance. Some developed countries wasted no time to impose travel restrictions on selected Southern African countries of which South Africa was the main target and the big economic loser owing to its vibrant aviation and tourism industry in the sub-region. The pattern of travel restrictions and the hasty manner of their imposition re-enkindled the ever present and hidden racial divisions among developed and developed countries.

It was argued by many particularly in developing countries that racism was at play as there was no plausible explanation to convince anyone why the United Kingdom for example would ban flights from South Africa and not do the same to her European neighbours where the same Omicron variant had already been dictated. However, some other analysts who did not want to stretch the racial argument rather argued that political exigency, expediency or survival constituted the major drivers of such hasty decisions to impose travel restriction on South Africa and her neighbours. It was equally argued that South Africa should be commended rather than punished for identifying the Omicron variant classified as 'Variant of Concern' (increased risk of infection or simply dangerous) by the WHO.

The President of South Africa, Mr. Cyril Ramaphosa, had decried the ban as discriminatory and damaging to the economy of South Africa. He, therefore, called for the lifting of the ban. The government of Nigeria also described the travel ban against South Africa by Western nations as discriminatory. Coincidentally, Nigeria went ahead to host Mr. Ramaphosa on a State visit on Wednesday December 1, 2021 at a time when the controversies surrounding the Omicron 'Variant of Concern' were still raging across the world. The visit also coincided with the discovery of the Omicron variant in Nigeria among people who had recently travelled to South Africa. By her action, the Nigerian government elevated political interest above public health interest.

In conclusion, Nigeria's response to the controversy surrounding the Omicron variant, was an inappropriate show of political solidarity to a fellow African country, forgetting that its own healthcare system is weak and indeed fragile. Hosting the South African President at a period when a 'Variant of Concern' detected in his country, was spreading across the world, might have been politically courageous, but certainly it was at a great risk to Nigeria's weak health system. Nigeria's policy response to such *variant of concern* failed to be one of cautious approach for a government that this author has been commending for her proactive measures.

Part Ten
Managing the Return to Normalcy

CHAPTER SIXTY FOUR

Policy Response to a Receding COVID-19 Pandemic

Despite its resurgence in some countries (China, Hong Kong, Germany, among others) as of early 2022, for many, COVID-19 pandemic is on its receding trajectory, and it is only a matter of time that its pandemic status would be a thing of the past. Across much of the world, COVID-19 pandemic is no longer seen as the most dangerous life-threatening disease facing society today, as was the case a year or two years ago. This is because the pandemic is gradually receding into an epidemic. Although the war against this hitherto ravaging virus is not yet completely over, there is however palpable relief in many countries over its retreating trend. Many countries across the world are lifting the restrictions previously imposed in order to reduce the spread of the virus. If this is accepted as a confirmable hypothesis, then the concern of health experts would (among others) be on how to manage a gradual return to normalcy.

Nigeria's full policy cycle

In Nigeria, public policy response to the devastating effects of COVID-19 pandemic has gone through a full cycle namely (a) lockdown stage (most dangerous period) when restrictions were fully imposed, (b) lifting of lockdown and/or relaxation of restriction stage (imposition of mask mandate and other Non-pharmaceutical interventions), (c) vaccination stage (combined with the observance of Non-pharmaceutical interventions), (d) stage of near or full lifting of many of the hitherto imposed restrictions, and (e) the return to normalcy stage. These stages witnessed a plethora of policy responses aimed at (a) controlling the spread of the virus, and (b) treatment of victims to mitigate the severity or devastating impact of the virus such as increased hospitalisation or death.

With the pandemic gradually retreating, many countries have started reversing some of their existing policy responses through the lifting of the restrictions. Some of these policy reversals positively affect citizens of these countries, while some positively affect international travellers entering their countries. Whichever way one looks at these policy reversals, one thing is clear and that is the near possibility that the world is inching closer to a complete victory over COVID-19 as a pandemic. It may continue to exist, but it would no longer threaten public health in a devastating scale across the world.

Nigeria's reversal of COVID-19 containment polices

In Nigeria, the Presidential Steering Committee (PSC) on COVID-19 was not left out in this reversal of COVID-19 containment polices. First, the PSC announced that the wearing of face masks in public places was no longer mandatory. It further announced that the wearing of face masks in open spaces was now discretionary. It was in this regard that the Nigeria Centre for Disease Control (NCDC) clarified that the rules on face mask have not been completely abolished because wearing of face mask is still recommended in high risk places such as in crowded indoor events. Broadly seen, this policy reversal on mask mandate and its associated practices, can be regarded as the first step in the gradual return to normalcy.

It would be recalled that COVID-19 Disease Health Protection 2021 (which itself derived from Section 4 of the Quarantine Act, Cap. Q2 Laws of the Federal Republic of Nigeria 2010) made the wearing of face masks mandatory in public spaces. The law empowered the president to protect the health and wellbeing of Nigerians against the rising number of COVID-19 cases. Specifically, apart from government offices, the regulation stipulates that no person shall be allowed within the premises of a market, mall, supermarket, shop, restaurants, hotels, event centres, gardens, leisure parks, recreation centres, motor parks, fitness centres, or any other similar establishment except he or she is wearing a face mask covering the nose and mouth. The person is also required to wash his or her hands or clean the hands using sanitizers approved by the National Agency for Food and Drug Administration and Control (NAFDAC). The person's body temperature should also be checked and any person found to have a body temperature above 38 degrees Celsius shall be denied entry and advised to immediately seek medical attention.

The second step in the gradual return to normalcy was the issuing of international travel guidelines for international passengers which took effect on 4 April 2022. The guidelines removed the mandatory Polymerase Chain Reaction Test (popularly called the PCR Test) for fully vaccinated returning passengers. It then prescribed stiff penalties for (a) unvaccinated travellers who violate the new rules, and (b) for airlines that bring in passengers that violate the new rules. The Guideline which was titled 'Provisional Travel Protocol for Travelers Arriving Nigeria' and released by the PSC Chairman Mr. Boss Mustapha, on Sunday, 3 April 2022 was a revised version of the November 29[th.] 2021 Interim Travel Guidelines for Passengers Arriving in Nigeria.[332]

Other provisions of the revised 3 April 2022 Guideline include: (a) Fully vaccinated passengers arriving Nigeria will not also be required to carry out Post-arrival PCR test or a Rapid Antigen Test upon arrival in Nigeria; (b) Children below the age of 18 years will be accorded the same privileges as person who are fully vaccinated; (c) In-bound passengers who are unvaccinated or partially-vaccinated for COVID-19 shall take the PCR test 48 hours before departure and undergo Days 2 and 7 post-arrival PCR tests at their own cost; and (d) All in-bound passengers must register via the online Nigeria International Travel Portal (NITP).

The third step so far in the gradual return to normalcy in Nigeria was the announcement by the PSC of the revised social restriction recommendations in line with three established thematic areas namely movement, industry and labour, as well as community activities.[333] With respect to the reversal of policy in these areas, the PSC announced among other things that (a) there are no more formal restrictions on movement within the country as the nationwide curfew imposed from 12 midnight to 4 am has been lifted; (b) all categories of workers should resume work fully in their offices as against working from home; and (c) the ban on social and religious gatherings has been lifted.

These three broad areas of policy reversals (lifting of restrictions) became necessary (according to the PSC) "following the reduced risk of

---

[332] See Vanguard, April 3, 2022 in its report titled 'COVID-19: New travel guideline takes effect from April 4 – PSC', for details.

[333] See The Guardian, April 6, 2022 in its report titled 'Nigeria lifts COVID-19 restrictions on party, gatherings, curfew,' among others for details.

importation of new variants and the availability of vaccines and the increasing number of people vaccinated in Nigeria and globally."

In conclusion, these revised measures are quite in order but one important point worth underscoring is that the war against COVID-19 is not completely over. The implication of this is that we all have the personal responsibility to manage our gradual return to normalcy. The PSC and NCDC should not be left alone with this responsibility. People should therefore allow part of the new normal behaviour (wearing of mask in crowded places, and observance of other non-pharmaceutical interventions which displaced our old way of life) to still be part of their behaviour in public places as we gradually move into our old ways of life. More importantly, increased efforts at the vaccination of people is key in the management of our gradual return to normalcy. We can proudly say goodbye to COVID-19 pandemic with immense gratitude to God by all of us who survived it since 2020.

CHAPTER SIXTY FIVE

Conclusion and Key Policy Lessons

Given the nature of the subject matter under discussion, conclusion and the key policy lessons are tied up together and captured in such a way that both are inseparable. For example, a major conclusion of this book is that in a novel pandemic as COVID-19, science rather than politics should always constitute the pathway for a national policy response of any country. This conclusion also constitutes a key policy lesson for any future action in a pandemic. It is important to note however, that in many of the chapters, policy lessons formed part of the discussions especially at the concluding part of each chapter. Consequently, on the basis of the detailed analysis in this book, the following key policy lessons are found relevant in the management of COVID-19 pandemic.

(a) Temporizing or Delaying Attitude over Policy Response to a pandemic is dangerous
The first policy lesson is that delay is dangerous in managing a pandemic of this type, while a quick adoption of proactive measures is key to stopping the rapid spread of the virus. In fact, policy response must be ahead of the virus, otherwise the measures will have difficulty catching up with the devastating effects of the virus. As the former Governor of New York, Andrew M. Cuomo rightly said during his COVID-19 update,[334] time matters, minutes count, and the time for action was at that material time. Experience in both Nigeria and the United States of America clearly demonstrate that a temporizing attitude of a president was part of the major reasons why proactive measures could not be taken earlier enough to check the rapid spread of the virus. Although, the Nigerian president Muhammadu Buhari acted well by setting up a national policy coordinating machinery called the Presidential Task Force on COVID-19 (PTF on COVID-19), however the same president

---

[334] Andrew Cuomo (Governor of New York State) COVID-19 Update, Sunday, March 22, 2020 via CNN.

delayed unnecessarily before taking proactive measures in such areas as closing the international boarders (air and land), the failure of which made it possible for infected international travellers to bring the virus into Nigeria. As shown in the early part of this book, the president's temporizing attitude was a major cause of the rapid spread of the virus beyond Lagos and Abuja during that early period. On the part of the US, the former president Donald Trump adopted the same temporizing attitude which was however driven by selfish politics. His policy inaction made the US to become the new epicentre of the pandemic (after China and Italy) then and thereafter recorded heavy fatalities and infections during the period.

(b) Science rather than Politics should always dictate Policy Response
The second major policy lesson is that following science in understanding and managing a novel coronavirus (COVID-19) pandemic is key to a successful containment of the virus. The opposite is that the abandonment of science in preference for politicization of the virus is dangerous and would never allow any good policy response to achieve the desired results. The dismal performance of the USA under the Trump administration is an instructive lesson as the jettisoning of science led to the death of many people under preventable circumstances. Nigeria however did commendably in following science rather than politics in managing COVID-19. It achieved this by allowing its policy response to be coordinated and guided professionally by the PTF on COVID-19, and later the Presidential Steering Committee on COVID-19.

(c) A Twin Containment Policy on Coronavirus and Hunger-virus is essential to sustain health and livelihood
Nigeria's experience during the lockdown amply demonstrates that a single-minded policy that focused on controlling the spread of the coronavirus and neglected people's livelihood was bound to be ineffective. A prolonged lockdown that deprived the majority of those in the informal sector the means of daily livelihood generated more

problems in efforts to control the spread of the virus. The concept of hunger-virus emerged during the lockdown period to describe a situation whereby poverty was killing as many people as the coronavirus itself. Consequently, a twin containment policy targeting both the coronavirus and threat to means of livelihood was a more effective means of managing the pandemic. Nigeria's experience in this regard is a mixed-bag of successes and failures. Its initial failure was quickly arrested by the implementation of social protection measures. The role of the private sector through its Coalition Against COVID-19 (CACOVID) – a task force in partnership with the Federal Government in the fight against the virus and against hunger - was noteworthy.

(d) Nigeria's modest Success in managing its COVID-19 policy response is mainly due to its management by technocrats

The modest success recorded in the execution of Nigeria's COVID-19 policy response is mainly attributable to its management by technocrats (i.e. experts and professionals). This enabled decisions to be driven mainly by professional knowledge and less by political considerations. Nigeria's success confirms the time honoured and tested principle that when less politics is involved in the management of a policy programme, the outcome is optimum results. This confirms the saying that the lesser the politics in programme management, the higher the probability of a programme success.

(e) The lesser the Corruption in programme management, the higher the probability of programme Success

A follow-up policy lesson is that the lesser the corruption in programme management, the higher the probability of programme success. The management of Nigeria's COVID-19 policy response was not associated with disturbing incidence of reporting of corruption scandals by the press. As far as public knowledge is concerned, corruption was not a major issue in the management of Nigeria's COVID-19 policy response. Although analysis carried out in this book did not cover the financial management aspect of the programme - the job of financial experts and auditors - the reporting of corruption scandals (in programme management) in Nigeria a common occurrence in the press was not the case in COVID-19 financial management issues. It was noted however that issues were raised concerning the social investment programme in relation to the management of the conditional cash transfer and the home grown school feeding programme during the COVID-19 pandemic.

(f) Citizens' Cooperation is Key to Effective Implementation of Policy Response

A national policy response to a pandemic without an accompanying buy-in and cooperation of the citizens, is bound to achieve sub-optimal results. Experience across much of the world demonstrates that the resistance of the people to the measures aimed at checking the spread of the virus, led to greater ineffectiveness of the measures. In Nigeria and many parts of the world, lack of cooperation of the citizens in the enforcement of the lockdown policy, like face masks policy, social distancing policy, and other Non-Pharmaceutical Interventions (NPIs), led to the resurgence of the virus in different waves and variants. Europe and the United States of America suffered a lot of setbacks in controlling the virus because sizeable part of their citizens saw such measures as limiting their liberty. These two continents witnessed a harvest of demonstrations by the citizens at different times under the pandemic. As a result, some countries experienced up to fifth waves of the virus, with many of the new variants devastating their citizens. The cooperation of the citizens is therefore key to the success of a national policy response to a pandemic. The successful case of New Zealand, Australia, South Korea among others at different points in time in 2020 and 2021, is a demonstrative evidence of citizens' cooperation in the fight against the virus.

(g) Effective Enforcement of NPIs and other Measures reduces the rapid spread of the Virus

A resolute and effective enforcement of containment policies such as the Non-pharmaceutical Interventions (NPIs), and other safety measures, reduces the rapid spread of the virus. Put differently, if enforcement is weak, the spread of the virus would even be more and rapid too. The case of China during the early period of the outbreak of the virus, is a good evidence of a resolute and effective enforcement of the containment policies. The point here is that no responsible government would allow her citizens to die carelessly in the guise of protecting liberty rather than public health.

(h) *Irrational Scepticism is counter-productive to public health protection*
In science, rational scepticism is a virtue but irrational scepticism is
certainly a vice. In a pandemic, irrational scepticism is counter-productive
to public health protection. When some citizens keep doubting a
scientific fact (like an outbreak of a pandemic) up to the point of
endangering the lives of many others, (as a result of their non-observance
of preventive measures), then the government should step in to take
immediate actions to protect the larger society. This irrational scepticism
is even more dangerous when it is found among the leaders who should
lead by example. Nigeria's experience shows that a good number of the
citizens were sceptical about the fact that COVID-19 was (is) real. This
group of people formed part of those who did not cooperate in the fight
against the virus. However, in some countries such as the US, Brazil,
Mexico, Tanzania and Burundi, their leaders were the ones who were
sceptical about the reality of COVID-19. These adversely affected the
management of the virus in their countries which they paid heavily for
with high number of infections and fatalities. It was as a result of this
irrational scepticism that Tanzania and Burundi lost their presidents in
circumstances that could have been preventable.

(i) *The Existence of a weak Health System prior to a pandemic is catastrophic to*
public health
Nigeria's experience shows that the existence of a weak health system
prior to an outbreak of a pandemic, is catastrophic to the protection of
public health. The Chairman of the PTF on COVID-19 and Secretary to
the Government of the Federation (SGF) Mr. Boss Mustapha confessed
then that he never knew Nigeria's healthcare infrastructure was in such a
bad state until he was appointed the Chairman of PTF on COVID-19.[335]
The poor state of health infrastructure generated a lot of anxieties for
health workers who had to struggle to provide services at great risk when
infections were rapidly spreading. Unfortunately, the country lost many

---

[335]Premium Times, (2020): "I never knew Nigeria's healthcare infrastructure was in such bad state –
SGF." April 10. See: https://www.premiumtimesng.com/health/health-news/387036-i-never-knew-nigerias-
healthcare-infrastructure-was-in-such-bad-state-sgf.html

of them under such preventable circumstances. It was as if the Director-General of the WHO had this in mind when he said on January 30, 2020 during a speech on the declaration of COVID-19 as a *public health emergency of international concern* (PHEIC) that "our greatest concern is the potential for the virus to spread to countries with weaker health systems, and which are ill-prepared to deal with it."[336] He made the point that the situation in China would have been more catastrophic if not for the efforts of the government. According to him: "we would have seen many more cases outside China by now – and probably deaths – if it were not for the government's efforts, and the progress they have made to protect their own people and the people of the world."[337] Although some countries in the developed world (with strong health system) were devastated by the pandemic, the reality is that it would have been more catastrophic if their health systems were weak.

(j) Poor management of Health Workers' welfare is a serious threat to the successful management of a Pandemic

The Nigerian experience in COVID-19 policy management shows that when the welfare of health workers and other health professionals is not well taken care of, the result would be low morale and low commitment to their highly needed duty. It was a sad and embarrassing experience that Nigeria witnessed a harvest of preventable strikes during the pandemic and more dangerously during the lockdown period from health workers and professionals. It is bad enough that Nigeria has a weak health system, but it is even more catastrophic to neglect the welfare of health workers and professionals who are managing a dangerous pandemic at the risk of their lives. The neglect of their welfare led to the death of some during the most dangerous period of the pandemic.

(k) Massive Vaccination of Citizens should be a priority

Experience in Nigeria and across the world amply demonstrate that vaccination is an important pharmaceutical intervention that greatly

---

[336]WHO (2020): WHO Director-General's statement on IHR Emergency Committee on Novel Coronavirus (2019-nCoV). at: https://www.who.int/director-general/speeches/detail/who-director-general-s-statement-on-ihr-emergency-committee-on-novel-coronavirus-(2019-ncov)
[337] Ibid.

reduces the spread of infection, severity of infection, hospitalization and fatality. Since the administration of COVID-19 vaccines, it is as if the entire world is out of the danger zone of the deadly virus. However, there has been serious resistance to vaccination in different countries of the world leading to the adoption and enforcement of the vaccine mandate policy in some countries of the world. The enforcement of a vaccine mandate policy has also received stiff opposition from vaccine-hesitant persons or opponents. Based on the usefulness of the vaccine in the resolution of this public health crisis of immense proportion, massive vaccination of citizens should be a priority and should continue to be.

(l) A Vaccination Mandate Policy (with in-built flexibility) is a way to go
Although massive vaccination is the way to go, a strict enforcement of a vaccine mandate policy should be accompanied with some level of flexibility to accommodate some peculiarities where they exist. When people resist vaccination, an alternative policy which requires compulsory testing and a presentation of a negative test result, should be adopted and enforced. This is a fair treatment to vaccine-hesitant persons who are doing so for religious or other cultural reasons. This policy-alternative was implemented by Nigeria in 2021 when it announced that "federal government employees shall be required to show proof of COVID-19 vaccination or present a negative COVID-19 PCR test result done within 72 hours, to gain access to their offices, in all locations within Nigeria and our Missions."[338] Such a vaccine mandate policy- alternative takes care of the fears of vaccine-hesitant persons.

(m) In a Pandemic, some aspects of Normality become Abnormal with a New Normal emerging
One big surprise which emerged during the most dangerous period of the COVID-19 pandemic, was how some normal ways of doing certain things suddenly became abnormal with a *New Normal* emerging in their place. This was the case of *abnormality of normality replaced with a New*

---

[338]See for instance Obasi, I. N. (2021): 'Enforcing FG's 'Compulsory' COVID-19 vaccination policy'. Sundiata Post via https://sundiatapost.com/enforcing-fgs-compulsory-covid-19-vaccination-policy-by-isaac-n-obasi/, October 22.

Normal. Nigeria's experience shows that *old habits die hard* leading to obstinacy in obeying the New Normal. This wrongheadedness manifested in the enforcement of the face mask policy, as well as the social distancing policy. Other social practices such as the shaking of hands, hugging, and giving a peck on the cheek among others, were discouraged and abandoned, thereby becoming abnormal. In their place, new ways of greeting emerged. The lesson for our health policy makers is the challenge of devising new ways of coping in such a situation and followed quickly with enforcement rather than merely appealing to the people, as old habits die hard.

Generally and lastly, this book concludes that Nigeria's policy response to the COVID-19 pandemic, was on the average not a disappointment. This was because first, Nigeria's response followed science rather than politics, and secondly, it was managed by a task force driven largely by technocratic and professional ideas. This overall conclusion is in spite of what we have referred to as policy lessons based on peculiar Nigerian experience as presented below.

Key Policy Lessons based on peculiar Nigerian Experience

> Many public officials and VIPs in Nigeria flagrantly violated COVID-19 safety protocols. They saw themselves as those operating above the law even when some of them were the ones that made the law or to enforce them. Impunity reigned supreme among this class of Nigerians during the COVID-19 lockdown period.

> Impunity among public officials as well as among the ordinary people, remains a major governance challenge in Nigeria. The number of people arrested and subsequently prosecuted by the Mobile Courts for violating the lockdown order in the FCT, was a clear evidence of widespread disobedience to the law. The impunity disease in Nigeria is as bad as the COVID-19 disease itself.

> Nigeria is one of the countries where trust deficit has been high over many decades. It even grew to an all-time high under COVID-19 policy implementation.

> The two-pronged government approach of attacking COVID-19 disease and improving economic livelihood of the people was good and deep thinking, as a neglect of either of them could lead to

➢ death whether through disease or through hunger.

➢ Looking back now, one can say that the dilemma and politics of school reopening under the lockdown in 2020, was one of the most difficult policy responses faced by the Nigerian government to the COVID-19 pandemic. Luckily enough, the right decision was eventually taken.

➢ There is enough evidence under the COVID-19 pandemic that government across levels in Nigeria failed to prioritize the safety and welfare of health workers.

Appendices

Appendix 1

Address by H.E. Muhammadu Buhari, President of the Federal Republic of Nigeria on the COVID-19 Pandemic Sunday
29th March, 2020

1. Fellow Nigerians,

2. From the first signs that Coronavirus, or COVID-19 was turning into an epidemic and was officially declared a world-wide emergency, the Federal Government started planning preventive, containment and curative measures in the event the disease hits Nigeria.

3. The whole instruments of government are now mobilized to confront what has now become both a health emergency and an economic crisis.

4. Nigeria, unfortunately, confirmed its first case on 27th February 2020. Since then, we have seen the number of confirmed cases rise slowly.

5. By the morning of March 29th, 2020, the total confirmed cases within Nigeria had risen to ninety-seven.

6. Regrettably, we also had our first fatality, a former employee of PPMC, who died on 23rd March 2020. Our thoughts and prayers are with his family in this very difficult time. We also pray for a quick recovery for those infected and undergoing treatment.

7. As of today, COVID-19 has no cure. Scientists around the world are working very hard to develop a vaccine.

8. We are in touch with these institutions as they work towards a solution that will be certified by international and local medical authorities within the shortest possible time.

9. For now, the best and most efficient way to avoid getting infected is through regular hygienic and sanitary practices as well as social distancing.

10. As individuals, we remain the greatest weapon to fight this pandemic. By washing our hands regularly with clean water and soap, disinfecting frequently used surfaces and areas, coughing into a tissue or elbow and strictly adhering to infection prevention control measures in health facilities, we can contain this virus.

11. Since the outbreak was reported in China, our Government has been monitoring the situation closely and studying the various responses adopted by other countries.

12. Indeed, the Director-General of the Nigeria Centre for Disease Control (NCDC) was one of ten global health leaders invited by the World Health Organisation to visit China and understudy their response approach. I am personally very proud of Dr Ihekweazu for doing this on behalf of all Nigerians.

13. Since his return, the NCDC has been implementing numerous strategies and programs in Nigeria to ensure that the adverse impact of this virus on our country is minimized. We ask all Nigerians to support the work of the Federal Ministry of Health and NCDC are doing, led by the Presidential Task Force.

14. Although we have adopted strategies used globally, our implementation programs have been tailored to reflect our local realities.

15. In Nigeria, we are taking a two-step approach.

16. First,. to protect the lives of our fellow Nigerians and residents living here and second, to preserve the livelihoods of workers and business owners to ensure their families get through this very difficult time in dignity and with hope and peace of mind.

17. To date, we have introduced healthcare measures, border security, fiscal and monetary policies in our response. We shall continue to do so as the situation unfolds.

18. Some of these measures will surely cause major inconveniences to many citizens. But these are sacrifices we should all be willing and ready to make for the greater good of our country.

19. In Nigeria's fight against COVID-19, there is no such thing as an overreaction or an under-reaction. It is all about the right reaction by the right agencies and trained experts.

20. Accordingly, as a Government, we will continue to rely on guidance of our medical professionals and experts at the Ministry of Health, NCDC and other relevant agencies through this difficult time.

21. I, therefore, urge all citizens to adhere to their guidelines as they are released from time to time.

22. As we are all aware, Lagos and Abuja have the majority of confirmed cases in Nigeria. Our focus therefore remains to urgently and drastically contain these cases, and to support other states and regions in the best way we can.

23. This is why we provided an initial intervention of fifteen billion Naira (N15b) to support the national response as we fight to contain and control the spread.

24. We also created a Presidential Task Force (PTF) to develop a workable National Response Strategy that is being reviewed on a daily basis as the requirements change. This strategy takes international best practices but adopts them to suit our unique local circumstances.

25. Our goal is to ensure all States have the right support and manpower to respond immediately.

26. So far, in Lagos and Abuja, we have recruited hundreds of Adhoc staff to man our call centres and support our tracing and testing efforts.

27. I also requested, through the Nigeria Governors Forum, for all State Governments to nominate Doctors and Nurses who will be trained by the NCDC and Lagos State Government on the tactical and operational response to the virus in case it spreads to other states.

28. This training will also include medical representatives from our armed forces, paramilitary and security and intelligence agencies.

29. As a nation, our response must be guided, systematic and professional. There is a need for consistency across the nation. All inconsistencies in policy guidelines between Federal and State agencies will be eliminated.

30. As I mentioned earlier, as at this morning we had ninety-seven confirmed cases. Majority of these are in Lagos and Abuja. All the confirmed cases are getting the necessary medical care.

31. Our agencies are currently working hard to identify cases and people these patients have been in contact with.

32. The few confirmed cases outside Lagos and Abuja are linked to persons who have travelled from these centres.

33. We are therefore working to ensure such interstate and intercity movements are restricted to prevent further spread.

34. Based on the advice of the Federal Ministry of Health and the NCDC, I am directing the cessation of all movements in Lagos and the FCT for an initial period of 14 days with effect from 11pm on Monday, 30th March 2020. This restriction will also apply to Ogun State due to its close proximity to Lagos and the high traffic between the two States.

35. All citizens in these areas are to stay in their homes. Travel to or from other states should be postponed. All businesses and offices within these locations should be fully closed during this period.

36. The Governors of Lagos and Ogun States as well as the Minister of the FCT have been notified. Furthermore, heads of security and intelligence agencies have also been briefed.

37. We will use this containment period to identify, trace and isolate all individuals that have come into contact with confirmed cases. We will ensure the treatment of confirmed cases while restricting further spread to other States.

38. This order does not apply to hospitals and all related medical establishments as well as organizations in health care-related manufacturing and distribution.

39. Furthermore, commercial establishments such as;

a. food processing, distribution and retail companies;

b. petroleum distribution and retail entities,

c. power generation, transmission and distribution companies; and

d. private security companies are also exempted.

40. Although these establishments are exempted, access will be restricted and monitored.

41. Workers in telecommunication companies, broadcasters, print and electronic media staff who can prove they are unable to work from home are also exempted.

42. All seaports in Lagos shall remain operational in accordance with the guidelines I issued earlier. Vehicles and drivers conveying essential cargoes from these Ports to other parts of the country will be screened thoroughly before departure by the Ports Health Authority.

43. Furthermore, all vehicles conveying food and other essential humanitarian items into these locations from other parts of the country will also be screened thoroughly before they are allowed to enter these restricted areas.

44. Accordingly, the Hon. Minister of Health is hereby directed to redeploy all Port Health Authority employees previously stationed in the Lagos and Abuja Airports to key roads that serve as entry and exit points to these restricted zones.

45. Movements of all passenger aircraft, both commercial and private jets, are hereby suspended. Special permits will be issued on a needs basis.

46. We are fully aware that such measures will cause much hardship and inconvenience to many citizens. But this is a matter of life and death, if we look at the dreadful daily toll of deaths in Italy, France and Spain.

47. However, we must all see this as our national and patriotic duty to control and contain the spread of this virus. I will therefore ask all of us affected by this order to put aside our personal comfort to safeguard ourselves and fellow human beings. This common enemy can only be controlled if we all come together and obey scientific and medical advice.

48. As we remain ready to enforce these measures, we should see this as our individual contribution in the war against COVID-19. Many other countries have taken far stricter measures in a bid to control the spread of the virus with positive results.

49. For residents of satellite and commuter towns and communities around Lagos and Abuja whose livelihoods will surely be affected by some of these restrictive measures, we shall deploy relief materials to ease their pains in the coming weeks.

50. Furthermore, although schools are closed, I have instructed the Ministry of Humanitarian Affairs, Disaster Management and Social Development to work with State Governments in developing a strategy on how to sustain the school feeding program during this period without compromising our social distancing policies. The Minister will be contacting the affected States and agree on detailed next steps.

51. Furthermore, I have directed that a three month repayment moratorium for all TraderMoni, MarketMoni and FarmerMoni loans be implemented with immediate effect.

52. I have also directed that a similar moratorium be given to all Federal Government funded loans issued by the Bank of Industry, Bank of Agriculture and the Nigeria Export-Import Bank.

53. For on-lending facilities using capital from international and multilateral development partners, I have directed our development financial institutions to engage these development partners and negotiate concessions to ease the pains of the borrowers.

54. For the most vulnerable in our society, I have directed that the conditional cash transfers for the next two months be paid immediately. Our Internally displaced persons will also receive two months of food rations in the coming weeks.

55. We also call on all Nigerians to take personal responsibility to support those who are vulnerable within their communities, helping them with whatever they may need.

56. As we all pray for the best possible outcome, we shall continue planning for all eventualities.

57. This is why I directed that all Federal Government Stadia, Pilgrims camps and other facilities be converted to isolation centres and makeshift hospitals.

58. My fellow Nigerians, as a Government, we will avail all necessary resources to support the response and recovery. We remain committed to do whatever it takes to confront COVID-19 in our country.

59. We are very grateful to see the emerging support of the private sector and individuals to the response as well as our development partners.

60. At this point, I will ask that all contributions and donations be coordinated and centralized to ensure efficient and impactful spending. The Presidential Task Force remains the central coordinating body on the COVID-19 response.

61. I want to assure you all that Government Ministries, Departments and Agencies with a role to play in the outbreak response are working hard to bring this virus under control.

62. Every nation in the world is challenged at this time. But we have seen countries where citizens have come together to reduce the spread of the virus.

63. I will, therefore, implore you again to strictly comply with the guidelines issued and also do your bit to support the Government and the most vulnerable in your communities.

64. I will take this opportunity to thank all our public health workforce, health care workers, port health authorities and other essential staff on the front lines of the response for their dedication and commitment. You are true heroes.

65. I thank you all for listening. May God continue to bless and protect us all.

President Muhammad Buhari

29th March 2020.

Appendix 2

Address By H.E. Muhammadu Buhari, President of the Federal Republic of Nigeria on the Extension of COVID- 19 Pandemic Lockdown at the State House, Abuja
Monday, 13th April, 2020

1. Fellow Nigerians
2. In my address on Sunday, 29th March, 2020, I asked the residents of Lagos and Ogun States as well as the Federal Capital Territory to stay at home for an initial period of fourteen days starting from Monday, 30th March 2020.
3. Many State Governments also introduced similar restrictions.
4. As your democratically elected leaders, we made this very difficult decision knowing fully well it will severely disrupt your livelihoods and bring undue hardship to you, your loved ones and your communities.
5. However, such sacrifices are needed to limit the spread of COVID-19 in our country. They were necessary to save lives.
6. Our objective was, and still remains, to contain the spread of the Coronavirus and to provide space, time and resources for an aggressive and collective action.
7. The level of compliance to the COVID-19 guidelines issued has been generally good across the country. I wish to thank you all most sincerely for the great sacrifice you are making for each other at this critical time.
8. I will take this opportunity to recognise the massive support from our traditional rulers, the Christian Association of Nigeria (CAN) and the Nigerian Supreme Council for Islamic Affairs (NSCIA) during this pandemic.
9. I also acknowledge the support and contributions received from public spirited individuals, the business community and our international partners and friends.
10. I must also thank the media houses, celebrities and other public figures for the great work they are doing in sensitizing our citizens on hygienic practices, social distancing and issues associated with social gatherings.
11. As a result of the overwhelming support and cooperation received, we were able to achieve a lot during these 14 days of initial lockdown.
12. We implemented comprehensive public health measures that intensified our case identification, testing, isolation and contact tracing capabilities.
13. To date, we have identified 92% of all identified contacts while doubling the number of testing laboratories in the country and raising our testing capacity to 1,500 tests per day.
14. We also trained over 7,000 Healthcare workers on infection prevention and control while deploying NCDC teams to 19 states of the federation.
15. Lagos and Abuja today have the capacity to admit some 1,000 patients each across several treatment centres.
16. Many State Governments have also made provisions for isolation wards and treatment centres. We will also build similar centers near our airports and land borders.
17. Using our resources and those provided through donations, we will adequately equip and man these centres in the coming weeks. Already, health care workers across

all the treatment centers have been provided with the personal protective equipment that they need to safely carry out the care they provide.

18. Our hope and prayers are that we do not have to use all these centres. But we will be ready for all eventualities.

19. At this point, I must recognise the incredible work being done by our healthcare workers and volunteers across the country especially in frontline areas of Lagos and Ogun States as well as the Federal Capital Territory.

20. You are our heroes and as a nation, we will forever remain grateful for your sacrifice during this very difficult time. More measures to motivate our health care workers are being introduced which we will announce in the coming weeks.

21. As a nation, we are on the right track to win the fight against COVID-19.

22. However, I remain concerned about the increase in number of confirmed cases and deaths being reported across the world and in Nigeria specifically.

23. On 30th March 2020, when we started our lockdown in conforming with medical and scientific advice, the total number of confirmed cases across the world was over 780,000.

24. Yesterday, the number of confirmed COVID-19 cases globally was over one million, eight hundred and fifty thousand. This figure is more than double in two weeks!

25. In the last fourteen days alone, over 70,000 people have died due to this disease.

26. In the same period, we have seen the health system of even the most developed nations being overwhelmed by this virus.

27. Here in Nigeria, we had 131 confirmed cases of COVID-19 in 12 States on 30th March 2020. We had two fatalities then.

28. This morning, Nigeria had 323 confirmed cases in twenty States. Unfortunately we now have ten fatalities. Lagos State remains the center and accounts for 54% of the confirmed cases in Nigeria. When combined with the FCT, the two locations represent over 71% of the confirmed cases in Nigeria.

29. Most of our efforts will continue to focus in these two locations.

30. Majority of the confirmed cases in Lagos and the FCT are individuals with recent international travel history or those that came into contact with returnees from international trips.

31. By closing our airports and land borders and putting strict conditions for seaport activities, we have reduced the impact of external factors on our country. However, the increase in the number of States with positive cases is alarming.

32. The National Centre for Disease Control has informed me that, a large proportion of new infections are now occurring in our communities, through person-to-person contacts. So we must pay attention to the danger of close contact between person to person.

33. At this point, I will remind all Nigerians to continue to take responsibility for the recommended measures to prevent transmission, including maintaining physical distancing, good personal hygiene and staying at home.

34. In addition, I have signed the Quarantine Order in this regard and additional regulations to provide clarity in respect of the control measures for the COVID-19 pandemic which will be released soon.

35. The public health response to COVID-19 is built on our ability to detect, test and admit cases as well as trace all their contacts. While I note some appreciable progress, we can achieve a lot more.

36. Today, the cessation of movement, physical distancing measures and the prohibition of mass gatherings remain the most efficient and effective way of reducing the transmission of the virus. By sustaining these measures, combined with extensive testing and contact tracing, we can take control and limit the spread of the disease.

37. Our approach to the virus remains in 2 steps – First, to protect the lives of our fellow Nigerians and residents living here and second, to preserve the livelihoods of workers and business owners.

38. With this in mind and having carefully considered the briefings and Report from the Presidential Task Force and the various options offered, it has become necessary to extend the current restriction of movement in Lagos and Ogun States as well as the FCT for another 14 days effective from 11:59 pm on Monday, 13th of April, 2020. I am therefore once again asking you all to work with Government in this fight.

39. This is not a joke. It is a matter of life and death. Mosques in Makkah and Madina have been closed. The Pope celebrated Mass on an empty St. Peter's Square. The famous Notre Dame cathedral in Paris held Easter Mass with less than 10 people. India, Italy and France are in complete lockdown. Other countries are in the process of following suit. We cannot be lax.

40. The previously issued guidelines on exempted services shall remain.

41. This is a difficult decision to take, but I am convinced that this is the right decision. The evidence is clear.

42. The repercussions of any premature end to the lockdown action are unimaginable.

43. We must not lose the gains achieved thus far. We must not allow a rapid increase in community transmission. We must endure a little longer.

44. I will therefore take this opportunity to urge you all to notify the relevant authorities if you or your loved ones develop any symptoms. I will also ask our health care professionals to redouble their efforts to identify all suspected cases, bring them into care and prevent transmission to others.

45. No country can afford the full impact of a sustained restriction of movement on its economy. I am fully aware of the great difficulties experienced especially by those who earn a daily wage such as traders, dayworkers, artisans and manual workers.

46. For this group, their sustenance depends on their ability to go out. Their livelihoods depend on them mingling with others and about seeking work. But despite these realities we must not change the restrictions.

47. In the past two weeks, we announced palliative measures such as food distribution, cash transfers and loans repayment waivers to ease the pains of our restrictive policies during this difficult time. These palliatives will be sustained.

48. I have also directed that the current social register be expanded from 2.6 million households to 3.6 million households in the next two weeks. This means we will support an additional one million homes with our social investment programs. A

technical committee is working on this and will submit a report to me by the end of this week.

49. The Security Agencies have risen to the challenges posed by this unprecedented situation with gallantry and I commend them. I urge them to continue to maintain utmost vigilance, firmness as well as restraint in enforcing the restriction orders while not neglecting statutory security responsibilities.

50. Fellow Nigerians, follow the instructions on social distancing. The irresponsibility of the few can lead to the death of the many. Your freedom ends where other people's rights begin.

51. The response of our State Governors has been particularly impressive, especially in aligning their policies and actions to those of the Federal Government.

52. In the coming weeks, I want to assure you that the Federal Government, through the Presidential Task Force, will do whatever it takes to support you in this very difficult period. I have no doubt that, by working together and carefully following the rules, we shall get over this pandemic.

53. I must also thank the Legislative arm of Government for all its support and donations in this very difficult period. This collaboration is critical to the short and long-term success of all the measures that we have instituted in response to the pandemic.

54. As a result of this pandemic, the world as we know it has changed. The way we interact with each other, conduct our businesses and trade, travel, educate our children and earn our livelihoods will be different.

55. To ensure our economy adapts to this new reality, I am directing the Ministers of Industry, Trade and Investment, Communication and Digital Economy, Science and Technology, Transportation, Aviation, Interior, Health, Works and Housing, Labour and Employment and Education to jointly develop a comprehensive policy for a "Nigerian economy functioning with COVID-19".

56. The Ministers will be supported by the Presidential Economic Advisory Council and Economic Sustainability Committee in executing this mandate.

57. I am also directing the Minister of Agriculture and Rural Development, the National Security Adviser, the Vice Chairman, National Food Security Council and the Chairman, Presidential Fertiliser Initiative to work with the Presidential Task Force on COVID-19 to ensure the impact of this pandemic on our 2020 farming season is minimized.

58. Finally, I want to thank the members of the Presidential Task Force on COVID-19 for all their hard work so far. Indeed, the patriotism shown in your work is exemplary and highly commendable.

59. Fellow Nigerians, I have no doubt that by working together and carefully following the rules, we shall get over this pandemic and emerge stronger in the end.

60. I thank you all for listening and may God bless the Federal Republic of Nigeria.

Appendix 3

Address by H.E. Muhammadu Buhari, President of The Federal Republic of Nigeria on The Cumulative Lockdown order of Lagos and Ogun States as Well as The Federal Capital Territory on COVID- 19 Pandemic at the State House, Abuja Monday, 27th April, 2020

1. Fellow Nigerians

2. I will start by commending you all for the resilience and patriotism that you have shown in our collective fight against the biggest health challenge of our generation.

3. As at yesterday, 26th April 2020, some 3 million confirmed cases of COVID-19 have been recorded globally with about 900,000 recoveries. Unfortunately, some 200,000 people have passed away as a result of this pandemic.

4. The health systems and economies of many nations continue to struggle as a result of the coronavirus pandemic.

5. Nigeria continues to adapt to these new global realities on a daily basis. Today, I will present the facts as they are and explain our plans for the coming months fully aware that some key variables and assumptions may change in the coming days or weeks.

6. Exactly two weeks ago, there were 323 confirmed cases in 20 States and the Federal Capital Territory.

7. As at this morning, Nigeria had recorded 1,273 cases across 32 States and the FCT. Unfortunately, this includes 40 deaths.

8. I am using this opportunity to express our deepest condolences to the families of all Nigerians that have lost their loved ones as a result of the COVID-19 pandemic. This is our collective loss and we share your grief.

9. Initial models predicted that Nigeria will record an estimated 2,000 confirmed cases in the first month after the index case.

10. This means that despite the increase in the number of confirmed cases recorded in the past two weeks, the measures we have put in place thus far have yielded positive outcomes against the projections.

11. The proportion of cases imported from other countries has reduced to only 19% of new cases, showing that our border closures yielded positive results. These are mostly fellow Nigerians returning through our land borders. We will continue to enforce land border arrival protocols as part of the containment strategy.

12. Today, the Nigeria Centre for Disease Control (NCDC) has accredited 15 laboratories across the country with an aggregate capacity to undertake 2,500 tests per day across the country.

13. Based on your feedback, Lagos State Government and the FCT with support from NCDC have established several sample collection centers. They are also reviewing their laboratory testing strategy to further increase the number of tests they can perform including the accreditation of selected private laboratories that meet the accreditation criteria.

14. Several new fully equipped treatment and isolation centres have been operationalised across the country thereby increasing bed capacity to about three thousand.

15. I commend the State Governors for the activation of State-level Emergency Operation Centres, establishment of new treatment centres and the delivery of aggressive risk communication strategies.

16. Over 10,000 healthcare workers have been trained. For their protection, additional personal protective equipment have been distributed to all the states.

17. Although we have experienced logistical challenges, we remain committed to establishing a solid supply chain process to ensure these heroic professionals can work safely and are properly equipped.

18. In keeping with our Government's promise to improve the welfare of healthcare workers, we have signed a memorandum of understanding on the provision of hazard allowances and other incentives with key health sector professional associations.

19. We have also procured insurance cover for 5,000 frontline health workers. At this point, I must commend the insurance sector for their support in achieving this within a short period of time.

20. Nigeria has also continued to receive support from the international community, multilateral agencies, the private sector and public-spirited individuals. This support has ensured that critical lifesaving equipment and materials, which have become scarce globally, are available for Nigeria through original equipment manufacturers and government-to-government processes.

21. The distribution and expansion of palliatives which I directed in my earlier broadcast is still ongoing in a transparent manner. I am mindful of the seeming frustration being faced by expectant citizens. I urge all potential beneficiaries to exercise patience as we continue to fine-tune our logistical and distribution processes working with the State Governments.

22. Our Security Agencies continue to rise to the challenge posed by this unusual situation. While we feel deeply concerned about isolated security incidents, I want to assure all Nigerians that your safety and security remain our primary concern especially in these difficult and uncertain-times.

23. As we focus on protecting lives and properties, we will not tolerate any human rights abuse by our security agencies. The few reported incidences are regrettable, and I want to assure you that the culprits will be brought to justice.

24. I urge all Nigerians to continue to cooperate and show understanding whenever they encounter security agents. Furthermore, for their protection, I have instructed that the personnel of all the security agencies be provided with the necessary personal protective equipment against infection.

25. As we continue to streamline our response in the centers of Lagos and the FCT, I am gravely concerned about the unfortunate developments in Kano in recent days. Although an in-depth investigation is still ongoing, we have decided to deploy additional Federal Government manpower, material and technical resources to strengthen and support the State Government's efforts, with immediate effect.

26. In Kano, and indeed many other States that are recording new cases, preliminary findings show that such cases are mostly from interstate travel and emerging community transmission.

27. Drawing from these, I implore all Nigerians to continue to adhere strictly to the advisories published by the Presidential Task Force and the Nigeria Centre for Disease Control.

28. These include regular hand washing, physical distancing, wearing of face masks/coverings in public, avoidance of non-essential movement and travels and avoidance of large gatherings.

29. Fellow Nigerians, for the past four weeks, most parts of our country have been under either Federal Government or State Government lockdown. As I mentioned earlier, these steps were necessary and overall, have contributed to slowing down the spread of COVID-19 in our country.

30. However, such lockdowns have also come at a very heavy economic cost. Many of our citizens have lost their means of livelihood. Many businesses have shut down. No country can afford the full impact of a sustained lockdown while awaiting the development of vaccines.

31. In my last address, I mentioned that Federal Government will develop strategies and policies that will protect lives while preserving livelihoods.

32. In these two weeks, the Federal and State Governments have jointly and collaboratively worked hard on how to balance the need to protect health while also preserving livelihoods, leveraging global best practices while keeping in mind our peculiar circumstances.

33. We assessed how our factories, markets, traders and transporters can continue to function while at the same time adhering to NCDC guidelines on hygiene and social distancing.

34. We assessed how our children can continue to learn without compromising their health.

35. We reviewed how our farmers can safely plant and harvest in this rainy season to ensure our food security is not compromised. Furthermore, we also discussed how to safely transport food items from rural production areas to industrial processing zones and ultimately, to the key consumption centers.

36. Our goal was to develop implementable policies that will ensure our economy continues to function while still maintaining our aggressive response to the COVID-19 pandemic. These same difficult decisions are being faced by leaders around the world.

37. Based on the above and in line with the recommendations of the Presidential Task Force on COVID-19, the various Federal Government committees that have reviewed socio-economic matters and the Nigeria Governors Forum, I have approved a phased and gradual easing of lockdown measures in FCT, Lagos and Ogun States effective from Monday, 4th May, 2020.

38. However, this will be followed strictly with aggressive reinforcement of testing and contact tracing measures while allowing the restoration of some economic and business activities in certain sectors.

39. Furthermore, new nationwide measures are to be introduced as follows;
a. There will be an overnight curfew from 8pm to 6am. This means all movements will be prohibited during this period except for essential services;
b. There will be a ban on non-essential inter-state passenger travel until further notice;
c. Partial and controlled interstate movement of goods and services will be allowed for the movement of goods and services from producers to consumers; and
d. We will strictly ensure the mandatory use of face masks or coverings in public in

addition to maintaining physical distancing and personal hygiene. Furthermore, the restrictions on social and religious gatherings shall remain in place. State Governments, corporate organisations and philanthropists are encouraged to support the production of cloth masks for citizens.

40. For the avoidance of doubt, the lockdown in the FCT, Lagos and Ogun States shall remain in place until these new ones come into effect on Monday, 4th May 2020.

41. The Presidential Task Force shall provide sector specific details to allow for preparations by Governments, businesses and institutions.

42. In respect to the above guidelines, State Governors may choose to adapt and expand based on their unique circumstances provided they maintain alignment with the guidelines issued above.

43. To support our businesses and traders, the monetary and fiscal authorities shall deploy all the necessary provisions needed for production to continue and thus, jobs restored.

44. These revised guidelines will not apply to Kano State.

45. With regards to Kano, I have directed the enforcement of a total lockdown for a period of two weeks effective immediately. The Federal Government shall deploy all the necessary human, material and technical resources to support the State in controlling and containing the pandemic and preventing the risk of further spread to neighboring States.

46. I wish to once again commend the frontline workers across the country who, on a daily basis, risk everything to ensure we win this fight. For those who got infected in the line of duty, rest assured that Government will do all it takes to support you and your families during this exceedingly difficult period. I will also take this opportunity to assure you all that your safety, wellbeing and welfare remain paramount to our Government.

47. I will also recognise the support we have received from our traditional rulers, the Christian Association of Nigeria, the Nigerian Supreme Council for Islamic Affairs and other prominent religious and community leaders. Your cooperation and support have significantly contributed to the successes we have recorded to date.

48. I will urge you all to please continue to create awareness on the seriousness of the coronavirus among your worshippers and communities while appealing that they strictly comply with public health advisories.

49. I also thank the Nigeria Governors' Forum and the Presidential Task Force for all their hard work to date. Through this collaboration, I remain confident that success is achievable.

50. I also wish to thank corporate organisations, philanthropists, the UN system, the European Union, friendly nations, the media and other partners that have taken up the responsibility of supporting our response.

51. And finally, I will thank all Nigerians again for your patience and cooperation during this difficult and challenging period. I assure you that government shall continue to take all necessary measures to protect the lives and livelihoods of our citizens and residents.

52. I thank you for listening and may God bless the Federal Republic of Nigeria.

Appendix 4

Implementation Guidance for Lockdown Policy Section I: Guidance for Lockdown Enforcement

As part of the measures in place to enforce social distancing and limit the spread of the SARS-CoV-2, the Federal Government of Nigeria has decided that schools, organizations and businesses in FCT, Lagos and Ogun States will close effective from 30 March 2020 at 23:00h for an initial period of 2 weeks.

• For the period of the lockdown, every person is confined to his or her place of residence, unless strictly for the purpose of performing an essential service, obtaining an essential good or service, or seeking medical care.
• All borders linking the two States and FCT to the rest of the country are shut during the period of the lockdown, except for the transportation of persons on essential duty, food, fuel, manufactured goods or donated relief items. Security agencies should note this.
• Mass gathering is prohibited, except for funeral services as guided by infection prevention and control regulations, for which social distancing rules apply and crowds are limited to not more than 20 persons.
• Movement between and within the affected States and FCT is restricted, except for workers involved in the delivery of authorized essential services, duties, food and goods.
 • Retail shops and malls must be closed, except where essential goods are sold. Shops and malls that are open must enforce social distancing and hygiene measures in line with issued guidelines.
• Any business or organization providing essential goods and services must identify the staff who will perform those services.
• Commuter services between cities and States including passenger rail services, bus services, e-hailing services, maritime and air passenger transport are suspended for the period of the lockdown in the affected States. ○ Limited transport services are allowed for the movement of workers, services and goods in response to COVID-19 and for the purpose of seeking medical attention or provision of essential services. Transport services available during the lockdown must implement social distancing and hygiene measures. The table below lists the essential services and businesses that are exempted: Services and Businesses Exemptions Medical:
• Private and public hospitals • Dental clinics (emergencies only) • Specialist Clinics • Pharmacies and chemist shops • Opticians and ophthalmologists (emergencies only) Retail : All should ensure social distancing and increased hygiene measures are in place
• Food markets, open from 10:00h -14:00h daily) • Supermarkets and shops selling food and essential non-food items (groceries) • Shopping malls (only shops selling food and essential groceries shall open) Food and drink • Food delivery services (no eating-in) Logistics and transportation • Fuel stations • Registered repair garages • Company car services for essential staff • Post offices • Courier and distribution companies • Private security companies • Trucks carrying essential goods including food,

439

pharmaceuticals and manufactured goods related to the COVID-19 response ● Airline ground handling staff and essential aviation staff Accommodation ● Hotels with guests and/or hosting essential staff (no restaurants, bar services or night clubs shall open to the public) ● Orphanages and homes Financial institutions ● Banks: skeletal services to maintain ATMs, essential online operations and cash services. Government institutions and public utilities ● Agencies involved in essential duties (see list below) ● Utility companies ○ Electricity distribution and Transmission company ○ Waterboards ○ Waste management ○ Environmental Health Services ○ Telecommunications Places of worship ● Small funeral services limited to 20 persons only.

Section Ii: Protocols For Lockdown Road Movements: 1. With regards to the carriage of passengers: a. Ensure adequate spacing in between passengers Agriculture ● Farms, distributors of food and perishable commodities Manufacturing ● Manufacturers of food, drugs, pharmaceuticals and essential products related to the response Aviation ● Cargo and specially approved flights only Communications ● Telecommunication companies, newspaper, TV, radio and broadcasting companies ● Workers allied to this sector including newspaper vendors ● Internet service providers Legal and Security ● Public and private security agencies ● Criminal justice and correctional services as necessary to maintain law and order Diplomatic Missions, International development partners and honorary consulates ● Critical diplomatic staff necessary for essential embassy functions including security, consular issues, plant maintenance etc. b. Clean and disinfect frequently touched parts e.g. door and window handles/buttons, steering wheels and dashboards. c. Encourage passengers to frequently perform hand hygiene.

Super Markets and Food Stores: 1. All owners and managers of supermarkets and food stores must strictly adhere to the following: a. On arrival, all staff must be screened for high temperature. Those found to have a body temperature above 38.0^0C should be denied entry and advised to immediately seek medical attention. b. Ensure staff and customers wash their hands before entry to the store. Make provision for regular hand hygiene for staff during working hours. c. Ensure all deliveries of supplies and products are made between 5:00 am and 9:00 am. Porters should wash their hands before offloading products and goods. d. Store opening hours should be between 10am to 4pm daily for customers e. At any point in time, the total number of customers inside each store must not on average exceed a third of the store's maximum capacity. Where necessary, store owners should assign security personnel to ensure strict compliance with these measures. f. Ensure that from 4pm all shelves, aisles and stores are cleaned and disinfected g. Ensure that by 6pm, all stores are closed, and staff conveyed back to their respective homes.

Pharmacies: 1. The rules above for supermarkets shall also apply to pharmacies. However, 24-hour pharmacies may continue to operate as usual.

Markets: In order for markets to operate, State and local government authorities as well as leaders of market associations must take full responsibility for strict compliance with the following protocols: 1. Only shops and stalls selling food and groceries shall be allowed to open to customers between 10:00am to 2:00pm every 48 hours or less frequently. 2. All market associations must make provision for hand washing for all sellers and buyers. At entry and exit points of the market, both sellers and buyers must wash or sanitize their hands. 3. Each stall/shop in the market should ensure that their customers queue and are attended to serially while complying with social distancing measures and avoiding overcrowding. 4. All shop owners and staff must arrive and set up at least 30 minutes before the market is open to customers. Each store owner is responsible for cleaning and disinfecting their shops. 5. All markets should strictly comply with social distancing policies. A safe gap should be ensured between shop/stall owners and customers.

Banks: 1. All banks shall comply with the guidelines, mode and scope of operations issues by the Central Bank and Federal Ministry of Finance as it related to the COVID-19 response. 2. All banks shall make provision for hand hygiene at the entry of the premises and temperature monitoring of all staff and customers. 3. Those customers and staff found to have a body temperature above 38.0^0C shall be denied entry and advised to immediately seek medical attention. 4. Banks should develop a schedule for cleaning buttons and surfaces of ATM machines.

List of Exempted Government Agencies

Due to the essential nature of their functions, the following MDAs are exempted from the lockdown order (this list is not exhaustive): 1. The Presidency a. Office of the Secretary to the Government of the Federation b. Federal Road Safety Corps c. Bureau of Public Procurement d. National Agency for the Control of AIDS e. Offices of all permanent secretaries, CEOs/accounting officers of all MDAs in the public service 2. Department of State Services 3. Central Bank of Nigeria 4. Federal Ministry of Agriculture a. National Grain Reserves 5. Federal Ministry of Aviation a. Accident Aviation Bureau b. Federal Airports Authority of Nigeria c. Nigerian Airspace Management Agency d. Nigeria Civil Aviation Authority e. Nigerian Meteorological Agency 6. Federal Ministry of Communications a. Galaxy Backbone b. Nigeria Communications Commission c. Nigeria Information Technology Development Agency 7. Federal Ministry of Environment 8. Federal Ministry of Finance, Budget and National Planning a. Nigeria Customs Service b. Nigerian Sovereign Investment Authority c. Debt Management Office 9. Federal Ministry of Health a. All teaching hospitals and federal medical centres b. Nigeria Centre for Disease Control c. National

Primary Healthcare Agency d. National Health Insurance Scheme e. Nigerian Institute of Medical Research 10.Federal Ministry of Humanitarian Affairs, Disaster Management and Social Development a. National Agency for Prohibition of Trafficking in Persons b. National Emergency Management Agency c. National Cash Transfer Office d. National Commission for Refugees, Migrants and Internally Displaced Persons e. National School Feeding Programme 11. Federal Ministry of Information and Culture a. Federal Radio Corporation of Nigeria b. National Orientation Agency c. News Agency of Nigeria d. Nigeria Broadcasting Commission e. Nigeria Television Authority f. Voice of Nigeria 12. Federal Ministry of Interior a. Federal Fire Service b. Nigeria Immigration Services c. Nigerian Correctional Services d. Nigerian Security and Civil Defence Corps 13. Federal Ministry of Justice 14. Federal Ministry of Petroluem a. Nigeria National Petroleum Corporation and allied petroleum sector agencies b. Upstream oil and gas companies (operating, services and logistics) 15. Federal Ministry of Transport a. Nigerian Ports Authority 16. Federal Ministry of Industry, Trade and Investment 17. Federal Ministry of Water Resources 18. The Armed Forces 19. The Nigeria Police Force.

Appendix 5
Implementation Guidelines for Phase 1 of Gradual Easing of Lockdown
(May 4 – 17, 2020)
May 1, 2020

Further to the pronouncement of Mr. President in the broadcast of Monday, 27th April, 2020, in which he directed the Presidential Task Force on COVID-19 to provide implementation guidelines on the new measures to control COVID-19 pandemic, the following are hereby issued for:

– General Information to the Public;
– Guidance to States and Security Agencies; and
– Description of the types of activities allowed under Phase 1 (4th -17th May, 2020)

Section I: General Information on New Covid-19 Measures
2. Following improvements in the multisectoral response to the Coronavirus (COVID-19)
pandemic, the Federal Government of Nigeria has decided that there will be a phased and gradual easing of the lockdown in Lagos and Ogun States as well as the Federal Capital Territory (FCT) effective from Monday, 4th May, 2020.
3. The easing of the lockdown will be characterised by the following enforceable actions:
• The mandatory use of non-medical face mask/covering for all persons while in public spaces. Latex hand gloves should not be worn except for specific medical purposes;
• The mandatory provision of handwashing facilities/sanitizers in all public places;
• All interstate travel is prohibited except for essential travels & services, such as: transportation of agricultural products, petroleum products, relief items, goods, commodities related to the COVID-19 response and persons on essential duty;
• Mass gathering of more than 20 people outside of a workplace is prohibited;
• There will be controlled access to markets and locations of economic activities;
• Mandatory temperature checks will be conducted in public spaces;
• Social distancing of 2 metres must be maintained between people in workplaces and other public spaces;
• Retention of the ban on all passenger flights;
• Religious gatherings are still restricted; and
• Mandatory supervised isolation of person(s) arriving from outside the country for at least 14 days.

General Rules and Regulations:
• Anyone who presents a temperature of above 380C will be mandated to return home and call NCDC for evaluation;
• Anyone without a face mask/covering will be asked to return home and will be prosecuted;
• Anyone violating the curfew in a non-emergency situation will be prosecuted;
• Anyone attending a gathering of more than 20 people will be prosecuted;
• Institutions that fail to comply with these protocols and guidelines will be prosecuted; and

• Any member of the public who violates the ban on Inter-State movement as outlined in this guideline will be prosecuted.

Section Ii. Protocols for Containment of COVID-19
Activity: Recommendations & Obligation of Operators
PHASE 1: 4th -17th May 2020
Curfew: Imposition of overnight curfew nationwide from 8pm to 6am

General movement:
i. May go out for work, to buy necessary foods and for exercise
ii. Movement between LGAs (except metropolitan areas) is strongly discouraged unless for critical reasons such as healthcare and work
iii. Avoid unnecessary contact with people
iv. Mandatory use of face mask/coverings in public

Inter-state travel (Across State borders):
All inter-state travel for supply chain & services allowed, such as: goods, agro-products with a limited capacity of accompanying personnel, petroleum products, relief items, supplies, construction supplies, registered courier services (DHL, FedEx, etc) and security services

Intra-state travel (public transport- buses, tricycles, taxis)
(Within State borders):
i. Ensure provision of hand sanitizers to all passengers
ii. Reduce occupancy to half for buses (maximum 50% of usual occupancy)
iii. Mandatory Use of face mask/coverings
iv. Mandatory temperature checks
v. Taxis to carry only 4 persons (driver and 3 persons)
vi.Tricycles to carry only 3 persons (driver and 2 persons)
vii.Daily motor park sanitation
viii.Travel should be between 6.00am and 6.00pm

Bus stop/motor park:
i. Provide hand washing facilities
ii. Maintain social distancing
iii.Mandatory Use of face mask /coverings
iv.Mandatory temperature checks
v.Provide hand sanitizers and hand washing
vi.Should only open between 6.00am and 6.00pm

Agriculture & Rural development:
i. Mandatory use of face masks and social distancing
ii. Persons above age of 65 years and those with underlying chronic illness e.g. diabetes, high blood pressure are advised to remain at home

iii.Trucks bearing agricultural and animal products to be allowed easy passage
iv. Companies involved in food processing can commence operation
v. Ensure provision of hand sanitizers and hand washing facilities

Construction sites (large and small), Public Works:
i. Limit number to maintain social distancing
ii. Construction of critical roads to resume
iii. Waivers to be provided by State Govts to enable movement
iv. Mandatory use of face masks/coverings
v. Provide hand sanitizers and hand washing facilities
vi. Open between 6.00am and 6.00pm

Banks and other financial institutions:
i. Ensure provision of hand sanitizer to all employees and customers
ii.Limit staff physically working in the office to between 30% to 50%
iii.Limit number of customers to allow social distancing
iv.Mandatory Use of face mask/coverings
v. Encourageonline banking
vi.Mandatory temperature checks
vii. Open between 8.00am and 2.00pm

Manufacturing and Pharmaceutical industries, pharmacy shops:
i. Ensure provision of sanitizer and hand washing facilities
ii.Limit staff working to between 30-50% to maintain social distancing
iii.Shift work is encouraged; pharmacy shops may remain open overnight
iv. Mandatory use of face masks/coverings

Government offices /other corporate offices and entities:
i. Ensure provision of hand sanitizer to all employees and customers
ii. Limit staff physically working in the office to between 30% to 50%
iii. Government staff limited to essential workers and those from GL 14-17 on Monday/Wednesday/Fridays
iv. Limit number of customers to allow social distancing
v. Mandatory use of face masks/coverings
vi. Encourage work from home policy
vii. Mandatory temperature checks
viii. Offices to open between 8.00am and 2.00pm

Neighbourhood Markets:
i. Ensure provision of sanitizer and hand washing facilities
ii. Control entry to reduce number to ensure social distancing
iii. Mandatory use of face masks/coverings
iv. Temperature checks
v. Local authorities to determine date and time for opening of the neighborhood markets not more than 3 times a week

vi. Warehouses to open on neighbourhood market days to serve shops

vii. Abattoirs to open three days a week

viii. Ensure strict sanitation compliance

ix. Time of opening 8.00a.m. – 3.00p.m.

Supermarkets:

i. Ensure provision of sanitizer and hand washing facilities

ii. Limit number of customers to allow social distancing

iii.Mandatory use of face masks/coverings

iv.Ensure handwashing

v. Mandatory temperature checks

vi.Open 8.00a.m.-3.00p.m.

Restaurants:

i. Not open to the public, encourage home delivery

ii. To remain closed to eat-in, until further evaluation

iii. Allow social distancing always

iv. Eateries to practice the takeaway system

v. Open 8.00a.m.-3.00p.m.

Clubs, Bars, Beer Parlors, Gardens, etc:

i. To remain closed

ii.The use of recreational parks, communal sports, concerts, social parties, movie theatres are suspended until further notice

Academic institutions and Social engagements:

i. All schools to remain closed till further evaluation

ii. Schools are encouraged to continue with e-learning and visual teaching

3. State Governments and Security Agencies are enjoined to ensure effective and strict enforcement of these guidelines.

4. The level of compliance with these guidelines will be reviewed in 2 weeks before additional guidelines for phase 2 is issued.

(Signed)

Boss Mustapha

Secretary to the Government of the Federation

Appendix 6

Samples of PTF National Briefing Remarks by Chairman of PTF and Minister of Health

6 (a) National Briefing, May 4, 2020 – Remarks by SGF / Chairman of PTF

Good afternoon ladies and gentlemen. I welcome you to the National Briefing for today, Monday, 4th May, 2020.

The World Press Freedom Day was celebrated yesterday Sunday, May 3rd, 2020 and I want to join Mr. President in congratulating our hard working and diligent men and women of the Nigerian Media who had consistently served as a necessary watchdog of the society. This role has been made more manifest in our current efforts at tackling the COVID-19 pandemic. Your complementary support in drawing Government' attention to areas of improvement, creation of awareness and broadcasting the daily press briefing in a professional manner is highly appreciated.

Let me reiterate a significant portion of Mr. President's goodwill message, in which he decried the negative impact of the on-going disinformation, fake news and hate news perpetuated through the digital platforms. This is fraught with undesirable consequences for a country like Nigeria because this is the time for us to remain united as a nation, to fight the COVID-19 pandemic.

In line with Mr. President's plea to the media, I also wish to urge you to continually work together to eliminate this unpleasant phenomenon.

Today marks the beginning of Mr. President's directives to ease the lockdown in Lagos, Ogun States and the Federal Capital Territory and the introduction of new measures nationwide. The guidelines on the first phase of the new measures spanning 4th -17th may, 2020 have been published in eight newspapers. Awareness is also being created through broadcast on electronic medium, on line platforms as well as dissemination in local languages by the National Orientation Agency (NOA) and other sources.

The PTF has been monitoring the level of compliance with some of the measures and early observations showed lack of compliance with social distancing and wearing of masks. We note particularly the chaotic scenes around the banks and other financial institutions. We must reiterate that the danger of infection is not over and that individual actions will contribute to the success or failure of our measures.

We urge citizens to minimize the risk of getting infected while trying to transact in the banks. We similarly urge the banks to ensure that their ATMs and online banking systems are in good order and stocked regularly to avoid convergence of customers in their premises.

The PTF fully understands the desire of Nigerians to come out to continue their lives after five weeks of lockdown. States Governments and Security agencies have however, been advised to enforce the measures rigidly and violators will be prosecuted. Let me remind you, once more, that this easing up is in phases and those who are permitted to open have clearly been defined. Our admonition to Nigerians is that it is still desirable to stay at home if there is no compelling reason to go out and to comply with the measures always, whether at home or not.

The PTF has also received reports on the level of compliance with the nationwide ban on inter-state movement. The objective of the ban is to slow down the spread of virus across state boundaries. The determination of government to enforce this policy is not in doubt and as we progress, we believe that proper alignment with the directives of Mr. President would be pursued.

There has been very noticeable relocation of Almajiris from one state to another, up until yesterday. With the ban on interstate movement, the continuation of this exercise will not be in alignment with the guidelines issued. The PTF shall engage with the respective State Governments on how to achieve their objectives. 11.As we journey into this new phase of measures, it is imperative that I re-iterate the importance of adherence to the guidelines more so that preliminary reports indicate that there is observable high level of breaches by the citizenry.

I wish to at this point convey the assurances of the security forces that the rights of Nigerians will be protected and their lives and property protected. Therefore, I passionately appeal to Nigerians to desist from attacking security personnel in the discharge of their duties and not recourse to taking the laws into their hands.

With regard to Kano, the teams dispatched from Abuja have continued to work with the State Structure and appreciable achievements have been recorded in improving manpower support, deploying appropriate equipment, increased testing capacity and treatment centres. Efforts are also on-going to upscale the training of medical personnel in the Kano and neighboring States on the management of infectious diseases and to provide them with PPEs for protection. Private hospitals have also been advised to seek accreditation before taking up the management of infectious diseases.

Our collaboration with the Kano State Government still remains focused on strengthening their existing structures, especially for sustainability. The results coming out from the state is a comforting indication that efforts put in place, which are being strengthened, would yield expected results.

The PTF has also received reports about medical facilities and doctors turning back sick patients for fear of their illnesses being COVID-19 related. The PTF appeals to these facilities especially public hospitals not to neglect treatment of other ailments because such actions have resulted in avioidable deaths. The Honourable Minister of Health will engage the management of our tertiary health institutions to address this.

Ladies and gentlemen, I must as always, appreciate the tremendous support of all Nigerians during the previous phase. Worthy of mention are our Religious and Community Leaders, our frontline health workers, administrators, the members of the Press as well as all individuals and groups that have contributed to the successes achieved then. The battle is still ahead of us as a nation. Together we shall overcome.

As we commence this new phase today, we would require your greater understanding and support to ensure that our decision does not result in compromising our health for our wealth. I count on the resilient Nigerian spirit and call on all of us to make this phase work. It can only be done with the active cooperation of the citizenry.

I will now call on the Minister of Health, the DG-NCDC and the National Coordinator to provide updates you on new developments.
I thank you for listening.

6 (b) National Briefing, May 15, 2020 – Remarks by Minister of Health

1. 193 new covid-19 cases were confirmed in the past day in 15 states- Lagos(58), Kano(46), Jigawa(35), Yobe (12), FCT(9), Ogun(7), Plateau(5), Gombe(5), Imo(4), Edo (3), Kwara (3), Borno (3), Bauchi (1), Nasarawa (1), Ondo(1), bringing the total number of confirmed cases in Nigeria over the 5,000 line to 5,162 in 34 States and the FCT. Till date, 1180 patients have been treated and discharged from hospital care and 167 deaths have sadly been recorded. The case gender ratio remains about 70 to 30 percent for men and women respectively, while case fatality hovers around 3%. A steady rise in these figures is what we envisage with more diligent testing, treatment, Isolation and tracing. Ability and capacity to keep up and align these activities with each other will determine the course of events as time goes on. We implore States and partners not to relent, but to keep up with the pace, which, in some States will increase well before it begins to decrease. Adherence to advisory against interstate travel and compliance with other simple measures like use of masks and avoiding crowds will significantly mitigate the burden.

2. The situation in Kano has largely stabilized, thanks to the good relationship between the visiting Federal task team and Kano State Task force on COVID-19, one manifestation of this being the high number of new cases recorded daily from the fact that all labs in Kano are now functioning and clearing the sample backlog, with over 350 tests done daily. The State government has been doing well in opening up more treatment and Isolation centers.

3. A strategy document of National Primary Healthcare Development Agency is being developed and repurposed for application to Kano; but also to similar high density, high burden metropoles like Lagos to respond more specifically to the challenges of COVID-19 tracing, tracking, testing, Isolation and treatment in congested communities. If implemented, it could go a long way in addressing many challenges looming before us.

4. An innovation of the FMoH Kano task team is the Training of journalists to take place tomorrow, the aim of which is to ensure reporters are in a better position to interpret covid-19 related data and information and also learn to take necessary infection prevention measures. I shall use this opportunity to thank His Excellency, the Governor of Kano State for providing the necessary support for the Federal team to function.

5. A Federal Ministry of Health team has been assembled to proceed to Sokoto and Bornu on fact finding and support missions; to engage with State authorities and determine material and technical needs. A most immediate probability is the prioritization of these States for the deployment of repurposed Gene Xpert machines as soon as we start receiving the cartridges in a few weeks to bring speed to testing.

6. As mentioned earlier part of the mission in Kano is to assist State pathologists and scientists to unravel the mysteries around unexplained deaths in some States. The tools for forensic investigation have been jointly developed for a uniform approach and balanced results.

7. We were able to persuade Mrs Susan Idoko-Okpe, now popularly known as the Benue Lady, to allow a test sample to be taken to our laboratory for testing yesterday; the result is being awaited any time now and it will be given to her in person. Please note that, while a patient may disclose their result by themselves, the FMoH cannot do so, except with the permission of the one concerned.

8. The annual World Health Assembly, held every year in Geneva, shall begin on Monday 17th May, and hold this year for the first time by teleconference. I shall be leading the Nigerian team to the virtual meeting, the focus of which is expected to be the global spread and response to COVID-19, require individual and collective effort.

9. Finally, I shall reiterate again the importance of adhering to public health advisories (wearing our face masks, observing social distancing, practicing hand washing or sanitizing, standard respiratory hygiene, avoiding crowds and all non-essential travel). The importance of these and similar measures is such that compliance should be taken as a civic duty and obligation for every citizen, where each should be responsible for the other. As such, enforcement or policing should not be necessary, for what is meant to preserve life and health. Therefore I call for considerate attitude and social adjustment to the challenges we face at this moment.

10. Thank you for listening.

Appendix 7

How my husband survived COVID-19
By celebrity journalist, Moji Danisa[339]

Moji Danisa and husband, Olawale Dawodu Snr

My name is Moji Danisa, I am a journalist based in Abuja. This is my story:

It all started like a bad dream. The ailment which creeped in just like malaria, the usual Agbo remedies, then the cough and frightening total weakness...he

---

[339] This testimony by Moji Danisa and published by *Yes International Magazine*, (Also in *The Eagle Online* of June 8, 2020 & reproduced equally by *Sundiatapost*) was included here to show how dedicated some of our health personnel were during the lockdown in spite of their poor working conditions. This is to pay tribute to them for their commitment and sense of patriotism during that most difficult and risky period. Please note that except for in few cases (such as correction of few spellings and minor addition of the word 'week'), this piece was reproduced as published. Apart from the picture, the version used here however is that of *The Eagle Online:* https://theeagleonline.com.ng/how-my-husband-survived-covid-19-by-celebrity-journalist-moji-danisa/).

would tell his story, but let me narrate mine; the night COVID-19 went beyond research and Facebook posts and landed on my doorstep. When I noticed that a strongman was going down, struggling to stand but failing, I put a call through to the dynamic chairman of the NUJ FCT council, Emmanuel Ogbeche. He sent me a number. I came to know her as Dr Joe. Josephine Okechukwu, DG, Public Health Department, FCT.

I called and she was not happy I had not called much earlier knowing my husband was asthmatic. When you seek permission and its not granted, what do you do? She insisted I should have called, given the times, nevertheless, within the hour, the Public Health Department sent a team to our house and we both got tested. Waiting for the result was perhaps the worst traumatic 22 hours of my life. Promptly next evening, Dr Joe called and gave me the results. My husband was positive, mine returned negative.

"Pack some of his things for two weeks. They are picking him up. He will be okay, do not be afraid", she counselled. As if she could hear my heart beating in terror on the phone. "Will we pay anything"? I queried, after she told me he would be taken to the Asokoro General Hospital Isolation Center, assuring me she had put a call through to the MD who was waiting to receive him and commence treatment immediately, "No," she said: "Government foots all the bills."

Like a zombie, I packed. Efficiently, the Ambulance came and without fanfare or drawing any unwarranted attention, my husband was taken away, after we prayed, a very short prayer. I did not sleep. As a matter of fact, I do not think I slept for the whole week. We went for my son's test at the testing center, it was no stress at all. He got tested and returned negative.

Then I began to feel the effect of the whole (week) emotionally and physically exhausting experience. Chills and cold and lack of appetite. I cried to Dr. Joe again. Promptly, I got another test. Another wait, at this point, I thought I'd run mad, my husband was on oxygen the whole (week) while as doctors battled to pull him through at Asokoro. Every time I went there, I would be at the gate until someone came to pick up what he needed (glasses, charger, fruits, etc).

I did not know what he faced inside but he kept assuring me he would pull through, though his breathing was hollow and his voice almost non-existent. I was terrified but I kept praying…friends and family kept my hope alive with calls, prayers and other support. My second result came out negative and Dr Joe advised me to rest.

I have never met this Angel called Dr Josephine Okechukwu. I came to realize how tasking her job is right now as she is always in and out of meetings, her phone always busy…yet, when she misses a call, she calls right back to listen and not just listen but act. I came to realize the great burden our health officials are carrying right now, working and putting life at risk so we can be safe.

I am now 100% convinced that our negative comments on the social media about the government's handling of COVID-19 is based on false information.

A day after my husband was admitted, a team from the WHO, Public Health Department, NCDC and PTF came to the house for contact tracing. The team headed by Emma Okala, a consultant with WHO, FCT gave us thermometers, all recognisable contacts, I mean, a chart and we all monitored our symptoms for 14 days.

Scholarstica of the PHD kept track of all contacts while Emma became like my personal counsellor, always calling, always checking, always giving hope. As my husband grew stronger, having used up about nine giant oxygen canisters and five small ones, as he regained his appetite, he would laugh and say, wow, "They are really packing us full with protein, fruits, and all the nutrients here o"…As I said, he would tell his story.

Mine today is to celebrate our Angel, Dr. Joe Okechukwu, a most diligent, efficient, humane public servant, and Emma Okala of WHO. I nominate these great front liners for awards when they start rolling in. If you think government is not doing anything, it is because you do not have the right information, the government and NCDC must be commended for their handling of the pandemic so far.

Oh, though decontamination came late, it was finally done (This Is An Area For Improvement. If We Lived In A Smaller Or More Populated Apartment, It Would Have Been Highly Risky). COVID-19 is very real. I did not contact it but I have been through HELL and back.

I call it the lonely sickness. Once positive or when someone close to you tests positive, you are on your own. I had nowhere to run to. It was me and mine alone in our own space.

Pls be very careful. Wear your face masks, insist on social distancing anywhere you are (as I always do), wash your hands often, sanitise as much as you can…and please stay safe for your family and our tireless health officials. God bless you all. Let us celebrate and keep praying for our own doctors here as well. The Lord reward them!

Index

www.ingramcontent.com/pod-product-compliance
Lightning Source LLC
Chambersburg PA
CBHW040255290326

41929CB00052B/3383